NO TIME FOR YOUTH

A publication of the

INSTITUTE FOR THE STUDY OF HUMAN PROBLEMS
Stanford University

NEVITT SANFORD, Director
JOSEPH KATZ, Executive Director

NO TIME FOR YOUTH

GROWTH AND CONSTRAINT
IN COLLEGE STUDENTS

Joseph Katz & Associates

Harold A. Korn

Marjorie M. Lozoff

Ving Ellis

Max M. Levin

Peter Madison

Nevitt Sanford

Susan Singer

Jossey-Bass Inc., Publishers
615 Montgomery Street • San Francisco • 1969

NO TIME FOR YOUTH
Growth and Constraint in College Students

Joseph Katz and Associates

Jossey-Bass, Inc., Publishers
615 Montgomery Street
San Francisco, California 94111

Library of Congress Catalog Card Number 68-21317

Standard Book Number SBN 87589-014-8

Manufactured in the United States of America
 Composed and printed by
 Hamilton Printing Company, Rensselaer, New York
 Bound by Chas. H. Bohn & Co., Inc., New York
 Jacket design by Willi Baum, San Francisco
FIRST EDITION
 First printing: May 1968
 Second printing: September 1969

Code 68054

6/24/70 p.l. 1000

THE JOSSEY-BASS SERIES IN HIGHER EDUCATION

General Editors

JOSEPH AXELROD and MERVIN B. FREEDMAN
San Francisco State College

❧ PREFACE ❧

No Time for Youth
is based on an intensive study of college students over a four-year
period. Data were obtained from several thousand students. A random group of over 200 students was selected for intensive interviewing by a staff of experienced psychologists. The students were
interviewed at least two times each year about their academic and
nonacademic experiences and the meaning these had for them. The
result was an exceedingly rich collection of materials.

Our focus throughout has been on what is universal in the
development of college students and not on what was of primarily
local significance in the student populations we studied. The intensive interview is a particularly good tool for obtaining knowledge about the underlying and pervasive dynamics of personality
development. We offer this book as a guide to the understanding
of college students everywhere.

In *No Time for Youth*, the reader will get a close view of
the lives and problems of undergraduates, the achievements and
the burden of four turbulent years. He may react with distress
at the realization of just how much is left undone in higher education, and he may even come to agree with our conclusion that radical changes are necessary.

Part One, "How Students Change," describes how students change during their college years. Two chapters give an overview and a third presents two detailed case studies. Part Two, "From Curriculum to Career," describes and documents the profound differences in the way students learn, their motivations for learning, and the interplay of choice and coercion in their career decisions. Part Three, "Student Life and its Problems," follows the students into their lives outside the classroom and presents a long description of their off-campus life. A chapter on drinking traces the role of impulse expression in student culture. Another concerns students troubled enough to seek psychiatric help and aware enough to realize that they need it. A chapter on authoritarian students deals with the problems of those whose rigidity of character seems to make them particularly inaccessible to education. A chapter describes the activist, a new kind of student who emerged before the researcher as the study progressed. Part Four, "Recommendations," proposes a new type of undergraduate education that would better develop the potentialities of students. (Some readers may want to read this Part first, as it assembles the earlier themes in a pragmatic context.) Part Five, "Appendices," offers a methodological note and a brief guide to further reading.

ACKNOWLEDGMENTS

In an undertaking as extensive as ours, we cannot mention and thank all of the many people who helped us. Invaluable help must be properly acknowledged. The United States Office of Education and the Danforth Foundation provided the funds that enabled us to carry on our research. The following administrators at Berkeley and Stanford sponsored and facilitated our work, and we thank: John D. Black, Henry B. Bruyn, John Moore, Harvey Powelson, Saxton Pope, and Robert J. Wert. In addition to the authors of this book, the following participated as senior researchers, and we thank: Elizabeth Alfert, Louise Farnham, Mervin B. Freedman, Richard Fresco, Mary C. Jones, and Robert Suczek. The following were research assistants, and we thank: Mallory Jones, Paul Kanzer, Nanci Moore, Dana S. Power, Susan Roberts, Barry H. Sokolik, Ronald Starr, John Stelzer, and Fred Strassburger. Among the many secretaries Phyllis Gardiner and Linda Horn were associated with the research for long periods.

The study owes much to Saxton Pope and his masterful knowledge of the psychological development of college students. Nevitt Sanford was a friend throughout. His superb command of psychological theory and his understanding of the dynamics of personality development and educational processes benefited out study at every step. Max M. Levin was a constant participant in the planning of this long study. Harold A. Korn played a major role in the planning of the analyses of the data. He kept a sharp eye on the utilization of data for the development of theory and on making psychology relevant to education. Marjorie M. Lozoff's unusual sensitivity to the complexities of human beings was a great asset to our work. Ving Ellis gave his psychiatric competence and his humaneness from the planning stage through the completion of this study.

In the preparation of this book for publication in the Jossey-Bass series, we are greatly indebted to the fine editorial skills and judgment of Joseph Axelrod, Mervin B. Freedman, and William E. Henry.

We express deep gratitude and thanks to the students who shared their college lives with us in the hope that they might contribute to the improvement of the education of future generations of college students. We hope they will not be disappointed.

Stanford, California   Joseph Katz
April 1968

❦ CONTENTS ❧

Preface   xiii

The Authors   xix

PART ONE: HOW STUDENTS CHANGE

1. Four Years of Growth, Conflict, and Compliance
   Joseph Katz   3

2. Dynamics of Development and Constraint: Two Case
   Studies
   Peter Madison   74

3. Personality Scale Changes From the Freshman Year to
   the Senior Year
   Harold A. Korn   162

PART TWO: FROM CURRICULUM TO CAREER

4. Differences in Student Response to the Curriculum
   Harold A. Korn   187

5. Careers: Choice, Chance, or Inertia?
   Harold A. Korn   207

xvii

6. Incomplete Liberation: Two Premedical Students
   Harold A. Korn   239

PART THREE: STUDENT LIFE AND ITS PROBLEMS

7. Residential Groups and Individual Development
   Marjorie M. Lozoff   255

8. Students Who Seek Psychiatric Help
   Ving Ellis   318

9. Drinking and Personality
   Nevitt Sanford and Susan Singer   348

10. Changes in Authoritarianism
    Max M. Levin   376

11. The Activist Revolution of 1964
    Joseph Katz   386

PART FOUR: RECOMMENDATIONS

12. Recommendations for Policy and Philosophy
    Joseph Katz   417

PART FIVE: APPENDICES

Note on the Collection and Analysis of the Data   449

Guide to Further Reading   454

Index   457

❧ THE AUTHORS ❧

Ving Ellis received his M.D. from the University of California Medical School in 1950 and took his psychiatric training at the Langley Porter Neuropsychiatric Institute. Before his death in 1969 he was associate psychiatrist at the Student Health Service at the University of California, Berkeley; assistant clinical professor of psychiatry at the University of California Medical School; and research associate at the Institute for the Study of Human Problems at Stanford University.

Joseph Katz received his Ph.D. in philosophy in 1948 from Columbia University. He is executive director of the Institute for the Study of Human Problems at Stanford University. He has been a staff member of the Institute since its founding in 1961 and has been director of its Student Development Study. Previously he was a research associate in the psychiatry department of Cowell Hospital at the University of California, Berkeley. He has taught at Amherst, Vassar, and Columbia.

Harold A. Korn did his graduate work at the University of Minnesota, completing his Ph.D. in clinical psychology in 1958. He is director of the University Counseling Center and professor of psychology at Florida State University.

Max M. Levin received his Ph.D. in psychology from the University of California, Berkeley, in 1946. He is senior preceptor at Crown College at the University of California, Santa Cruz. Previously he was associate director of the Institute for the Study of Human Problems at Stanford.

Marjorie M. Lozoff did her graduate work at The University of Chicago, completing her master's degree as a psychiatric social worker in 1941. She is a research associate at the Institute for the Study of Human Problems at Stanford. Formerly she was associated with the Menninger Foundation.

Peter Madison received his Ph.D. in psychology in 1953 from Harvard. He is professor of psychology at the University of Arizona. Previously he was associate professor of psychology at Swarthmore and director of counseling and testing at Princeton. He has been a visiting research fellow at the Institute for the Study of Human Problems.

Susan Singer received her Ph.D. in psychology in 1966 from the University of California, Berkeley. She is a psychologist at the Institute for Childhood Aphasia at Stanford Medical Center. She was a consultant on the Student Development Study at the Institute for the Study of Human Problems.

Nevitt Sanford received his Ph.D. in psychology in 1934 from Harvard. He is director of the newly established Wright Institute and of the Institute for the Study of Human Problems, and professor of psychology and education at Stanford University. Previously he was professor of psychology at the University of California and coordinator of the Mellon Foundation study at Vassar College.

NO TIME FOR YOUTH

Enforced learning will not stay in the mind.

Plato

PART ONE

How Students Change

❧ 1 ❧

FOUR YEARS OF GROWTH,
CONFLICT, AND
COMPLIANCE

Joseph Katz

The picture that
emerges from our four-year study of college students is that of a
wide variety of patterns in which individuals react and develop
during the college years. The college environment is a highly controlling one, and it creates stress in many students. Some individuals are well enough equipped psychologically to utilize both
the opportunities and the obstacles of the college environment
for the purpose of their own growth. At the other end of the spectrum are those whose needs for passivity—for being told what to
do—have become so much a part of their life-style that they do
not experience the conditions of the environment as stressful or

inhibiting. In between are the bulk of students, whose lives never reach an adequate expression of their potential because they are handicapped by inadequate self-awareness and inadequate self-assertion, as well as by the environment, whose demands and constraints discourage their spontaneity.

For many students, the academic-intellectual offerings of the college do not connect adequately with their own motivations. There is a consequent loss of adequate learning and of personal involvement in the process of intellectual inquiry. Moreover, many students do not learn how to utilize their reasoning capacities in the service of the problems they face in their own development. Major life decisions, such as occupational or marital choices, as well as minor ones are made without sufficient use of the perspective that intellect and awareness can bring. The consistent encouragement of abstract thinking, at the expense of experience and involvement, leaves the student with insufficient practice in the art and science of applying thought to the clarification of feelings and to decision-making. Higher education seldom gives the student sufficient opportunity to develop the non-intellective parts of his character. The development of more autonomous identity, of the capacity for intimate communication with other people, and of taking responsibility for others is not brought to the fruition that most students implicitly desire but cannot realize without further educational help.

The college years bring many difficult psychological tasks and problems. Separation from home and parents, confrontation with a wide variety of peers, and high standards of academic performance create insecurities and a questioning of one's powers and identity. Older problems and feelings, often dating back to childhood, are revived once more, and many students find themselves more or less consciously struggling with derivatives of earlier feelings of narcissism, omnipotence, or passive dependency. At the same time, there are the demands of the new roles that the student is about to fill, which call for greater social, sexual, and occupational maturity. The tasks are so staggering that many individuals let some or most of them go by default; and institutions rarely address themselves in sufficient detail to the problems of helping their students cope with these many-faceted problems. Effective education during the college years may well depend on the degree to which the student can do justice to his various tasks simultaneously.

The present chapter gives an overview of the passage through college of two groups of students we followed from the freshman through the senior year—the classes that entered Berkeley and Stanford in 1961. This chapter includes data from the Senior Questionnaire responses of our students, and utilizes interviews and psychometric data as well. We begin by briefly considering some theoretical questions concerning change and development.

How do students change in college? Our study has shown us that fewer students than one might expect report or are concerned with change. Thus, only about a third of the men and close to half of the women in our questionnaire samples said that they had changed much in personal characteristics after entering college; and even fewer indicated that they had changed much in their moral, religious, and political views.

As one conducts interviews, what strikes one about many students is the relative passivity with which they view life. For many, their coming to college has not been a deliberate choice, but a matter of course. When asked what their occupational plans are, students say that their parents leave that choice up to them; yet upon probing, it becomes clear that they are strongly influenced by their parents' wishes and aspirations as well as by the prevailing fashions and opportunities in the society. By the end of the senior year, students are heading toward various schools and professional training; but to the interviewer, it seems that further schooling is viewed by many as an opportunity for finding stimulation and achieving commitment there. For many, there never will be a clear-cut decision. Each step, channeled by educational and other social institutions, will gradually determine their "decisions" for them.

Nevertheless, changes do take place during the college years. Students learn to make certain decisions without seeking permission from parents. They learn to regulate their own time and handle their own money. Starting from an original position of rather undifferentiated dating and distance in heterosexual relationships, they move toward closer relationships and toward the assumption of the marital role. As time goes by, they express their own impulses more freely, and are more able to pursue their own desires. At the same time, they lessen previous constrictive and restrictive controls over their own impulses, and adopt more tolerant and permissive attitudes toward the behavior of others.

These changes were apparent in varying degree in nearly all the students we studied, and may be considered a part of normal maturation. Such maturation may be heavily influenced by the social setting and social expectations. Society considers certain tasks and performances, such as leaving home, developing greater freedom of expression, and assuming marital or occupational roles, appropriate to certain ages or stages in people's careers. Normal maturation must be distinguished from more profound alterations of character, that is, from the more or less major relocations of the psychological systems—the id, ego, and superego—in their relations to each other. For instance, a student may move toward the adoption of the role of husband without any profound change in his dependency reactions—simply transferring them from the home to the college to the marriage. By contrast, a student who moves toward greater psychological autonomy—for example, the replacement of self-punitive demands with task-minded and pleasure-giving work in an occupation of his own choosing— would have undergone change in a more profound sense.

When we speak of development, we often confuse these two meanings of change. Both normal maturation and profound character changes constitute development. ("Change," strictly speaking, is a more general term, as a person can "change," for example, in his political affiliation, without this indicating either maturation or character alteration. Change also can denote direction opposite from development, as in regression.) Normal maturation does not take place without psychological effort; whenever people cannot assume the usual marital, occupational and other social-psychological roles, the presence of a more or less disabling pathology may be assumed (although the assumption of these roles is, of course, no guarantee against pathology). Profounder alterations of character are a function of factors in the environment other than those an individual would normally encounter, and are as well a function of greater psychological effort within the person—whether that effort is made through analysis, through more intense and open relations with other people, or through mobilization of intuitive and esthetic capacities.

When we began our research, the distinction between the two kinds of changes was not clear to us. Perhaps because of a too idealistic reading of Erikson's developmental timetable, we had a greater expectation of profound alterations of character among our interviewees than was warranted.[1] We postulated for at least a fourth or a third of the students several conscious and more or less sharply defined identity crises in their relations to themselves, their parents, peers, and other authorities, and in their study and work patterns, all eventuating in a redefinition of their character. This did not turn out to be the case. Moreover, many students who did experience crises and conflicts did not move toward the postulated resolution, at least by the time of graduation. While some of them may achieve such resolution within a longer time span, we would not make such a prognosis confidently, for their behavior during the college years suggested rather the likelihood of a life-long pattern of conflict.

Instead of dramatic changes, we did, however, find changes confined to some segment of the character, for example, a more adequate self-conception, or a lessening of previous masochistic tendencies in relationships with others. This experience has led us to question our original assumption of dramatic changes for the age span we studied. Perhaps partial change is all one ought to expect during any period of life, except for the first few years. Beyond childhood, profounder changes may only come slowly— an implicit lesson for our educational institutions, which are often in too much of a hurry. It may well be that our present educational setup is not sufficiently supportive of beneficial characterological alteration.

The term "development" may suggest normative or valuational judgments. Such judgments need not be subjectivistic. Our conception of development includes such indices as increase in autonomy, relatedness, complexity, and differentiation of character. Such factors may be necessary conditions for the human

[1] Erikson, Erik H. "Growth and Crises of the Healthy Personality," in *Identity and the Life Cycle*. New York: International Universities Press, 1959.

organism to achieve dynamic equilibrium within itself and with its environment. Whether such equilibrium has been achieved is discernible by objective testing after the empirical criteria have been defined. The search for norms must, however, include a recognition of human diversity, and possibly a conceptual ordering of human behavior into types.

Students come to college with a great variety of agenda. Some come with a desire to define their own identity. Others come with a desire to learn the occupational and social skills that will allow them to acquire a functional competence in the world. Still others come because that is the thing to do during these years; they seek acceptance by their environment and are less concerned with scrutinizing their environment than with being liked. Still others approach college as one more burdensome task imposed on them by society; they obey reluctantly, and "gripe" when they can.

If one probes deeply enough, one will find doubts and uncertainties in everyone about the roles, controls, and restrictions into which life, that is, previous environments, has cast them. Even the most rigid express some dreams of escape. Others engage in fantasies of a prolonged motoric state; for instance, leading the life of a racing driver. Almost everyone, even the freshmen who had just entered college, said that if they did not have to be in college, they would like to travel—the most common motoric fantasy. A longing for profound transformation seems to live in nearly every human soul. But on a day-to-day level, many of our students seemed to have decided many years ago that transformation was out of their reach, and to have settled for a more restricted responsiveness to stimuli, seeking security by finding out what the rules of the game were, and by playing accordingly. Those who chafed against restrictions and who battled the rules did not necessarily find the way to peaceful integration. Only some, in some areas, found the avenues toward modification of their own selves or of aspects of the environment that would permit a greater unfolding of their potentialities and a greater scope for expression and differentiation of their impulses and desires. Our study has not given us the impression that the skills of men to further their own happiness are in a particularly advanced state.

Let us turn directly to the Senior Questionnaire. First of all, what indications did our students give of perception of change within themselves? The Senior Questionnaire contained a series of open-ended questions, one of which was: *How have you changed since the fall of 1961?* [2]

Roughly a third of those who responded made statements that fell into a category we coded as "more self-confidence, poise, independence." This category was defined in our coding manual as including "a feeling of independence, of improved social skills, and of leadership ability, as well as self-confidence per se, and willingness to express and stand up for one's beliefs." Less frequently, but still relatively often, students also described themselves as having become more stable and as having achieved self-understanding, self-satisfaction, self-criticism, a better defined philosophy and interests, better emotional control, and the ability to face limitations. Next in frequency they reported changes in their awareness of others—better relationships with people or greater tolerance of their behavior or convictions—and often they reported change in the direction of increased intellectual activity and curiosity.

It is worth noting that the students' responses have a strong egocentric slant. Uppermost in their minds is self-improvement and greater independence. In this they actually conform to the social system—for the college rewards, by grades and other incentives, such attempts at self-improvement, and it puts verbal, though not necessarily operational, emphasis on independence and originality. At the same time, the student's sense of greater self-confidence and independence reflects inner psychological changes. Both psychological and social factors are reflected in their report of better relations with and greater tolerance of others. Psychologically, they have moved in varying degrees to greater comfort with and responsiveness to other people, having been both challenged and aided by the heterogeneity of the college population. Though it sounds somewhat paradoxical, greater conformity during the college years actually requires a greater amount

---

[2] The students' open-ended responses were coded in accordance with a coding manual developed by Nanci I. Moore, and checked for reliability.

of tolerance of others, because of the need to adjust to a wide variety of peers. This is rather dramatically illustrated in the way conservative students react when they confront what seem to them majority liberal sentiments. Liberal feelings go against their own grain and yet they feel pressure to accept them; or at least they feel less sure of their own views. It is difficult, therefore, to disentangle a broadening of attitudes and greater closeness to people from the learning of the arts of accommodation. The relatively low frequency with which an increase in intellectual activity and curiosity is mentioned introduces a theme of major interest: in the student's own mind, other aspects of his development loom larger than the academic or even the intellectual requirements and opportunities of the college years. To him, "education" seems only secondarily to be the education of the mind.

Contrasting statements made by two senior male interviewees serve to illustrate the students' own perceptions of how they had changed. The first one is from a student who underwent much development during college. Asked how he was different as a senior from what he had been when he entered college, he replied:

> I was probably less concerned [in the freshman year] with the academic sort of things. I was more concerned with having a good time, with going out, getting drunk. . . . I always felt myself independent whether I was or not. The image had really nothing to do with reality; I'm more independent now as to viewpoint. . . . When I first came here, I had the confidence of ignorance . . . just coming to college is enough to make anyone lose their confidence. Now my confidence is starting to come back. By the end of last year, I discovered that I could do some things better than anyone else, and that I'm really basically able. . . . I doubt people more now. . . . The thing that I valued most was being in a position of power, being a leader—an organizer. Now the thing I value most is being able to solve problems. . . . I'm more of an idealist now. I'm concerned with equality of opportunity. I'm willing to go to bat for ideas. [My principles] probably are a little more strict now than they were then. Then my views were just empty. I was free in a sort of anarchistic way.

This student indicates considerable growth through the development of true competence, which allowed him to find meaning in problem-solving activities rather than in a more primitive release of impulse. At the same time, he worked through some of his narcissism and power striving, though traces of them are still very visible. He reports more strictness in the way in which he controls his behavior. Many other students report the opposite— a relaxation in strictness—but they refer to the liberalization of the harsher or more punitive aspects of their superego, while this student refers to the growth of realistic and task-oriented ego controls. When asked what accounted for the changes in him, this student mentioned the proofs he had received of his academic ability; his exposure to different points of view and different people in the university community; an intimate and intellectually meaningful relationship with a girl, which cut him off from the "carefree," less responsible standards of his former peer group.

The other senior male student, who, in his interviewer's judgment, in his test scores, and in a self-report, seemed to have changed little, expressed regret that this should be so. He had not changed much in his freedom to do things, nor had he changed much with regard to moral principles.

> I should have changed more from the experience. I was not sure [in the freshman year] about my goals, and I'm not sure now. [He had gained, he said, a wider perspective of what is going on in the world: when he came, he was not interested in reading *Time* magazine, but now he is.] I definitely feel more independent; when I came here, I thought completely along the lines of my parents. I am probably less close to people now. I have trouble finding a common bond—perhaps because others have changed more than I have. They are more experienced in different things. I have not become as interested in different things as they have. I was not prepared for the freedom: study when you want, and so on. . . . I never had any great goals in my life.

It is clear perhaps even from this brief excerpt that here is a student who is in a relatively torporous state at the end of his four college years, and probably has been injured in his passage through college by feeling rebuffed and inadequate in the college environment. But even so, he registers some maturational gains in independence. It is of interest to note that at the end of college, this student was accepted at a major graduate school.

The responses of the students to the open-ended questions were parallel to those they gave to the structured ones.

> Over half of them report much greater self-understanding. About half say that during their college years it has become less difficult for them to feel close to people. Half or more say that academic pressures have become much easier to handle. Their social life in their junior and senior years compares very favorably with that in the freshman year. Their sense of personal mastery is relatively high. Less change is reported in values. About one-fifth of each group report much change in their moral views, their religious views, and their political views. One-third report much greater freedom to express their feelings and desires.
>
> The changes that have taken place have caused only a portion of the students great conflict. For about 30 per cent, deciding on a major and planning their life's work has created inner turmoil. With regard to sex, a third of the women and less than a fifth of the men describe themselves as having been involved in a struggle of conflicting thoughts and feelings.

Struggle and conflict are marked for only minorities of the students. For most students, adaptation to the role demands of their college environment and to their anticipated future roles in society seems to take place without conscious conflict. The question arises as to whether the absence of conflict and struggle indicates that alternatives were not faced up to with sufficient vigor, so that the students adopt roles without sufficient examination of how they fit them, and without sufficient exploration and nurturance of their half-dormant proclivities and potentialities.

Analyses of responses by students who report a higher degree of conflict than their peers seem to indicate that conflict and development go together. Students who report having experienced a greater degree of conflict than their peers in college also report themselves more frequently as having engaged in creative activities, and as having changed more in their personal characteristics, in the freedom to express their feelings and desires, and in their moral and political views. More frequently than their peers, they feel that being away from home has had a great influence on their understanding of themselves and others, and on their relations with their families and with friends of both sexes. They also attribute greater influence to ideas in books they read on their own. The students with a history of conflict also report participating more frequently in activities, changing more, and being more deeply affected by various influences upon them. It is also of interest that the more conflicted students tend to report themselves as having engaged in social activities less than their peers did.

After having asked the seniors how they had changed since they entered college, we asked them: *What do you think contributed most to these changes?*

> Between one-third and one-half of the students said that personal relationships contributed most. These percentages increase further if one includes other responses to questions mentioning relations with other people, such as living groups, the contact with a variety of people on campus, dating, love, and marriage.
>
> Next in order of frequency are responses in which the student reports his own inward disposition as a major source of change: his self-awareness, personal philosophy, self-reliance, and responsibility.
>
> Between a fifth and a fourth of the students single out course work and professors as an important source of change. Additional numbers (a fifth or less) mention the challenge and difficulty of academic life. Relatively small percentages of respondents single out student government, political activities, and job experiences as influences on them.

It will be remembered that when they were asked how they had changed, the students mentioned change in their personality more frequently than change in relationships with others. In the question above, the order of the two is reversed. This could be interpreted to mean that students tend to locate the causes of change outside themselves more frequently than within themselves (caution is necessary in phrasing such questions, for the word "cause" may induce the one questioned to look for external factors). At any rate, the different distributions of the replies to the two questions are expressive of the college situation: there success is measured in terms of individual accomplishment—for example, grade-point average. At the same time, paying attention to what is expected by the environment of professors or peers also is important—hence the frequent mention of external influence. There is thus an intriguing interplay between expectations of individual achievement and social conformity.

Intellectual and academic activities trail considerably behind personal relationships as a source of change. It is one of the many pieces of evidence we have found indicating that the intellectual and academic aspects of the college are secondary or tertiary for most students when compared with other concerns of emotional and social growth. This is corroborated by the students' responses to another open-ended question: *Please indicate the most meaningful experience during your last three-and-a-half years. How did it affect your life?*

> In response to the first of the two parts of this question, the highest percentages list love, marriage, friendship, and living-group experiences, with love and marriage listed far more often than the rest. At Stanford, very high percentages list their overseas experience as an unusual opportunity to establish meaningful friendships and good social relations. Only between 2 per cent and 5 per cent spontaneously mention course work or student-professor relationships as the most meaningful experience.
>
> In response to the second part of the question, *How did it affect your life?* the largest proportion is composed of replies listing self-understanding, self-awareness, or self-evaluation. This percentage is swelled by those who list improved self-confidence and increased meaning to life. Second in order of frequency are responses that fall under the heading of relationship to others: insight into others, greater awareness of the world, and greater tolerance. Last are responses regarding choosing or changing one's major or career. These [percentages] are very small, about 3 per cent.

Again the open-ended responses of the students are corroborated by their replies to structured questions. We asked them,

To what do you attribute the changes that have taken place in you during the past three-and-a-half years? and then gave them a list of 18 difference influences.

About half of the men and two-thirds of the women checked their gaining understanding of themselves as persons as having had much influence on them. Next frequently checked was confrontation with problems and conflict within themselves. Next came close relations with friends of the opposite sex, close relations with friends of the same sex, being away from home, and associating with the living group. That the influence of other people is primarily that of peers rather than adults is indicated by the fact that having had close relations with teachers or other adults is assigned great influence by about only 13 per cent.

Academic influences trail far behind personal and interpersonal influences. About one-fourth said that ideas presented in courses or by teachers had much influence. Still lower are participation in student organizations, committees, and so on, to which about 10 per cent assign much influence. Idealistic activities fare even less well. Participation in activities directed to social or political improvement is endorsed by about 9 per cent of the students.

Once more it is the sphere of their private lives, rather than academic pursuits or public concerns that receive the lion's share of the students' attention.

One way of corroborating what students say about influences on them is to go to their behavior and see what influences they submitted themselves to. We gave them a list of 21 different activities or experiences and asked them to tell us how frequently they engaged in them during the college years.

The categories that the students most often check as having engaged in frequently are reading of non-fiction and reading of fiction. [Unfortunately, the question did not distinguish between required and non-required reading.] Next in order of frequency, the students said they engaged in social activities, parties, and the like. Frequent participation in sports activities as a spectator is checked as often or more often than social activities by the men, and somewhat less often by the women. Participation in sports activities follows next in line.

A quarter of the Stanford women and a fifth of the Berkeley women report going to museums, symphonies, and dramas as a frequent activity, and the same proportions check creative expression, such as writing and painting. The men check this only half as often. A little more than a fourth of the students check frequent attendance at the movies. Travel is a frequent activity for over a third of the Stanford students and a fifth of the Berkeley students. Relatively small percentages of students—never more than 10 per cent—list the following: campus political activities, and off-campus, national, or community political activities.

These responses indicate a hierarchical structure. For both sexes, idealistic and humanitarian activities are at the bottom; for the men, artistic activities are at the bottom, too. On top are social activities, sports, movies, and travel. The preeminence of social activities should be viewed not just as gregarious and rather superficial socializing, but rather as evidence of the deep concern students have with getting closer to other people and establishing more satisfactory communication. However, their social growth does not seem usually to extend to activities that involve broad social concerns. Personal growth and private pleasures seem to be predominant. Particularly for the men, private pleasures do not include esthetic activities, but do include sports; men describe themselves as participating in sports three times more often than writing creatively or painting.

The last two questions on the Senior Questionnaire were: "Are there changes you wished for that have not occurred?" and, "If it were 1961 again, what would you do differently?"

To the first of these two questions, about 17 per cent of the students did not respond, and about 33 per cent said "No." About a sixth wished they had acquired more self-confidence and poise, or more a sense of purpose, or otherwise had developed further. Over a tenth expressed the desire for better relationships with other people.

If it were 1961 again, close to a third of the students would have sought out different social arrangements— that is, they would have tried to meet more people, become involved in more extracurricular activities, or join a different living group. An almost equally substantial percentage would have arranged their academic programs differently, that is, would not have settled on a major or career so quickly, would have taken a greater variety of courses, or would have been more careful in their choice of courses. Finally, about a sixth would have tried to be less self-conscious and more outgoing, would have taken themselves less seriously, or would have attempted other changes in personal attitude. Once more, nearly a third either did not respond, or said "No," to this question.

The relatively large proportion of students who single out their problems about academic program deserves special attention. The students' statements in the interviews suggest the kind of problems confronted by them. For instance, a premature career choice may saddle a student with a series of courses that have no great appeal to him, and that in the end, when he turns to another career, will not serve even a preparatory purpose. Another student, by the structure of the requirements or the nature of the grading system, may be kept from exploration in areas in which he has a potentially keen interest. Other students are kept by the inadequacy of advising, and by the relative inaccessibility of professors, from finding out what is available to them and what individual modifications are allowed under the complex rules governing the curriculum.

Over a fifth said that if it were 1961 again, they would study harder. One might say that in distinction to the group just discussed, these are the people who do not question the academic system as such, but wish they had succeeded better under it. For many students, studying is desirable not so much for the sake of intellectual growth, as for the sake of more self-esteem through more successful performance as measured by grades. Moreover, good grades are necessary for admittance to many desirable college activities, as well as for admittance to graduate school.[3]

About a tenth say they would have gone to a different school, a smaller or a larger one, a school with a different atmo-

[3] For the centrality of the "grade-point average" perspective in the students' life space, see Becker, Howard S., et al. *Making the Grade*, New York: Wiley, 1968.

sphere, or the like. This is one response in which the students focus on an environmental factor; the sociological perspective is rarer for them. Usually, when they think of changing, they say that something within them, for example, an attitude or a capacity, needs mending, rather than their environment.

> Among the students at Berkeley who express a wish for different social arrangements, about 10 per cent say that they would have chosen different living situations. [At Stanford, less than 2 per cent said so.] Of those who wish their living arrangements had been different, the largest group say they are against living at home; a large proportion of the men wish for fraternity life. The remaining responses are scattered between those who would have preferred apartments and those who would have preferred dorms. A few express the wish for having exposed themselves to different types of living arrangements during their college years.

It was somewhat surprising to find huge percentages of students who left the two "wish" questions unanswered or said that they wished for no changes, or would have done nothing differently. Such poverty of wishing or imagination seems particularly unsuited to their time of life, when one might expect the expression of more regrets, fantasies, desires, perhaps even passion. This response pattern may corroborate the passivity and lack of idealism we have noted previously. It is perhaps also an index of the confinement of the imagination by the tight structuring of the college situation. Significantly, about 60 per cent of the students said they were depressed at least as often as a few times a month.

When we started this study, we somewhat naïvely assumed that the students would proceed in a more or less straightforward fashion from a fairly vague conception as freshmen of what occupation they wanted to a relatively firm position by the time of graduation. In making this assumption we did not sufficiently consider two important factors: first, that students do not usually have much direct experience of what the work world is like, and second, that career plans are very much a part of the student's growing identity. Our study has impressed us with the incompleteness of students' identity at the time of graduation.

Many students seem to undergo little struggle and little change in occupational plans from the freshman to the senior years. Only a third of the men and women in our study report that planning for their life's work has involved them in a pronounced struggle. About half of the seniors say that when they entered the university, they already had a fairly clear idea of what career or occupation they wanted for themselves. For many students, there is little change in plans from the time they fill out their entrance application to their senior year, when they list in our questionnaire what occupations they plan to enter. In a count of our Stanford interview sample, the following percentages were obtained in regard to changes in occupational plans between the end of high school and the end of college. No change: men, 52 per cent; women, 34 per cent. Moderate change: men, 17 per cent; women, 9 per cent. Much change: men, 31 per cent; women, 27 per cent. Marriage plans only at end of college: women only, 30 per cent.

For some, this relative stability means that they have found their life's work early. For others, it means a persistent rigidity and a failure to seriously consider more appropriate alternatives. It is our impression from the interview data, however, that for the bulk of the male students, there is a certain amount of "nominalness" in their listing of an occupation: that is, they need to have an answer ready when asked what they will do later, and to have a guiding principle when selecting their courses and majors while in college. (There is an element of artificiality here, because undergraduate courses frequently are not "vocational," and are often repeated in one fashion or another in graduate school.) We found that many students enter graduate or professional school with the expectation of finding activities there that will really interest and involve them. For example, a student may enter law school in pursuit of a "plan" he had voiced even as a freshman, but he may be thinking of law school primarily as a refuge from definite action. Later on, after the hoped-for involvement takes place, he can use his knowledge of law in any of a number of careers. Meanwhile, he waits for the really absorbing interest to develop—the interest that somehow never developed in undergraduate school. In his last senior interview, one student replied, in a somewhat rattled fashion, when asked why he planned to go into law:

What else could I go into? I don't want to go on and study economics in graduate school, because I don't want to become a professor of economics or an economist. I'm very happy I majored in economics; I enjoyed it, but I'm not trying to make it a career. I don't want to go in the Army now, because I want to go to graduate school and now is the time to do it. I want to study law; it's going to be a tool. Even if I don't become a lawyer, I've got to know something about it, and I think it's fairly valuable knowledge. I think studying law demands logic. I think also the ability to express myself well and to think clearly is going to help me, no matter what I do. I think I can do a lot of things with a law degree and I think I'm going to enjoy studying law—at least after the first year, I'll enjoy it. But this is the only reasonable course I have open to me, I think. It's the one that's the most appealing. I haven't set myself toward the law. In fact, I can see I don't really want to become a practicing lawyer. I don't have that desire. I may over time. But I'm a neophyte. Even though my father's a lawyer, I really don't know what it entails, or how much I like it. My father loves what he's doing—he just wouldn't want to do anything else. Yet I'm not sure that I would be happy working 60 to 70 hours a week.

Search for a continued moratorium on occupational and life commitments may also be expressed in the large percentage of students—close to a third—who are either planning to enter the Peace Corps or are considering it as a possibility. Part of the appeal of the Peace Corps seems to be that it is one legitimate avenue for taking more time for further development and the sorting out of motives.

In a list of 14 adult activities, "career or occupation" is ranked first by the men more frequently than any other activity. For the women, the highest percentage rank "future family" first, and "career" fourth. This is not a surprising pattern. By virtue of our societal arrangements alone, career looms larger as an objective for the men, as family does for the women. But what is the motivation behind an interest in career? We have found the uncertainties and lack of orientation displayed by the student just quoted quite common among our interviewees. Robert Mogar, who used an earlier version of our list of 14 interests and activities in a study of a group of San Francisco State College freshmen, also found that the men ranked career first. But in analyzing their responses to open-ended questions, he found that "few students discussed career in terms of intrinsic interest, social usefulness, or self-fulfillment, although this was the intent of the question. Rather, career was treated as a means [to income, material security, or status], not as an end in itself." [4]

The lack of orientation in regard to career has many roots. Education at school and at home may not have succeeded sufficiently in connecting work with pleasure (hence the underdevelopment of the spirit of good workmanship). Another cause may be the egocentricity of people of college age, who still are so involved in achieving their own identity that they lack energy and direction for concern with the objective world outside of their own selves. In addition, the college situation encourages the student to be concerned with his own performance, rather than putting him to work on tasks useful to others and making him a genuine participant in realistic work. Finally, there is the student's lack of exposure to the work world. For some it will be many years before they are actually doing the work for which they "prepared" during their academic years.

The prolonged moratorium on action and the lack of real acquaintance with or involvement in the work world make it very difficult for the student to make an occupational decision. It seems likely to us that many never do make a decision. They "select" each institution—college, graduate school, corporation, or university—with many reservations, and while seemingly keeping an open mind. But in fact, with each step some of the decision is made for them. Their sojourn in each institution keeps on determining their outlooks, skills, and character. Moreover, years of investment in schooling of a particular kind are not easily repudiated. The student may be committing himself to a basic life plan with insufficient attention to his interests and aptitudes, and too much regard for the expectations of parents, peers, and other reference groups.

Finally, our data indicate that the students studied by us conform to the pattern of upward mobility that has been one of

[4] Mogar, Robert E. "Value Orientations of College Students." *Psychological Reports*, 1964, *15*, 747–48.

the traditional functions of the American college. Moreover, they show a trend away from business occupations. We asked the seniors what they expected to be doing ten years after graduation. In comparing the career aspirations of Berkeley and Stanford students with the careers chosen by their fathers, we found no students who wished to become skilled workers, tradesmen, or clerics, though their fathers were in these occupations. Only half as many sons expected to go into business as there were fathers in business. None of the sons wanted to become owners of small businesses, and only a small proportion planned sales or managerial careers. Medicine and law registered large gains, and so did engineering at Berkeley. The greatest gain was in education or teaching. Only very small percentages of the sons planned to enter the fields of natural science or the arts, though they did so in larger proportions than their fathers.

The women in our study exhibited even more traditionality. About half of the Berkeley and Stanford mothers were listed as housewives by their daughters, and about half the daughters expected to be housewives ten years after graduation. If one adds to this the 24 per cent of the daughters at Berkeley and 14 per cent of the daughters at Stanford who listed education as a future occupation, the figures for potential housewives might be put even higher, because many of these students may have viewed education as a very temporary occupation. Large percentages of the Berkeley and Stanford mothers are described as holding clerical and accounting jobs, while almost none of the daughters expect to be in these occupations.

Women are still primarily oriented toward the role of wife and mother. The interview data make clear the potentialities for conflict. Women develop capacities during the college years that they cannot easily let remain unused, and interests that they cannot easily give up. Moreover, they develop habits of self-assertion that may conflict with their marital roles. Corresponding to the men's lack of clarity about what the occupational world will bring, there is lack of clarity among the women as to what marriage will bring. It is worthy of note that the student activists, who have raised many provocative questions regarding education, have thus far said little (except for criticizing college residential restrictions) about the role of women in the world, and about social changes in their behalf.[5]

For some students, the academic program is intimately connected to their career plans; it is like a means to an end. For others, it is a way of finding themselves. Perhaps for the bulk it is simply what society asks them to do.

> How do students see the place of intellectual activities in their own lives? When asked to single out their most important future activity from a list of fourteen, about 6 per cent of the students named intellectual and artistic activities. About a quarter of the students rank intellectual and artistic activities among their first three preferred activities, and a like percentage say that ideas presented in courses or by teachers had great influence upon them. About 3 per cent rank curiosity and knowledge as the most important of a list of eleven needs, and about 15 per cent rank them among the first three. Compare this with the rankings given to emotional well-being, love, and affection, maintaining self-respect, and being accepted and liked by others: 73 per cent of the men and 89 per cent of the women list one or the other of these four as their first choice. Achievement is listed first by about 16 per cent of the men and about 6 per cent of the women.

These figures, as well as what we have reported earlier about students' academic and intellectual involvement, tend to support the assertion that the current academic-intellectual program of the college has a strong intrinsic interest for no more than a quarter of the students.[6] The 25 per cent figure is probably high, since students are likely to pretend to more involvement—even to themselves—than they really have. (They have different "masks," they told us, to put on for different people: one mask for the teacher,

---

[5] See the subsequent chapters by Peter Madison and by Harold Korn for detailed discussions of career choice.

[6] Richard E. Peterson reports that of 12,949 entering freshmen at 23 different institutions, 19 per cent said that "academic orientation" was the most accurate self-description; the other three orientations were "collegiate" (51 per cent), "vocational" (27 per cent), and "nonconformist" (4 per cent). Peterson, R. E. *A Summary of Responses to College Student Questionnaires.* Princeton, N.J.: Educational Testing Service, 1964.

another for the Dean, another for the psychologist.) If even at highly selective institutions, only a fourth are strongly committed to the intellectual program in its present form, serious questions concerning educational procedures are raised. What about the education of the other 75 per cent?

Perhaps at the present time we favor students whose relation to the world is strongly conceptual and neglect those who relate to the world by way of action, feeling, or involvement with other people. To win these last for reflective thinking and pleasure in intellectual pursuits, we need to pay much attention to the different ways of cognitive, psychological, and social development, and to the students' intrinsic purposes and wishes.

> About 60 per cent of the students in our study say that when they entered the university, they had a fairly clear idea of what they wanted as an academic major. About a fourth report that deciding on a major involved them in a pronounced conflict. A count of student records of persistence and changes in major confirms the students' self-report of relative stability.

Such stability might indicate maturity of commitment, but as in the case of occupational choice, it seems more a function both of student drift and of the academic requirement according to which a major must be declared at a certain point. Sometimes the anticipated requirements of graduate or professional school more or less force the student's hand. Where there is more freedom in the choice of a major, a simple factor like the friendliness of a department secretary, or greater opportunity to obtain higher grades may tip the scales between one department and another.

Grades are, for many students, the central reality of academic life. Grades control access to graduate and professional schools, as well as to desirable extracurricular activities and institutions such as fraternities and overseas campuses. Retention of scholarships and many other privileges hinge on them. Grades also have great emotional value in the eyes of many peers and parents. Above all, they often deeply involve the student's self-esteem. The grade-point average is a steady presence; the student usually knows his to two decimal points, and is forever calculating and recalculating its contingencies. Like a Calvinistic deity, it allows for no transgressions; every slip is forever included in its cumulative record.

> What attitude do the students in our samples take to grades? About half of the men and 40 per cent of the women say that the emphasis on grades in college has stimulated them to greater achievement. But nearly half say that the grading system has kept them from trying out courses and fields they otherwise might have tried; that it was the cause of much anxiety; that it had little influence on their achievement; and that it lowered their self-confidence. Similar divisions appear in a questionnaire we administered in 1963 to 600 Stanford freshmen at the end of their freshman year. Thirty-nine per cent expressed acceptance of the grading system as it is, while 36 per cent endorsed the "pass-fail" system.

Student reactions to the grading system are mixed. The large proportions of seniors who say that the grading system has stimulated them to greater achievement may be an indication that the grading system owes its persistence to the fact of its resemblance to other externalized reward systems in our culture. Grades may be particularly useful to those who need external judgments and rewards—who need others to tell them how well they are doing. It is also noteworthy that more than a majority of those who see grades as a stimulus to achievement also say that the emphasis on grades has not made them happy. (Who says that achievement and happiness should be related?)

Students make their own adjustments to the grading system. One method is "psyching out" the professor, that is, determining what he wants on examination papers by means of studying his previous tests, his intellectual and emotional preferences, and other clues he provides in the classroom. Lectures are preferred by many students because they tend to present material in an organized and comprehensive fashion, and thus serve as a convenient basis in preparing for exams, regardless of the student's interest or involvement. Avoidance of courses where a low grade may be earned is another attempt to better one's chances—often at an educational loss.

The pattern just noted—that of different groups of students responding quite differently to the same situations—is a frequent occurrence. Students often split three or four different ways when they are asked to evaluate a teacher, the contents of a course, the examination, the grading, and so on. When such differences are found, a common reaction on the part of faculty and administrators is to say that the variety of the responses justifies leaving things as they are. For us, the variety of the responses points to the existence of different needs, styles, and phases of development among different students.

The educational task, therefore, would seem to be to identify these differing groups better, and then gear teaching methods and contents differentially toward them. For instance, the large number of students who think that the grading system interferes with their education seems to need different arrangements than those who are satisfied with it. One cannot assume that either one or the other group is "right." In regard to those who are satisfied with the grading system, one would have to explore to what extent this satisfaction is based on their underdevelopment of internal incentives for learning. Those who are dissatisfied may not have come to understand fully the benefits of a realistic evaluation of one's work. (One can envisage a freshman course in which students are allowed to select voluntarily sections in which there are letter grades, "pass-fail" grades, or no grades. One could learn much from this about the causes of these different preferences; and the students could be confronted by the different consequences of different choices.)

In contrast to the importance students attach to grades, they attach little importance to getting to know their professors in or out of class, or getting recognition from them. About 83 per cent of all the men, 76 per cent of the Berkeley women, and 60 per cent of the Stanford women rank getting good grades first, second, or third in importance. By contrast, only 11 per cent of the men and women rank getting recognition from their professors as having the same degree of importance. With the exception of the Stanford women, not quite a fifth rank getting to know their professor "in class" as either first, second, or third in importance. Twelve per cent rank getting to know him "outside of class" at the same degree of importance; the figures for the Stanford women are higher: 40 per cent and 20 per cent respectively.

Such low ranking may result from the fact that most students have little close contact with their professors; and they may rank knowing and getting recognition from professors low, not because they consider the professors undesirable to know, but because they find them relatively inaccessible. To make things more complicated, many observations show that students are highly ambivalent about closeness to professors; that they wish as much to be left alone by them as to gain their attention and approbation. This is in spite of a certain kind of professorial vanity that assumes that if professors would only spend more time with students, the students would be much happier—an assumption that is frequently belied by the facts. It is the nature of the contact, not its frequency, that is crucial.

Over the four years of college, students often feel that they have changed in academic efficiency. Over a third of our student sample say that they have gained much in efficiency as students since they entered college. As they look back and compare their senior year with their sophomore year, over half say that the academic pressures have become easier to handle. (In a junior-year interview series dealing especially with academic matters, many students seemed to feel that they had improved particularly in their ability to "psych out" their professors.)

The first quarter or the first semester of the freshman year seems to loom over all others as particularly difficult academically. At Stanford, there is an easing off in the second and third quarters, with a slight increase again in the first quarter of the sophomore year. The greatest ease is reported for the spring quarter of the junior year and for the senior fall quarter—the quarter just preceding the taking of the Senior Questionnaire. At Berkeley, the spring freshman semester is reported difficult by double the percentages of people at Stanford. In addition, at Berkeley there is a sharp rise in the percentages of students who report satisfaction with their academic work in the spring of their sophomore year and the fall of their junior year.

The rise in satisfaction at Berkeley may mean that the transition from lower to upper division status, which is more marked at Berkeley than at Stanford, gives the students a new assurance of their staying power. By contrast, Stanford seems to be able to reassure people earlier about their academic status. This may be a function of both its greater academic selectivity and its larger staff, such as deans, graduate student resident advisors, and upperclassmen sponsors, who give information and moral support, and indicate the university's personal interest in the student.

Many freshmen (and upperclassmen, in retrospect) assert that they came to the university with high intellectual expectations, only to find them stifled not just by the academic requirements and the nature of many courses, but also by the anti-intellectual attitudes of their fellow students. We heard complaints about the lack of intellectuality of the other students so often that we inferred that at least some of those who complained about this must be among those whom others complained about. How might one explain this phenomenon? It suggests the absence of curricular or other sufficiently effective arrangements to respond to this intellectual willingness. A senior, Stephen B. Hurlburt, who served as a sponsor in a freshman dormitory writes: "When talking privately with me, a few would express genuine liking of some Civics and English readings much more strongly than they usually did to their peers. [A group of] 'underground intellectuals' participated in the freshman literary magazine, art show, creative writing groups, and freshman seminars, often without their hallmates knowing."

Peer pressures, and particularly the fear of competing with peers, can militate against active involvement in intellectual pursuits, and one may assume that both fear of competition and fear of intellect are among the causes. Further, intellect is feared because the student perceives intellectual pursuits not just as the cold amassing of facts but as a style of life that threatens his established ways of feeling and acting: letting oneself think differently might lead to letting oneself feel differently. Apart from peer pressures, the incongruity between what is presented in the classroom and the student's own intellectual inclination and phase of cognitive-affective development make intellectual involvement difficult. Moreover, many students have a passive orientation to learning.

Even "good" students expect to be stimulated. When the academic environment fails to provide such stimulation, and at the same time makes one feel that one ought to be more interested, guilt is inevitable. Not surprisingly, this guilt may be projected onto others: the others are not intellectually interested; one would do better oneself if only the others were more interested. Finally, freshmen in particular often do not know how to approach other students for serious conversation. They fear that they may be exposing too much of themselves, and that they may be rejected. Hence they play it safe by staying on a superficial level. It is precisely because their thinking is tied to deeper levels of their personality that they find it difficult to talk.

In view of the relatively small proportion of students whom one might describe as genuinely active intellectually during college, one might suggest that if the freshmen's intellectual eagerness had a more secure base, it would not so easily be discouraged either by peer resistance or by faculty incongruity. The spark is there early in the freshman year, but we fail to use it. The psychological potency of the moment of entrance to college is worth much further exploration.

Our questionnaire was given at the height of the FSM crisis at Berkeley early in 1965; similar, though not as strong, tensions were being felt at Stanford. We asked the seniors how satisfied they had been with their relations with the university administration.

About 55 per cent of the students at Stanford declared themselves either satisfied or neutral about administration-student relations, and about 40 per cent of the Berkeley students did so. About 10 per cent of the Stanford students said they were very dissatisfied with the administration, in contrast to about a quarter of the Berkeley students.

We also asked the students, in an open-ended question, to name two or three things about the administration that they would like to see improved. By far the largest number of responses appeared under the heading of greater cooperation between administration, faculty, and students in administrative affairs. The students asked for a lessening of the control of the bureaucratic structure at the university, an increase in personal contact with administrators, more attention and real listen-

ing to student needs, and more student and faculty
authority. Sixty-three per cent of the Berkeley men and
81 per cent of the Berkeley women mentioned this,
while 31 per cent of the Stanford men and 43 per cent
of the Stanford women did so. About a quarter of the
students at Stanford and a fifth of the students at Berkeley called for changes in administrative personnel or
their attitudes. About a fifth of the Stanford students
and 13 per cent of the Berkeley students wanted to do
away with "paternalism" or with "arbitrary" decision-
making. Only very small percentages—1 per cent of the
Stanford men, none of the Stanford women, and about
5 per cent of the Berkeley students—suggested stricter
control of students, especially "the unruly element."

In their answers to these questions, many students are expressing
their search for more attention to individual values in an impersonal society. They are also expressing the special need that people
their age have for recognition from adults, to strengthen their still
shaky conviction that they, too, can make it into an adequate
adulthood. They want more attention from "Papa," and at the
same time, they reject his paternalism. Thus they exhibit their developmental problem, which requires both a leaning on and mod-
eling after "father" as well as a shaking loose from dependence and
submission. Given such ambivalence on the part of the student,
the administrator can maneuver himself into a position where
whatever he does, he cannot win, because he will do "wrong" in
terms of one facet of the student's conflict. But he can also learn
to discern where guidance and where "keeping off" are preferable,
and thus help to make the student more independent without
depriving him of some of the controls he needs and which, hope-
fully, he is in the process of internalizing.
    We now turn from the academic life of the students to their
other activities and their residence and friendship patterns.

Apart from reading, students describe themselves as engaging most frequently in social and in sports activities.
About half the Stanford students and somewhat over a
third of the Berkeley students say they engage in social
activities frequently. Nearly half the men and over a
third of the women are frequent spectators at sports
events. Over a third of the Stanford men, a quarter of

TABLE 1

DIFFERENCES BETWEEN MEN AND WOMEN IN ACTIVITIES FREQUENTLY
ENGAGED IN DURING COLLEGE
(FIGURES ARE PERCENTAGES)

	Men Berkeley and Stanford (N = 560)	Women Berkeley and Stanford (N = 480)
Reading fiction	34	55 **
Service activities, off-campus (frequently and occasionally)	21	40 **
Sports as a participant	34	20 **
Climbing, diving, flying, and so on	35	21 **
Museum, symphony, drama ᵃ	10	22 **
Reading non-fiction	53	64 **
Student committees (frequently and occasionally)	41	52 **
Creative expression: writing, painting ᵇ	12	23 **
Seeking out off-beat places and people (frequently and occasionally)	48	58 **
Sports as a spectator	46	36 **
Lectures	19	28 **
Civil rights	19	26 *
Breaking rules for the fun of it (frequently and occasionally)	22	16 *
Church attendance or church-connected activities ᶜ	17	22 **

** p < .01   * p < .05

ᵃ Forty-one per cent of the men and 16 per cent of the women report themselves as never having attended a museum, symphony, or drama.

ᵇ Fifty-six per cent of the men and 37 per cent of the women report themselves as never having engaged in creative expression.

ᶜ Sixty-three per cent of the men and 51 per cent of the women report themselves as never having attended church or engaged in church-connected activities.

the Berkeley men, 29 per cent of the Stanford women, and 16 per cent of the Berkeley women are frequent participants in sports activities. Attendance at movies is next in order of frequency, followed by lectures. Next in order is attendance at church or church-connected activities, reported by nearly a fifth. Only very small percentages of students describe themselves as participating frequently in civil rights activities (about 5 per cent), national or community political activities (about 4 per cent), or even campus political activities (about 7 per cent). About 8 per cent say that they engage frequently in service activities off-campus. Six per cent of the men and about 12 per cent of the women seek out "off-beat" places and people frequently.

TABLE 2

DIFFERENCES BETWEEN BERKELEY AND STANFORD STUDENTS IN
ACTIVITIES FREQUENTLY ENGAGED IN DURING COLLEGE
(FIGURES ARE PERCENTAGES) [a]

	Stanford Students (N = 486)	Berkeley Students (N = 554)
Student committees	58	36 **
Travel	39	22 **
Social, parties	49	37 **
Sports as participant	34	23 **
Reading fiction	47	40 *
Movies	25	31 *
Breaking rules for the fun of it (frequently and occasionally)	22	16 **
Museum, drama, symphony	17	14 *
Lectures [b]	23	24

** $p < .01$ * $p < .05$

[a] In addition, the following statistically significant differences obtain: Stanford women students report reading fiction more frequently than Berkeley women, but the men in the two schools do not differ from each other in this. Twenty-two per cent of the Stanford women and 11 per cent of the Berkeley women report having broken rules for the fun of it frequently or occasionally. Twenty-five per cent of the Stanford men and 17 per cent of the Berkeley men report themselves as having engaged in off-campus service activities frequently or occasionally.

[b] Sixty-four per cent of the Stanford seniors and 51 per cent of the Berkeley seniors report themselves as having attended lectures occasionally.

What differences are there in favorite activities between (1) men and women and (2) Berkeley and Stanford students?

As far as male-female differences are concerned, the women read more often than the men. They attend lectures, symphonies, and the theatre more often, visit museums, write, paint, and seek other creative expressions more often. They engage more often in service activities off-campus, serve more often on student committees, attend church or church-connected activities more frequently than the men. But the men engage more frequently in sports activities, both as participants and as spectators. In sum, the women show a greater orientation toward intellectual, artistic, and service activities. This is true not only at Stanford, where the women are more highly selected than the men, but also at Berkeley, where they are more evenly matched.[7] It is particularly worth noting that this male-female intellectual and esthetic discrepancy persists at the end of four years of liberal education.

There are fewer differences between the Stanford groups and the Berkeley groups than there are between the men and women students.

Stanford students more frequently read fiction, attend lectures, engage in social and sports activities, serve on student committees, and travel. The Stanford men report themselves as going to the museum and the symphony and engaging in sports activities as participants more often than the Berkeley men—65 per cent as compared to 55 per cent. Sixty-one per cent of the Stanford women say they read fiction frequently, as compared with 48 per cent of the Berkeley women. Twenty-two per cent of the Stanford women say they occasionally break rules for the fun of it, as compared with 11 per cent of the Berkeley women.

These responses point toward somewhat more intellectual involvement, involvement with social activities, and student self-rule at Stanford. These differences may be due to the more selective entrance requirements at Stanford, and to the higher social class background of Stanford students.[8]

The students' reported behavior is usually consistent with their expressed attitudes. In response to the question of what

[7] The mean SAT verbal score for the entering Berkeley men in 1960 was 548 (SD 93); for the women, it was 544 (SD 86). The score for the entering Stanford men in 1961 was 617 (SD 70); for the women, it was 664 (SD 63).

[8] It is to be kept in mind that Berkeley is highly selective, too, taking only the top 12 per cent of the graduating seniors of the California high schools. As Martin Trow has pointed out: "In 1960, Berkeley admitted . . . 420 students with SAT verbal scores of over 650, and almost 1,000 with SAT scores of over 600, more at that level than enter MIT and Amherst com-

would be important to them in their future lives, they give low rank to participation in community affairs, activities directed toward national or international improvement, religious activities, and helping other people. There are two instances where the students' attitudes and behavior seem to diverge. Between 35 per cent and 51 per cent of them reported themselves as engaging frequently in social activities, parties, and the like. At the same time, they rank social life and entertainment quite low in importance for their life after graduation. (Nine per cent or less rank it among the first three of a list of fourteen.) But when one considers that love and affection are ranked among the first three by nearly half of the men, and between two-thirds and three-quarters of the women, the discrepancy seems to dissolve, and we understand what the students are really after in their frequent social activities. They seek for deeper engagement and meaningfulness. As we will see later, their relationships with other people are a source of both problems, pleasure, and progress to them during their college years.

The second discrepancy is not so easily resolved. Four per cent or less of the students anticipated that athletics would be important in their lives after graduation. Yet about half of the men and more than a third of the women reported frequent attendance at sports events, and larger percentages said they often actively engaged in sports as participants. In their interviews with us, the students also often mentioned sports activities spontaneously as sources of pleasure. The denial of future importance to an activity that, to judge by the students' behavior, seems quite important to them, raises an interesting question. Perhaps the academic emphasis of college, uneasiness about pleasure, and a sense of the infantile components of pleasure in sports all combine to account for this low ranking. Sports, of course, are not the only area in which students fail to integrate their impulses, plea-

---

bined." It also admitted 1,500 students with scores below 500—more than triple the number with scores that low who were admitted to Kutztown State College in Pennsylvania. Trow, Martin. *Notes on Undergraduate Teaching at Large State Universities.* Stanford: Center for Advanced Study in the Behavioral Sciences, 1966 (mimeo). This study is cited by Lipset, S. M., and Altbach, P. G. "Student Politics and Higher Education in the United States." *Comparative Education Review,* 1966, *10,* 347.

sures, and interests into their growing adulthood. Sex, for instance, is also ranked as low importance, even though it is a frequent object of their talking and thinking.

Residence requirements differ between Berkeley and Stanford. At Stanford, women undergraduates are required to live in college dormitories throughout their four years; the men are required to do so only in their freshman year. At Berkeley, the students are free to live wherever they want to; the university provides housing, and has built many additional dormitories in the recent past, but can house only a portion of all undergraduates. Particularly the freshmen in 1961 experienced difficulty in obtaining housing. Joining a fraternity or sorority upon entering Berkeley solved the housing problem for some of them.

The fact that Berkeley allows choice of residence provides us with an instructive opportunity to ascertain the residential preferences of students when left to themselves.

Of the Berkeley senior men reporting, 26 per cent had started out in dormitories as freshmen. Only 11 per cent of the seniors lived there. For apartments, the trend was reversed. Ten per cent started out in apartments and 44 per cent were still there in their senior year. Fraternity residence began with 13 per cent in the freshman year, reached the highest point of 20 per cent during the sophomore year, and then dropped to 11 per cent during the senior year. The figures for the Berkeley women are similar. Thirty-nine per cent were in the dorms as freshmen, and 10 per cent were still there as seniors. Sorority residence began with 13 per cent, reached its peak during the sophomore year with 17 per cent, and slightly dropped to 15 per cent during the senior year. Eight per cent of the freshman women were in apartments, but 49 per cent of the senior women were. About 19 per cent of the students of both sexes lived at home as freshmen, and about 10 per cent of the seniors did. Elizabeth Alfert reports that those who lived at home dropped out of the university in much larger proportion than those who lived in dormitories, apartments, fraternities, or sororities.[9]

[9] Alfert, Elizabeth. "Housing Selection, Need Satisfaction, and Dropout from College." *Psychological Reports*, 1966, *19*, 183–86. Alfert's study is based on data collected in our study.

Some students start out their college residence in a hotel. A woman student among our interviewees who felt very shy with people began in a hotel room. She gradually invited other students to her room to listen to music and to talk. The following semester, she moved into a dorm. Step by step, she developed closer and more mutually gratifying relations with other people. One wonders how many freshmen who have a need for privacy and even distance from other people are excessively intruded upon by the present dormitory system, which is compulsory in many places.

Individuals differ sharply—the same individual may differ in any college year. We were impressed by how important the sorority was for some Berkeley freshman women as a means of bridging the gap between the more or less protected home environment (particularly if the student happened to come from a small town), and the big and somewhat frightening university. The sorority behaves like "Mama," and a fairly strict Mama at that— setting down specific hours at which freshmen must study, and giving more or less precise rules as to how to behave on a date, including whether a boy is to be kissed or not on a first date. These rules become more relaxed as the freshman year continues. For some, the sorority becomes less important, and later, some leave it. In general, sorority or fraternity membership seems to become less important in the junior and senior years. But our observations have impressed us with the important support provided by small group membership. Wherever fraternities are restricted or abolished, attention needs to be given to finding proper substitutes.

At what point does group membership become less supportive and more constrictive? That question transcends the subject of fraternal organizations. We have observed a common tendency for students to associate with people similar to each other, even at the expense of broadening their cognitive and imaginative capacities. It suggests to us that attention to "mixing" students is a problem that cannot be confined to the freshman year. For some students, the freshman year is the worst one for mixing because the shock of the difference of other people is often too severe.

At Stanford, all women undergraduates remain in college dormitories for four years. The men are allowed to move off-campus from the beginning of the sophomore year. Eleven per cent of our respondents report themselves as having lived off-campus during their sophomore year. This rises to 29 per cent in their junior year, and to 37 per cent in their senior year. About a third of the men live in dormitories from the sophomore through the senior years. A fourth report themselves as residing in their fraternities during their sophomore and junior years, and a fifth as residing there during their senior year. Eighteen per cent of the Stanford men among our respondents, and 27 per cent of the women, were on overseas campuses during their sophomore year. This dropped to 5 per cent for the men and 14 per cent for the women in their junior year.

About the same proportions—roughly a third—of the Berkeley and Stanford men students live in university dormitories in their sophomore year. But while in both universities there is a strong trend toward off-campus living, the Berkeley men leave the dorms in much larger percentages. Even higher percentages of the Berkeley women do so; 41 per cent resided in dorms during the sophomore year, and 10 per cent did so during the senior year.

This dramatic tendency of women to leave their campus residences is an important factor for consideration by institutions that require their women to live in. Moreover, when left to choose freely, students, particularly upperclassmen, tend to move into apartments or houses of their own. The reasons for this tendency are many. Some prefer the intimacy of one or two partners or of a small group. Others want to save money. Some have the more negative incentive of fleeing from the noise and intensiveness of the dormitories. Still others leave because, in spite of appearances, residential living does not provide enough opportunity for friendships and closer relationships with a group, nor does it necessarily facilitate that participation in campus culture that the "commuter colleges" often so longingly ascribe to the residential institutions. For some, moving off-campus is a flight from, or protest against, the perceived coerciveness of the institution. In recent years, students at many different residential colleges have increasingly argued for the right to move off-campus. We are probably dealing with a phenomenon that is subject to some extent to the spirit of the times—a difficult problem for institutions who have to make heavy financial investments and would like to plan for an indefinite future. But it is probably safe to say that in the foreseeable future, dormitories will remain viable for many students only if changes are made that take into account more fully the students' desire for more genuine companionship. It is conceivable that the residential principle is in the process of some partial erosion, just as the cohesiveness of college classes (for example, the class of 1965) has dwindled in many places.

How important to our students were their places of residence, and the activities and relations these places made possible? We asked the seniors to list the three organizations that had been the most important to them during their college years (the question was open-ended). From the high percentages of responses, it would appear that practically everyone who belonged to a fraternity, sorority, or eating club listed these as important (48 per cent of the Stanford men and 25 per cent of the Berkeley men listed fraternities; 24 per cent of the Berkeley women listed sororities). Stanford has no sororities, and it is of interest that the living groups are listed as important by only 33 per cent of the women. But next to fraternities and sororities, the living groups draw large, though proportionately much lesser, percentages. About a fifth of the Berkeley men and women, and 14 per cent of the Stanford men list their living groups as important. These responses may be compared with preferences for other groups. At Berkeley, 20 per cent list civil rights and other "action" groups. Similar proportions list professional clubs, religious groups, and hobby clubs. At Stanford the overseas campuses, student government, international relations activities, and hobby clubs are singled out by between 14 per cent and 20 per cent of the students. Athletic groups are listed by 13 per cent of the Berkeley men, 19 per cent of the Stanford men, and about 7 per cent of the women.[10]

Having looked at what students do while in school, let us examine the question of what they do during the summer. This question was raised early in our study because we were aware how much the university structured the students' time and activities, and we wished to know what students do when they

[10] For a full discussion of the differing patterns of residence or living of Stanford men, see Chapter 7.

are not under the direct control of the university. Our expectation was that we might find many students making creative use of their freedom. But from the first series of interviews after the summer of the freshman year, it became clear that there was no strong tendency on the students' parts to make the summer an especially meaningful experience. We found that many tended to submit themselves to controls of their time and activities similar to and sometimes even more coercive than those of the university. Other students more or less drifted along. The instances of coherent, meaningful summer experience, in terms of either work or personal growth, were relatively rare. One may ascribe this to the need for a period of relaxation and recharging; however, it is not our impression that the summer experience is guided by a more or less implicit desire for purposive rest, but rather that it is an expression of a relatively passive attitude on the students' parts. (A meaningful summer, however active, would probably have been more useful to many students than the rest they were getting.) As will be seen later, however, confrontation with parents and a move toward independence was a marked feature of the summer after the freshman year.

> About three-fourths of the men students and about two-thirds of the women students work during the three college summers. (There is a drop for the summer after the sophomore year at Stanford, probably because many students are then on their way to or from the overseas campuses.) In the summer after their freshman year, the largest percentages of men students were engaged in summer employment that we had coded under the heading of "general labor," that is, work that requires minimal or no skills, but a certain amount of physical strength and stamina. Thirty-one per cent of the Stanford men and 23 per cent of the Berkeley men were found in this category in the summer after their freshman year. For the women, office work was the highest category. Further, in the summer after the freshman year, twice as many women as men were engaged in such service jobs as those of camp counselor, waiter or waitress, babysitter, and casino worker, but the percentages for the women go down over the two subsequent summers.

One may assume that most of the activities just listed are not primarily educational in character; nor is real financial need an incentive for most students. But these jobs seem to have a major root in our social ideology, which stresses the value of work and the making of money for their own sakes, and another root in our psychological disposition, which makes keeping busy an important security device. It must also be remembered that making one's own money is for the students an important step in their growing independence from their parents. Many students are burdened by a sense of obligation to their parents for financing their education.

There is, however, one category of summer activities that is educational in character and that we coded as "semi-professional apprenticeships." Included in this category are all occupations that require a certain amount of skill and can be considered as a step toward a given profession. Fifteen per cent of the Stanford and Berkeley men were engaged in such jobs in the summer after their freshman year, and about 5 per cent of the women were. By the third summer, about 23 per cent of the men were engaged in such jobs, while percentages for the women had risen to only 9 per cent. Thus, during their last summer before graduation, only relatively small portions of the students engaged in work that might have had bearing on their occupational choice.

It is interesting to note that there is little difference between Stanford and Berkeley with regard to the nature of the summer jobs held by students. There is also little difference over time: the distribution of jobs in the summer after the junior year is nearly the same as that in the summer after the freshman year, except that among the men there is a decrease in general labor jobs and an increase in semi-professional jobs.[11]

[11] In a pilot study of male Berkeley and Stanford interviewees reporting on their summer experiences, Barry Sokolik found that people who make different uses of their summers differ significantly on several personality scales. His data suggest that while some students may be predisposed to make a more autonomous use of the summer, others may need the help of institutional arrangements. Mr. Sokolik suggests that "universities might allow students holding jobs to live in coeducational dormitories during the summer, and provide appropriate educational arrangements. Or universities might arrange for community projects headed by professors or student personnel staff and, where appropriate, sponsored by local businessmen, government, or other agencies." In spite of its importance, the summer experience has gone unstudied. Barry Sokolik reports that "a search of the *Education Index* and the *Psychological Abstracts* from 1950 to the present failed to produce even a single relevant study concerned with the nature or function of the summer experience for college students—except for studies concerning summer school."

How important is the experience of living at an overseas campus to the student's overall development; and how important does the student perceive it to be? For the Stanford students, attendance for two academic quarters at one of the overseas campuses was one of the most important experiences of their college careers. Under this system, a group of 40 men and 40 women go to a common overseas residence and are taught by Stanford professors and specially selected native instructors.

Thirty-one per cent of our men and 53 per cent of our women respondents had gone to overseas campuses. Thirty-three per cent of the men and 46 per cent of the women said that being overseas had had great influence on them.[12]

What, in particular, did they get out of it? In their interviews with us, the students said regularly that one of the important aspects of their overseas residence was the opportunity it afforded for establishing meaningful relations with members of both sexes, and that these relations did continue even after the group returned home. Similarly, in a dissertation by Emily Stevens Girault, it is noted that 16 per cent of the students interviewed before departure for a Stanford overseas campus gave establishing friendships as one of the anticipated outcomes.[13] Sixty-six per cent of the students interviewed six months after their return from an overseas campus listed friendships among the outcome. Of a third group, interviewed 18 months after their return from their overseas campuses, 80 per cent did so.

The overseas campus gives a natural demonstration of some of the conditions for establishing meaningful and growth-producing relations between people: a common purpose, so that members of the groups can help each other; ease and informality of meeting (in contrast to the dating system); and a mixing

12 Unfortunately, we asked for the influence of "being overseas" instead of "being on an overseas campus." Some, therefore, must be referring to overseas experiences other than campus residence. But it seems plausible that most of them meant overseas campus residence. When one compares the Stanford with the Berkeley figures, only 5 per cent to 8 per cent at Berkeley assign great influence to having been overseas. (Berkeley has a numerically much more restricted overseas program.)

13 *Effects of Residency at an Overseas Campus on Some Social Attitudes of Stanford Students.* Unpublished doctoral dissertation, Stanford, 1964.

of different kinds of people in a non-threatening way. In addition, there is an academic communality, and greater leisure time than on the home campus (only four days of classes). During the period of our study, however, the students demanded consistently that their overseas courses be made to relate more fully to their overseas experience.

One may also raise the question of the "safety-valve" value of overseas residence. Given the students' restlessness, their desire to travel, and their frequent or occasional dissatisfaction with college life, the prospect of two quarters of residence abroad may well inhibit unrest. When the students return, the time until graduation is much shorter, and the memories of their overseas stay are vivid and pleasant enough to make it seem less worthwhile to press for changes. At the same time, the overseas experience sharpens many students' perceptions of their home institution, and leads them to voice criticisms.

What of relations with others? Relations with their fellows are of great importance to college students. They enjoy them, and attribute to them great influence on personal development. They also find them a source of strain and suffering. At the end of their college years, many students expressed the wish that they might have been able to establish even more meaningful, intense, and less self-conscious relationships. In an area as deep as relations with other people, one must expect many complexities and levels of feelings.

> In the Senior Questionnaire, about 42 per cent of the men and women say it had become much less difficult for them to feel close to people. Nearly a fifth report that it has become slightly more difficult or much more difficult. Very few, 6 per cent or less, say that during their college years they have not made any close friends who significantly influenced them or whom they significantly influenced.

The picture of progressive ease in social relationships is also borne out in the periods the students single out as difficult or easy socially.

> The period of greatest difficulty is the freshman year. A decisive break toward a good social life seems to come for about half of the men and over a third of the women

in the spring of their junior year or the fall of their senior year. Fifty-one per cent of the Stanford men and 39 per cent of the women list their freshman year as the most difficult socially.

The discrepancy might be explained by the Stanford sex ratio of two-and-a-half men to one woman. But given this ratio, the discrepancy is small, and it is noteworthy that at Berkeley, with roughly a one-to-one sex ratio, 43 per cent of the men and 42 per cent of the women declare that their freshman year is particularly difficult. It is to be kept in mind that social difficulties do not include only relations with the other sex. The dormitory experience, and the encountering of hordes of strangers, many of whom seem more accomplished than oneself, is a rather sharp transition from a relatively protected home.

While the women report less social difficulty than the men for their freshman year, the men report greater ease than the women during the end of their junior and senior years. This may indicate in part that men's social development is slower; but it also may be an indication that "difficulty" and "goodness" in social relations may mean different things to the two sexes. The men may refer to their greater ease in obtaining and entertaining dates, while the women are beginning to look for greater depth of relationship and for marriage partners.

The increasing proximity of the two sexes is also reflected in the fact that by the middle of their senior year, about one-half of the men and two-thirds of the women report that they had been going steady during college. About a sixth of the men and a quarter of the women are engaged or have been engaged. Nearly one-tenth of the men and women are married.

The picture of relative interpersonal serenity that has been conveyed by several of the data just cited seems to be further confirmed by the fact that few students report themselves as having frequently seriously disagreed with or having taken a different attitude from their friends.

About one-sixth say that they had serious disagreements with friends of the same sex, and slightly lesser numbers disagreed with friends of the opposite sex. Over a quarter say that during their entire college career, two or more friendships had either broken up or been severely strained. Half of the men and more than a third of the women say that this never occurred.

But the relatively low incidence of disagreement and conflict may betoken not so much the peacefulness of social relationships as their relative superficiality. If one remembers the student's turbulent development during late adolescence, his shaky identity and struggle for self-definition, the situational factor of his being exposed to many different and dissonant peers, and his attempts to try himself out in new heterosexual roles and new types of friendships closer to the adult model, and considers these tests and the inevitable mistakes they involve, the vagaries of impulse, the hazards, the hopes, and the fears, one may be surprised that a much larger number of students do not experience break-ups, strains, disagreements, or at least strong feelings of difference. There are indications that these feelings exist, but are glossed over by a compelling sense that they must, if possible, never be expressed. In our interviews, the students exhibited deep resistance to admitting negative feelings about others; and we often found that they would go to great lengths of inconvenience or pain before they would dare to tell a roommate about some habit or action of his that greatly interfered with their own studying, or sleeping. Thus, they might walk every night to a distant study room on campus rather than facing up to a "criticism" of their roommate.

This resistance to admitting negative feelings about others prevents them from finding out more fully what they themselves feel and want—a precondition for establishing a relationship with others based on self-respect and devoid of resentment and self-deprecation. The apparent smoothness of relations with others seems in part to be bought at the price of developing a more profound self-definition. It is also bought at the price of the selection of inappropriate peers or partners for closer relationships. The progress of students during the college years in mutual tolerance and in ease and graciousness of social behavior must be viewed in the light of this loss. As a socialization agency, college contributes to the education of people toward that "consensus" which is a marked characteristic of American social and political behavior. Such "consensus" training at the moment seems to inhibit differentiation and assertiveness of personality.

Our hesitations about the depth of the students' relationships to one another are supported by their responses to our question about whether they had found in college one or several friends with whom they had a deep, meaningful, and lasting relationship.

> Fifty per cent of the Berkeley men said that they were not sure, or had not found such a relationship with members of the opposite sex, and 34 per cent said this about members of their own sex. The figures are lower for the Stanford men (37 per cent and 22 per cent respectively), and lower for the women (23 per cent of the Berkeley and Stanford women for the opposite sex, and 18 per cent and 12 per cent for their own sex).

These figures seem to indicate in many students, particularly in the men, a sense of dissatisfaction in their relations with others.

Is the capacity for making friends such that those who have it will tend to make friends with members of both sexes? Analyses of our data indicate that this tends to be so. People who have close relations with members of the same sex tend to have close relations with people of the opposite sex, and vice versa. But there is a sex difference in regard to the people who have not found close friends of their own sex. Women who do not have close friends of their own sex are much more likely than men to have close friends of the opposite sex. The women also have a much more pronounced tendency than the men to be close to members of both sexes, and the women rarely have no close friends of either sex (see Table 3). There also seems to be a tendency for more men than women to be close to their own sex alone.

On the basis of some observations, we had assumed that there would be a tendency for the men in particular to seek out women rather than men when they wished to express their deeper feelings, or to engage in self-revelation or self-exploration. We thought that among other things, the frequently observed fear of homosexuality in men would be a barrier to intimacy between them. The figures in Table 3 show a small percentage to whom this may apply. Only about a tenth of the men say they have close friendships with the opposite sex only. However, more detailed investigation might uphold our hypothesis, if it revealed that there are different definitions of intimacy in the two sexes. It is also worth noting that between 22 per cent of the Stanford men and 36 per cent of the Berkeley men report no close friendships with other men during college.

TABLE 3

CLOSE FRIENDSHIPS WITH MEMBERS OF THE SAME AND
OF THE OPPOSITE SEX
(FIGURES ARE PERCENTAGES)

	Stanford Men (N = 274)	Stanford Women (N = 214)	Berkeley Men (N = 284)	Berkeley Women (N = 266)
Close with the same sex and with the opposite sex	54	70	38	66
Not close with the same sex or with the opposite sex	14	4	24	8
Close with the same sex but not with the opposite sex	24	18	26	15
Close with the opposite sex but not with the same sex	8	8	12	11
Not close with the same sex	22	12	36	19
Not close with the opposite sex	38	22	50	23

While students in college have relatively infrequent relations with adults, they seem to include at least one group of older people in their circle of friends. Somewhat to our surprise, we found that only small percentages—about one-seventh—said that they had not come to know any graduate student well. About a fourth of the students had come to know between one and three graduate students well; about a third, four to ten; about a fifth, ten to nineteen; and about a tenth, twenty or more. This availability of the graduate students is worth further exploration. Our impression is that it contributes much to the informal education of undergraduates. (One should compare otherwise similar institutions with and without attached graduate schools.) Particularly in our observations of the student activists did we find that graduate students often supplied what the undergraduates were looking for, given the infrequency of support from faculty and administration: adult support by people who are apparently successful in the academic enterprise, are articulate, and possess a longer time-perspective than undergraduates.[14]

We also asked the seniors whether they still had close friends near their own age whom they had known before college.

We found that about half of the seniors have between one and three close friends of both sexes whom they knew before college; and a fairly large number have four or more such friends. Males tend to have more male friends and females more female friends from their precollege days, but about half have remained close friends with members of the opposite sex.

We had assumed that friendships would be much more a function of the environment; that with the shift to college, old friendships would dissolve; and that by the senior year most of the precollege friendships would have more or less come to an end. Our data point to greater permanence than we had expected.

Finally, the importance of social relations to the student is underlined by our discovery that

close to two-thirds of the men and 58 per cent of the women find only moderate enjoyment in being alone. Twenty-three per cent of the Stanford men and 14 per cent of the Berkeley men, and 37 per cent of the Stanford women and 23 per cent of the Berkeley women say that they find much enjoyment in being alone. At the opposite end of the spectrum, 14 per cent of the Stanford men and 22 per cent of the Berkeley men, and 6 per cent of the Stanford women and 17 per cent of the Berkeley women say that they find very little enjoyment in being alone.

These data show interesting differences both between the schools and between the sexes.

According to developmental theory, achievement of a relatively stable identity is a condition of forming adequate relations with other people. Enjoyment of self and enjoyment of others

[14] See Katz, Joseph and Sanford, Nevitt. "Causes of the Student Revolution." *Saturday Review*, December 18, 1965, *48*, 64–66, 76, 79.

are intimately related. Our data show that 21 per cent of the men and 28 per cent of the women who say they have close friends of the same sex also report great enjoyment in being alone. The same is said by 17 per cent of the men and 29 per cent of the women who have close friends of the opposite sex.

We now turn to the sexual aspects of social behavior and attitudes, and to developing attitudes toward marriage. The data on sexual attitudes and behavior run parallel to those on social attitudes and behavior already reported.

> The students say that during their college years, their sexual impulses have become increasingly more acceptable to them. Only 13 per cent or less express a contrary opinion. By their senior year, a fifth of the senior men and less than a third of the senior women disagree with the statement that full sexual relations are permissible for males before marriage; and only a little more than one-tenth of the students disagree strongly. About a third say that during college, they have reached a high degree of physical intimacy. About a third of the men and a fifth of the women say that the degree of physical intimacy they have reached has been low. The women report experiencing more conflict with regard to sex and also achieving a greater amount of acceptance of sex.

Despite the differences in the students' backgrounds, the different sex ratios at Berkeley and at Stanford, and the differences in social opportunities, the figures for both institutions are remarkably similar. This similarity extended to frequency of dating. The women tend to make close friends of either sex more frequently than the men do.

What are the students' attitudes toward heterosexual relations and what changes have taken place over the four years? Very high proportions of senior men and women say that they think about sex often, take pleasure in various activities relating to sex, do not find sex objectionable, and do not believe that there is widespread sexual misconduct. They approve of premarital intercourse, intermarriage between the races, and abortion. They think that women should be given as much sexual freedom as men.

(These assertions are made by between 75 per cent and 95 per cent of the senior men and women.)

Between the freshman and the senior years, dramatic changes take place in attitudes toward premarital sex, with both men and women moving toward acceptance or even advocacy of premarital sex (Table 4).

> In the Senior Questionnaire, 69 per cent of the men and 60 per cent of the women said they believed that full sexual relations should be permissible to the male before marriage. A fourth of the men and more than a third of the women stated that their sexual impulses had become much more acceptable to them during college; and with the exception of about 13 per cent, the rest reported that these impulses had become moderately more acceptable.

In addition, many more seniors than freshmen are not set back by unconventional behavior in women, are in favor of sexual equality, intermarriage, and abortion, and otherwise take a freer and less censorious attitude to sex and sex-related activities. These changes did not come about without struggle.

> Only a third of the men and about a fifth of the women say that during their college years their attitudes toward sex have not involved them in a struggle of conflicting thoughts and feelings. The rest report either moderate or great struggle. A third of the women report great struggle. Close to 60 per cent of the men and women report moderate or great difficulty in controlling their sexual impulses during college.

Our data indicate that the higher the degree of intimacy reached, the greater the intervening struggle. There is a widespread lessening of the moralistic outlook. For instance, about two-thirds of the freshman men and women said that a large number of people are guilty of bad sexual conduct; only a third of the seniors so replied. This is one of many pieces of evidence we have that sex and guilt are becoming more dissociated from each other.

TABLE 4

DIFFERENCES IN FRESHMAN AND SENIOR ATTITUDES TO SEX [a]

	Stanford Men (N = 185)		Stanford Women (N = 148)		Berkeley Men (N = 286)		Berkeley Women (N = 265)	
	F	S	F	S	F	S	F	S
No man of character would ask his fiancée to have sexual intercourse with him before marriage	52	11	52	11	47	13	54	21
A large number of people are guilty of bad sexual conduct	70	33	63	30	67	35	67	35
In illegitimate pregnancies, abortion is in many cases the most reasonable alternative	45	78	42	64	46	71	24	60
I dislike women who disregard the usual social or moral conventions	51	22	59	20	46	24	55	26
People would be happier if sex experience before marriage were taken for granted in both men and women	33	60	18	45	41	63	18	51
There is nothing wrong with the idea of intermarriage between different races	59	80	67	74	67	79	56	77
I never attend a sexy show if I can avoid it	25	6	41	19	30	11	51	28
I believe women ought to have as much sexual freedom as men	61	77	32	57	59	76	35	60

[a] Percentages are those answering "True." The *same* people are responding as freshmen (F) and as seniors (S).

There is some difference between men and women in sexual attitudes. Often the difference is one of degree of endorsement. For instance, both men and women students move toward endorsing sexual equality or advocating premarital intercourse, but the women do so in smaller proportions. Hardly any men say that they are embarrassed by dirty stories, but about a quarter of the senior women say so (Table 5). About two-thirds of the men say that they like to talk about sex, but only half the women say they do. Less women than men say that when a man is with a woman, he is usually thinking about things related to her sex. A third of the senior men still think so; that is, they seem to think of women primarily as sex objects. Strikingly different endorsements are given to the item: "There was a time when I wished that I had been born a member of the opposite sex." About one in seven of the senior men agree, and 55 per cent of the Stanford women and 40 per cent of the Berkeley senior women do. This response may be influenced by the fact that it is harder for the men to admit this wish, because of fear of the label of homosexuality; and that men may be less aware of their feelings in this area than women. But the response also lends support to those who claim that envy of the male sex and "phallic" strivings are a frequent female characteristic.

TABLE 5

DIFFERENCES IN ATTITUDES TO SEX OF MEN AND WOMEN SENIORS
(FIGURES ARE PERCENTAGES)

	Stanford Men (N = 185)	Stanford Women (N = 148)	Berkeley Men (N = 286)	Berkeley Women (N = 265)
There was a time when I wished that I had been born a member of the opposite sex	12	55	15	40
People would be happier if sex experience before marriage were taken for granted in both men and women	60	45	63	51
I am embarrassed by dirty stories	4	25	6	28
I believe women ought to have as much sexual freedom as men	77	57	76	60
I like to talk about sex	62	46	64	51
When a man is with a woman he is usually thinking about things related to her sex	34	19	36	20

To what extent is frequency of dating associated with movements toward greater heterosexual intimacy? For the men in our samples, the frequency of dating increases considerably between their freshman and senior years.

Over half of the Stanford and Berkeley men said that they had no evening dates in an average week during their freshman year. [Because of inaccuracies in the key punching of this item, the data about frequency of college dating are to be taken as approximations.] By the senior year, about a third of the men report no evening dates. While only about 12 per cent of the men dated two times or more per week as freshmen, about a third of the seniors did so.

But mere frequency can be misleading, and the extent to which dating facilitates intimacy is open to question. (In a sense, dating is an equivalent of the chaperone system. It allows for some indirect expression of the sexual impulse, while at the same time inhibiting it.) As we reported earlier, our interviews with the Stanford overseas students indicate that opportunities for more informal contacts and participation in common tasks seem superior avenues toward better acquaintance and close friendship.

The dating behavior of the women tends to support what we have just said. While there are many indices of increased intimacy, the actual frequency of dating remains fairly stable.

About a quarter of the women report no dates in an average freshman year week. About a quarter report no dates for an average senior week. The increase in the amount of dates per week is less than for the men. Forty-seven per cent of the Stanford women and 37 per cent of the Berkeley women date two or more times per week in their freshman year; 54 per cent and 47 per cent do so as seniors.

In the interviews we learned that many freshman women engage for a period in rather "promiscuous" dating, often to convince themselves that they are desirable even though intellectual. After they have gained reassurance, they turn toward fewer dating partners, and eventually move toward a closer relationship with one man.

How do sexual attitudes and behavior in college relate to previous development?

About 60 per cent of the women and about 35 per cent of the men report that they first began taking a more intense interest in sexual matters between 17 and 21.

There is other evidence that interest in sex does not seem to correlate with onset of the physical signs of puberty. We asked the women to indicate their age at the time of their first menstruation and the men to indicate their age at the time when they first underwent voice changes, body hair growth, or other signs of the onset of puberty.

> Over 50 per cent of the men and 75 per cent of the women said this had happened between 11 and 13, but only about 17 per cent of the men and 9 per cent of the women said that they first began to take a more intense interest in sexual matters between 11 and 13. It also appears that for the bulk of the men students, about 67 per cent, the onset of puberty, as reported by them, was between 12 and 14, and for the women, between 11 and 13.

It appears from the above data that while women develop physically somewhat earlier than men, large proportions of them take a more intense conscious interest in sex later than the men do. At the same time, it appeared in our interviews that the women had achieved a more mature orientation to sex: that is, they seemed to be more aware of the psychological complexity of sex and to think of members of the other sex more as individuals than as stereotypes. Perhaps once the women take strong interest in sex, they do so in a fairly sophisticated manner, while for the men, the integration of sex with the rest of their personality is a longer and more gradual process. At least in our society, there are possible discrepancies in this regard between many men and women throughout life.

There are fairly large numbers of students—roughly a third of the men and a quarter of the women—who seem to date little or not at all even as college seniors. Similar percentages obtain for infrequent dating in high school. One quarter of the Stanford men and around a third of the other respondents said they had dated no more than twice a year during their last two high school years. It is of special interest that in spite of the very favorable male-female ratio at Stanford, over a fifth of the women students reported having no dates in an average week in any of the four college years. Are we dealing here with a sizable group of people whose loneliness deserves special attention? Other analyses of the data indicate that while men who dated little or not at all in their last two years of high school tend to date little as college freshmen, this is less often the case for the women. Of those who do not date as college seniors, between 50 per cent and 75 per cent say they dated not at all or only once or twice a year during their last two years of high school. By the middle of their senior year, slightly less than a third of the men and women students report themselves as having reached a high degree of physical intimacy. The interview data support the Senior Questionnaire data. By the middle of the junior year, more than a third of our male interviewees and a quarter of the female ones had experienced sexual intercourse.[15]

TABLE 6

EXPERIENCE OF SEXUAL INTERCOURSE BY MIDDLE OF JUNIOR YEAR
(IN PER CENT)
(INTERVIEWERS' REPORT)

	Stanford Men (N = 47)	Stanford Women (N = 39)	Berkeley Men (N = 41)	Berkeley Women (N = 39)
Yes	36	23	39	26
No	60	62	61	72
Information uncertain	4	15	—	2

What is the relationship between sex and morality? Our data indicate that by their senior year, about 60 per cent of the men and about half of the women think that people would be happier if premarital sex were taken for granted; and even larger percentages approve of premarital sex and even abortion. But

[15] To help determine the accuracy and meaning of the students' self-reports of their degree of sexual intimacy, we checked the questionnaire responses against our interview data, which contain much more substantial information about sexual behavior. About 20 per cent of the seniors who reported themselves as having reached a "high degree of physical intimacy" had not had coitus during college—at least as far as our data showed. At the same time, 39 per cent of the men and 13 per cent of the women whom we knew to have had intercourse reported the degree of their sexual intimacy only as moderate. Caution must be used in interpreting these data, because these two computations are based on small numbers (one group of 40 people and one of 39). But they suggest the possibility that for the senior women, the percentages reporting high degree of physical intimacy are about the same as the percentage of those who have experienced coitus in college; while for the men, the percentages of those who have experienced coitus are higher than those who report a high degree of physical intimacy. Table 7 also supports this inference.

this liberalism does not mean that sexual conduct is not guided by moral standards. Our interviews show that students know each other for a protracted period of time before they engage in intercourse. Their relationship is usually a meaningful one and often the partners seriously think of marriage and do get married. If there has been a shift recently in sexual morality—which is difficult to determine in the absence of sufficient data in previous decades—one might say that it means not so much a decline of moral codes as a change in their contents; so that for large segments of college youth, premarital sex is consistent with morality and behavior ruled by principles of responsibility and concern for others. The thesis that heterosexual behavior is guided by moral standards is also borne out by the distinction students make between extramarital and premarital sex. In the interviews, the numbers of students who found premarital sex acceptable were at least three times larger than those who found extramarital sex acceptable. Presumably a moral principal—fidelity—is violated in the one but not in the other.

Our interviews corroborate Ehrmann's finding that for females, sex and affection are more closely associated than for males.[16] The percentages of women for whom sex and affection are closely linked is nearly double that of the men (Table 7). However, at least part of this discrepancy might be explained by the developmental and career lag of the men previously referred to. Fuller integration of sex and affection may have come later for them.

TABLE 7

COLLEGE JUNIORS FOR WHOM SEX AND AFFECTION ARE STRONGLY LINKED
(IN PER CENT)
(INTERVIEWERS' RATINGS)

Stanford Men (N = 39)	Stanford Women (N = 36)	Berkeley Men (N = 40)	Berkeley Women (N = 36)
48	86	32	63

[16] Ehrmann, Winston. *Premarital Dating Behavior.* New York: Bantam Books, 1960. Our interviews also corroborated Ehrmann's conclusion that both sexes are more lenient toward their peers than toward themselves with regard to permissible heterosexual behavior.

Other data support the thesis that physical sexual activity alone is not strongly desired by the students. In our list of fourteen adult interests and activities, only about one-tenth of the students interviewed ranked sexual needs among the three most important. Some denial of sex is probably involved in these responses, given the students' frequent talking and thinking about sex. But compare their response about sex to that about love and affection, which is ranked by 43 per cent of the men and about 71 per cent of the women as among the three most important.[17]

Our data also show that students who report a high degree of physical intimacy have a long history of frequent dating, stretching back to high school (Table 8).

The rather sparse dating history for those who are low in physical intimacy suggests that they tend to refrain not only from sexual contact but from other association between the sexes. Table 8 also shows that those high in physical intimacy also tend to drink beer and liquor more frequently than those who are low in intimacy; their greater freedom of expression in the sexual sphere seems to be correlated with greater freedom of impulse expression elsewhere. It is of interest also that women high in physical intimacy report great struggles concerning sex, while the men do not. This greater struggle may in part be a result of adult social feelings about premarital intercourse, which are more strict for women than for men; and with the possibility of pregnancy, the consequences of intercourse are more portentous for them. Moreover, young women tend to have a psychologically more complex understanding of sex than the men have.

Our investigations do not confirm the popular stereotype of widespread sexual promiscuity on campus. Where it occurs, sexual intimacy seems to take place in the context of a relationship that is serious rather than casual. Sexual behavior, however, is governed by a moral code which, in contrast to the "official" code,

[17] It is possible that institutions such as the two we have studied, which attract men of high "verbal" ability, may select men less defensive in regard to their own "femininity." Hence other student male populations may show greater separation of sex from affection. For a discussion of the role of sex in the specific development phase of the student, see *Sex and the College Student*. New York: Group for the Advancement of Psychiatry, Report Number 60, 1965. The report also describes various college policies toward sexuality and suggests new guidelines.

TABLE 8

DATING HISTORY AND SOME COLLEGE ACTIVITIES OF STANFORD STUDENTS HIGH, MIDDLE AND LOW IN SEXUAL INTIMACY

(IN PER CENT)

	Low		Middle		High [a]	
	Men (N = 74)	Women (N = 29)	Men (N = 113)	Women (N = 107)	Men (N = 81)	Women (N = 64)
Less than two dates a year in the last two years of high school	49	59	17	25	10 **	29 **
More than one weekly evening date:						
Freshman year	7	10	7	52	22 **	56 **
Sophomore year	11	10	27	52	44 **	58 **
Junior year	4	24	48	67	47 **	66 **
Senior year	12	28	53	60	49 **	64 **
High frequency of social activities in college	20	21	57	57	59 **	56 **
Drinking beer daily or once or twice a week	31	14	56	31	64 **	38
Drinking hard liquor daily or once or twice a week	7	10	31	22	33 **	17
Never drunk during senior year	59	79	22	55	21 **	38 **
Great struggle over sex	15	21	27	32	11 *	50 **

** p < .01   * p < .05

[a] Significance levels are from chi square tests for differences between low, middle, and high sexual intimacy groups, computed separately for men and women.

57

allows for premarital intercourse. Physical contact seems to be but one component of interest in the opposite sex. Establishing more communicative relations often is uppermost on the students' conscious agenda. We have found that administrators and faculty advisors often do not see the students' search for greater psychological intimacy in the proper perspective when they view student demands as primarily "sexual" in nature. Our interview experience has also taught us that beneath a layer of "coolness," the students still carry many anxieties concerning their sexual attitudes and behavior. The whole area of relations with other people contains much that is only partially resolved in college. In the sexual sphere, too, if we can be subtle and understanding enough, colleges can be more helpful to their students. This is of particular importance because sexual attitudes and behavior are so closely linked to choice of a marital partner.

According to our data, the women's interest in sex seems to develop later than the men's, but reaches a more fully developed state during college; many men seem less ready than the women to assume full heterosexual roles. The men participate in smaller proportions in the activities that may be deemed preparatory for marriage.

Two-thirds of the women and half of the men have gone steady during college; a quarter of the women and one-seventh of the men have been engaged. (Around 10 per cent of the men and women are married before graduation.) The men's lesser readiness for commitment is also expressed in the fact that about half of them say that they expect to get married at age 25 or beyond, while only a quarter of the women say so.

But there is great agreement between men and women in many of the things they expect in marriage. Men and women agree about the number of children that they expect to have. Very small percentages want to have less than two children. About a quarter want two children, and about 40 per cent want three; between a fifth and a quarter want four or more children. There is remarkable agreement between men and women about the wife's working after marriage. About three-quarters of the men and women expect the wife to work full-time before there are children. The same proportions, three-quarters, do not expect the wife to work if the children are under six. About half do not expect the wife to work when the children are between 6 and 12. But only 17 per cent of the men and 9 per cent of the women do not expect the wife to work after the children are older. About 45 per cent of the women expect to work full-time and 42 per cent part-time after the children are grown. The men tend to agree in this.

Differences seem to arise in the area of underlying feelings and attitudes. About half the men and women agree that a husband should control his wife, while the other half is either neutral or undecided. However, when asked whether they would prefer the spouse or themselves to have priority when it comes to making decisions, 82 per cent of the women say that they would prefer their husbands to have priority, while only 60 per cent of the men say so. In other words, there are more women who expect their husbands to have control than there are men willing to assume control. Other indications of women looking for more authoritative control come from the response of 44 per cent of the senior women who say they like men of whom they are a bit afraid; and from one-third of them saying that they are strongly attracted to older members of the opposite sex. We already referred to the fact that much larger percentages of women than of men say they wish they had been born a member of the opposite sex.

The issues to which these responses point are intricate and complex. The women's desire for "control" ought not to be interpreted as a desire for domination. Some of the women may well desire it. But many others may be calling for male decision-making and protective responsibility outside of the sphere of submission or domination. The hard battle of the last hundred years for equality of the sexes has obscured the search for non-invidious differences between them. Our data point in the direction of such differences, in that women may expect a leadership from their men that many men, at least in their senior year in college, are not ready to give.

A student's life in college is influenced by his past education at home and his developing relations with his parents. We have already described the occupational background of our students' parents. In turning to the psychological background, we note first that on the whole, our students' lives have been affected only infrequently by obviously adverse external circumstances.

Only 3 per cent or less do not have their mother living, and 8 per cent or less do not have their father living (with the exception of the Berkeley women, where the figure is 13 per cent). Eight per cent or less say that their parents are divorced. There are, however, more parents than one might expect whom the students report as having a serious drinking problem. About 6 per cent of the fathers and nearly 3 per cent of the mothers are so characterized.

When the students describe their parents' lives with each other, the general tone is one of mildness.

Only small percentages describe their parents' lives together as either overdependent or isolated from each other. About 30 per cent say that in the years before they entered college, their parents differed strongly from each other in their views either sometimes or often. The majority say that important decisions at home were usually made by both parents acting together. About a third of the men and only a fifth of the women say that important decisions at home were usually made by the father.

Does this difference between the men's and the women's responses mean that some men have a greater need to believe that their fathers make the decisions? Do some women have the opposite need, or are they simply better observers?

Only very small percentages say that as children, before the age of 13, they were punished frequently. Two-thirds or more say they were punished occasionally, and between a quarter and a fifth say they were never or almost never punished. Close to two-thirds were punished by both parents. More girls than boys were punished only by their mothers, and more boys than girls were punished only by their fathers. The most effective form of punishment (described by the students in response to an open-ended question) was verbal punishment, i.e., scolding, lecturing, reasoning, verbal expressions of anger and disappointment. The women list verbal punishment more frequently than the men, and they list verbal punishment three to four times more often than physical punishment; while the men list physical about as often as verbal punishment. A frequently listed punishment is denial of an object, activity, or privilege.

Students divide nearly evenly between those who say they resemble the parent of their own sex in emotional makeup and those who say they resemble the one of the opposite sex; but more men than women describe themselves as resembling the parent of their own sex. About 55 per cent of the men and 45 per cent of the women say they resemble their fathers, while 41 per cent of the men and 49 per cent of the women say they resemble their mothers.

From the interviews we know that the parent a student says he resembles may not necessarily be the one with whom he identifies at deeper levels of his personality; but it is interesting that at this more conscious level, students tend to pick a parent of either sex.

The mildness of the description of the parents is not surprising to us in the light of the information we obtained in the interviews. First of all, it is difficult for students to talk about their parents with adequate openness. Assessment and criticism are easily confused in their minds. (In their last senior interview, many students told us that their sexual behavior and their parents were the two topics they found it particularly difficult to talk about.) We have already noted that it is difficult for many students to admit to having such emotions as anger or hostility, or to admit their existence in people close to them. Some of them, even when they suspected disagreement among their parents, described it as taking place out of their hearing. At the same time, our impression from the interviews is that openness of disagreement at home is a helpful factor in people's development. If father and mother are open about their differences, it teaches the child that good people can legitimately differ; it frees him to differ too, and to explore his own ways. Obviously there are optimal degrees of disagreement. Where, as in the lives of some of our interviewees, disagreement was persistently hostile, the child came to embody part of both contending parents in himself, which resulted in a persistent inner conflict.

The process of separation from home is a lengthy one. Our impression is that many students are ready to leave home one or two years before college starts. There seems to be an intensification of the process of separation in the summer before the freshman year, and students begin taking leave while still at home. Then college, with its overpowering demands, brings a temporary intensification of dependence ("homesickness") that is often not consciously admitted. The summer after the freshman year is for many a major turning point in the struggle for independence. The students have been away from parental supervision and guidance for a year. They have not only survived, they have grown. Parents tend to act the same way they did before and thus seem out of step —lacking in respect for the student, who is discovering himself. Often the ostensible battles between parent and student center on relatively trivial issues such as what hours to be home at night, but the underlying issue is the student's attempt to achieve self-regulation. The student usually wins the battle, and reports much less of a repetition of the friction the following summer. (Do their parents give in, or do they become truly educated, or is it something of both?) The relative triviality of the stated issues is probably an obstacle to the achievement of full autonomy, since it hinders a more deliberate and aware striving after a differentiated identity.

For most people, college is the time of greatest exposure to different viewpoints on a wide variety of subjects and emphasis on the proper marshalling of evidence. This new outlook and methodology becomes for many another source of disagreement with their parents, particularly with their fathers. Many students in the later college years report difficulty in talking with their fathers, particularly about political issues, because, they say, the fathers tend to get too emotional and to lack a keen sense of what is appropriate evidence. One may assume that these debates are not entirely innocent and that the student is likely to pick the topics he knows his parents are sensitive about. It requires the parent's as well as the college administrator's wisdom not to be shaken out of equilibrium by the student's semiconscious provocativeness. It may help them to realize that autonomy is often bought at the price of some rebelliousness.

When reviewing their years at college, many students view their separation from home as very beneficial to them.

> Half of the Berkeley women and over a third of the other students say that being away from home had great influence on the changes that have taken place in them; and most of the rest say it had moderate influence. That separation from their parents is a serious and prolonged business for many students is indicated by the fact that more than a fourth say that during their college years they have frequently strongly differed from their father. A different, though overlapping, fourth say they have frequently strongly differed from their mother.

But apart from such attempts at separation and autonomy, we have been impressed by the large extent to which the students move within the life-space of their original family. In their activities during the college years, in their values, in their choice of occupation, the vast majority seem to conform to the behavior and expectations of their own family. Few define themselves as different from their parents and set out to fashion a different life style for themselves. Much of the domination of the family is unconscious, and can in some cases go together with conscious hostility to one or both parents. The lack of awareness was indicated to us in the first freshman interviews, when the students told us that their parents wanted them to do whatever the student wanted to do, while further probing revealed that parental expectations were actually quite definite and were well known to the students. Most students never reach a clear picture of some of their most binding determinations.

The influence of the family may express itself in different ways, for instance, in the choice of an occupation. A student may do exactly what his parent does: the son of a lawyer may plan to become a lawyer. Or he may go into a line of work or life style very similar to that of the parents: the son of a man involved in county politics may go into a law practice with a political orientation. Or he may select an occupational life style in accordance with his parents' wishes: the son of a man who wanted to become a doctor but could not may plan to become a doctor himself. In a count of a random sample of 23 interviewees, we found that 18 chose an occupational life-style like that of their parents and only five chose one unlike.

The interviews also exhibited to us that families differ very much in degree of closeness, and that this is so regardless of the degree of community of values and attitudes. In many families, each of the individual members go their separate ways. The father may be out evenings, working or engaging in some civic function. The mother may be involved in a club or social activity. Even if the members of the family are in the house together in the evening, father may be working away in his shop, or in the garden, or be watching TV; while mother may be sewing or talking to the children. Some families engage in common activities of a leisure kind, such as fishing or spending their vacations together. In some families, both mother and father hold jobs in order to put the child through college. When members of the family have a close interest in each other, this interest can range from intrusive domineering to affectionate understanding.

Many students transfer the sense of home from the family to the college. After the freshman year, they would make such comments as: "Stanford is my home now." The college thus provides a transitional experience and a "weaning" in the passage from the parental home to the home of their own. However, with some students one also wonders whether there is not a superficiality of relatedness, so that any group, provided it is ruled by congenial codes, will be satisfactory to them.

What of changes in values over the college years?

> When asked how they had changed in their moral views, about a fourth of the seniors report themselves as having changed much since they entered college. They respond similarly when asked about changes in their political and religious views. About a fourth report much change in the kinds of friends they have (changes in kinds of friends may be taken as a concomitant of change in values).

These changes do not seem dramatic when one considers the varied exposures and opportunities for exploration during college as well as the students' potential for inner turmoil and investigation. A still more static picture seems to emerge from a comparison of what freshmen and seniors say about the importance to them of various interests and activities. The similarities of the percentages are striking (Table 9).

TABLE 9

PERCENTAGES OF STANFORD STUDENTS WHO RANK THE FOLLOWING
INTERESTS AND ACTIVITIES AMONG THE FIRST THREE

| | 1962 Freshmen | | 1965 Seniors | |
| | Men | Women | Men | Women |
	(N = 375)	(N = 225)	(N = 271)	(N = 212)
Career or occupations	56	26	58	24
Relations and activities with future family	56	63	49	57
Love and affection	39	54	42	74
Developing a personal identity	39	47	29	43
Time for thinking and reflection	24	35	22	23
Participation in activities directed toward national or international betterment	15	6	13	5
Helping other people	14	14	18	13
Religious beliefs and activities	13	12	7	7
Sexual needs	11	7	7	10
Participation as a citizen in the affairs of your community	7	2	6	3
Social life and entertainment	7	1	6	2
Sports or athletics	5	3	3	1
Home improvement (for example, gardening, carpentry, decorating)	1	0	1	2

Career, family, love, and affection, and developing a personal identity are ranked highest by freshmen and seniors alike.[18] Participation in activities directed to-

[18] The great stress that students put on emotional well-being and security emerges also from other responses to the Senior Questionnaire. In a list of 11 possible needs, they rank (both as freshmen and seniors) as the first four a set of strongly similar items. The four are, in order: (1) love and affection, (2) emotional well-being, (3) maintaining self-respect, and (4) being accepted and liked by others. The great stress that students put on love and affection may spring from a sense that the cultivation of these qualities is not given sufficient support in their education. They are more often encouraged to be solitarily performing animals than social or communicating animals.

ward civic, national, or international improvement, religious activities, and helping other people are ranked low by freshmen and seniors alike.

Thus no change is indicated toward an outlook that stresses other people beyond one's immediate surrounding and self-improvement. The greatest increase is in regard to the importance of intellectual and artistic activities. After four years of exposure to academic life, only a quarter of the men and a third of the women rank intellectual activities high.[19]

But the static picture conveyed by Table 9 must be qualified by other considerations. In examining those items in our personality scales that show a great amount of change (20 per cent or more), we find a trend toward greater acceptance of impulse, a relaxation of rigid or punitive controls, greater assertion of independence, less of a tendency to self-blame, and greater readiness to look for objective conditions, rather than magic or moralizing, in accounting for misfunctioning, failure, and destructiveness (Table 10 lists some representative items indicative of this trend).

The trends just noted suggest that even though for many students certain values remain quite stable, there may be quite a difference in the ways in which these are held. Students may maintain the same general orientation and yet be much more flexible and tolerant in the way in which they express it. Hence although differing studies have come to differing conclusions concerning the degree of change during college, this may be the result of their tapping different aspects of values and the ways in which the values are held and expressed. At the same time, we must always keep in mind that the desire for and the rate of change varies considerably with different students. A look at Table 10 shows that larger portions of students did not participate in the described tendencies.

[19] An outlook toward doing things is also indicated by the fact that when asked whom they admire, the seniors select political figures in larger proportions than they do artists, writers, philosophers, and scientists combined. About 28 per cent of the students choose political figures. About 14 per cent choose artists, writers, philosophers, and scientists. It is also of interest to note that only 8 per cent of the women and none of the men choose a woman as a person they particularly admire.

TABLE 10

PERCENTAGES OF STUDENTS WHO AGREE WITH THE FOLLOWING STATEMENTS
(1961 AND 1965 RESPONDENTS ARE THE SAME PEOPLE)

	Stanford				Berkeley			
	Men		Women		Men		Women	
	(N = 185)		(N = 148)		(N = 286)		(N = 265)	
	1961	1965	1961	1965	1961	1965	1961	1965
In the final analysis, parents generally turn out to be right about things	83	59	77	53	79	53	77	49
No weakness or difficulty can hold us back if we have enough will power	64	36	68	45	68	47	73	46
Human passions cause most of the evil in the world	63	43	65	28	63	46	63	32
I have been quite independent and free from family rule	52	70	50	61	43	69	41	60
What youth needs most is strict discipline, rugged determination, and the will to work and fight for family and country	50	28	53	24	53	22	55	22
A person who lets himself get tricked has no one but himself to blame	46	24	38	22	50	28	47	22
The surest way to a peaceful world is to improve people's morals	45	25	43	17	37	25	40	12
Most of our social problems could be solved if we could somehow get rid of the immoral, crooked, and feeble-minded people	35	15	20	9	30	9	22	6
We should respect the work of our forefathers and not think that we know better than they did	32	14	28	17	40	19	44	18
Most people don't realize how much our lives are controlled by plots hatched in secret places	29	9	16	5	38	16	27	10

One of the vexing problems in trying to ascertain a person's values is that conflicting and even contradicting values can be held by the same individual on different levels of the personality. Thus in their evaluation of themselves, our students described themselves as satisfied with themselves and a little later described themselves as depressed quite frequently—a sign of a lower self-estimate.[20] Similarly, students expressed themselves as satisfied with the progress they have made in social relations, while on deeper probing they revealed a sense of incomplete communication with and partial isolation from other people. Much of the thrust of our research has been to get at the less obvious levels of personal development on which much of people's fate, including their educability, is decided.

Students differ widely in what they consider man's happiest age (Table 11).

TABLE 11

PERCENTAGES OF STANFORD STUDENTS WHO RANK THE FOLLOWING
AGES AS THE ONES WHEN MOST PEOPLE ARE HAPPIEST

| | 1961 Freshmen | | 1965 Seniors | |
Age	Men (N = 874)	Women (N = 409)	Men (N = 271)	Women (N = 212)
Birth to 3	19	21	16	17
4– 6	10	11	7	8
7–12	10	9	14	9
13–16	5	1	3	1
17–21	20	15	9	10
22–35	20	26	29	38
36–50	7	9	9	6
51–64	3	2	3	1
65 and older	4	2	1	2

About a fifth think that the first three years of life are the happiest, and this swells to between a fourth and a third for the first six years of life. But no more than 14 per cent think that beyond age 35 lies man's happiest time. The women put 13–16 at the bottom as far as happiness is concerned, and the men put it near the bottom—which confirms what psychologists say about the stresses of that part of adolescence. A comparison between freshman and senior responses shows that students change their

[20] Fifty-eight per cent of the men and two-thirds of the women say that they are depressed from a few times a month to at least once a day.

estimate of the happiness of people between 17 and 21 downward and that of the age 22–35 upward. Only a brave 10 per cent say in their senior year that life is happiest between 17 and 21—the phase of life just behind them.

Human consciousness seems to flicker between fantasies of a golden age in the past and of a rosy future. The present tends to get squeezed in, just as the ego is squeezed in between the archaic id and the authoritarian superego. Trying to reduce this squeeze constitutes still another insufficiently met task of education.

In the first interview of the senior year, we asked our students to take a retrospective look and tell us how they had changed during their college years. Their responses, as coded by us, reveal again that students' relations with other people are of paramount importance to them. They feel that they have made progress in their relations with others, and at the same time feel troubled by the fact that they have not come as close to other people as they desired. The seniors register a very strong sense of having become more independent during college, but they differ much in their description of the degree and manner of their independence. Some describe it in such relatively superficial terms as freedom to regulate their own hours or handle their own money, while others describe extensive changes in their views and values and greater independence from the expectations and pressures of their peers and the authorities.

The following excerpt is from the interview with George, a student with strong intellectual interests. His words illustrate the common concern of students to achieve greater closeness with others, the uncertainties and identity problems still active at the end of the college years, and the attainment of a fuller sense of the complexity of life and a more tolerant superego.

Interviewer: *How would you say you were different when you came to Stanford?*

George: Well, I was a lot different in my ideas. And I suppose this is kind of normal. A lot of ideas are different here. I just hadn't been thinking about a lot of things, or questioning a lot of the traditional things I grew up with. I think I'm a lot more secure now, about my ability to get along with people especially. I hadn't been very happy when I went to high school, and I came out here with kind of an aggressive get-to-know-people attitude. I had to have some way of proving to myself that I was accepted—a leader, and so I ran for office. I got along very well my first year here and made a lot of close friends, here and at the Stanford campus in France as well—I just became a lot more sure of myself, of my ideas of other people. I realized I didn't have to take a back seat to anyone.

Interviewer: *Can you tell me a bit more about this situation in high school?*

George: I moved in the tenth grade and went to live in a suburb called Mount Peter. My class had about 600 students. It was a real large school: about 1,800 in three classes. Mount Peter is known as being very snobbish. I guess it's upper-income groups, upper-middle class. The high school is good academically, but probably not as good as people think it is. People have the attitude that you're lucky to be allowed to live in Mount Peter. "We'll let you in, and after a while, if you're good, you can be part of our group." But it never occurs to them that you might have something to offer them. This is pretty much the attitude. My first year there I had some friends. Part of the problem was just geography; it's kind of a big place, about 40,000. Somehow the people that I liked best in school lived clear on the other side of town. This remained the case all during high school. I'm not a sociologist or anything, but I think the part I lived in was newer and more mobile in society. The part where my friends came from was very old and more settled; these people had lived there all their lives and so forth, and were a lot more squared away than the people who lived where I lived. The people in my section were a lot wilder—partied more and so forth— seemed of less intelligence, and were less interested in school and athletics, and leadership and so forth. So it was kind of hard for me to get into any kind of group. I know I met this one girl, right away, because we both started going there at the same time and while both of our families were building houses there, we both lived in the same apartment building in town. So we shared rides to school practically every day. Got to know her real well, real fast. But I didn't have very many close friends at all.

By the second year, I had a couple [of friends] but they seemed very impermanent because next year they weren't in my classes, and the friendships kind of dissolved. My junior year was the hardest. I really didn't have any friends at all. I was accepted in school—I was president of my home room and this kind of thing—but there was no way to develop anything outside of school. There was nobody in my neighborhood; there were very few people my age; and the people that were there I didn't particularly like and they didn't like me. But the next year things were O.K. I got to know Paul and I got to know some of his friends. Things were a lot better, but I was always kind of an outsider, especially in any kind of a group with Paul in it. In the group that he had grown up with, I was always an outsider, and I felt like it. This group had kind of broken up when I was home and he was there; there were some who had developed into harder drinkers than the others; and they were divided along this line, I think. I associated more with the non-drinkers, but I really didn't like them. The only guy I really liked was Paul. Most of those people, when they go to college they're never happy, always homesick and so on. Almost all of the people I knew in Mount Peter grew up thinking they lived in heaven. But I was very happy just getting away from there. One of the reasons I came to Stanford was to get as far away as possible. Consequently, when I got here I did seem to get along very well quickly, and this kind of redeemed my faith in myself. I didn't get to know any girls, and I had some misgivings about that. But when I was over in France I got to know girls—a lot of girls—and I felt pretty easy around both male and female.

Interviewer: *Have there been any other changes in you since the freshman year?*

George: I really didn't have any idea when I came about what I wanted to do for a living. I really didn't. I thought about being a lawyer, but I wasn't really sure. Everybody had to write a vocational theme in twelfth-grade English. I wrote on being a lawyer, and after that I was pretty sure I didn't want to be a lawyer. I guess I haven't changed in that respect. I have become a lot more aware of the problems—perhaps a little more disillusioned—I guess you're going to jump on me for using that term—perhaps I got a little better idea of what life offers and what some of the problems are that are insoluble. I've become a little more aware, at least, that some people consider life to be completely absurd

—Camus, for example—and I can see their point of view a little bit. Makes me consider ideas that I never had considered before. You know, you just don't think about this—like whether there's any meaning or not. This just doesn't come up in the high-school mind—at least it didn't in mine. As I said, about things like religion and so forth, my ideas changed pretty drastically; but they were in the process of change before I came here. One of the big things was being in Europe; I think I was developing myself in so many ways so fast there, that it hasn't been the same since. There were so many ways that I could learn new things—doing something new all the time, traveling around.

Interviewer: *Could you sum up the difference that Europe made for you?*

George: This is—I think—I want to beat around the bush for a second. Seems like almost everybody that goes over there—a lot of people—I think this is one of the ways that Stanford gets the highest per capita Peace Corps volunteer rate, for example. People come back from there, and they really don't know what they want to do. I know so many cases—everybody's grades drop when they come back the next quarter. Everybody gets all screwed up, as the saying goes—well, some people do. I just feel it's a kind of dissatisfaction with the way it is in the United States. Kind of a difference and so forth—a hustle and bustle. Never take your time to realize what you're doing here. Just live for the present, you know. Experience things, realize that the end of life is the present. I get very dissatisfied with myself, like this past summer, for example. Even now, the fact that I spend all my time waiting for something else, and not to being alive right this moment dissatisfies me. Except for a couple of rare times. And that's the way I've felt this quarter, too. Made me mad. But a large part of it is that I'm just so busy that I can't . . . if I'm going to do the things that I've signed up to do, I just can't spend too much time to enjoy a nice day like this one, go out and just maybe relax a little bit outside, go for a walk, instead of the books. It's such an entangled thing. I think it's just that if you didn't have to study, you could work on it. Really a definite effect on people who go to Stanford overseas campuses. And maybe that's what it is. I don't know. We talked about it, and so on, and everybody agrees that it's there. I'm not really sure what happens. I'd like to know.

Interviewer: *You mentioned talking about the effect [of the overseas campus] and why it has such an effect.*

George: Yeah, but I'm not sure really what it is. I think, it's maybe—you just realize. I remember one night, I went for a walk by myself in Rome. I'd kind of got dissatisfied with the people in the group, because we were all together. I don't know, I just wanted to get off by myself. I ended up just walking around Rome by myself; didn't know where I was going. At night. And I remember walking out in the Forum, you know, and seeing all these ruins—seeing Mussolini and so forth. Such an historical perspective there, that you don't get here. You realize kind of the impermanence of everything. And the relative nature of all the values that we place first. So few people come back the same, but some people come back with . . . not wanting to be a businessman or any of these mundane kinds of things, the kind of normal thing to do in American society. Nobody wants to do that. I don't know what it is. It would be the last thing I would want to do—to go to business school next year. And I couldn't go to law school. But there's some sort of kind of perspective, I guess; it doesn't seem like much of a word, but I guess that's what it is. [A few sentences are omitted.] The junior year, I guess, has probably had the greatest effect on me. I was a lot more of a teetotaler when I came. I'm not sure how much this had to do with a loss of religious conviction, but probably some. And I'm more tolerant of individuals now. My roommate, for example, who is probably my closest friend, gets quite drunk reasonably often. About every two weeks. I'm sure he's still asleep now because he was pretty late last night. Certainly when I came, in my freshman year, I would have pretty well looked down on him. I don't do it myself, but I know the guy and I think—I wouldn't want to say that I don't blame him—but I can understand what he's doing and I'm sort of glad I don't enjoy it the way he does.

❧ 2 ❧

DYNAMICS OF
DEVELOPMENT AND
CONSTRAINT: TWO CASE
STUDIES

Peter Madison

The emerging view of development in the college years is one of a dynamic interaction between stability and change. As Nevitt Sanford has expressed it, "We have to say that in order to induce desirable change—toward further growth or development or toward greater health—we have to think in terms of what would upset the existing equilibrium, produce instability, set in motion activity leading to stabilization on a higher level." [1]

[1] Sanford, Nevitt. *Self and Society*. New York: Atherton Press, 1966.

Let us examine the interaction of the forces that induce development or constrain it, as exemplified in the lives of two students, Bob and Nancy, whose cases illustrate the constant balancing of stability and change that characterizes personality development in college. The young person's strong drives to explore, to open himself to new experiences, are checked by protective security maneuvers whenever the instability induced by change becomes too great. As soon as sufficient equilibrium is restored, new ventures follow.

In ways that are largely unknown to the student, his pre-college past enters into the developmental picture. The new freshman is intensely aware of this past, but he tends to think of it in terms of his memories. When he shuts off his reminiscences and turns to the present, he does not consciously experience his current feelings and actions as being related to the past: the immediate situation appears to him to require the responses he is so reasonably making. But the past does enter in, often in the form of unrecognized constraints on development; and much of the student's effort is spent in discovering and dealing with that intrusion.

Both Bob and Nancy are typical students in terms of the test score dimensions that governed the selection of the student sample, and they were in the middle group on both the Impulse Expression and Social Maturity Scales of the Omnibus Personality Inventory. From this standpoint, they are representative of the students at a selective college.

Bob's case is interesting because he made such great developmental strides relative to his classmates, and because, as a freshman, he seemed an unlikely candidate for such growth. At the time of his first interview, Bob appeared to be the sort of inarticulate, constricted, vocationally-oriented engineering student who could be expected to retreat to his room with his slide rule, grind for four years, take a technical job with a large company upon graduation, and then settle down to the materialistic, family-centered life of the suburbanite. But in fact, after an initial shock period, Bob began to develop along those dimensions where he felt the least constraint, in response to stimuli he encountered in the college environment. In the end, he was able to directly challenge the strongest constraint of all: his feelings that he must fulfill his childhood conception of what his parents wanted of him before he could respond to what he wanted for himself.

For most boys, the question of what to major in and what to do with their lives after college deeply involves almost every element of their makeup. The personality theorist who keeps his eye on this dimension isn't going to miss much of the action. Like most high school seniors, Bob had made his initial choices of college major and career without knowledge of, or experience in, his proposed profession. He expressed this in his first interview.[2]

> (Fall, freshman year) I decided on chemical engineering as a major during my senior year in high school. As a matter of fact, I decided when I was filling out my application that fall. We were asked to put down what we intended to major in. Since I had such an interest in science and math, I felt my major should be somewhere in that category, and I liked chemistry so well—I thought that would be a good way to start. After I got into algebra in ninth grade, I'd always thought that my future plans should have something to do with math, because I've always liked math, and always did quite well in math. But I hadn't really considered chemical engineering until my senior year. In my junior year, the only thing I was sure of was that [my major] was going to be something in science and math.
>
> I don't have any idea as to why chemical engineering, rather than chemistry, physics, or some other science. As a matter of fact, when I put down chemical engineering I hardly knew what it was, except that it dealt with chemistry. I still think that's kind of my general idea of it. I can go ahead and take courses for at least two years, and then either become a chemist or a chemical engineer. I think I probably put down chemical engineering mainly because I enjoyed physics, and a chemical engineer employs more math and more physics than a pure chemist.

> *But as you envision it, what do you see a chemical engineer doing that might be of interest to you?*

> Well—there are many things. I've had interests in architecture, and one of the important phases of chemical

[2] In the following excerpts from interviews with Bob and Nancy, the interviewer's words appear in italics.

engineering is the design of machinery for use in the chemical industry. I'm also interested in research, which is more along the line of what a pure chemist would do, but still, research comes up in chemical engineering.

Do you have any general ideas about the kind of place you would like to work in when you become a chemical engineer?

Well, that's a little premature. I haven't had a chance to work in any place that employs large numbers of men. I've always worked in small groups, so I might prefer that. I don't know whether I would enjoy working in a large corporation as just one of the cogs.

Such vagueness about careers is not unusual, especially for boys like Bob, who have grown up in small and culturally isolated communities. His lack of information was such that he thought of chemical engineering as a field that would allow him to fulfill an architectural interest; and he knew too little to realize that such a vocation would inevitably mean involvement with a large organization. Nevertheless, he could see that his research interests would more likely be met by chemistry than by chemical engineering. These inconsistencies are characteristic of the freshman's decisions on such matters. The freshman year starting plan is not an indication of what the student seriously means to do with his life so much as it is an effort on his part to feel that he has a "place" in the college and in society's scheme of things.

In the usual course of events, the starting plans soon begin to dissolve under the impact of college and give way to a new synthesis better suited to the student's purposes. In Bob's case, this did not happen for a long time, but when it did, there was something of an explosion. As Bob began to develop, his starting plan became less and less suited to his maturing self, but he clung resolutely to chemical engineering for three years. When the dissolution finally came, late in his junior year, it was overwhelming. Bob graduated, liberated from a prematurely frozen life plan symbolized by chemical engineering, but liberated too late to resynthesize around an alternative before graduation.

At the end of his freshman year, Bob was still adhering to his starting plan. His strategy, one widely used by students, was to keep alternatives open, and to delay decision as long as possible while accumulating experience and judgment toward the day on which an unavoidable choice point would arrive.[3] By November of his sophomore year, the first explicitly recognized doubts had begun to appear.

(Fall, sophomore year) *Are you still vacillating between chemistry and chemical engineering?*

Actually, I'm kind of wobbling all the way around. I've had so much trouble—I'm still enjoying chemistry courses, but I'm having quite a bit of trouble with the organic chemistry, mainly because it is a lot of memory work, and I find it hard to study for the kind of test the instructor gives. I'm just not sure that chemistry is exactly what I want. I don't know what it is that I want. Once in a while I think that I'd do well in economics.

Is it a matter of what you're best suited for—what you would do best in?

Well, what I would like best.

By spring, Bob had returned to a firm stand on chemical engineering.

(Spring, sophomore year) *What are you majoring in, and why?*

I have decided that chemical engineering is the right field. I am taking organic chemistry. I am also seeing more of the mechanical side of the field. The job opportunities and pay are better in chemical engineering. The appeal of chemical engineering is the chance for travel, outdoor work, good money, and opportunities for advancement.

Note the interesting addition to Bob's perception of chemical engineering: that it will allow him to travel. This theme fre-

---

[3] This "many-option coping mechanism," as I have called it in *Personality in College* (Reading, Mass., Addison-Wesley, 1966, preliminary edition, Ch. 3), appears to be one of the main ways in which college students deal with important decisions under conditions where relevant facts are not known.

quently recurred throughout college together with the larger theme of "freedom," of which the appeal of traveling seemed to be a part.

Over the summer, Bob seemed not to have wavered, but he had, however, significantly modified his plan to be a chemical engineer: he would go into management, where he could satisfy his newly acknowledged interest in working with people rather than chemicals.

What accounts for that shift from research into the management and legal side?

> Well, I don't know. I enjoy lab work, but I can see that I would get tired of being in the lab day after day washing bottles and so on, and of research, which would involve lots of library work, lots of reading and compiling materials. Going into the laboratory would be a little more interesting, but I do think that I enjoy being a little higher up, where the overall picture is a little more clear—I like working with people. Besides that, there's more money in management, or in the legal side.

By the end of his junior year, Bob found that chemical engineering was "leaving him cold."

(Spring, junior year) *Let's start with how things have been going since we saw you last fall.*

> They haven't been going quite as well as they should be. I don't know whether it's just finding out that maybe engineering isn't what I want or not, but I've been very disappointed in all my chemical engineering courses this year. I'm not doing well because of my attitude. As it looks right now, I'm just barely going to squeak by on my scholarship grades again this year.[4] It's kind of bad.

Do you think it's related to your lack of interest in the courses?

[4] Bob's scholarship, which covered something over half his expenses, was contingent upon his maintaining a C+ average.

Yes, I think it definitely is. I know I just have been unable to work, unable to get any interest at all in anything. I have yet to get above a "C" in any of the chemical engineering courses. The only reason I've been keeping my average up is that I'm doing all right in some of the chemistry courses. But chemical engineering is kind of leaving me cold.

Has this led you to think about your major?

Yes, it certainly has. Of course, at the end of my junior year, it's a little difficult to switch over, so I think I'm going to go ahead and get my degree in chemical engineering, and then I can always get a job. The way things look right now, a chemical engineer is not what I want to be. The courses that I'm taking are indicative of the type of work that I'd be doing. If I don't like the courses, I won't like the work.

You've been debating this for some time, haven't you—chemistry or chemical engineering?

Yes. I'm still not that interested in chemistry, straight chemistry. The only thing that would be open there would be teaching and I'm not entirely sold on teaching.

So you really are up in the air about your career plans?

I just have no idea at all what to do.

Here is how things looked in the fall interview of Bob's senior year.

Well, what is your first impression of the senior year?

It is quite different, in that I did switch my major. I'm taking two language courses, Art 1 and Music 1. I'm taking no chemistry. All my remaining chemistry courses come later in the year, and I will have no straight engineering courses, since I dropped chemical engineering.

What led to the change?

I was tired of taking these required engineering courses which didn't seem to have too much that would be applicable to chemical engineering—they were simply departmental requirements. And I have been wanting to take a language all the way through college, and just never had the time for it. So I finally decided I might as well get a B.S. in chemistry, since I am now thinking about going into medical research—I need a chemistry background for that.

You are now thinking about medicine?

Well, the research side—medical school, or at least graduate school in biochemistry. I'm not really worrying too much about it yet, as I have to take a year or two in biology before I could get into either medical school or graduate school.

So your plan now is to stay on in college?

Not here—I want to go back East. If worst comes to worse, back to my own state university for a year or two.

To complete premed requirements, biology requirements?

Biology, and a little political science.

Well, now, this is a real change, isn't it? How did you . . . ?

I got to looking over my courses last year, which courses I had enjoyed and which I hadn't, and I found I hadn't enjoyed most of it . . . particularly those that were on the engineering side.

But medicine is a switch.

Well, it's still laboratory work, and it's something I might have gone into anyway.

So you are not sure?

I'm still not sure. I'm going to take the Peace Corps test, and maybe go into the Peace Corps before I go on. I don't know.

You are pretty much up in the air, then?

Probably one of the main reasons I did decide on chemistry rather than chemical engineering is that the change gave me the freedom finally to get a language, which I wanted, and also made it easier—not necessarily load-wise—but easier on me the rest of this year.

Did you find the engineering too hard for you?

Not enjoyable.

How about the grades?

They showed the lack of my enjoyment [laughs]. They weren't good at all.

Good enough to keep your scholarship?

I lost a good part of it last year. I have enough to get me through this year, and that's about it.

Why are you so keen on languages?

Well, I enjoyed high school Spanish, and always regretted that I hadn't been able to take any more Spanish, or at least some type of language—just interested, I can't really explain it.

Am I right—that underneath this was a kind of feeling that you weren't learning some of the things that you wanted very much to learn?

Right. This quarter I am really enjoying every course.

But until recently you didn't quite have the courage to make the break; you felt it wouldn't be terribly practical to do so?

I don't know whether it was courage, or what—I really
don't know—but I finally decided this last summer.

The eve of graduation found Bob's starting plan dissolved,
and his plans for his future confused.

Let's start out with what's been going on since the last in-
terview.

Well, I still don't know exactly where I'm going [pauses].
I still don't know exactly where I'm going, and it's still
pretty difficult to say; but at the present, the only thing
I'm worried about is graduating. I just don't know yet
exactly what I'm going to be doing next year. I have
three or four different plans. I still want to take some
biology and some more language, to see where my field
of interest is. I'm still considering three colleges to go to.
What I might do is to work for six months, and then I'll
be able to afford to go to an eastern university. It's not
so much the difference in universities as the difference
in country, people, and so on, that I want. I'd like to
go back East for a while. I have a good friend who is
trying to talk me into going to France with him, so it's
possible I might do that too; or work for more than six
months, so I'd have some money. But I don't really
know yet. It's kind of hard to say.

The confused state of Bob's career plans throughout his
senior year shows what a problem a major change of direction can
be when it comes so late in college. As a senior, Bob was just beginning the kind of exploration of his own interest in language,
biology, music, and art that would have been desirable in his first
two years. But Bob's developmental and academic timetables
were so out of phase that there was no chance to find out where
his enduring interests lay, or to regroup his forces around a new
career plan. He graduated, liberated but unintegrated—an outcome that may be more frequent than we know.

There is good evidence that a part of Bob wanted to make
such a breakout almost from the beginning, and that the whole
course of his development in college was away from the narrow
educational plan he came with. In many ways, Bob's shift out of

chemical engineering was very desirable from an educational standpoint; one only wishes it had come earlier.

The evidence that Bob persistently wanted to move in directions that were at variance with the course he set out upon and clung to so tenaciously is all too clear to the outside observer, who has the advantage of being able to look at the record of Bob's four years of college life; but what was happening did not look at all clear to Bob from within. Strong forces were at work to keep him on the course he had begun. Let us look at some of these.

The top graduate of a tiny high school in a rural, culturally isolated setting (Bob's home was located a few miles from the nearest town) who enrolls in a large, selective college full of able and culturally sophisticated students invites a set of shock experiences capable of unhinging almost any personality. Here is how Bob described his first response to college, as he looked back upon it from the perspective of his senior year.

How are you different from when you entered college?

For about the first two days, I had a pretty high opinion of myself, and from there on out for the rest of the year, I felt like a midget among giants. It was a case of a small frog in a small pond becoming an even smaller frog in a huge pond. In high school, I was a big man. I came down here with the thought that there would be no problems in college, and that I had a pretty good background; when I got here, I found out that this wasn't true.

Academically, mostly?

Academically, socially—just all around. Even right there from the first I would run into people who had definite ideas about politics and I hardly even knew who the people they talked about were, and this sort of thing. It didn't seem like I knew very much; my confidence level wasn't very high. I still don't, in a lot of respects, have an idea of where I am or what I think, but I do have more confidence in myself that when I do make up my mind, I have a right to say so and to feel that way.

Was it in terms of other students that you felt inferior, or in terms of what needs to be known and understood?

I think it was mainly in terms of other students, because that was easier to see right there. Well, in general, it was kind of an overwhelming situation. There is an awful lot to be known that I didn't have an idea of. It was most easily seen by talking with the other students. I was supposedly on their level, and yet I didn't seem to be.

They knew so much more? Or they had many more exposures, opportunities, advantages, or experiences? Was it because of their social class?

Because of the type of community they came from. I think that had a lot to do with it. Mainly I just didn't realize how much I had missed by being in a small community.

When measured by the Scholastic Aptitude Test, Bob proved to be more competent than his classmates. His Verbal Aptitude Score was 630, and his Mathematics Aptitude Score 798—as compared to the male class average of 617 (SD 70) for Verbal Aptitude and 652 (SD 71) for Mathematics. Nevertheless, at the outset he had a decidedly low opinion of his own competence.

(Spring, freshman year) *How would you like to be different as a person than you are now?*

I'd like to be a little bit sharper; to think a little more quickly than I do; to stand out a little bit more. I feel somewhat subdued by the fact that there's so much talent here. I don't feel nearly as competent as a lot of these people are.

"Background shock" is a particular form of identity shock. Discovering how inadequate his background was relative to that of other students would have been a difficult enough problem for Bob to deal with, but to find as well that he was not even in the running, academically, politically, or athletically, produced an effect so massive that one must speak of something like "identity shock": a fundamental challenge to the bases of his self-esteem. Bob's failure in athletics was especially difficult for him to take:

(Spring, junior year) *How come you dropped out of track?*

It was more a matter of frustration than anything else, because I worked very, very hard at track all during the last summer and got down to a point where I was running better than I ever had in my life. I could run a 4:20 mile without any problems; I could probably have made the squad in just about any other college, and here I was running ninth on the track squad. It just got kind of frustrating—seeing myself finish from a hundred yards back all the time.

(Fall, freshman year) *What do you think is the most difficult aspect of college for the entering student?*

For me, it's facing up to the competition—the high level of competition. To be frank, I never had much competition in high school. College is different from what I had expected. I hadn't had to work nearly as hard in high school, and I wasn't prepared for this difference.

(Spring, freshman year) The first semester of college was an eye-opener and a real shock. Just getting here and getting bad grades—not knowing how to study.

(Spring, senior year) *Looking back at your life before college, what are some personal characteristics in which you differed from the way you are now?*

One thing that was characteristic of me in grade school as well as the rest of high school was . . . being on top.

Bob graduated with a C+ average for his four years of college. His first term grades average C—. By contrast, his high school academic career had been so distinguished that he had been offered large scholarship inducements from the country's leading universities. But though Bob had been student body president in high school, he held no offices during his freshman year in college, and had practically no social life. He later described his freshman year as "study, study, study," and spoke of being "confined to a cubicle in the dorm."

That Bob must have suffered massive blows to all his high-school-associated bases for self-esteem seems plain. Although the effects of this shock were not directly disclosed by the interview data, one can guess at them from the overall pattern of Bob's response to college. As the material on Bob's choice of college major and career suggest, Bob stuck to his starting plan in a way that suggests a very great hesitance to change. As we will see, there was plenty of evidence available to Bob that could have told him he was on the wrong track, especially his early and persistent interest in courses outside his technical field. It is hypothesized here that the massive freshman-year shocks made Bob feel so insecure that he was not open to the evidence that he belonged elsewhere. Such shocks usually have the overall effect of closing up the person and leading him to cling in an exaggerated way to the remaining bases of security.

One of the great differences between the educator's concept of a college education and the incoming student's (particularly the student from a culturally limited background) is that of goals. The faculty and administration usually envision the college education as a liberating process that introduces the student to the whole range of man's culture and knowledge, and turns him into a mature adult who understands the world and wants to participate significantly in it. Many freshmen and their parents view these cultured benefits as "frills," or extras, and see college as primarily a place where one qualifies oneself for a good job—that is, for economic security. Bob put it very well when he arrived: "I've always figured that I was going to have to go to college to get what I wanted out of life. I don't think that job opportunities and the chance to pick up security are offered to the non-college person."

And you're thinking that what you want out of life is security?

Security and a chance to be able to support a wife and children in a good community, and be able to give them what I consider are the necessities, and more . . . I'd like us to be able to have television if we want it; hi-fi if we want it; a dishwasher, and so on.

Vocational orientation to college is probably the strongest factor working against the liberalizing effects of the curriculum. Bob made it plain that his desire for security in a vocation kept him studying chemical engineering long after he had ceased to take pleasure in the course work required for his major.

(Spring, junior year) *And you thought about switching, but decided it wasn't practical?*

> Well, financially it's not practical right now. I mean the degree from here will do me, will be, uh . . . let's face it, it means a dollar sign and a contract and all that. If you have something from this college, you've got it made. So I will go ahead and get my degree in chemical engineering. I can do that without too much of a problem.

The most damaging effect of vocational orientation on the student is that it prevents him from exploring the curriculum. In his freshman year, Bob wished that he could take only chemistry and mathematics and rid himself of "useless" general studies requirements.

(Fall, freshman year) *Suppose you could have college any way you wanted it, what would be the kind of an ideal college you would want?*

> I wish there wasn't quite so much emphasis on the general studies. I would like to go to college to study what I want to prepare for, what I am going into. I'd be satisfied now if I had two chemistry classes and two math classes straight.

One would never guess from this that Bob was to say later on that these same general studies courses had been the most satisfying classes that he had taken in college!

Personality formations developed in childhood often show up in student data. When no systematic effort is made to gather childhood information, the inferences about childhood personality must be made indirectly, from what the student reveals of his precollege life. Bob spontaneously spoke of his home values as "Puritanistic," and it is reasonable to infer that this describes the atmosphere of his childhood home life.

(Spring, sophomore year) *Have your moral convictions undergone changes since coming to college?*

> They are approximately the same—haven't changed much. I don't question the values I came with. Actually,

they have been strengthened by what goes on down here at college. Fellows talking about their prowess—makes me ill in some respects. It seems like they get more evil out of it than good. The fellows talk about petting that gets a little violent. The next day they feel miserable—went a little too far, felt guilty. I think I am different in my attitudes from my close friends. I have tended to keep my Puritanistic values—like those of my folks, but maybe not quite as Puritanistic as theirs.

Bob's direction throughout college is explainable if one assumes that the general outcome of his childhood interaction with his parents was the development of a central self that included his own interpretation of what was important to his parents, and to his relationship with them. These home-bound personality formations naturally included Bob's childhood strategies for dealing with his own inferences about his parents' wishes. As a college student, Bob acted as though there were a kind of a "home plan" that specified the priorities in life and the ways in which one must proceed in order to insure oneself against the temptations of the present. Several elements of this "plan" appear in Bob's college material. As intimated in the passage already quoted, one element has to do with sex. Another shows up in Bob's attitude toward drinking. A third includes the idea that authority must not be criticized. A fourth, and most important theme, is that one must carry out the wishes of one's parents before responding to one's own preferences.

Bob's early sophomore year interview shows the feeling he brought to college about drinking.

(Fall, sophomore year) *How did the drinking go this summer?*

I haven't started yet.

Not even an occasional beer?

No. I just don't care for beer. The other men in the construction crew I worked with last summer always had a couple of cases, but I always took along my carton of soda pop. [Laughs]

You have tasted liquor, though?

Oh, yes. I just don't care for it. I don't like the flavor, the strength of it. I never liked beer. My folks had a little once in a while, and I have had plenty of opportunities to taste it, but I have never acquired the taste for it. It doesn't appeal to me enough to bother acquiring a taste.

When Bob came to college, he left behind a girl with whom he had begun a dating relationship during the spring of his final year in high school. He did not consider that they were going steady, however, and the relationship broke up in the middle of his sophomore year. He had a few dates with girls he met in college, but avoided serious involvement. It seemed he was following his father's advice about girls; however, as we shall see, Bob also had his own reasons for keeping girls at a distance.

"Do what must be done before following your own wishes." As far as can be inferred from the interview data, if Bob's child self could have spoken, these words would have represented its central construct. One can see an underlying conflict between Bob's own impulses and his feeling that he cannot do the things he would like to do until he has fulfilled the wishes of his parents.

(Fall, senior year) *How did your father feel about your dropping chemical engineering?*

I think he was slightly disappointed, but he didn't try to talk me out of it. He just wanted me to look into all the angles first before I made any switch, which I did. Well, at times I talked about—in moments of fancy—going into the Peace Corps, and then coming back and finishing school. I always went along with his idea that I ought to get at least my B.S. before doing that.

Above all, this element of Bob's child self called for gaining a college degree before "fooling around."

How uncomfortable are you with this uncertainty? How does it affect you?

Well, I don't know, really. It doesn't scare me as much as some people, or some people think it ought. I think part of it is, in a way, I've at least fulfilled the major wish of my parents—that I get a degree—graduate and get a degree in something before I start fooling around.

Is that the way you kind of feel about it, that this is for them—for their sake?

Well, in some respects, because, if it wasn't for the fact . . . uh . . . it's kind of my own feeling too, to have a degree in my pocket so I have a little bit of security. But I sometimes have the feeling that if it wasn't for this fact, I might have dropped out of school, bummed around, maybe gone to Europe, or gotten a job for a year or so, just to see if I could find something outside that I could come back to. Sometimes I think that I'm . . . I just like the college life for the college life and not necessarily for what it means to my future. Just being here, and being able to study, and sit down and talk about things with other people. That's why I have enjoyed the outside courses I've taken so much—because I can bring in this, that, and the other thing without really worrying about how this is going to fit in with what I'm going to be doing in the future.

The origins of the proscription against drinking and sex are directly suggested in this interchange.

(Fall, sophomore year) *What do you talk to your father about?*

I remember trying to get the car for some reason or other. That is usually the signal for us to talk about my attitude toward life. He generally asks me whether I've changed any of my attitudes. Most of the time he simply says he's given up making me do what he wants me to do. I'm on my own now, and what I do is my own business . . . every once in a while, he wants me to reassure him that I'm not getting too serious with my girl. He just wonders how I feel about going around with guys who do a lot of drinking and smoking. The only thing he has ever said positively is not to get involved in any extreme relationships [with girls] or anything for a while.

Bob inferred that his father would be disappointed in him if he allowed his own wishes to deflect him from completing his present college program.

> (Fall, senior year) Oh, I think my Dad was a little perturbed at first about my switching from chemical engineering, because he always thought that I ought to finish what I started and then fool around and play around with the other things.

Bob's phraseology is interesting. To him, actions motivated by his own interests, as distinguished from what his parents wished, represented "fooling around." While "fooling around" included the type of activity the words connote, such as having a beer with the boys, it also carried the more general meaning of doing things that were interesting for their own sake: "Just being here, and being able to study, and sit down and talk about things with other people. When I take a literature course, I like to sit down and wonder why. . . ." The dynamic of the Puritan child self operates in such a way that the liberal arts educator's invitation to browse among the best literature and to investigate the curriculum just because it is interesting is experienced by the student as an invitation to sin—to "fool around."

It is consistent with Bob's central childhood value of doing what was expected of him that the strategy he used against such enticements was to "tighten up." This ego mechanism is one of restricting oneself to the preservation of what is absolutely essential when the general situation becomes overwhelming. Only activities directly supporting the values that matter are permitted, and these are intensified far beyond what is usual. In Bob's college situation, this meant severe restriction to a grueling program of study.

> (Fall, freshman year) As to how college compares to life before I came, I can't say too much, because the difference is so great. The time I spend studying now is so much greater than the time I spent at home. I haven't kept an accurate record of the time I've put in studying, but it must be about five hours a night, plus five or six hours more during the day—altogether, at least eleven or twelve hours a day.

If competition is one of the things that worries you, how do you deal with the problem?

I'll have to dig in a little bit harder . . . study harder. I can't see any other way out of it.

In his freshman year interview, Bob did not say on what basis his decision to become a chemical engineer had been made, other than that his preferences for mathematics and sciences among his high school courses had led him to it; but his senior year interview was more revealing on this point.

I think part of it is due to the fact that I had stated when I was in high school that I wanted to be a chemical engineer—without ever really knowing—because I liked chemistry and math. I was talking with my college counselor in high school, and he felt chemical engineering was my mold, and that was where I leaped.

He said that to you?

Well, aptitude tests showed that I was headed toward engineering of some type, and chemistry was a strong point, and one that I liked. So I combined the two, and for two years here I took essentially all chemistry, and I enjoyed it—I enjoyed the whole program, until getting into the straight engineering courses.

Sometimes it is the content of a program that is not congenial in terms of our interests and tastes. Sometimes we are not successful in it, and then we don't like it. How was it with you?

I think it was the content. I simply got no thrill at all out of electrical circuits, or electric magnetism, or other things I ran into in electrical engineering courses. It was tough, too; but I think a lot of it was tough because I didn't like the subject to begin with. In physics, I had had an introduction to electricity and circuits and so on, but they left me cold there.

And how did your folks feel about all these changes?

Oh, I think my Dad was a little perturbed at first about my switching from chemical engineering, because he had always thought that I should finish what I started, and then fool around and play with the other things. I suppose my mother felt about the same way; she didn't really voice a strong opinion either way.

What do you think your Dad would have liked you to do?

Well, basically, I know what he wants me to do, and that is to finish my four years and get my B.S. degree before I do anything like joining the Peace Corps, or anything . . . that is the main thing he worries about, just to be sure that I get through and have something as a backlog. But I think he would have liked to see me continue in chemical engineering, just because that is a little more monetarily rewarding than chemistry as far as an occupation is concerned. If you have a B.S. in chemical engineering rather than in chemistry, the first year's salary is much higher. I don't intend to be a straight chemist or a straight chemical engineer either. It doesn't make that much difference to me.

The curriculum for any field of study tends to be organized like a pyramid, with the courses most closely related to the student's chosen vocation at the top. There are rational reasons for this in some cases, since some preparation may be needed before the student is able to do the work in courses pertaining to his final vocational objective. These often do not come until the senior year—in some fields, not until graduate work. An extreme case would be that of the entering freshman who thinks he wants to become a psychotherapist. He can follow several avenues to this objective, all involving postgraduate work. The longest avenue is through psychiatry, which involves four undergraduate years, then four years of medical school, followed by a year of hospital internship in general medical work. Finally, as a first-year resident, the young doctor may be allowed to treat his first psychiatric patient. Even if he chooses a shorter route through clinical psychology or psychiatric social work, the student cannot hope to try his hand at treating a patient of his own short of six or seven years after he first enrolls as a college freshman. While such a pyramidal structure may be defensible from certain standpoints, it has a serious flaw, in that the graduate, who will have developed as a person during his long period of study, may no longer care about the goal to which he committed himself as an undergraduate. If a student's strong exploratory tendencies are curtailed, he may never find out what he really wants to do.

Bob was overjoyed when, in the fall of his junior year, he came into personal contact with a real, life chemical engineer who for ten years had been earning a living doing what Bob planned to do when he graduated. Nevertheless, when he finally had a chance to take upper-division chemical engineering courses, Bob found that he did not like them.

Looking at the junior year overall, what has been most satisfying?

Well, frankly, I'd say the academic side, overall—just the fact that I've been unable to get interested in any of my courses this year. It's really very disappointing to go through three years of college, headed toward a degree in chemical engineering, and finally get around to taking some concentrated chemical engineering courses and find you don't like them.

It is not only the organization of the college curriculum that frustrates the student's efforts to learn what field he wants; the job world outside seems to be even more determined to keep the student from exploring it until he has completed his studies. Bob showed a very strong drive to find out about his proposed vocation. He was aware that he had decided for chemical engineering without any first-hand information about the field, and he felt a strong urge to test out his interest.

(Spring, junior year) *What about this summer? What are your plans?*

Well, I'm not really sure yet what's going to happen. Something that made me rather irritated with chemical engineering was that none of the companies who are hiring chemical engineers seem to want you as an undergraduate. They want you as soon as you've graduated. I can see their reasons, because they're never sure whether you're coming back, and they probably don't get their full measure out of you during the summer; but, then, again, it seems to me that a large part of your education as a chemical engineer would have to come from industry, because they don't have as big a lab system here, or anything else. And yet I went to ten to twelve interviews during the year trying to get jobs. All the companies offer a very limited number of positions. They interviewed at seven or eight different colleges, and gave only two or three jobs. It just kind of disappointed me to see that companies weren't really interested in your undergraduate education. All they wanted to do was grab you as soon as you were through with college.

In the interaction between student and college, some of the forces that work against constraint seem to be within the structure of the student's personality, while other influences seem to emanate from the environment. (The distinction is obviously a relative one, since both person and environment are involved in every interaction, but, for the purposes of a preliminary analysis, there is a certain heuristic value in dividing the problem in this way.) Youngsters do not, of course, simply accept the mandates they perceive as emanating from their parents. While on the one hand; Bob accepted his interpretation of his parents' wishes for him, on the other, his natural vigor drove him to explore and to reach out beyond the boundaries he had set for himself. One part of Bob valued freedom from the constraint that his child self urged him to accept.

(Fall, junior year) *If you could have all the money you want at the time of graduation, what would you do with yourself?*

I'm quite sure I'd go on with my plans. Even if I had money, I wouldn't be capable of doing what I wanted to do without education. I think it might make a difference in one respect: I might take a couple of years off and maybe join the Peace Corps, or something like that —while I'm still pretty young. But I'm sure I'd finish college sometime.

A more indirect sign that Bob was chafing under his self-imposed restrictions is suggested by his perception of certain aspects of the social sciences as threats to the independence of the human spirit.

What is the last course in the world you would consider taking?

It seems to me that both sociology and psychology tend a little to try and put everything down: because of this, you do this; and it doesn't seem to leave too much room for independence, or much room for the overall picture.

The theme of freedom from restraint, which was to become an open concern in Bob's senior year, pervaded his thoughts about chemical engineering as well. Even at the end of his sophomore year, he had emphasized the opportunities for travel offered by his proposed career. But he drew his first clear line against giving in wholly to constraint at the end of his freshman year, when he refused to do what he saw that he would have to do in order to maintain a position of academic superiority. One of the interesting facts about Bob's freshman year is that after earning a C— average during his fall quarter, he tightened up his whole program, and did B+ work in the next two quarters. He seemed on the road to academic excellence in his major; then, in his sophomore year, he turned away from studies. Why did he not follow up this dramatic improvement in grades and go on to be outstanding, as he had always been in the past? The following interchange tells us: he saw that he could do it only by totally sealing himself in.

How has it affected you, having once been at the top, and then at college being further down?

[Very long pause] Well, I don't exactly know how to say it, but, in a sense, I think that it's enabled me to broaden my experience. Because, if I were to try and drive enough to be Number One all the time, well, I'd have to take an awfully narrow road.

Well, if you were to limit yourself, do you feel that you could be Number One?

Well, I think that if I'd done like I did my second term here . . . I didn't have a single date, stayed in my room; I think I went to see one movie during the term, and almost all the time I was in my room studying, just day in and day out. And I came out with a high grade point average. I was getting A's in chemistry.

So you more or less made the decision that it's not for you?

Right. I think towards the end of my spring term of my sophomore year, when I joined the House, I decided there was—it sounds kind of corny—but I decided that there was more to life than studies.

(Fall, senior year) *How has education affected you as a person?*

We can go back to that old cliché—the more you know, the more you realize you don't know. I think that is definitely true. The longer I am in college, the more people I talk with and the more I am exposed to classes of this type and that type, the more I realize that I don't have any conception of what there is to know. When you try to decide what you want to be and do, you realize that no matter what path you take, it will have to be a fairly narrow one. And I think that has been one of my problems. I don't really want to narrow myself down that much in order to become really adept in anything.

Bob's refusal to "narrow down" reminds us how vigorous the exploratory drive is in young people: he was willing to sacrifice the security of high academic achievement to find out about the world. The fundamental instincts of youth support the educator's goal of liberation through discovery.

A highly selective college presents talented students with a problem: most can only maintain their accustomed position at the top by an extreme effort, in which they shut out many of the opportunities for intellectual and personality development that a college offers. The problem would not have existed for Bob if he had gone to his home state university: there he could have continued on top while exploring the possibilities of the curriculum and the environment.

Although Bob ultimately changed his attitudes towards such home values as drinking, sex, and authority, he changed very little over four years in his avoidance of going steady. Judging from his responses, going steady was not just something his parents would have disapproved of. While girls represent sex, and therefore freedom from parental constraint prior to fulfillment of obligations, the girl herself becomes a constraining influence once the relationship has developed to the point where the boy begins to center his plans around her and around the implied constraint of marriage.

(Spring, senior year) I every now and then get an idea that if I found somebody that I would enjoy living with the rest of my life . . . I would be able to settle down and find my niche or whatever. I mean a lot of people have said that the best thing that could ever happen to me would be for me to find . . . a steady girl friend, and that maybe I could see where I was going then.

They're concerned about your not settling down?

I don't know whether they're really concerned about it. It's just that I've talked to them, and they suggested that that might be one way of doing it: find someone that I was interested in enough to draw some purposeful lines for her.

Does that make sense to you?

Oh, it makes some sense [laughs]. Maybe that's what kept me from ever deciding to get a permanent girl friend [laughs]. Then you have to make a few decisions!

What do you expect your life will be like ten years from now?

If I had to bet, I would bet that within the next five or six years, I'll decide that what I do want is a married life, and whatever I'm doing at the time—whether I'm going on in chemistry, or whether I finish chemical engineering, or whether I'm in medical research, or what—well, I'll find some pretty permanent job, settle down and have a wife, I don't know. Not sure about kids—things like that. You can only get so far, I guess, in giving up an ideal of some independence.

You think that marriage, and especially kids, will tie you down more than you want to be now?

Yes.

Bob's sophomore year breakup with his girl friend back home confirms the point. His feelings of depression following the breakup tell us that he had given up something that meant a great deal to him.

(Spring, sophomore year) *What sophomore year experience or activity was particularly unpleasant?*

> The breakup with my girl friend back home. I received a cryptic letter from her, and called her. She named conditions. She was ready to settle down, and I wasn't. She found a guy who was. It came at midterm, and I got behind for a lot of the quarter. I felt depressed; it was hard to study. Finally went to the student health service about it, and was referred to the college psychiatrist. I saw him several times—a little bit helpful.

Bob's willingness to break with his girl friend in spite of the pain involved indicates how strong his resistance was to the constraints inherent in a close relationship leading to marriage.

As every educator knows, the richness of the fare provided by the college curriculum may not even be perceived by the student. We saw that Bob's first response was to wish that he could get rid of all but the vocationally relevant courses. But that was only a part of Bob speaking. The other part fought against the constraint of the technical curriculum, irrepressibly ventured to look over his roommates' shoulders at what they were reading, and kept up a steady pressure against constraint over the first three years of college. This resulted in Bob's switching in his senior year to a program consisting of music, art, and two languages.

(Fall, freshman year) *How do you feel about some of the fields outside of your major interest?*

> Well, I've always been interested in music—my dad is very interested in it. I had eight years of music before

college. I was a little disappointed at not being able to take any music this year—it takes time. I would like to take up some sort of language, if I have a chance to do so. I had two years of Spanish in high school and I enjoyed it very much. But I was never able to—it won't do me much good in chemistry. And I like literature. I'd rather read than sleep. That's one thing that has disappointed me this year: I haven't had time to do any outside reading at all.

Although in the fall term of the sophomore year a part of Bob was jubilant over being done with required non-major courses (he had been required to take English and history in his freshman year), another part of him was finding that math, his favorite high school subject, was often painful, and he found it "odd" that he was enjoying his one non-chemistry, non-engineering course more than any of his other courses.

(Fall, sophomore year) I've had a chance to see what several other courses look like—one of my roommates is taking archaeology, and it's quite interesting, and two of my roommates are in the humanities. I think I'd really enjoy some of the reading they are doing . . . one is taking a political science course that parallels my economics course, which I am enjoying very much. I don't know . . . I have no room in my schedule for any of these courses.

Bob found himself envying his roommates. Moreover, when he tried to work on his science and mathematics courses, he had trouble concentrating on them. By spring of his sophomore year, at the very time when he had, in his formal statements about his major, returned to a firm stand on chemical engineering ("I have decided that chemical engineering is the right field"), Bob was reacting strongly against his chosen curriculum. His underlying feelings come out in his responses to several questions about what he would do if circumstances allowed him more freedom.

(Fall, junior year) *If you were required to take only half of your courses in order to graduate, what would you do with the free time?*

> I would probably take a lot of general courses like the sociology I'm taking now, and political science, or a couple of religion courses, or philosophy—just about anything to make me the well-rounded graduate.

Bob still ignored his strong drive to look deeply into matters outside his own field. He could not see the implications of his interest in his roommates' studies for his own decision about a career. Chemical engineering was an obligation. These other courses were just fun—"fooling around"—something that must be postponed until what was obligatory had been carried out.

Nevertheless, he refused to be completely confined by his technical curriculum. He found himself developing a growing interest in people and in social life.

(Fall, sophomore year) *What is different about the sophomore year?*

> I'd say the main difference is I'm living a lot more free a life now. I've been doing a lot more socially—been just sitting around and talking a lot more than I did before. I think it's definitely more fun. All of us [four roommates] are finding it pretty difficult to study, but one of my roommates has been doing what I would call "exorbitant non-studying." He has had as many as eight dates in eight days. Last year, he never went below an A— average, and he was not sociable at all. But he got a car, and that seemed to turn him on. It's somewhat baffling to me . . . the car has something to do with it. The car had something to do with me, as well, because his having a car enables me to go on more dates. He generally looks for someone to go with him, and I'm the only one of us roommates who dates much. People told me all last year that I ought to take more part [in social events]. Just getting to know people, that's a big part of life. I'm beginning to agree with them that it is a lot of fun to be out with other people and just relax.

Bob was doing more and more "fooling around" on the social front. Despite his childhood-based perception of his father as disapproving of such exploration, his interests kept leading him into developmental and highly educational experiences. The student's primary emotional response to college life is made toward other students rather than toward the faculty or the curriculum. Most of the developmental effects on personality and, apparently, many more educational influences than anyone has suspected, come from student encounters. In Bob's case, this influence seemed to be of two kinds: the effects of contacts with a great variety of personalities, and the special power of close friendships.

Any college is likely to contain a more diverse selection of personalities than most students have encountered before. The heterogeneity of the student body at the college Bob attended was probably particularly great, since most selective private institutions consciously attempt to guarantee a diversity of background, experience, talent, and personality among their students through selective admissions policies. Bob became conscious of diversity in every aspect of his college environment, especially after he had pledged a fraternity.

(Fall, senior year) *Can you give me a picture of the different kinds of people one finds at this college?*

Just about anybody: from beatniks to the very conservative sophisticates. I'd say, first, that most students here are on the conservative side. They are neither raving liberals nor solid John Birchers—a little to the right of the middle of the road. There does seem to be a rather strong element of these pretty wild people—you might call them immoral by social society standards of immorality—who just don't care about what others think.

You mean sexually? Or in other ways?

Oh, sexually, and in the lack of respect shown to their elders, to other people—they simply don't care. They are not too large a group, but there are quite a few. Then there are others who are completely on the other side, who go through the whole four years of college on a very reserved basis and have contact with only a few people. The first couple of years it seemed to me I met many non-intellectuals who are just here because the college gives them a degree and really do not care about their education much. I think getting into the House [his fraternity house] has got me away from that side of it. In my freshman year, I knew fellows who were here just for a good time; their folks had money, and they didn't have to worry about that. I think that attitude still exists, but I don't see so much of it anymore.

How would you say your present friends are similar to you?

I'd say the only similarities are the fact that we are all in the same House. We're about as diverse a group of guys to be close friends as is possible. My friends differ from me in that we are in different courses of study; have different ideas towards girls; towards drinking. About the only similarity among the four of us who are closest is that none of us smoke, and three of us are ex-track men.

How many of your present friends have a religious background different from your own?

Two of them are Jewish. Two or three are Catholic, I guess. I think there's a Lutheran and an Episcopalian.

Do any have a different racial or national background?

One roommate is a Negro, and one friend is a Costa Rican.

About how many of your present friends' parents are in income groups different from your own parents?

A few are in the same category—otherwise I think it runs the gamut. Fred's parents, for instance, are in a quite low income group, while Alfred's father is pretty high up.

(Spring, junior year) *If someone were to ask you to describe the students in your House, what would you say?*

There are those who are the grinders—I suppose you'd call them the "educational machines"—who just simply sit there and work their slide rules all the time and try to get the best grades—the grade-grubbers. There are those who are quite liberal, always worrying about other people, worrying about civil rights, worrying about what's going on in poverty, and so on—working outside the House in various areas of general welfare. There are those in the House who, sometimes I would say, are just there to have fun. They don't work that hard at grades and they don't work that hard at outside activities; they just spend their time going to movies or going out, or just kind of enjoying life. There are the executive types, the future business men, guys who are already getting businesses going for themselves. They are pretty serious about their studies, but don't care about their grades. They're trying to get what they can out of college to benefit them in what they're already setting up for, or what they intend to set up when they get out. Then there are the athletes—fellows who are pretty much devoted to their running. To them, school seems to be somewhat secondary.

(Fall, junior year) *So you have three roommates? And how's that working out?*

Oh, there are a few conflicts, but it's working out all right. One of the fellows we have is a Turk from Nigeria and his ideas are somewhat divergent from ours. He's a segregationist, and in some respects a warmonger [laughs]. Being a member of the minority of the population in Nigeria, he's also an imperialist. It makes a rather interesting situation for arguments.

How is he as a person?

He's immature. He's only 18 years old, and he has lots of things to learn. He's pretty obstinate, and quite dogmatic. He will not change his views, and will rarely really listen to anyone else's opinions. It's interesting, because my older roommates and I have a mutual friend who is a Negro. The Turk from Nigeria spends quite a bit of time in the room, and it sets up some pretty good arguments when we get this older roommate and the Negro and the Nigerian into arguments. I think basically it's a good situation, because it helps you to make your own convictions concrete.

(Spring, junior year) During the fall quarter, I've dated a Catholic, a Jewish girl, and an Oriental girl . . . a history major, a music major, a writer, and a math major.

Bob gave a telling account of one of the effects of student diversity upon his own development.

(Fall, junior year) Aside from your academic work, what has been happening in your life during the past two years that has been of particular importance to you?

> The most important has been due to a combination of influences from both academic and campus life, and that is the formation of ideas of my own. When I came out of high school, I was just a blob of putty being ready to be molded. I had no real opinions about anything— political, moral, or anything else. I know that I've developed educational, occupational, and moral goals and ideas. One example would be this racial problem that's been so predominant on campus the last year or so. My mother's father, for instance, was a Southerner, and was very definitely a segregationist; and members of her family are very opinionated about racial problems— segregationists and integrationists. This last summer we had quite a discussion. Here [in college] I was able to have a definite opinion on the matter; not just sit there and nod at the obvious statements of one and then nod at the obvious statements of another.

How did you come to have particular ideas about political, moral, and other matters?

> I think it's mainly been through discussions with my fellow students. For instance, our House has about as diverse a group as you can find, and there are constantly arguments being waged about this, that, and the other thing. It's difficult not to have a stand on something when you hear ideas being presented that you know you don't agree with. This sort of discussion makes you want to find out something about the case. I read *The Organization Man* and two or three other books mainly because of discussions we got into.

So there is a difference of opinion in your family too. You said there were segregationists and integrationists . . . and you had heard these discussions and yet that didn't lead up to your becoming firm about your own views. Was there something different about hearing it here at college as compared to back home?

Yes, I think so, because here at college the thing seems a little bit closer to me. Back home I never really had any . . . well, I had never even met a Negro before I came here, for instance. The people I talked to and had discussions with at home were generally involved within the community—they were either lawyers or teachers. There wasn't too much else. Down here [at college] I was exposed to sons of steel workers, and sons of bankers, and so on. It's an association with the world.

Bob's account illustrates the difference between mere exposure to environmental differences and personal involvement with these differences. For example, he had heard discussions about segregation at home, but had experienced what he heard as just another remote aspect of the adult world.

Another important developmental influence on Bob was friendship. Some friends are special. And when they are not only very close, but are also very different from oneself, they can exercise a powerful influence upon the course of a young person's development. A close college friend named Fred influenced Bob's development in many ways.

(Spring, junior year) *Would you describe your two closest friends, preferably one male and one female—the one in each category that you would consider your best friend? You want to start with the male?*

Well, that would be Fred, I guess. Fred is shorter than I am . . . fairly good physical condition. His dates are usually made on the basis of his intelligence, not his looks; he's not really too good-looking, but he gets along. He's quite impressive. Partly this is in the man, partly because he always has something to say, and generally has something to back up what he says. It's kind of like talking to a term paper, because if you ask him to footnote it, he'll footnote it.

He's quite a scholar?

Yes, his grades are pretty close to a B. I think they're a little bit above that, but the thing that amazes me is that he doesn't get A's on all his papers. Well, it doesn't really amaze me that much, because he doesn't spend the time on it that some of the other fellows do, but most of the time in discussions, or when he is really writing, I find him hard to surpass. My other roommate, Alfred, has close to an A average, and he takes about the same courses that Fred does, but he spends all his time working on these things. If he has a thirty-page paper to write, he'll spend three or four weeks on it, while Fred will just sit down and write it in a week and a half, or something like that. Fred will probably read more books. Alfred will read fewer books, and perhaps use more out of the books than Fred. Fred uses a lot out of his head.

When did you meet Fred?

My freshman year. He was the first person I really knew well here. We came in on the same day, and because our names sound alike, another student said, "Hey, there's a track man by the same name on the second floor." So we got together that way.

What would you say your relationship is like now? What are your roles in this relationship?

I'd say that I hold more respect for Fred than he does for me. I'm not by any means as lucid as he is, and, therefore, in most discussions, he carries the ball most of the time.

What are you getting out of this relationship? What is there in it that's satisfying?

I'd say that Fred has been responsible for a good deal of my education; otherwise I'd simply have been a slide-rule manipulator for the three years that I've been here. He makes you think. He'll come out with some answer which is so cynical or so . . . well, if I come up with some statement like, "I want to be a tutor in the educational program for deprived children," Fred says, "What for?" Even though he is also a tutor there, he'll ask me exactly why; he'll give me a lot of reasons why I shouldn't be. He just makes you look at every side of every question and think about it, and not in terms of just simple equations. If I have any philosophy at all, I know most of it has been dredged up by Fred.

How are your backgrounds different?

Fred comes from a less well-to-do family. His father is a mechanic. Fred went to a large high school in a big city, and ran around with a pretty wild group of fellows, most of whom were quite intelligent. He started tackling philosophical problems in high school, while I barely knew what philosophy was.

What do you see as his outstanding positive and negative traits?

Positively, I'd say just the effect he has on other people. I've known people who almost despise Fred, but still respect him because he'll make anybody think about something. And he's so completely capable of being coherent all the time that you never have any doubt about what he's saying; usually you don't even doubt that what he's saying is true. That may also be somewhat negative in the sense that some of the guys, like perhaps myself, sometimes take everything that he says for granted, simply because we have no reason to believe otherwise, or because he presents it in such a good manner that it's difficult to believe otherwise.

What kind of difficulties do you have with each other?

Well, my main difficulty with him is trying to communicate. I'm not nearly on his level of communication most of the time. The places where we are in communication with each other are generally on everyday things, such as our common interest in track, and our drinking together.

Do you ever have any arguments with each other?

Oh, now and then. Not any really strong arguments except . . . I don't know . . . it usually ends up with Ralph and me against Fred, and we hold our own fairly well.

What do you think you do for him?

I think that what I do for him is, perhaps, holding him down to the worldly level every now and then, and specifically, quite often I keep him from drinking too much. Sometimes he'll get carried away on some idea of his, and it takes the practicality of an engineer to pull him back down. He gets pretty wound up on something like getting an idea of quitting school, or something like that, and, after arguing with me, he sees the practical side of the situation.

Have there been any changes in your relationship over a time?

I'd say it's much closer now, and much less superficial. In our freshman year, most of our relationship was based on our participation in track. Since we've roomed together for over a year and a half now, it's changed.

In his senior year interviews, Bob added to his description Fred's approach to life.

What would you say about his general beliefs and values?

It's hard to say because, in a lot of respects, he is a humanist. It doesn't always show, because of his sarcasm and cynicism, but I think his basic belief in humanity is that humanity is good. On the moral side, he drinks, but doesn't smoke—not because he thinks smoking is immoral, but because he doesn't like to smoke. Girl-wise, sex-wise, I think he can take it or leave it—just one of those things. He doesn't really seem to have too much respect for other persons unless the other person shows that he is capable of meriting respect—unless he has a sharp wit, or uses what he has to the best.

You once said that if it weren't for him you might have ended up being a slide rule.

Yes, I think that is probably pretty true. In order to ever sit down and argue with him on any point, I knew that I had to have a lot better background than just the science and math that I was going through . . . I used to read scientific journals, math journals, and things like this instead of reading *Time*, or *Harpers*, or some of the broader magazines. I just didn't realize, until I met him, exactly how narrow my past was.

Is your relationship with him a mutual one? Is there a kind of equality about it, or is he more dominating, controlling?

> Well, I don't know, frankly. I feel inferior to him, mainly because of the knowledge he has, and the way he can use it. And I think that if he does have any feeling of superiority—well, he merits it. It is pretty much of a reciprocal friendship.

Fred had some qualities that Bob's father would not have approved of. As a high school student, he had been "wild," and in college he drank heavily. Could it have been Bob's own suppressed tendencies in this direction—his strongly controlled rebelliousness—that drew him to Fred? He may have been equally attracted to Fred because of the latter's ability to criticize and question. As a freshman, Bob felt extremely reluctant to question authority; as he ended his senior year, he felt that he had changed most by becoming able to criticize. Fred's fearlessness in this regard may have exerted a powerful attraction.

During three summer vacations, Bob worked on a construction crew—first as a laborer, then as a foreman. It proved to be a significant experience for him. As foreman, he was forced to deal strictly with a malingering laborer on his crew.

And this crewman who didn't want to work—how did you handle him?

> Well, fortunately he left before the summer was over. The main thing was that I did have to become pretty dominating over him towards the end, because he started griping about every little thing that went wrong, and causing dissension among the crew. Actually, the whole matter kind of alleviated itself, because he not only alienated himself from me, but he got the other crew members rather irritated at him too. There were a few times when I had to use—well [laughs]—you might call it disciplinary action, but it just amounted to insisting that he do something instead of us, or insisting that he be quiet about something.

In the semester following this incident, Bob entered into leadership roles within his House. Quite possibly, the experience as construction crew foreman laid the groundwork for his junior-year developments on campus. Bob's talent for political compromise was evidenced by the way in which he managed to look after the best interests of the crew and enlist their support in handling the difficult crew member.

Student organizations serve as developmental pathways to a good many students. Their developmental function lies in their organizational structure, which provides an opportunity for students to hold positions of responsibility. Carrying out the obligations of these roles serves to bring the student into activities that he would otherwise not engage in; this happened in Bob's case.

(Spring, sophomore year) *What sophomore year experience was particularly pleasant?*

> Just the fact that I participated in the House. It brought a lot of new things into my life. I was able to see more of the world instead of just the dormitory cubicle. I saw more of the university—more controversial types of faculty, administration, and students.
>
> I take a good part in fraternity activities. As Faculty Guest Chairman, I arrange for faculty guests to come over for informal discussions. I work out the faculty list program, issue an invitation to the professor, and try to work out some dates when he can come over. Then when he comes, it is my job to introduce him to the club. A history professor was over last week, and talked about the department; everybody was interested in that. Another professor discussed university policy—he is connected with the Dean's Office. One of the guests we had was from Harvard, and we discussed what went on at other campuses.

What about non-academic life?

> Well, I quit track, so I'm spending more time on House activities, House social life. I was the athletic chairman for the House during the fall, and rush chairman during the last half of this year. I'm to be president of the House next fall.

What junior year experience has been particularly satisfying?

My work . . . as rush chairman. In some respects, it's a leadership position. You've got to get out and work on an awful lot, take care of the freshmen, find the right ones, and get them over. It's a position of power in some respects, because you have a big part of the say over who the members are for next year. What was most pleasing was that even though the other Houses had their problems in getting pledges this year, well, we were quite successful . . . we actually got more pledges than we needed.

By his senior year, Bob was handling his presidential office with the relaxed ease of an experienced politician. The job even seemed a little tame.

(Fall, senior year) *Are there any new things you are doing this year?*

Oh, outside of the classroom, mainly I have been involved in being an officer of the House. This includes sitting on the Inter-House Council which is a little different, but so far not too much different.

What's it like being president?

Not too much different than being any officer in the House. Except I get served first at dinner [laughs]. It's good in that I have somewhat of a talent for organizations, and so I am in a position now where I can get things going; but it's not too much different than being, for instance, rush chairman in the spring. There you are doing the same kind of thing . . . trying to organize a group to take care of this, and so on.

What are you getting out of it?

Oh, seeing a few things accomplished that probably wouldn't be accomplished if I hadn't been there, such as revising the Constitution. The House has needed a revised Constitution for years, but nobody ever got around to it. I got a committee going on that. A couple of weeks ago, a lady from town called me up about the United Fund drive; I took care of that. It didn't involve too much work, and didn't have to have a big committee, so I took care of it. Usually it is a matter of delegating a little authority here and there.

What of the influence of the faculty, whom we presume to have such great powers to stir young minds and to free them? Bob's response to the faculty was mostly in terms of the instructor's skill in making his presentations understandable.

(Fall, freshman year) *And what are your teachers like?*

I find them all very interesting. Our English teacher is a young lady . . . it must be her first year of teaching . . . but she's all right for the course. My chem instructor is tops, along with the math instructor. I don't think much of the graduate student who is my math discussion leader . . . he acts entirely bored with the whole thing. I can see why: it's elementary to him. But to me . . . having had no calculus in high school, I'm behind. He brings in a lot of things we haven't had, shows them to us, and says, "Well, you'll get to them later on." My math teacher goes at a rapid rate, but she presents it in a way which we can completely understand . . . you don't have any trouble at all getting what you should out of the lesson . . . she's a very good instructress.

(Fall, junior year) *What is the physics teacher like?*

He's a good presenter of the materials. He does a lot of preparation for his lectures, in that he always has ex-experiments or illustrations . . . he tries to explain everything in terms which you can understand . . . illustrates them well enough that you don't have any trouble understanding. He's not one of these fellows, as the last two physics profs that I had were, who stands up there and says, "It is obvious that this follows this," though it is not always obvious. Probably the first quarter physics prof was about as boring as they come. He took his lectures almost exactly from the book. He didn't add many illustrations or experiments, and when he tried, he generally failed. Just a dry lecturer. He was one of those types who just sits there and goes rattling through his lectures, rarely with any time out for questions or anything like that.

Can you think of an exciting teacher and tell me what he was like?

> I'd say probably my chem prof. Wild as he is, he's probably the most exciting. The main reason that he's exciting is that he brings things from industry right into the classroom and really arouses the interest of the class. He has just come out of ten years of industrial work, so he tends to throw problems at us that you might run into in industry. I think that is about the main reason I enjoy it so much.

Social scientists who have been looking into faculty influence on student development are beginning to feel that a reaction like Bob's is fairly typical. Bob knew little about the faculty, and did not care to change the relation.

How much contact have you had with your college teachers?

> Well, some contact with those in chemical engineering and chemistry. Probably not more than going in and seeing them personally a couple of times a term. Our chemical engineering class at present has only twenty students in it, so you become fairly familiar with your teachers just through class discussion.

Did you see any of the instructors in others fields outside of sciences?

> I did see my history prof a couple of times . . . each term.

Would you like to have more contact with your teachers, or less?

> Oh, I think the more the better. Now and then I feel that I don't see them quite often enough, but if I really felt that way, I'd probably go and see them more often.

Constraining forces held their own against liberalizing influences during Bob's first year, and there was little change during his sophomore term. But Bob's junior year was decisive. A sensitive indication is the difference between the summer (June 1st) and fall interviews that year. In the fall interview, Bob said he still did not drink. By June, he had changed.

How much drinking do you do these days?

Considerably more than I did my first two years—about once a week I will go out and just have one or two beers, and talk. Sometimes it's a little more extensive: maybe four or five.

Although Bob graduated without having had sexual relations, his verbal attitudes, at least, had definitely been modified. Again, it was the junior-year interview that showed the change.

How intimate are you now, physically, with the girls?

Oh, nothing beyond a little make-out.

Nothing beyond a little necking? Are you still a virgin?

Yes.

What are your thoughts about premarital relations?

It isn't really of very great importance to me. I have a good friend at home, for instance, who wouldn't think of premarital relations, but I think it's completely up to the people involved.

But for yourself?

I don't know. If the situation arises that I have to make a choice, well, I'll make it; but I don't know which way it would be. There's nothing that . . . I still have in the back of my mind the fact that I know my folks would not condone it, but then I've changed—changed so much—so many of my other ideas from what my folks have advocated, that if I ever made that decision, it wouldn't bother me that much. Like I say, it depends completely on the people involved. I know fellows in the House who've had premarital relations, and they see nothing wrong in it as long as neither person is hurt, and that kind of thing; but I feel that if you have real doubts about whether it's right or wrong, well, it's probably wrong in your mind, because you've got those doubts there.

His attitudes towards grades had changed as well. Bob's freshman year reaction to suddenly finding himself a C— student instead of an A student, as he had been, was to "tighten up" and study much harder. As a matter of fact, this hard work paid off: he made better than a B average the second and third quarters of his freshman year—the best he was ever to achieve in college. But his junior-year grades had a different emotional importance to Bob.

I want to ask you whether your feelings about grades have undergone any changes in college.

I'm less worried about grades now than I was before. These past two years, it's been constant worrying about keeping the grades up so I could get my scholarship back. But right now the pressure is completely gone on that, because I have enough money at home, and even if I don't win my scholarship back for next year, I could make it through. I've got my scholarship for this year, so . . . there's no question about my finishing college. I think that's been the main consideration before. I'm mainly just worried now about how much I'm actually getting out of the courses, rather than whether or not I'm making A's and B's.

By the end of his senior year, Bob's only motivation for study was that good grades would allow him to graduate.

Bob's personality changes seem to have been a part of a general breakup of the constrained organization of personality that had prevailed over his first two years and during part of his third year. Bob's new freedom to criticize authority is described in a senior year interview on impulse expression and control:

Well, if you can think back to when you were a freshman —was there any sphere of thinking, feeling, or acting that you might at some time have felt tempted by, but just didn't dare to feel free to give in?

Possibly, to criticize . . . criticizing the class, if I had something to say. Or, if a member of our House were to ask what was wrong with the House, something like that. As a freshman I probably would have been quite reticent. I think probably I feel more free in [pause] talking with professors than I did at that time.

What stands out in the past three years that you have enjoyed doing just for fun or pleasure?

Quite a few things. Playing on intramural teams, and other sports I was out for. Just about any of the social life—just for the fun of doing it.

If you had to pick out something that you found most pleasurable, what would you pick out?

Probably the beer and bull sessions with the gang.

That wasn't so when you came?

In the first place, I wasn't twenty-one, and in the second place, I didn't feel as free with the fellows.

Not only the general growth of impulse expression, but the directions it took are significant: Bob now felt freer to criticize authority, and he most enjoyed "beer and bull sessions." One could hardly get a clearer statement of the tug-of-war that had been going on inside Bob: to follow uncritically the implied dictates of parental authority, or to give in to "fun"—to what he liked to do. It would be difficult to find an activity less likely to be approved by Bob's father than "beer and bull sessions with the fellows," unless it were serious involvement with girls, a prohibition that Bob hesitated to challenge as much because of the constraint attendant upon a serious relationship as because it was "fooling around."

We have already reviewed a major type of evidence for Bob's "breakout"—his long-delayed shift from chemical engineering. That the critical developments took place in Bob's junior year can be seen by comparing his fall interview, when he spoke of his plans for a master's degree in chemical engineering, and his late spring interview, when he said that chemical engineering was leaving him "cold." Here is a final example of Bob's changed attitude away from technical courses and toward the humanities:

Well, what academic areas have capitivated you so far?

I've enjoyed literature, the one literature course I've taken. I've enjoyed English—mainly the second half, because that involved literature—and I took one other literature course this last term.

That the developments Bob made represent big changes is confirmed by large standard score changes in five of the six scales of the Attitude and Opinion Survey. The figures below show the extent of Bob's changes between entrance and graduation as compared to the average change made by the men in his class.

Scale Change (in standard points)	Bob	Class
Increase in Social Maturity	+23	+8
Increase in Impulse Expression	+10	+3
Decrease in Schizoid Functioning	−3	−3
Decrease in "Masculinity"	−14	−3
Increase in Estheticism	+18	+2
Increase in Developmental Status	+27	+10

Development and instability go hand in hand. When changes come as fast as they did in Bob's final two years, they are bound to create instability and great subjective uncertainty— even confusion. In Bob's case, there was the added problem that there was no way of integrating the changes with a new educational plan for his final year: it is not possible to shift from a technical curriculum to a liberal arts major in the junior year of college and still graduate with one's class. The total effect of Bob's extensive changes in his final two years added up to a senior-year picture that sometimes bordered on chaos.

(Spring, junior year) *What are you getting out of this diversity of friends and diversity of girls that you date, and why do you prefer it?*

[Laughs] Confused. I don't know, it sometimes bothers me, because it seems like all of my friends are different and I like something in each of them, but I'm never really sure of what I feel myself, or . . . whether or not they're right. I don't know, after, uh . . . after those small groups of friends that I had in high school, I mean, high school was pretty limited as far as the number of friends and the feelings that you get out of that. It's kind

of like trying to sample every piece of cake around because there are just so many different people, and their
feelings are so different. It's like reading a number of
different books . . . for instance, during high school,
I think that I practically ran the gamut of every type of
literature that it's possible to read. Everything from
scientific documents to western fiction. It has been in
some respects a habit of mine to look at everything that's
different. I can't really tell whether it's good or bad.

What would be bad about it?

The fact that I can never set myself in any specific
train of thought. Now and then I'll get really up in arms
about civil rights, and then something will happen to
cool me down a bit. When you know so many different
people, and you get so many viewpoints, it's hard to
figure which is right and which you should choose. It's
like last year when I came in. After reading this Ayn
Rand novel, well, I was impressed by the way she put
things down and I felt that was part of the way I wanted
to be—just think about material things, let nothing else
bother me. Then after talking to other people, I realized
that that wasn't all there is to life. I don't know, it's just
like I said before—confusing.

By fall of his senior year, Bob's state was one of acute dissolution.

What aspects of yourself do you like best and least?

Best? Well, I think it is that when I am given something
to do, I can accomplish it in a fairly practical method.
I guess the best way to say it is that I am pretty practical
in most situations. I don't get carried off by a lot of hare-
brained, wild ideas. I guess what I like least about myself are my vacillating ideas—I never seem to get a clear
viewpoint of what I am doing, or what I want to do, or
what I have done. It all just kind of waves back and
forth. I don't know—there doesn't seem to be any definite pattern, because of the way I have done things and
the way I continue to do them.

*This is mostly with respect to your career, or are you
talking about other things?*

This is just about everything. When I was running for president last spring, there was never any point in the campaign when I was absolutely sure that this was what I wanted. And it just seems that this is the way everything happens. I get a date for Friday night, and then by Friday night I am not so sure I want to go out on a date. At the beginning of the term when I decide my courses, for a while there, I think they might be fine; then I have reservations about it. It seems like my whole life has been [this way].

Then you start doubting? You say your whole life has been this way? It has been characteristic of you for a long, long time? Even during high school?

I don't think it was so evident in high school. I don't think I really thought about it that much; but particularly since I have been in college.

(Fall, senior year) *How often do you find yourself getting depressed—feeling blue?*

Well . . . every other hour [laughs]. Actually, quite often, because I can't really seem to make heads or tails out of what I am doing.

What is it like?

More a feeling of being lost . . . no sense of direction. Kind of . . . for a few minutes you feel like you have got to start doing something, but when you get on something, a few minutes later you can't quite turn around. What good are you doing when you don't know where you are going?

Has this been rather steady in the last three years of college, or has it fluctuated?

Oh, I think it has fluctuated. My freshman year I don't think it was quite so evident, because I was still pretty much in the groove. I was depressed after the first term because of the grades I had received, and then I got my grades back up. I can't remember too many times when

I was a freshman; but the past two years the depression
rate has been going up.

There are several noteworthy points about Bob's account.
One is that indecisiveness has always been something of a problem to him. What we see in his senior year is an acute exaggera-
tion of trends that have long been a part of his personality. It is
characteristic that such breaks take place along the line of old
fractures. Secondly, Bob's experience confirms the general sequence and timing of the constraining and liberating processes
postulated here. In his freshman year, things were especially bad
when the academic basis of his self-esteem was knocked out, but
his depression lightened when his tightening-up response improved
his grades. The general constraining reaction that was a part of
the whole freshman-year response Bob called being "still pretty
much in the groove." The "groove" is the whole family-associated
frame of reference by which he guided his life, including the plan
of becoming a chemical engineer, which he brought to college
with him. Thirdly, the dissolution was definitely identified by
Bob as a junior-senior year phenomenon. As we have seen, Bob's
original plan for his college career began to break down at an
accelerated pace between the fall and spring of his junior year.

Finally, the dissolution was not a general personality breakdown, even though Bob's uncertainty tended to creep into many
aspects of his life. He still felt secure in his House relationships,
the one place where through his own efforts, he had established
a secure identity after coming to college. Even the original leadership experience that preceded and probably helped this development took place away from home, during summer work with the
construction crew. It is quite possible that Bob's possession of such
a strong, self-made anchor point as his House position was instru-
mental in making him feel secure enough to risk opening up as
suddenly as he did on the college major and career fronts.

There is one curious but highly significant aspect of Bob's
wishes for his future as he experienced these in the midst of the
senior year chaos:

*What would you consider a good life for yourself about ten
years from now?*

It's hard to answer. Sometimes I just get the feeling that all I want to do is sleep the rest of my life but, uh [laughs] . . .

Well, what are some of your dreams of glory, ten years from now; what kind of life; what would you like to be doing?

It may sound strange, but I don't really have any, uh, grand ideas, or any grand dreams, of what I want to do. I . . . I don't know [laughs]. Well, sometimes I just get the feeling that, uh, all I want to do is be in some sort of position, I really can't say what, but some sort of position in which I can kind of float along and not have too many things to tie me down—be able to just leave when I want to, be able to study when I want to, and so on.

Would it be too much to suggest that what is seen above is the subjective correlate of the liberating forces that had always been a part of Bob's makeup but had been nurtured in college to the point where they had produced an explosive effect? The following interchange, which took place on the eve of graduation, seems to reveal the pure impulses of liberation and constraint as seen from within.

How is this indecision? Uncomfortable or . . . not too unpleasant?

I . . . at times when I sit down and think that I really have to get more serious on this and try to see exactly what I'm doing and where I'm going. . . . Then there are other times I think, "Well, I'm still young and I'm not tied down, so there's no reason not to . . . not to play around a little bit and find out if there's something else that I'm interested in, instead of sticking myself in a trap again and trying to force my way into something that I might not like."

Bob's feeling that he had been in a trap is particularly interesting. Indeed he had been. What he wanted most was to get out of it—be free—avoid any more traps. A final interchange seems to confirm the whole idea of the child self as central among the forces of constraint, and the college environment and Bob's inner explorations as principal liberating forces.

(Spring, senior year) *Well, how do you account for this great need for freedom and independence? Where does it come from?*

> I suppose part of it is just a kind of rebellion of sorts. I mean, before college I was quite dependent; my parents made me so. But I was dependent on them too. I mean, it was kind of a mutual thing—they didn't have me tied to the family, or anything. But when I got down here . . . well, it seems to me that there are an awful lot of things you can do when you don't have real close ties that I'd like to do, like traveling and studying . . . things that might not have anything at all to do with what I'm going to do or be in the future. If I had a lot of ties, a lot of needs to get into a position of security rapidly, well, I couldn't take the time and the effort to do them.

So a lot of it stems from—what? Just general intellectual curiosity and a need to travel?

> It's just . . . you could probably just call it curiosity. Period.

Which you haven't been able to satisfy thus far?

> I'd like very much to go to Europe, for instance, but thus far, because of the education things that I've tied myself to, I haven't been able to take the time to do it.

Bob's state of mind at graduation should make any educator who talks about "liberating" the student pause and reflect.

How do you feel about yourself in terms of relative maturity? What are your feelings about your own development in college, and the state you're in now?

> Well, I don't know. I'd say that when I first came, I had a single purpose in mind, and now I have lost all purpose entirely. Well, that's an oversimplification, of course, but. . . .

Things got more complicated?

Yes, that's it in a nutshell. What I've learned and what I've seen and done over the past four years have all just led to a state where I don't really know what I want.

Are you that uncertain?

Yes, I think so. I don't really know for sure what I want. I can sit down every other week and mark down a new goal, and still not be any more sure.

Has there been any change in the rules or principles by which you guide your conduct?

I suppose I have less rules now than I did when I came in. Just "hang loose."

Do you find it difficult to live up to your own standards?

I think that is one of my problems. My standards haven't really gotten definite, so it is pretty hard to say. I don't know . . . it just seems that even basic standards of decency. . . . Be good to your fellow men. That's about the only standard I have. Try to be a nice guy, and not hurt anyone else, and yet be as independent as you possibly can.

Taken at face value, this report would seem to indicate that Bob approached graduation without values or purpose. Is this a desirable outcome for one of the country's choicest high-school graduates—a student who was much sought after by the most selective colleges? One can't help wondering if Bob was ready for entry into a college filled with sophisticated and highly talented students. If he had gone instead to his home state university, he would have been able to maintain a high academic standing while pursuing the various new experiences that a college campus has to offer. He would still have had difficulty in establishing his independence, but he would have been spared the shock of having his identity knocked out from under him, and his development would not have been delayed by the tightening-up response that followed. Moreover, he would not have been forced to cling in self-defense to the career plan he supposed his parents wanted him to pursue. On the other hand, he would not have been forced to come to grips with the great problem facing all talented young people—that of learning to work effectively and comfortably among equals and superiors—nor would he have learned as much about diverse personalities. He probably would not have had a Turk from Nigeria for a roommate, nor a Negro for a friend, nor would he have encountered Fred, who did so much to educate him.

Finally, how does one know that a massive identity shock at Bob's age is a completely bad experience? Having once "trapped" himself by his constrained response, perhaps Bob stands in less danger of sealing himself in at a more critical point in later life. And how does one judge whether graduating "dissolved" is bad or good for a man Bob's age? Perhaps as the research staff follows him through later life, they will find that he is more able to respond effectively than he would have been if his life-plan had become hardened too soon.

Bob's case raises other questions for educators, but we will delay them until we have examined the case of Nancy, an undergraduate at the same school. Nancy's college career presents interesting parallels and contrasts to Bob's and illustrates the special ways in which a girl's situation is different in college from a boy's. Both Bob and Nancy were at the tops of their high school classes scholastically, and had nearly the same score (640) on the verbal aptitude section of the Scholastic Aptitude Test. Nancy's mathematical aptitude was very high for a girl (681). The two tested within a point or two of each other on five of the scales of the Omnibus Personality Inventory, with Nancy scoring higher on the sixth scale, Estheticism.

Nancy and Bob had similar high school dating patterns. By and large, each had avoided involvements with the other sex. They had devoted themselves with great effectiveness to studies and to accomplishments of the kind that teachers and parents approved. They were both very ambitious—Nancy more overtly so than Bob. She came to college determined not only to have a career, but to become an influential public figure. They were in every way model youngsters, the pride of parents, school, and community, and of the college admissions office that persuaded them to come.

This may be why both faced, as the major developmental task of their college years, the great problem of the young who represent ideals to adults: differentiating between what they want for themselves and what adults (their parents) want for them, and learning to implement this distinction with action.

The great contrast between Nancy and Bob was in their backgrounds—not so much in basic home values, since both families valued education, hard work, and achievement, and shared the usual middle class and professional family attitudes—but rather in the difference between the cultural isolation of Bob's home and Nancy's urban home environment. Bob's family did not have the money to travel, and his experience of the world did not extend beyond working up the river on a construction crew. Nancy's family was relatively well-to-do, and her father's relatives were among the social elite of a large city. She had traveled abroad with her family, and her father was a corporation executive with cultural and philanthropic interests.

One direct consequence of their great difference in background was that Nancy suffered only the most transitory qualms about her status in the student culture, while Bob suffered greatly from background and identity shocks. Poised and attractive, she was the member of a select sorority, from the outset, a campus "queen." But Nancy's sensitive and thoughtful reflections on her college career reveal the ways in which a girl's situation produces a distinctive kind of interaction between education, career, marriage, and the normal developmental problems of the college years. This interaction comes out with special clarity in Nancy's case, because she differed in certain respects from her group. Her high ambition, devotion to studies, and lack of pre-college dating experience are unusual in a good-looking girl whose family background assures her of a secure place in high school and college campus social life. Moreover, Nancy had a high degree of social consciousness—an interest in doing something about the problems of the disadvantaged. Finally, her very strong attachment to and admiration of her successful father, though not unusual among college women, was distinctive in its intensity and in the role it played in her college career.

The talented and ambitious girl who wants a career faces conflicts from the start if she wants marriage—a vocation in itself

—as well. Not that the boy differs in his ultimate interest in being married and having a family, but boys do not look upon marriage and family as a career—something that will occupy a major portion of their lives. Most boys want marriage, assume that it will come readily enough when they are ready for it, and picture it as a source of personal and vocational support. The vocational future is a single, integrated whole for the boy. For the girl, the marriage issue is divisive.

For Nancy, the conflict between marriage and career was to become particularly acute. She had already enjoyed considerable gratification in receiving affirmation of her talents from meaningful people in her life, especially her father. She prized her capacity for logical, clear thinking, and welcomed the challenges of rigorous intellectual work. She gave keen attention to the conversation and comments of stimulating adults. The accumulation of facts intrigued her, and she had been encouraged by her brilliant father to utilize her perceptions in problem solving and expression of opinion. However, she lacked feminine models who had carried the excitement of acquiring and applying knowledge to the field of work. She described the adult women she had known as intelligent, supportive, gracious, and cultured women who had been respected because of their husbands' status. She had observed the affection and respect shown these women by their husbands and children. During our interviews, she made no mention of knowing women who combined a gratifying family life with serious pursuit of intellectual or career interests. She appeared to lack any personal knowledge of able women who had realistically achieved a functional balance between family and professional responsibilities. It is not surprising, then, that as a freshman, Nancy was not very clear about her occupational future. Here is how she described it:

(November, freshman year) *As you look ahead at the next four years, are there things that you look forward to with a little apprehension?*

> Well, I think the biggest obstacle, or whatever you want to call it, is that I'm not sure exactly what I want to do. There's no problem right now, because I don't have any decision to make right now. But the problem would be whether I would go on to get a graduate degree . . .

and then go into a profession, or whether I'd be willing to settle down. This question may never even come up, but I think that even if it did come up, it would be a hard decision to make, because I've always wanted to have an outside career.

Interestingly enough, Nancy did not reveal the high level of her initial career ambitions until her junior year.

(November, junior year) When I first came to college, I had all these aspirations: maybe I'd be the first woman Assistant Secretary of State, or something . . .

Of course, Nancy was probably not using "Assistant Secretary of State" as a specific career goal, although it may well have been a fantasy-level goal, but it suggests that she entered college with the idea of preparing for an influential role in society. Nancy's initial feelings about some of the traditional roles for women are clear from this interchange.

(May, sophomore year) *What kind of life would you consider bad for yourself ten years from now?*

It would be unbearable being stuck with a job that you didn't like, whether it involved staying at home and taking care of the house, or doing secretarial work.

Nancy's feelings about possible college majors were appropriate to her hope that she might become an influential figure. They also reflected some of the high school and home influences that supported her career interest.

(November, freshman year) *Have you thought about a major?*

Yes, I have. I think somewhere in the field of political science or history. The first thing that made me even start thinking of these possibilities was a teacher I had as a freshman in high school who taught a course in government. She took me with her to several meetings. We heard the Secretary of State speak at a conference. Anyway, I became very interested in current affairs, and she told me at the time that she thought this was probably my best field. It always has been something that I think held my interest more than anything else. Then in my junior year in high school, the World History teacher taught such a stimulating class that I decided then, I think, that this was what I wanted to go into. And there's nothing else that interests me nearly as much.

How do your parents feel about this?

They think this is a good thing to go into if you're really interested. Before I came to college this summer I was talking to my father, and he feels that at least during the first year he wants me to try lots of different things. My father has always had the feeling that I had musical talent. Well, I enjoy playing a number of stringed instruments, but I don't think I play well enough to ever make it into a career. This is the only conflict I've ever had with my father. So I don't think he's completely satisfied. I think my mother is. She thinks it's fine, if this is what I want to do.

(Fall, freshman year) *Do either of your parents have special interests?*

They both enjoy classical literature very much. My father is very interested in the history of music, and I think he knows as much about it as a good many semi-experts do. My mother had it in college, so she's followed right along with it. They both love to travel. When I was in the ninth grade, by brother and I went to Europe with them, and I got more out of that summer than anything else I have ever done in my life. Before we went, my father made my brother and me study a certain amount of history of music. So we spent a month working together, and this was very helpful. When we heard concerts, they meant something to us.

An important part of Nancy's initial plan for herself was that she would avoid commitments to boys that would interfere with her freedom to explore college life freely and to find and develop her potentialities.

(November, freshman year) *Have you gone out with the same person, or with a variety of people?*

For the first three weeks I went out with the same boy, one whom I knew before coming to college. I really enjoyed being with him, but I realized that it is foolish for anyone to come to college to date just one person, especially a freshman. You tend to depend on them. Right at the beginning of your freshman year, you have an unusually good opportunity to meet all different kinds of people, and if you tie yourself down with one person, your're hurting yourself. You're limiting your friendships—friendships that will pay off later. He started dating other people and I did, too. So lately I've been dating all sorts of people. I really find that it's a much better sort of experience.

Nancy's initial way of viewing the going-steady situation was consistent with her high-school attitudes.

(November, freshman year) *Did you ever go steady before you came to college?*

I don't really think I've ever gotten that deeply involved, mainly because my parents had always emphasized that going steady is really a serious mistake. I think that this developed a reaction in me; I just never was really interested in boys. If you really go steady, you have to give up too many of your individual wants. If I ever give them up, it's going to have to be for someone who really means a lot to me.

(May, freshman year) *How were the teen years?*

I didn't date much when I was in high school. Frankly, it was a good thing for me. You grow up a lot when you come to college. In high school, I mainly studied, and I think I learned how to get along with girls. If there are any girls in the dorm who are unhappy, I think it's because they can't get along with the girls.

Nancy's relationship to her parents emerges clearly only in the material from her upper-class years, during the period when the relationship was undergoing major changes, but a great deal about how matters stood when she entered college can be inferred from her freshman interviews:

(Fall, freshman year) I think that my parents are pleased with my career plans. Actually, they've never told any of us children what we have to do.

What effect has your father's position had upon your life?

Maybe I made too much of it, but I was very sensitive to it, in that I didn't like to have my last name mentioned in a lot of places, because then people would associate me with him. I felt as though I could never really be myself, because whatever I did would reflect upon him. People tended to expect a lot from me, which, in a way, was an advantage because . . . people seemed to have a good opinion of me, and it was up to me to maintain it. I didn't like to do a lot of things with other kids, because deep down inside I could never really be sure whether they fully accepted me just for myself. So although my father's position had great advantages, I tended to feel sorry for myself because of it.

Your mother must have had quite a challenge to meet.

She was kind of in the public light too. My mother is a fairly shy person anyway, so I think it helped her. People were very fond of her, because you can't help but feel as though she's a very sweet person.

(Spring, freshman year) *What gets you into trouble at home, and who punishes you?*

The thing that gets me into trouble most is that I talk back to my parents. My father always punishes me for this.

Does he punish you for talking back to him, or to your mother?

If I talk back to Mother and he's in the room, well, he just won't take this at all. To a certain extent, he will argue with me, because I think he realizes that I have inherited this from him. He does punish me—I can't think of anything, though. They are really very lenient with me. Occasionally, they'll send me to my room. If we are arguing at the table, and if I get up and start to leave, he will say, "Come back," and for about five seconds there's inner conflict as to whether I should just go on, or whether I should come back and do as he says, but I always go back.

Who is boss in your family, and what sort of things do you disagree about in the family?

My father is boss; there's just no doubt about that. He and my mother agree on most things.

Would you say they get along, or bicker?

When I was little—my room's right next to theirs—I would hear them arguing, and I would get very upset. As I have grown up, I have realized that my father's short-tempered, and so he will get angry with my mother, but then he will be sorry afterwards, and she's learned that you just accept him. He has to have someone to be angry with; so these [quarrels] are never serious. I think they have a completely ideal marriage.

If you could change whatever you wanted from your past, including your family, what would have been different?

I wouldn't change my attitude towards my family, because I feel very close to them. But I'm impatient with my brother and sister; and with my mother, because I know she will take it. I would change this, because they are so good to me, and I sometimes really feel badly when I think back at some of the ways I've been.

What disagreements did you have with your father this summer and how did you react?

The biggest disagreement with my father was over makeup and the sort of clothes I wore. I think my appearance is my private domain, and all summer long he kept making suggestions and critical comments. My mother sided with me on this—that my appearance was my own personal matter. This summer it seemed to me that Daddy was just more unreasonable than ever over minor things. I think it was partly that he was trying to prove to himself that he had authority. He doesn't want to let go, I think. Maybe the tendency of the father to hold on is stronger if there is a close father-daughter relationship. It's kind of a compliment to me. Mother is more understanding at this point . . . she is growing right along with me. . . . The more people I meet, the more grateful I am that Mother and Daddy are the way they are. I had no conflict of any kind with Mother over summer.

In Bob's case, one could speak meaningfully of the forces of liberation and constraint. Not only were there two broad sets of forces opposed to one another, but the onlooker was in no doubt about the desirability of Bob's freeing himself from a too-confining life plan. In Nancy's case, the forces that came into play were just as powerful and the conflict just as acute, but the outcome was more difficult to evaluate. Nancy herself was very unsure at times whether she liked what was happening to her.

A pretty freshman girl on a campus filled with vigorous young men cannot avoid facing the demands of some boy that she commit herself to going steady. Nancy was not seen by the research staff between November and May of her freshman year. In the interim, some critical changes had developed in her decision to avoid going steady. An interview in which she reflected on the freshman girl's situation gives some hints as to the pressures she must have felt.

(October, sophomore year) *If you were advising an entering freshman girl about the first year of college, what would you tell her?*

> The main thing would be not to succumb to social pressure. There is a tremendous social pressure on a freshman girl. Some people don't feel this pressure because they're only interested in study, and couldn't care less about it. However, among girls who do like to date, and to whom it has any meaning at all, there is the pressure to have dates, and then it becomes a matter of prestige. For instance, at the beginning of the school year, the fraternities have parties to which they ask a small percentage of freshman girls, based entirely on just wandering around and picking the ones they think are most attractive. There is a pressure among girls to get these invitations, which is ridiculous. . . . But still, there's

this initial pressure, which is too bad. So I think my advice would be not to succumb to this pressure. The freshman girl should worry more about relationships with girls, and getting her studies done, relating to her classes, keeping up with the work, and everything else.

(May, freshman year) *What sort of dating practices do you approve or disapprove of?*

At the beginning of the year, I would definitely have said that it was wrong to date just one boy. But, naturally, my views on this have changed. I still think it is good to date lots of different people, but it's hard to do that here at this college. For instance, I know one girl on our hall who does date lots of different people, and I've heard freshman boys say, "Why take her out, when you know that she may not have time to go out with you again?" They feel as though there's no hope, because even if they wanted to take her out a lot, she would consider them just one of the many. So that you're put in a hard situation, in a way. I think it really depends on the person. If you find someone that you would like to date exclusively, I think that is fine. I think too many girls are looking for one particular boy whom they can date exclusively. I think this is wrong. I think you have to meet someone; it can't be something you plan to do.

By the end of the freshman year, Nancy herself was going steady.

Has there been any change in your dating habits?

Now I'm dating just one boy, and before I wasn't. I just met someone. It was fine before, just dating when you wanted to on weekends, but frankly, you get to the point where you are spreading yourself thin. I wasn't looking for one person to date—it just happened. Usually we go out one night on the weekend, and we study together. And you're not so tired from going out different places. I really enjoy it very much.

At the end of her sophomore year, Nancy has "pinned" to the boy she had been dating steadily.

Has anything else happened since last fall?

> Neil and I are pinned, but it doesn't make much dif-
> ference, because there's no change in the relationship at
> all. Actually, we thought more about the formality of
> getting pinned last fall, but Neil was not an active mem-
> ber of a fraternity and he didn't have a pin . . . then,
> although I don't really care about what other people
> think, it really began to be funny. People would ask,
> "Why aren't you pinned? What's wrong?" We'd say,
> "Nothing is wrong." So when he finally got a pin, we
> just got pinned.

Nancy's quick capitulation may be interpreted as indicating
that her protests about the undesirability of going steady were only
a superficial attitude and hence easy to change, or it may be an
indication that the power of the forces involved are far greater
than we appreciate. That Nancy's attitude was not superficial is
suggested by her senior year restatement of the matter, in which
she strongly endorsed the idea of remaining uncommitted, while
recognizing that she had done exactly what she disapproved of.

(October, senior year) *What do you do now that you felt
you ought not to do when you entered college?*

> When I first came here, I thought definitely that when
> I was my present age I would not be thinking about
> marriage; that I would not be relating my goals or fu-
> ture plans to any other person. I thought that it was un-
> wise; that it was wrong—not in a moral sense, but a
> mistake. I thought this because this is what my father
> told me for a long time. And I believe it; I really do.
> I think it is a mistake, and I would teach my children
> the same thing. But I am doing it now.

As Nancy was soon to discover, the decision to go steady
brought a new force into her life. Discussions with Neil about
their mutual aspirations appear to have had a profound effect
upon her educational and personality development, and to have
set her life upon a course she had not anticipated. By the fall of
her sophomore year, the potential conflict between her career and
her marriage wishes had begun to materialize.

(October, sophomore year) *What career do you lean toward?*

Well, this is actually . . . a personal conflict. Since I
was in high school, I have always wanted to get a bachelor's degree and then get a master's. Then do something
with either the government, such as the information
agency, or in the foreign branch of some kind of private
institution, such as a corporation. This is what I want
to do, ideally. However, I would have to admit that
[now] Neil enters in. In a way, I'm really sorry that I've
met Neil as early as I have because . . . if it came to
choosing between someone I really liked and getting a
job, I think I would probably get married. But yet, it
would be so much easier if I didn't have to make any
decision like this. If there was not the complication of
having someone I might possibly marry, this [working
with the government] is what I would ideally like to do.
But now I don't know how it would be modified. It's
too early to say.

It is unclear from the data just what changes went on
during the sophomore year, but there are some suggestive clues,
For one thing, after committing herself to Neil, Nancy found that
her scholarly drive was gone.

(May, sophomore year) This quarter I loved my courses
and I loved my instructors, but I had no motivation.
. . . It's the most disappointing thing in the world, as
a personal thing in yourself.

Nancy began talking of "success" in different terms:

What do you think you will be like ten years from now?

My views have changed since I first came to college.
When I first came here, I thought a good life—well, a
basic part of it—was success. I think I equated success
with importance and influence in a really large sphere
of things that went on. I have changed my opinion. I
think I now equate success with doing whatever you are
doing well, and having something to do that is constantly new, so that you never get to the end and you
never lose interest in it. It is success if you can find
something like this; and if you find something like this,

you will be happy. I think you also have to have a happy
relationship with someone else if you want to have a
happy family life. And this is what I would consider success.

But in a different corner of her personality, Nancy's self-
ideal of being a figure of power and influence was still with her.

(May, sophomore year) *Whom do you admire among living,
fictional, and historical figures, and who would you wish to be like?*

I think I would like to be like Professor Owen. He was
in China in the Second World War, and he formulated
a lot of the American policy. Well, nobody could ever
go back and do exactly the same thing, but to have the
interest and experience he has. I think I'd like to be like
this.

Over the summer following her sophomore year, Nancy
developed a plan to implement her wish for a career.

(November, junior year) *What is your major?*

History. Last year I decided I wanted to specialize in Far
Eastern history. So then I started to think about what I
was going to do when I got out of college. And actually
the only thing I could do with an interest like Far Eastern history would be some kind of research work, which
would require an advanced degree—or just teach, and I
do not want to teach. So I thought that the only way I
could use this interest in Far Eastern history and really
get involved in this interest, was to learn one of the
Indian languages. India appeals to me. So I decided to
learn Bengali.

And this with what purpose in mind?

I really don't know. I don't know what I will do. I think
I'll probably get a master's degree in Indian Studies,
because at graduation from college, I won't be competent enough in the language. And then I would like to
get some kind of job. I don't really know what. Something like an import-export firm, or I might find something I was really interested in and go on with it—do
some kind of research. I don't know, really.

Can you tell me a little bit about your experience with Bengali and your reaction to the History of Modern India course?

Well, I love Bengali. It's really an interesting language to learn. Somehow, I just like it. I like the way it sounds, and I like the grammar. We haven't gotten into it far enough so that I can read it very well as yet, so I don't know how it will be. But I always thought the language had a very pretty sound. So I think it will be interesting to learn it. One of the things I like about the people of India is that they have a concept about individuals as human beings that is reflected in the language.

What made you pick India and Bengali?

I don't really know. I like Far Eastern history very much. One of the things I liked was that the people of India have been a pretty tolerant people as far as religion goes. And they have been a people who were able to take foreign ideas and be able to take the things that were good and yet keep a certain part of their own character, their own heritage; they could accept and reject according to their history and their way of thinking. I like this very much. They didn't have this superior view that some Far Eastern people have. . . . I think, to a certain extent, my idea of India is somewhat romantic. You think of places like Taj Mahal and things. To be perfectly practical about it [the career], it's a good type of foreign exchange to be involved in right now, because the Indian people are trying to improve their economic status. And America will have quite a few economic relations with them. That's just from the practical viewpoint.

What would you say was your best course thus far in college?

Overall, Indian Literature is my best course. I have a wonderful teacher. He presents the material as well as anyone could present it. I just love it. The professor is an extremely gentle person. He tries to make it as clear as he can. He understands that certain people in the class don't grasp it, and he drills these people a little more than others. He never becomes angry, he never becomes upset with anyone. He just kind of expresses the attitude, "Well, you'll get it. Keep trying." And he has a wonderful sense of humor, so his classes are always enjoyable.

Have your interests changed since high school?

I've always been interested in history. This was true in high school. I don't think that I had any definite interests that I wanted to pursue when I was in high school. I wasn't certain about anything.

Do you feel definite about it now?

I felt better than I ever have when I decided for sure I wanted to take Indian Studies. It was as though someone had given me a wonderful gift, because it was something I really wanted to do and I wanted to do well, and I knew that I would always have this interest from now on, and it was something I could take that would be mine. I think everyone should have a little interest they can call "just mine."

Do you remember the circumstances when you made this decision for Indian Studies?

It was my father who suggested that I think about it. And then I heard that they were coming out with a special program, and this really seemed to be the answer to everything. I don't remember when I made the decision, though.

At the end of the interview, Nancy commented thoughtfully on her college life and on the meaning of the changes she had undergone.

Apart from academic work, what has been happening in your life in the last two years that has been of great importance to you?

There are two most important things. The first one is that I decided what I wanted to do—which to me settles so many things. And secondly, I think that I've found a person I want to marry. Which is [pause], it's not really very satisfying, because then I think the ideal thing to do is to go through college and then have two years or three years of your own, and then get married. But [pause] things just don't always work in what would seem to be the most practical way. I really think a person who can go through school and then have two years of his own, and not be particularly interested in anybody, but just enjoy a lot of people and have lots of relationships, has a great advantage. Theoretically, this would be the ideal way to do it. But if you find somebody you want to share with, well, then this is the best way, under the circumstances. But, if you make a generalization and plan for people a best way, you shouldn't encourage them to look for someone to marry that young.

Then you plan to get married?

Oh, not for a long time, not at least [pause] we're both juniors, and then he has graduate school. And certainly his first year of graduate school, he'll have too many adjustments to make as far as that goes to have to worry about a wife or anything. And I have to finish with my Bengali so that I can start using it. So I don't know; it will be at least four years, I imagine. But it ties you down to definite plans. And it's kind of fun if you can decide, "Well, I want to use Bengali . . . maybe I'll go to India for two years." Which would be a wonderful thing to do. I don't want to go to India for two years now, if Neil couldn't come with me.

Does he agree with the way things are?

Oh, yes.

Would you like to add anything?

No, except that there's something very funny. I've been thinking about this—about how—how I've developed in the last few years. And it's really funny because when I first came to college, I had all these aspirations, like maybe I'd be the first female Assistant Secretary of State, or something, and I think you're going to find that my aims on the surface seem a lot lower than they did before. I'm much more satisfied with me. I think I'm much more realistic. And I somehow don't seem to think of my role in the world as being anything particularly outstanding. I used to think you had to be someone really important to contribute anything. I somehow think now if you can just be a sensitive, understanding, intelligent, and constantly growing person in your own tiny little capacity, how much better everything would be. So as I said, on the surface, I think my aims have seemed to drop, but I don't really think they have.

That is sort of a shift. What do you ascribe it to?

I think the reason I had these views before was the influence of my father. He and I are a great deal alike, and we're very close, and I probably respect him more than anybody I know. He's a great man, and I used to think I had to try to live up to what he'd done; but I realize now that . . . you're born with the spark in you. I mean some people have it, and some people don't. And . . . I just wouldn't. I'm not the kind of person who would add anything—try to do something that was really important—because this just isn't me at all. So perhaps getting away from my family and finding out what I'm really like and the kind of tendencies that I have has helped changed this idea that I had before. Before, I put it on the basis of looking about me, you know, and seeing what I was going to do. And I think it is more looking inside and seeing, not what I'm expected to do, or not what would look best to other people, but seeing what I really want. All through high school, I was a very aggressive person. I was one of the smarter students; therefore I had some illusions as to my intelligence. I think I thought I was much smarter than I am—and it was very important that I prove to people how intelligent I was. Now, somehow, this isn't really important. The only thing my intelligence really means to me is that I can always be interested in something. But as far as being on display, or as far as making my intelligence overt, that just doesn't matter at all any more. And so I'm much less aggressive. I used to think that it was really good for a woman to strive to do things that men did. And I still think that this is true. I think that a woman should use her intelligence to the fullest. However, I really wouldn't approve of a woman making important decisions in the State Department, because I really think that this is a man's field.

Even for someone like the late Eleanor Roosevelt?

No, Eleanor Roosevelt wasn't a typical woman. She had a good many feminine qualities, but also she was able to incorporate a lot of the qualities that I think make a man better than a woman in politics. She was able to incorporate these and still be gracious, nonetheless. But she was an exceptional woman. On the whole, I wouldn't vote for a woman.

What qualities come to mind that a woman statesman should have?

Well, in the first place, she needs to have the confidence of people. And I don't think our society has gotten to the point where men, or even a lot of women, would have confidence in the political decisions that a woman would make. Also, I think that a politician has to be shrewd, and somehow know when to make compromises, and I think that most women in general can't make hard-line compromises. Of course, this has to be judged on the basis of what I know about women, which is my mother or people like her, me, or my sister. Not only that, I don't think that a woman who would be this way would be very happy, because I think she wouldn't belong—would be kind of lost in society, you know.

Since meeting Neil, several important readjustments had occurred within Nancy. With her capacity for serious reflection, she was aware of the more dramatic changes, but some of the full impact of what was happening to her eluded her consciousness. To us, it appeared that she was now able to make the transfer of strong affection from her father to a man of her own age. Few girls had fathers whom they admired and loved as much as Nancy did her father. In a way, such high regard facilitates the transfer of loyalty and trust to another male, but there is always the danger that a girl will find no one who measures up to her concept of her father. Another danger is that the girl may settle for a man so limited that the father will remain the major figure in her life. Nancy was attracted by a dynamic, ambitious young man. She was emotionally healthy enough to expect from him performance and behavior appropriate to a young man rather than to a mature man like her prominent and well-established father.

The resolution of such an intense father-attachment by a

young woman is a major achievement, and it is not surprising that some of Nancy's energy was now freed for a more realistic goal than that of being a member of the President's Cabinet. Although she now referred to this ambition in a joking way as a fantasy, it did reflect her evaluation of her own potential. It also reflected an introjection of a fantasied parental wish. Her relationship with Neil may have been an important factor enabling her to renounce the child-like fantasy of pleasing her father by her abilities and success. However, her transfer from a fantasy of administrative achievement to imagined success in the international field reflected in part her limited but special life experiences. She had been given the opportunity to meet prominent people from foreign lands and to understand their problems and values, but she had not been given the opportunity to work at a paid job within her own country. She knew the wives of successful men, but had no acquaintance with professional women who had successfully combined marriage and career. When she was freed from her earlier fantasy, and attempted to replace her goal as an Assistant Secretary of State with another occupational goal, she could turn only to personal experiences that had been stimulating to her. In this respect, she was a "poor little rich girl."

In part, Nancy's new plan was a transitional one. Her commitment to Neil was developing, but it had not solidified. She continued to balance her attachment to him with a life-plan harmonious with her fantasy of her father's expectations. Later, she became more aware of her serious involvement with Neil, and was able to face the renunciation of this fantasy. Renunciation of gratifying fantasies and of closeness to an admired father can be painful experiences. Nancy's brisk matter-of-factness at the next interview suggests that although this renunciation was painful, it was a necessary part of her movement toward a more realistic and mature assessment of her life.

(May, junior year) *What has happened since our fall interview?*

> Well, I was taking Bengali then. I had signed up for two quarters. I stopped this spring quarter, because it got into the written part, and it's just too much for me to handle right now. So I stopped that, and started taking

history courses again. But I'm still going to India this summer to live with a non-English-speaking Indian family.

What junior year experience did you find particularly unsatisfactory?

Well, when I gave up Indian Studies I went through a period of self-reassessment or something. I'm thinking back about how I have changed in the past three years. When I first came here, I was going to be an Assistant Secretary of State or something like that. I realize that Bengali was just a part of it. But it made me look at myself and realize that I have changed quite a bit. And I tried to figure out if I really like the change or not.

There were some things that I [pause] thought were positive, but then there were a lot of things that were negative. I think most of it was that I had fallen into the rut of living too much in the present. I didn't have any excitement over things that I used to have, and it was really depressing for about two weeks, but in the long run, it was good. It wasn't just Indian Studies—there were big, influential things involved. It was a combination of three things. First of all, Bengali had gotten to the point where the script was very difficult to learn— a real mental impossibility. I just got depressed. I realized that I didn't really want to have to do this every day . . . I decided that perhaps starting Bengali had been a mistake—a sudden decision about something I didn't really know anything about, but which I would be doing for the rest of my life. At the same time, I realized that if I dropped it and couldn't read the language, the possibilities of getting a job inside India wouldn't be great. So I lost a bit of self-confidence, and then— looking back on it—then it was just a downward slide . . . all sorts of things.

Another thing was a wedding of a friend of mine who was geting married to a best friend of Neil's whom she had known since summer. I admit I was really jealous of her. Neil was in the wedding, so this took a lot of time, and I didn't get to see him very much. This is the thing that made me start thinking about getting married. Boys always say it is so much easier for a girl to decide what she is going to do, because a girl doesn't have to support a family, but I don't agree with this. I think it is equally hard, because if you find someone that you want to marry, you still have to think about how you are going to prepare yourself so that once you get married you don't get into a rut. I realized that was going to happen. I had almost become a married woman before even getting married. I really didn't know what to do about it. The thing that depresses me most about married women is that they are not individuals. And I really wasn't an individual. Everything I did was geared to Neil's convenience. It was really that I had gotten to be a shell. I really had. This is what I mean by being in the rut of a married woman. I wasn't really a person any more.

The third thing was the loss of self-confidence I felt because I had been a failure in Bengali. This was the only way I could see it at that time. I had this class for two hours every day. I was extremely fond of my teacher. I was really committed to this class, and I was making the best grades in the class. When I say that dropping out meant that I was a failure, I mean that I just had let myself down. I really wanted to stay in the class, and I really missed it for a while. I had made this commitment to myself at the beginning of the whole thing, not realizing that to be fully competent in the language would take four or five years. Everything—all about the future and what I was going to do—had been wrapped up in Indian Studies. I had no alternatives open to me. There had been no doubt in my mind at all that this was what I would be doing, so I had to readjust. That was one of the factors that I resolved—well, I wouldn't say resolved, but I just kind of got things straightened out— back into perspective maybe. After a while, I realized that even if I don't go into something requiring the Bengali language, this doesn't really matter. It will still have been a valuable experience.

I'm not sure now what kind of a job I would like to get. I decided not to worry about this problem of jobs. I have seen a lot of people working who I am sure are more stupid than I. If they can do it, I can do it. So I convinced myself maybe it wasn't the end of the world; that there would be something I could do in the future; and that everything didn't hinge on Indian Studies. It's not that I'm not concerned about the question of what to do when I get out of college, but there's nothing really I can do about it now.

The other thing, as I said, was this wedding of a friend of mine, and I really don't think it would have bothered me so much if it had not been for this wedding. It really upset me—but after the wedding was over I decided I really didn't want to be married anyhow, and that re-solved it.

I don't know exactly what it was that brought me out of it. My parents came for a meeting, and when they came I was already fine again. But I talked to Daddy at length about the whole thing. I decided for a while that I wasn't going to go to India. I didn't see any point in spending money to go there, because I had been think-ing of going to India in terms of preparation for a job. I hadn't even thought of it as something of an experi-ence in itself.

Were you able to talk to your friends during the period when you were reevaluating your objectives?

Well, they knew that I was depressed. I couldn't really explain it to them at the time. I could explain it to them in terms of dropping Bengali or I could explain it in terms of just thinking about getting married, but I couldn't exactly define or relate anything. I don't think anybody really knew why I was depressed.

Why did you decide you didn't want to be married?

Well, I don't know . . . there just seemed to be more things to do here. In the first place, I don't know enough outside of marriage to be married, and in the second place, I suppose I don't want to be a housewife yet.

When do you expect to get married?

Well, I really don't know. When Neil was planning to go to graduate school, we were going to wait until after his first year in graduate school. Whatever he does, he is going to have to go to graduate school, and I'm going to have to be supporting him, because we've both de-cided we won't ask our parents to help. In terms of when it's wise, we don't know. It depends upon what he finally decides—whether he wants to get a Ph.D., or whether he wants to go to graduate school in business.

And what is your decision about getting a job?

I'd like to get a job as soon as I get out of college.

With a bachelor of arts degree?

Yes. I don't want to go on to graduate school. Not just because I want to get married. Even if I didn't have any marital prospects for the future, I want to get out. I really have led such a sheltered life. I may get tired of working after a while, but I want to see what it is like.

What can you visualize yourself trying to do?

Well, I'm not really sure. I don't want to teach. I thought I might like to work in a bank. I don't know what I could do in a bank, but I just like the atmosphere. Actually, I have no idea. I've been looking through catalogues about jobs available, and I don't know. The only criterion I have is that it be a job that is interesting every day, and that I'm with people.

How do you feel about marriage and a career?

Well, I think if you don't have children, a career is a must. At least for me it would be. By career, I mean doing something outside of the house—even if you are just in charge of the volunteers in a hospital. As far as children go, I really don't know. I can't see sitting home all day taking care of a baby. But yet I feel as though a mother should be with her child. So I think I'll have to wait and see how it works out. When your children are grown, you should get back into something.

During your junior year, you can see a lot of girls are getting engaged. When people say the women at this college, or any girls, go to college to get married, this really infuriates me, because none of these girls came to college with this idea at all. But when you see so many people around you getting married, it doesn't necessarily mean that you'd like to get married, but I think a lot of them would feel more secure if they could at least find somebody with whom to have a meaningful relationship. Maybe not even somebody that they'd marry, but if there'd be just this sense of security there. Most of my friends don't have this, and I think that, therefore, the future really does look to them like a huge, nebulous, blank spot. They think, "Good grief,

I'll be graduating from college—where will I meet people?" Most girls are really concerned. When you are an underclassman, you don't even think about marriage. Now people are thinking about marriage. Some people talk about it more than others, but I think basically most girls who come here have fairly good minds. I think they are really scared of getting into a rut, because you look around and you know how easy it is.

Nancy's sensitive analysis tells its own story. It only remains to point out that it was no small crisis that she underwent. She knew she was giving up something that had been very precious to her—something that she could hardly explain to her friends. The girls in Nancy's sorority were more conventional than she—more interested in being a part of a comfortable social group. For many girls, achievement of a mature feminine identification appears to involve renunciation of the intellectual and achievement-oriented part of themselves. For some, this provides a sense of relief, while for others, a mild depression seems to accompany this perception. There are individuals, religious institutions, and mass media in our culture that exalt the mothering and alluring aspects of femininity. Depreciation of the importance of intellectual and professional competence for women can have an infantilizing effect on young men. Expectations that young women should be primarily supportive and ornamental colors their relationships with women. Under these circumstances, it is not surprising to find young men taking for granted sacrifices and services. It also may explain the grateful and apologetic attitude sometimes expressed by able women whose boy friends, husbands, or fathers give them permission to develop intellectual and professional aptitudes.

During the summer following her junior year, Nancy found that her lifelong wish for a career would not die so easily. It revived, but it took a different form.

(October, senior year) *What changes have there been in your major or career plans?*

Well, the dressmaker I have gone to for years told me that a daughter of hers is going into child welfare. Always before, I thought of child welfare as just lugging babies to clinics for checkups or giving out money. My dressmaker told me that her daughter is going to the university to get her master's. I had been thinking vaguely about child psychology, but I'm not very good in statistics and such. I looked into the program at the university, and then I read some books on it this summer. Then I talked to somebody in the department at the end of the summer, and decided that this is really something that I want to do.

By spring, Nancy was having some qualms about her choice.

(April, senior year) *Have you thought any more about child welfare work?*

A lot of people are very critical of it, which has made me really think about it. I have to defend myself to a lot of people, and it is really hard, because there are some people who are never going to really understand. If they do understand, they don't want to think about it; they prefer to let you worry about it. There are a lot of people who come up with the old clichés. They say that you are just encouraging people who shouldn't have children in the first place to go ahead and have large families. . . . It has gotten to the point where I'm not numb to this criticism. I realize that you can't just give millions of dollars and think things are going to work out.

However, Nancy was no longer in doubt that commitment to husband and family took priority over all other considerations.

What would be a good life ten years from now?

I plan to be married. I would like to wait two years before I have children. I only want to have two, and have them three years apart. So, ten years from now, I'd have two young children, and I couldn't be working. If I go into child welfare, I can get a part-time job. I think I would like to keep working. My husband will be working at whatever he wants. He's going to try graduate school and go into business administration. My relation with my future family is going to be the most important thing to me. I know that my husband will be the most important thing to me—maybe even more important than my children.

The general readjustment of Nancy's aspirations that had begun in her sophomore year when she became pinned to Neil continued and solidified.

(October, senior year) I used to think that the only way a person could really contribute to a problem was to become somebody really important whom a lot of people would listen to. Now I think that if chance, or whatever it is, happens to put you into a position like that, fine; but I look at it in terms of a very small area. For instance, if you can prove or set up something, or do something in a very small community, it is just as meaningful as going out and doing something big.

The senior year is a trying period for many students, and in Nancy's case, the cumulative impact of the tensions she had experienced had an adverse effect on her senior-year studies.

(October, senior year) In a way, this whole year seems kind of a waste, in that I'd really like to start doing something. I want to get an M.A. in child welfare. I still enjoy history courses; yet I feel kind of passive about the whole thing. I'd really like to be working for something, and now that I'm not going into Far Eastern history, it seems like the last three years have been a long extended intellectual hobby.

(April, senior year) *What has the senior year been like?*

First of all, I don't really care about this college any more. I don't really care about being here. I'm not that interested in my classes. I really would have rather gone to graduate school this year.

Nancy was aware that momentous things had been taking place during her college years. In her reflective moments, she wondered about her life and tried to understand what had happened to her.

What major mistakes do you think you made in college?

In a way, I think getting pinned was a mistake. I would advise people not to get pinned. Once you get pinned, if you take it, as I did, as a commitment to getting married, then you are limited. If things get to the point where there are a lot of troubles, if you want fresh air, if you want to look at things objectively, the only way you can do it is by not seeing the other person and by getting close to other people. If you are pinned, you have to go through the huge trauma of getting unpinned. I had a tendency to let things slide, simply because it was too much to bring them out. I think this is a mistake.

What were the rough periods in your college experience?

The only thing that really stands out was the spring of my junior year, which was a real trauma. I guess I was looking at myself for the first time. Either my perspective had gotten better, or my rationalization had gotten better, I'm not sure which. First of all, my family is an intellectual one. My father, with whom I strongly identify, had this idea that I was to be the one who was really going into politics: I was the one who wasn't going to be emotionally involved. I was going to be a doer, an emancipated woman. So I kind of incorporated this. I was going to be an intellectual, and I was going to do something really important, and he was going to be really proud of me. If I didn't do it, he wouldn't be proud of me. I finally realized that, in the first place, I'm not an intellectual. In the second place, I don't want to be something like that: be Assistant Secretary of State, or be in the President's Cabinet, or something like that. And I do want to be a kind of homebody. I think it will be fun. Daddy may look at me with disgust—"There she goes into the old rut. Count her out!"—but I realize that I don't really think he's going to be disappointed. In a way he may be, if my brother doesn't turn out to do something terribly important. Daddy always says that the second generation should be better than the first. But I really don't care any more, because if anything, this is his problem, and comes from a certain lack of insight on his part. I had to live with myself. I had to recognize that. For the first time [in the junior year], everything that I had planned on, the whole picture that I had of myself, was wiped out. And then I started thinking what I really had to care about. I don't think I really found out, but at least I think I'm making decisions more on my own.

In her final interview, Nancy made a reflective analysis of her overall development in college. It is interesting to note that as Nancy separated herself emotionally from her strong attachment to her father, her perception of her parents changed. She became more critical, though not rejecting, of her father. At the same time, she was able to recognize in her mother qualities of wisdom and independence that had not been evident to her earlier in her college career.

I am very close to Daddy in an emotional sense. This is a problem, because I can see a lot of faults in Daddy, and a lot of things I wouldn't want in my husband. But he really has a powerful hold over things that I do. Sometimes I even wonder if I have a conscience of my own—if it's me talking, or something that Daddy would be saying. One thing I've learned is not to argue with him, because the things that he tells me he really believes in, and I'm not going to change him. He's a really opinionated man. He's broad-minded in that he will accept other people's point of view, but with me, he really doesn't understand. He thinks I'm just misguided for the moment, and will come around eventually. I don't argue with him; I will value his advice. I think what he says is important, and I really weigh it carefully, but I don't swallow all of it like I used to. I don't know, it's really hard. I feel much younger than I am. The reason why I do, I think, is that although he has always given me full rein, I always feel a rein, and I think that part of the fact that I feel so young is that I know that the decisions that I make and the things that I do are so highly influenced by him.

Mother influences decisions a lot more than she used to. More and more I respect Mother, and we are a lot closer than we used to be. In fact, if Mother ever gave an opinion about something, I think I would listen even more closely, or consider it more valuable. Daddy is always giving advice, but Mother rarely says anything. I really think that a lot of the time when he says these things he is not thinking of the context—that I'm a woman. Some of the things that he says aren't the things that I want. Mother understands a lot more the emotions involved. But in a more mature way, I'm even closer to Daddy. Now I view what he says critically; before, there was no questioning at all.

Detailed biographical studies like those run on Nancy and Bob are not popular in personality and educational research, not only because of the expense involved in gathering the necessary data, but also because the value of such data for exploration of the basic dimensions of a new problem area is not widely appreciated. The area of personality changes during the college years is one in which there is much need for exploratory studies in depth. Here is a brief description of the kinds of problems and theoretical ideas that such data can suggest.[5]

Although it is well known that the achievement of independence from parents is a general developmental task of the college-age person, it is not clear just how this is accomplished, nor how the processes involved affect the education and social development of the student. In studying the cases of Bob and Nancy, it is hard to escape the impression that the most important thing that happened to them both in college was their achievement of differentiation from their parents—specifically, from their fathers.

This phenomenon suggests that educators need to remember that the personality of the incoming freshman includes a child self as a part of its central structure—a childhood-developed organization of cognitive, emotional, and motivational structures that enter into and strongly influence the student's personal and academic progress. The child self does not appear as such to the student, but manifests itself as an irresistible pull in a certain direction. For Bob, it appeared as a feeling that he must carry out certain obligations prior to exploring his own interests. For Nancy, it seemed to appear both as an attraction to a career in which she might become an influential person, and also as an attraction to Neil, who had enough of her father's qualities to reactivate the emotional residue of that powerful relationship.

Of course, the student does not consciously think of the process of maturing in college as one of differentiating himself from a parent. To him it consists of discovering that he does not really want to do what he earlier felt impelled to do. Bob found eventually that what he was so sure he wanted as a freshman held

---

[5] This section is a much abbreviated version of certain ideas that are developed in detail in my book *Personality in College*. Reading, Mass.: Addison-Wesley, 1969.

no attractions for him by the end of his junior year. Nancy found that she no longer wanted to become a figure of power and influence. She was able to move from a strong father-attachment to emotional involvement with a man of her own age. This dramatic developmental move forward took precedence over other involvements. If she ever returns to her interest in government as a career, she will probably be motivated by an intrinsic interest in the area rather than by a fantasy of pleasing her father by her brilliant performance.

Both of these perceptive young people were finally able to understand what had been happening to them. They saw that what they had thought they wanted as freshmen were the things they had supposed their parents wanted, and that they themselves no longer wanted those things. But it must be remembered such formulations are afterthoughts, and may even be uncharacteristic of the normal course of events. It is possible that Bob and Nancy were facilitated in this verbalization and understanding by their roles as research subjects. Not all young people are so fortunate.

Differentiation from the parent is, then, a change in a basic aspect of the person's internal structure. This structure, having been formed at a stage of cognitive and emotional immaturity, may well impose qualities of immaturity upon the subject's otherwise reasonably grownup behavior. Bob's stubborn adherence to his starting plan in the face of so much evidence that his interests lay elsewhere is an example in point.

As to how the change of child self is accomplished, the two cases we have examined here suggest that it's not a simple matter of giving up the child self entirely. Obviously, what is given up is only a component, or a set of components, of the childhood organization. What seems to happen is that the college experience acts to develop certain components of the child self, and as these become stronger and more mature, they increasingly come to occupy a central place. When these developments take a course that conflicts with a frequently dominant component, a struggle ensues and, if the newly augmented and more mature components are stronger, an aspect of the child self is given up. This renunciation is usually accompanied by depression. In Bob's case, his House leadership experiences, his stimulating association with Fred, the diversity of the campus culture, and, finally, his contact with chemical engineering as it actually was led to a development of the social, administrative, and service aspects of his child self. These aspects had previously been subordinate to his "Puritan" child self, which they now began to dominate.

Nancy's "political" child self, which represented her childhood relation to a loved and idealized father, received no developmental support in college. The college faculty and Neil may not have actively resisted her implementation of this part of herself, but they certainly provided no positive experiences that could have developed it. The campus culture generally, and Nancy's circle of girlfriends especially, gave it no encouragement. Her friends found her depression over giving up Bengali puzzling; and they encouraged her to develop the feminine component of her child self, which the long relation to Neil must have fostered as well.

Ultimately, the outcome does not consist of giving up the nonfitting component of the child self, but of integrating it with a new organization in a different way. Although in the heat of the crisis, Nancy disclaimed any intention of going to graduate school, and proclaimed the value of a "homebody" role, this is not, in fact, the role she finally chose. Instead, in her senior year she developed a new synthesis, which appeared in the form of the intention to go to graduate school and major in child welfare. The feminine side of her child self asserted itself as a desire to help others. But her desire to get a graduate degree may just as well have been the result of a reassertion of her ties to her father. Her political child self is not gone; it is a part of her makeup, and may easily become active. It would not be surprising if she were to go into an administrative job within social welfare or even to enter politics later on.

Nancy's depression is an example of a certain sadness observed in other students as an accompaniment to major changes in plans or personality. This not uncommon phenomenon suggests the need for reevaluating our understanding of temporary depressions in the lives of young people. Our usual attitude toward crises is that we should help the person suffering achieve relief as quickly as possible. The urge to ease the other's pain becomes imperative. If we know of an impending crisis, we try to head it off, on the assumption that emotional pain is a bad thing. As Nancy and Bob have shown us, pain can be symptomatic of development. Crises can be good things. One might even suggest that a college experience that does not have a good share of crises has probably not produced much that is worthwhile.

Depression, too, is a puzzling phenomenon. One wonders if it isn't a sign that a central aspect of the self is threatened, or is being subordinated to a newly developed component. Its appearance in college-age persons may signify growth more often than it signifies pathology. But while accepting signs of discouragement, vacillation, and sadness as necessary accompaniments of change and growth, we must not become unconcerned, or treat them lightly. One cannot be certain that the depression is a temporary growth phenomenon rather than evidence of deeper despair. In every case, supportive understanding and acceptance of the painfulness of the feelings of depression as well as appropriate guidance seem indicated.

Some recent psychoanalytic formulations concerning the time at which one establishes his own identity independent of the father have led theorists like Erik H. Erikson to new formulations of their own.[6] The concept of identity is still a vaguely conceived set of ideas about what is probably the most important single topic in human psychology: the fact that persons come to act as though certain features of themselves and their situations have special significance. In ways that he often cannot express and may have little awareness of, the person acts and sometimes consciously feels as though these special features of self or of surroundings represent him—in fact, are him. Identity is a conception of oneself as being a certain kind of human being and having a particular place in the social surroundings. It is a highly emotional concept, in the sense that it tends to have powerful motivational properties. A sense of identity is apparently a fundamental condition for feeling secure, at least for persons reared in our particular culture. Not having a sense of identity is a peculiarly disquieting and panicky state. It arouses strong feelings of being exposed, vulnerable, endangered— feelings akin to the fear of death. The threat of non-existence is particularly intolerable to the Western man. The vagueness of

[6] Erikson, Erik H. *Childhood and Society.* New York: W. W. Norton, 1950.

the identity concept is not the result of any lack of theoretical capacity on the part of those who have grappled with the topic. But identity is manifest in a particularly intangible set of phenomena in which the facts are as shadowy as they are important. A satisfactory theory of identification and identity would advance psychology more than any dozen other achievements one could name. The need for such a theory should be constantly kept in mind.

Although most of Nancy's energies were absorbed in the separation process, friends and faculty perceived her as actively involved in many aspects of college life. Her capacity to live vigorously in the present showed itself in many ways. When she was in the interviewing situation, she threw herself wholeheartedly into self-examination and communication. When she was in the classroom, she was effectively absorbed in the subject at hand. By the beginning of her senior year, she had experienced much that was meaningful to her at the university. She had developed a gratifying relationship with the man she hoped to marry, and had decided on a professional career necessitating further education. It is understandable that after finding earlier career choices inappropriate for her life plan, she was eager to explore a profession that seemed meaningful to her. In her three years of college, she had lived more fully than many students. She had had more than the average share of parties, football games, academic honors, student-faculty committees, close friendships with girls, and exposure to a variety of intellectual and cultural ideas. She had struggled with the problem of appropriate feminine behavior, and had developed what appeared to be a workable compromise. She had settled on a profession which enabled her to utilize her keen interest in people and her idealism in regard to service to others, and had chosen a field that would allow her to adjust her working schedule as her family demands fluctuated. It is no wonder that her senior year seemed anticlimactic and that she was eager to get on with the business of the future. A young woman of Nancy's impressive intelligence and energy who desires a gratifying family life as well as opportunities to test her personal competencies is faced with a real challenge. Achievement of these multiple goals depends on environmental supports and personal capacity to utilize time and energy.

An important fact for college educators to keep in mind is that the able woman student probably will have an interrupted professional career. It is probable that when such women return to their professions, many of them bring with them something rich and humanizing as a result of their interim dedication to family members or to the community. The main type of support that intelligent and vital young women need from their professors is recognition that devotion to family and devotion to intellectual, artistic, or professional pursuits are both worthy investments of time and energy. Most important, young women should be encouraged to feel free to fully enjoy both career preparation and family responsibilities, in the knowledge that flexibility and creativity on their parts will enable them to reenter the professional world when they wish to do so.

From an educational standpoint, it is important to remember that the changes in the child self are accomplished in part through the student's reaction to the curriculum. The issue of whether to relinquish precious components of the child self may be fought out in terms of what major to choose—a fact of obvious educational importance. For Nancy, this issue came to a head in her junior year, at the time of the wedding of Neil's friend. The outcome of the clash between her feminine component and her political child self led her to abandon Bengali, Indian Studies, and the whole father-associated idea of becoming an expert in Far Eastern matters. Naturally enough, these changes were not immediately evident to others—to Nancy's teachers and friends, for example. Even Nancy herself hardly knew what was happening at the time. It wasn't until her senior year that she saw clearly that she had been in the process of reorganizing her child self and fitting it into a new whole in which the political child self took a minor role.

Although experienced educators know intuitively that a shifting around of majors and courses such as that which took place in the college careers of Bob and Nancy is indicative of important changes going on within the student, they are unable at the present time to gauge accurately how much effect the curriculum has on this inner development. Social science has not yet provided the educator with ideas to help him implement the findings of his intuition. It would seem that the curriculum should be thought of primarily as a medium for accomplishing developmental ends. Once the student has achieved these ends, he may discard a given program of studies and take up one more meaningful to his newly integrated self. Bob threw out chemical engineering; Nancy found the whole senior year tasteless.

The fact is, serious and meaningful education can only take place when the curriculum is serving a developmental purpose. This thought—that education in the academic sense is secondary to a higher purpose—may be a distressing one to the educator. Certainly no one has yet been able to formulate an adequate theory concerning what the primary end of the educational process should be. But one clue may be found in the cases of Bob and Nancy: developmental processes, properly understood, may be exploited for both the personal and the academic good of the student.

Should such an expensive educational complex as the university be used to help the student achieve independence, or are there less expensive and possibly more suitable means? There may be some advantage to investigating the suitability of other means and organizations. If Bob had been allowed to join the Peace Corps or to "bum around" Europe with his friend before coming to college, he would probably have been able to make much better headway with the problems of achieving independence from his parent-associated goals and developing some sense of direction from within. It is unlikely that his seemingly aimless explorations would have led him into the wayward life his parents feared as the result of "fooling around." As for Nancy, she tells us that her senior year was "wasted." Would a year abroad, or one spent working, or a term in the Peace Corps have led to a different educational outcome? What might have happened if she had been allowed to spend some time before entering college in a setting that facilitated her differentiation from her father?

The cases of Bob and Nancy make it clear that individual developmental timetables may be quite different from the academic timetables set up by the administration and faculty. Because educators have no developmentally oriented framework of ideas to guide them in setting up the curriculum, they are forced to fall back on the traditional four-year college plan. Freshmen are thought of as new and undeveloped, and seniors as the finished product of this cycle. Within the four-year sequence, the underclass years are defined as the time for exploration and for settling upon a major, as well as for deciding upon the life career for which the college major is a preparation. In the fall of his senior year, Bob was just beginning to explore the curriculum and his own interests in the way that the educator prescribes for the freshman year. That same senior year was a "waste" for Nancy, since it came at the end of a developmental cycle she regarded as complete at the end of her junior year.

What are the usual relationships between the developmental and the educational timetables? The two sequences may often be related to one another in only the most accidental way. The four-year college cycle may come as a random intrusion upon a cycle of personal development that is completely unrelated to it. There must be systematic studies of these relationships before the two cycles can be brought together in a fruitful way.

Able students are increasingly taking such problems into their own hands by "dropping out"—taking leaves of absence at points when they realize that they need something that college cannot give. Clearly it is time for colleges to experiment boldly with educational and developmental sequences, and to exert every effort to improve the scope of the curriculum in terms of developmental aims.

❧ 3 ❧

PERSONALITY SCALE
CHANGES FROM THE
FRESHMAN YEAR TO THE
SENIOR YEAR

Harold A. Korn

Every year, more and
more colleges and universities administer psychological inven-
tories to entering freshmen. Often the same testing is repeated
at later points in the student's college career. The rationale behind this practice is concern with the impact of the college experience on the lives of students. Implicit in this concern is an
acknowledgement of the unified nature of the student's personality, values, and intellectual functioning, and of the profound
effect of the college curriculum on the student's whole develop-

ment. The study of the personality characteristics of students and the changes that occur during college is seen also as a means for evaluating the impact of the college curriculum.

Although the importance of studying the interrelationship between personality characteristics and the college experience seems to be gaining increased recognition, the methods of study now used leave much to be desired. Some of the difficulties that face the investigator will become apparent as we examine the types of personality measures used with our test groups of Stanford and Berkeley students in 1961.

Six scales of the Omnibus Personality Inventory (OPI), plus the Authoritarianism (F) and Ethnocentrism (E) Scales, were given to the entering freshman classes at Stanford and at the University of California at Berkeley in 1961.[1] These included the SM, or Social Maturity Scale (144 items);[2] the IE, or Impulse Expression Scale (124 items); the SF, or Schizoid Functioning Scale (107 items);[3] the MF, or Masculinity-Femininity Scale (103 items); the Es, or Estheticism Scale (51 items); and the DS, or Developmental Status Scale (72 items). The Ethnocentrism Scale (E) contains twenty items, and the Authoritarianism Scale (F) twenty.[4] A brief description may be helpful here:

Social Maturity (SM). High scorers on this scale are not authoritarian, and they are flexible, tolerant, and realistic in their thinking. They are not dependent upon authority, rules, or rituals for managing social relationships. In general they are impunitive, although capable of expressing aggression directly when it is appropriate. High scorers are also frequently interested in intellectual and esthetic pursuits.

Impulse Expression (IE). This scale assesses a general readiness to express impulses and to seek gratification either in conscious thought or in overt action. The high scorers value sensations, and have an active imagination. Their thinking is often dominated by feelings and fantasies.

[1] A fuller description of these scales can be found in *The Omnibus Personality Research Manual.* Berkeley, California: Center for the Study of Higher Education, University of California, 1962.

[2] A briefer version of this scale is called the Autonomy Scale.

[3] This scale has been rechristened the Social Alienation Scale.

[4] For descriptions of these two scales, see Adorno, T. W., *et al. The Authoritarian Personality.* New York: Harper, 1950.

Schizoid Functioning (SF). The high scorers admit to attitudes and behaviors that characterize socially alienated persons. Along with feelings of isolation, loneliness, and rejection, they may intentionally avoid others and experience feelings of hostility and aggression. The ego weakness of high scorers may be characterized by identity confusion, daydreaming, disorientation, feelings of impotence, and fear of loss of control.

Masculinity-Femininity (MF). This scale assesses differences in attitudes and interests between college men and women. High scorers (masculine) express interests in science and problem solving; they admit to few adjustment problems, feelings of anxiety, or personal inadequacies. They also tend to be somewhat less sociable and less esthetically oriented than low scorers.

Estheticism (Es). The high scorers endorse statements indicating diverse interests in artistic matters and activities. The content of the statements in this scale extends beyond painting, sculpture, and music to interests in literature and dramatics.

Developmental Status (DS). This scale differentiates between older and younger college students. High scorers among freshmen are more like seniors in their attitudes and thinking. They express more rebelliousness toward authority, especially when it is institutionalized in family, school, church, or state. They are less authoritarian than the low scorers and express impulses more freely.

Ethnocentrism (E). Ethnocentrism is based on a pervasive and rigid ingroup-outgroup distinction: it involves stereotyped negative imagery and hostile attitudes regarding outgroups; stereotyped positive imagery and submissive attitudes regarding ingroups; and a hierarchical authoritarian view of group interaction, in which ingroups are rightly dominant and outgroups subordinate.

Authoritarianism (F). Authoritarianism is a more general form of ethnocentrism. Rather than being tied to specific minority groups, the authoritarian has a general disposition to respond to the world with a stereotyped conception of the importance of all authority. Authoritarianism involves rigid ingroup-outgroup distinctions; stereotypical imagery; dogmatism; intolerance of ambiguity; and denial of certain needs, for example, dependence, weakness, and sexual urges.

When the freshmen of 1961 had become seniors, they were again invited to take this battery of tests. About 60 per cent of the eligible students at Berkeley and Stanford accepted. As part of our attempt to determine whether or not this senior sample was representative of the entire class, a random sample was selected of all those students who had taken the tests as freshmen but had not taken them as seniors. Their scores as freshmen were compared with the freshmen test scores of those who had repeated the tests. Tables 12 and 13 show the results for the Stanford men and women. A similar comparison made with the scores of the Berkeley men and women yielded substantially the same results. Of the 32 *t* tests computed, four were significant at the 5 per cent level of confidence. Three of these four significant differences occurred for the Berkeley women, but the magnitudes of the differences were not very large. It would seem reasonable to assume that the results for the group taking the tests both as freshmen and seniors are representative of the larger class.[5]

TABLE 12

OMNIBUS PERSONALITY INVENTORY—STANFORD MEN [a]

Random Sample (N = 200)			Freshman Results of Senior Sample (N = 185)		
X	SD		X	SD	*t* test
49	10.0	SM	50	10.0	NS
50	10.0	IE	47	10.3	$< .05$
49	10.6	SF	48	10.4	NS
49	10.6	MF	50	10.2	NS
49	10.6	Es	50	10.3	NS
50	10.5	DS	49	10.9	NS
113	25.8	F [b]	110	24.2	NS
53	17.6	E [b]	51	18.2	NS

[a] Means, standard deviations, and *t* tests for eight personality scales between a random sample from the freshman class and other freshman students who took the inventory again as seniors. With certain exceptions, which have been noted, raw scores from the freshman testing appear as standard scores both here and in the tables that follow.

[b] Raw scores.

[5] Another measure of the representativeness of our sample comes from the Senior Questionnaire described in Chapter 1, which was taken by the same students for whom we have freshman and senior personality test scores. There were negligible differences between a random sample of respondents and the rest of the students for a wide variety of questions.

TABLE 13

OMNIBUS PERSONALITY INVENTORY—STANFORD WOMEN [a]

| Random Sample (N = 291) | | | Freshman Results of Senior Sample (N = 148) | | |
X	SD		X	SD	t test
50	9.6	SM	50	10.8	NS
49	9.6	IE	50	10.6	NS
49	10.3	SF	50	10.0	NS
50	10.1	MF	50	10.7	NS
50	9.5	Es	49	10.9	NS
50	9.9	DS	50	10.5	NS
104	21.8	F [b]	103	21.8	NS
47	15.6	E [b]	45	14.5	NS

[a] See Note A, Table 12.
[b] Raw scores.

According to our observations, there was a consistent pattern of change among both Stanford and Berkeley students over the four undergraduate years. The eight scales we have used provide us with some clues as to the nature of these changes. The results for the Stanford men and women appear in Tables 14 and 15. In a similar analysis of freshman and senior scores, carried out for 286 Berkeley men and 265 Berkeley women, the results were substantially the same. For all four groups, and for all scales, the mean differences between the freshman and senior year were statistically significant. Four of these scales have enough in common to permit us to describe the changes as a composite. The SM, DS, F, and E (Social Maturity, Developmental Status, Authoritarianism, and Ethnocentrism) mean score changes all reflect a movement toward greater open-mindedness and tolerance, a rejection of a restricted view of life, and a humanization of conscience. The complexity of the world is more and more recognized, and there is less tendency to demand pat answers. Along with this, the stereotyped view of right and wrong gives way to a broader acceptance of human diversity. The increase on the IE (Impulse Expression) Scale indicates a further movement towards psychological acceptance of a broad range of human behaviors, and represents a greater willingness to experiment with aspects of life that have formerly been taboo. Along with these changes in

TABLE 14

OMNIBUS PERSONALITY INVENTORY—STANFORD MEN [a]
(N = 185)

1961			1965		
X	SD		X	SD	r
50	10.0	SM	58	11.0	.62
47	10.3	IE	51	10.0	.59
48	10.4	SF	45	10.0	.61
50	10.2	MF	47	12.4	.61
50	10.3	Es	52	11.0	.65
49	10.9	DS	59	10.7	.56
110	24.2	F [b]	94	25.8	.59
51	18.2	E [b]	44	17.0	.36

[a] Means, standard deviations, and correlation coefficients for eight personality scales administered in 1961 and 1965 (t tests were < .01 level throughout).
[b] Raw scores.

TABLE 15

OMNIBUS PERSONALITY INVENTORY—STANFORD WOMEN [a]
(N = 148)

1961			1965			
X	SD		X	SD	t test	r
50	10.8	SM	57	11.3	.05	.60
50	10.6	IE	54	11.3	.05	.64
50	10.0	SF	46	11.9	.05	.58
50	10.7	MF	48	11.7	.01	.53
49	10.9	Es	52	11.4	.05	.65
50	10.5	DS	61	11.9	.05	.57
103	21.8	F [b]	90	25.9	.05	.47
45	14.5	E [b]	42	16.8	.05	.40

[a] Means, standard deviations, t tests, and correlation coefficients for eight personality scales administered in 1961 and 1965.
[b] Raw scores.

the direction of greater psychological freedom, there is some evidence of a greater capacity for feeling close to others. The SF (Schizoid Functioning, or Social Alienation) Scale portrays a diminishing of feelings of isolation and rejection by others. The two other scales used in this study, the MF (Masculinity-Femininity) and the Es (Estheticism), reflect a general increase in awareness and appreciation of a variety of esthetic experiences.

Are the changes one observes in students during their college years the result of personality development or of socialization? We do not attempt to answer that question here, but merely to point out that "socialization"—learning what society expects and will tolerate—can greatly modify the individual's attitudes and behavior without touching his basic character structure. Between the freshman and senior years, a student's provinicial attitudes may give way to an ultra-sophisticated manner, even though his underlying disposition to fear that which is different remains the same.

In contrast to the seemingly dramatic changes that result from socialization, the changes associated with personality development are often subtle, but they are more pervasive and less subject to future change. Consider the freshman who focuses on his scientific or musical talents, and screens out other forms of experience and other intellectual modes of responding to the world. If this student were encouraged to respond to a broader range of human experience, his response to interpersonal relationships and to the varied realms of intellectual experience would increase in depth and scope. This increasing openness would involve a greater acceptance of the diversity of his own feelings, and would build up his confidence in handling the stress associated with new experiences.

We can achieve some perspective on our findings with respect to socialization and personality development by viewing them in the context of the prevailing attitudes and mores of our society. We noted earlier that the SM, DS, F, and E mean score changes all reflect a movement toward greater openmindedness and tolerance—a rejection of a restricted view of life, and a humanization of conscience. Since the movement is toward the prevailing operational moral standards of our society, many of these changes can be interpreted as part of a socialization process. It is possible that with increasing awareness and increasing breadth of contact, the adolescent loses his need to be puritanical. The liberalizing impact of higher education thus has its greatest potential for success in those areas where there is already a great deal of approval in the general culture.

The college experience is intended to be particularly potent in its effect on the intellectual development of the individual. Increased appreciation for the complexity of many problems and a greater commitment to the use of reason in solving them are among the most frequently articulated goals of a college education. Included in this concept of intellectual development is the ability to respond to a broad range of human emotion in relationship to other individuals, works of art, and the environment in general. The SM, DS, F, and E Scales all contain some items relating to intellectual development. The response to these items changes less frequently than the response to items relating to social attitudes and mores does. Further evidence that the college has less impact on the student's intellectual development than on his social attitudes can be found in the results for two other scales. For all four groups, the MF scores go up a few points; this is in contrast to the marked changes in the SM, DS, F, and E Scales, and suggests a slight broadening of esthetic interests. The cognitive processes involved in the capacity to respond to the esthetic domain demand that the individual integrate his feelings with his ability to think. It is this integraton of feeling and thought that distinguishes intellectual development from socialization.

One may be somewhat baffled by the suggestion that the college experience contributes more to the socialization of the student than it does to his intellectual development. However, the conditions that favor the changes we include under socialization are powerful and pervasive. In contrast, a variety of forces work against intellectual development, which is rooted in the character structure. By "character structure," we mean the complex set of attitudes, feelings, and accumulated knowledge that determines how an individual sees the world. At the least, intellectual development involves the student in an examination of why he has come to view the world in a certain way. More often, such an examination leads to the possibility of changing some significant segment of his attitudes and feelings or reorganizing his knowledge. This possibility often produces unbearable anxiety. Complementing the fearful reluctance of the student to seek out intellectual development is the reluctance of most college faculties to relieve student anxiety about intellectual expansion. Mastery of content is stressed as an end in itself, and little is done to help the student relate the course material to his personal goals and frame of reference. In addition to these specific barriers to intellectual development, a general anti-intellectualism and unintellectualism pervades the surrounding culture and is reflected in the student's peer culture.

Society seems to encourage the occasional expression of strong feelings, but not the continuing awareness of how one feels. Nevertheless, nearly all human behavior has an emotional or evaluational component; and if asked, most individuals can say that they like or dislike what they are doing at a given moment. But because of long training in the denial of feelings, we are often unaware of their presence or their manifestation. Students may feel bored, tired, or restless without knowing why, and without relating these feelings to their present situation. In addition, the academic establishment itself often sets intellect in opposition to emotion. Rather than emphasizing the interrelationship between reason and passion, many instructors caution their students against too much involvement with the subject matter. In view of this, and of the social forces working against the recognition of feelings, it may be surprising to find that all four student groups had an increase in their Impulse Expression scores. Such change is, in fact, a move toward what is condoned by society as a whole. For all four groups, there was only a slight decrease in social alienation (SF Scale). Since many of these students will never again have such an opportunity to move toward greater human closeness and shared understanding, one may raise the question why change was not more pronounced. A partial answer lies in the existence of those forces that tend to make encounters superficial rather than intimate and rewarding. Students learn the techniques of association with others, but there is little opportunity to learn about others in great depth. The socialization process permits students to learn a great many social skills, but it does not encourage the personality development necessary for psychological intimacy.

It is necessary to move to another level of analysis in order to arrive at a clearer picture of how much and what kind of personality change did take place among our samples. The dimensions tapped by the Social Maturity and Impulse Expression Scales are of particular relevance to the study of personality characteristics and the college experience. Intellectual development and personal growth depend upon the individual's capacity to be responsive to new experiences, and the possibility of those new experiences becoming meaningfully integrated with his past experiences. The SM Scale has as its focus the student's capacity for openmindedness and freedom from the power of arbitrary authority, while the IE Scale centers on the individual's capacity to be in touch with his feelings and to integrate them with his intellectual processes. The conceptual richness of these scales makes them important tools in the analysis of the varieties of student development.

How many and which individuals change in a direction opposite to the overall mean change? What is the psychological significance of these changes, and what does the data represent? We noted above that the direction of change was consistent with expectations based on society's mores and standards; but we did not focus attention on how greatly the magnitudes of these mean differences varied. A statistically significant difference between means can occur for groups of this size, even though the absolute difference is only two standard score points. Although the magnitude of change is a clue to how many individuals will have change scores consistent with the mean change, it must be remembered that certain trends may be masked.

In Table 16, we see the results achieved when Stanford students who took the Omnibus Personality Inventory both as freshmen and as seniors were classified on the basis of their freshman scores. (A similar analysis carried out with the Berkeley students yielded substantially the same results.) It was evident earlier that the SM scores for all groups (Stanford and Berkeley men and women) increased an average of eight standard scores. When we view the pattern of change, however, we see clearly that although some individual scores went up, many went down. This pattern appears even more interesting when we deal with a scale that has a small but statistically significant mean change. Despite the overall mean increase, large numbers of students had decreasing IE scores. In particular, more than 50 per cent of those students who were classified as high (standard score ≥ 60) had a lower senior score. This finding was true for all four samples.

The approach taken to the problem of what a scale measures has varied greatly among different investigators. Here we are primarily concerned with item content, and more particularly, with the relationships that exist between items in the mind of

TABLE 16

DISTRIBUTION OF CHANGE SCORES FOR INDIVIDUALS WITH
DIFFERENT INITIAL SCORES

	STANFORD MEN SM Standard Scores			STANFORD WOMEN SM Standard Scores		
Initial Score	High	Middle	Low	High	Middle	Low
Senior Score	(≥ 60)	($45 \gtrless 55$)	(≤ 40)	(≥ 60)	($45 \gtrless 55$)	(≤ 40)
Increase	24	63	36	20	40	26
Same	2	3	0	3	4	0
Decrease	11	7	4	9	6	0
		IE			IE	
Increase	10	40	52	9	39	23
Same	1	0	0	2	5	1
Decrease	12	21	3	17	11	3

the individual as he is taking the test. What is the likelihood that if one item is answered in a certain way, another item will be answered in a certain manner? A statistical technique that permits an answer to this kind of question is "cluster analysis," developed by R. C. Tryon.[6] Cluster analysis computes all the intercorrelations between a set of items, and then develops clusters of items based on patterns of correlations that fit together. These patterns of correlations are considered to be dimensions, or "clusters," and are open to a variety of mathematical treatments similar to those available in factor analysis. This technique permits the researcher to determine empirically how many dimensions, or clusters, exist within a single scale, and to observe how individual items change over time. Using this method, we analyzed separately the items from the Social Maturity and Impulse Expression Scales for the men at Stanford and Berkeley.[7] The items that comprise the key

[6] Tryon, R. C. *The Component Programs of the BCTRY System.* Berkeley: University of California, 1964 (mimeo).

[7] The program for cluster analysis permits a maximum of 120 variables; therefore, 24 items from the SM Scale and four items from the IE Scale were removed. It will be apparent to those familiar with the scales that large numbers of items are not included in the clusters presented here. Some of these items are added in the oblique cluster solution, but most of the missing items did not have communalities that met the criteria for this solution.

variables defining the several dimensions appear in Tables 17 through 20.

TABLE 17 [a]

STANFORD SM CLUSTERS [b]
(Men, N = 185)

	1961 Per cent True	1965 Per cent True
Cluster 1		
I have sometimes wanted to run away from home. (T)	36	38
At times I have very much wanted to leave home. (T)	51	55
My home life was always happy. (F)	53	49
I have often either broken rules or inwardly rebelled against them. (T)	34	48
Cluster 2		
I like to read serious philosophical poetry. (T)	36	36
I enjoy reading essays on serious or philosophical subjects. (T)	68	68
I like to discuss philosophical problems. (T)	80	73
I enjoy writing a critical discussion of a book or article. (T)	54	43
Cluster 3		
In religious matters, I believe I would have to be called a skeptic or an agnostic. (T)	37	64
We cannot know for sure whether or not there is a God. (T)	60	75
There must be something wrong with a person who is lacking in religious feeling. (F)	28	5
One needs to be wary of those persons who claim not to believe in God. (F)	18	3
Cluster 6		
What youth needs most is strict discipline, rugged determination, and the will to work and fight for family and country. (F)	50	28
More than anything else, it is good hard work that makes life worthwhile. (F)	51	30
Kindness and generosity are the most important qualities for a wife to have. (F)	43	35
Perfect balance is the essence of all good composition. (F)	39	23

TABLE 17 [a]—Continued

STANFORD SM CLUSTERS [b]
(Men, N = 185)

	1961 Per cent True	1965 Per cent True
Cluster 8		
I dislike women who disregard the usual social or moral conventions. (F)	51	22
I would disapprove of anyone's drinking to the point of intoxication at a party. (F)	52	17
Cluster 9		
I don't like to undertake any project unless I have a pretty good idea how it will turn out. (F)	37	30
I don't like to work on a problem unless there is the possibility of coming out with a clear-cut and un-ambiguous answer. (F)	25	27

[a] "T" or "F" in parentheses after each item in Tables 17, 18, 19, and 20 indicates the direction of response; if "T" appears, "True" is counted +1; if "F," "False" is counted +1.

[b] Clusters 4, 5, and 7 have been omitted.

TABLE 18

STANFORD IE CLUSTERS [a]
(Men, N = 185)

	1961 Per cent True	1965 Per cent True
Cluster 1		
I believe there is a God. (F)	75	47
God hears our prayers. (F)	66	37
I believe in a life hereafter. (F)	59	35
In religious matters, I believe I would have to be called a skeptic or an agnostic. (T)	37	64
Cluster 2		
I have never done any heavy drinking. (F)	64	29
I have used alcohol excessively. (T)	16	32
I would disapprove of anyone's drinking to the point of intoxication at a party. (F)	52	17
I enjoy playing cards for money. (T)	44	38

TABLE 18—Continued

STANFORD IE CLUSTERS [a]
(Men, N = 185)

	1961 Per cent True	1965 Per cent True
Cluster 3		
At times I have a strong urge to do something harmful or shocking. (T)	46	49
Sometimes I feel like smashing things. (T)	57	59
At times I feel like picking a fistfight with someone. (T)	42	41
I have periods of such great restlessness that I cannot sit for long in a chair. (T)	51	52
Cluster 5		
I have had periods of days, weeks, or months when I couldn't take care of things because I couldn't "get going." (T)	43	51
I find it hard to keep my mind on a task or job. (T)	20	29
I cannot keep my mind on one thing. (T)	22	28
Cluster 6		
My home life was always happy. (F)	53	49
I have very few quarrels with members of my family. (F)	57	72
Some of my family have habits that bother and annoy me very much. (T)	52	52
I have sometimes wanted to run away from home. (T)	36	38
Cluster 9		
I have had very peculiar and strange experiences. (T)	38	23
I have had strange and peculiar thoughts. (T)	60	46
I sometimes wake up to find myself thinking about some impractical or irrelevant problem. (T)	46	45
I often feel as if things were not real. (T)	34	24
Cluster 10		
It is all right to get around the law if you don't actually break it. (T)	35	43
It is a good thing to know people in the right places, so one can get traffic tags and such things taken care of. (T)	30	29
If I could get into a movie without paying, and be sure I was not seen, I would probably do it. (T)	36	44

[a] Clusters 4, 7, and 8 have been omitted.

TABLE 19

BERKELEY SM CLUSTERS [a]
(Men, N = 285)

	1961 Per cent True	*1965* Per cent True
Cluster 1		
I like to read serious philosophical poetry. (T)	29	32
I enjoy listening to poetry. (T)	49	49
I enjoy reading essays on serious or philosophical subjects. (T)	54	58
I like to discuss philosophical problems. (T)	66	74
I like to read about artistic or literary achievements. (T)	37	44
Courses in literature and poetry have been as satisfying to me as most other subjects. (T)	46	44
I enjoy reading Shakespeare's plays. (T)	64	66
Cluster 2		
I have sometimes wanted to run away from home. (T)	43	47
At times I have very much wanted to leave home. (T)	53	61
My home life was always happy. (F)	53	47
I have often either broken rules or inwardly rebelled against them. (T)	38	42
Cluster 3		
We cannot know for sure whether or not there is a God. (T)	56	71
In religious matters, I believe I would have to be called a skeptic or an agnostic. (T)	40	62
There must be something wrong with a person who is lacking in religious feeling. (F)	21	8
One needs to be wary of those who claim not to believe in God. (F)	24	6
Cluster 7		
I don't like to undertake any project unless I have a pretty good idea how it will turn out. (F)	39	31
I don't like to work on a problem unless there is the possibility of coming out with a clear-cut and unambiguous answer. (F)	42	28
I dislike test questions where the information being tested is in a form different from that in which it was learned. (F)	40	27
I prefer to have a principle or theory explained to me rather than attempting to understand it on my own. (F)	37	36

TABLE 19—Continued

BERKELEY SM CLUSTERS [a]
(Men, N = 285)

	1961 Per cent True	1965 Per cent True
Cluster 9		
More than anything else, it is good hard work that makes life worthwhile. (F)	52	36
What youth needs most is strict discipline, rugged determination, and the will to work and fight for family and country. (F)	53	22
No weakness or difficulty can hold us back if we have enough will power. (F)	68	47
No normal, decent person would ever think of hurting a close friend or relative. (F)	56	38
Cluster 10		
I dislike women who disregard the usual social or moral conventions. (F)	46	24
No man of character would ask his fiancée to have sexual intercourse with him before marriage. (F)	47	13
I prefer people who are never profane. (F)	31	17
I would disapprove of anyone's drinking to the point of intoxication at a party. (F)	51	24

[a] Clusters 4, 5, 6, 8, 11, and 12 have been omitted.

TABLE 20

BERKELEY IE CLUSTERS [a]
(Men, N = 285)

	1961 Per cent True	1965 Per cent True
Cluster 1		
God hears our prayers. (T)	64	38
I believe there is a God. (F)	70	48
I believe in a life hereafter. (F)	56	35
In religious matters, I believe I would have to be called a skeptic or an agnostic. (T)	40	62
Cluster 2		
I cannot keep my mind on one thing. (T)	26	29
I find it hard to keep my mind on a task or a job. (T)	28	31

TABLE 20—Continued

BERKELEY IE CLUSTERS [a]

(Men, N = 285)

	1961 Per cent True	1965 Per cent True
I have had periods of days, weeks, or months when I couldn't take care of things because I couldn't "get going." (T)	44	57
I often feel as if things were not real. (T)	38	30
Cluster 3		
I have never done any heavy drinking. (F)	67	44
I have used alcohol excessively. (T)	11	22
I would disapprove of anyone's drinking to the point of intoxication at a party. (F)	51	24
I enjoy playing cards for money. (T)	50	40
Cluster 7		
I have very few quarrels with my family. (F)	51	63
My home life was always happy. (F)	53	47
I have sometimes wanted to run away from home. (T)	43	47
Some of my family have habits that bother and annoy me very much. (T)	61	49
Cluster 10		
I sometimes wake up to find myself thinking about some impractical or irrelevant problem. (T)	51	49
Sometimes an unimportant thought will run through my mind and bother me for days. (T)	47	40
I have had strange and peculiar thoughts. (T)	67	51
I have often found myself, when alone, pondering such abstract problems as free will, evil, etc. (T)	59	49
Cluster 11		
People would be happier if sex experience before marriage were taken for granted in both men and women. (T)	41	63
Moral codes are relevant only when they fit specific situations; if the situations differ, they are merely abstract irrelevancies. (T)	49	57
The only meaning to existence is the one that man gives to it himself. (T)	70	78

[a] Clusters 4, 5, 6, 8, 9, 12, and 13 have been omitted.

A feeling for what the cluster analysis technique accomplishes can be obtained by reading through the items in a given cluster. In most instances, an examination of the content reveals why the items are intercorrelated. From this kind of analysis, it is also apparent that a very broad range of content is represented within each of the two scales. It is the breadth of this content that makes the interpretation of mean scores so difficult. Although individuals can achieve the same total score by a variety of item combinations, it seems likely that different combinations of items have different psychological meanings. This was clearly recognized by the authors of the tests. In the original papers, they presented a clustering of items, based on their own intuitive judgments, that are remarkably similar to those produced by the statistical techniques of cluster analysis. For instance, the authors noted the need to "separate the spontaneous from the defensive aspects of the tendency to impulse expression." [8] They also described in detail the complexity of the Social Maturity Scale, and pointed out the many subclusters of items that were part of the total scale.[9]

In the Omnibus Personality Inventory Research Manual, the Social Maturity Scale is described as a measure that reflects a certain approach to the world, rooted in the personality structures of the individual and characterized by flexibility of thought and capacity to see the world in an unprejudiced way. The results of the cluster analysis suggest that it is important to distinguish between the two possible levels of meaning in response to an item. The attitudes an individual holds may reflect his personality structure, or they may reflect some of the predominant themes of his family situation, or some other segment of his past or current environment. We would expect the entering freshman to be still very much involved with the attitudes he learned at home. By the time he is a senior, he will have learned from his fellow students and the faculty that prevailing attitudes in society are much more diverse than he had imagined. The SM Scale as a whole does not allow us to distinguish adequately between these two sources of attitude-formation and change; however, the cluster analysis does offer some clues by helping us to separate (1) those items that seem to be especially responsive to change brought about by the process of socialization from (2) those items that are

[8] Sanford, N., Webster, H., and Freedman, M. *Impulse Expression as a Variable of Personality.* Psychological Monographs, #440, 1957.

[9] Webster, H., Sanford, N., and Freedman, M. "A New Instrument for Studying Authoritarianism in Personality." *Journal of Psychology,* 1966, *40,* 73–84.

more reflective of the personality structure of the individual. We can see that many of the clusters showing change are made up of items that reflect themes on which many segments of society have taken a liberal stand or are now undergoing liberalization. The simplistic view of human behavior is frequently challenged by the assertion that human behavior is often unconsciously motivated. Even in popular culture, as expressed in magazine articles, movies, and folk-rock music, there are portrayals of man's complexity. In Cluster 6, Table 17, Stanford, and in Cluster 9, Table 19, Berkeley, we see some evidence that college seniors view human behavior in less categorical terms than freshmen do.

Still another question can be raised about the factors that contribute toward the change we observe. There is the likelihood that this shift away from a simplistic view of behavior reflects some developmental process rooted in the personality of the individual. At this point, we cannot assess the relative strength of this influence; however, we suggest that socialization is more likely to be influential than personality development, because change resulting from personality development is very difficult to achieve. This suggestion receives further support from the fact that when we look at those items related to personality development, we see less evidence of change. For example, there is not much change in attitudes toward problems carrying a high degree of ambiguity or a lack of certainty about the outcome (Cluster 7, Table 19, Berkeley, and Cluster 17, Table 6, Stanford). To grow intellectually, one must be able to tolerate uncertainty. This ability is intimately tied to personality structure.

The cluster analysis also helps to illuminate the findings for the mean change scores on the IE Scale (Tables 18 and 20). The scale itself reflects some of the contradictory attitudes prevalent in our society with regard to handling of feelings and impulses. There is some indication that intense feelings are seen as dangerous, unpleasant, and shameful. At the same time, feelings of excitement and adventure are highly valued. The Impulse Expression Scale reflects both these realms of experience. We noted earlier that many students who originally had very high IE scores had lower scores as seniors. It seems likely that the change for individuals who start at different points of the IE Scale will be quite different. For example, the freshman who is "wild" will gradually gain control over himself and feel more comfortable, while the freshman who is exposed to a very narrow range of stimulation will gradually try out many new things and find that he likes some of them.

Along with the great conceptual richness of our scales, there goes a danger of lack of precision or specificity in measurement. By casting a very broad conceptual net, we catch those individuals who have something in common, but we also lose something in precision of classification. Earlier we pointed out that both the Stanford and Berkeley men had a large and significant increase on the SM Scale (Table 14). Unless we consider which sets of items contributed to this increase, we are likely to conclude that when we see similar mean changes, the psychological processes accounting for the changes are also similar. For example, Cluster 1, Table 19, Berkeley, and Cluster 2, Table 17, Stanford, both contain sets of items centering on intellectual activities. For the Berkeley men, there was a slight to moderate increase in expressed interest in serious intellectual activities. In the Stanford scores, there was some evidence of a slight to moderate decline. The issue is further complicated by the fact that the men at the two schools had different initial endorsement frequencies on some of these items. The Stanford students tended to start off at a higher level of expressed interest in intellectual activities than the Berkeley students did, but by the senior year, there was much more similarity between the two groups of students. Although this finding raises a host of questions, we must view it as suggestive rather than conclusive, since we are dealing with relatively few items, and do not know whether they represent a broadly defined attitude toward the use of intellect or a more circumscribed attitude toward philosophical and critical thinking.

When we examine Cluster 7, Table 19, Berkeley, and Cluster 9, Table 17, Stanford, we see that there are differences between the two groups of students with regard to perceiving the danger associated with the free use of thought. In the Berkeley scores, we see some decrease of the perception of this danger; while in the Stanford scores, there seems to be no consistent trend. Once again, there is the problem of different initial endorsement frequencies. Nevertheless, the data from the SM Scale also reflect a great many similarities in the kinds of changes that were taking place. For both groups of men, there was a sharp decrease in puritanical attitudes toward a wide variety of behaviors and beliefs, accompanied by a decline in conventional religious attitudes.

In many respects, the Stanford and Berkeley men appear even more similar on the IE Scale than they did on the SM Scale. But when we see a moderate increase in the total score, we cannot be sure which component is changing. Furthermore, when we see large numbers of students who originally had high scores ending up with a lower score as seniors, our perplexity increases. Although no clear answers are available, we can obtain some clues from looking at the clusters of items and the changes in frequency from 1961 to 1965, which indicate a sharp decrease in conventional religious attitudes for both Stanford and Berkeley men (Cluster 1, Tables 18 and 20). There was an increase in tolerance for alcohol consumption on both campuses, with some evidence for slightly greater use among the Stanford men (Cluster 2, Table 18; Cluster 3, Table 20). Responses to these items led to an increase on the IE Scale. There was a sharp decrease for both groups of men in their reports of having strange and peculiar thoughts and experiences (Cluster 9, Table 18; Cluster 10, Table 20). The decrease in response to these items might suggest that some of the disturbing emotions of adolescence were quieting down by the senior year. When we look at other clusters, we see a marked increase in feelings of distractability (Cluster 5, Table 18; Cluster 2, Table 20), but little change in feelings of anger and uncontrolled hostility (Cluster 3, Table 18). A possible explanation for this might be found in the socializing effect of the college experience and in the psychological movement away from the adolescent years. Perhaps today's students realize as they mature that it is more socially acceptable to be intermittently angry or to be distractable than it is to have strange and peculiar emotional experiences. If this is true, it raises grave questions about the utility of the educational process. Earlier we discussed the importance of integrating the emotional and intellectual life of the student in order to ensure his chance to do meaningful and creative work. This integration can only take place in individuals who are encouraged to be aware of their feelings—even disturbing ones. If the social climate works against this kind of awareness, then it tends to perpetuate the split between the world of the intellect and the rest of life.

By reporting the fact that significant differences do occur over the four-year interval of college, we have raised many questions for which we do not have full answers. Some of these questions deal with matters of theory and facts, while others deal with methodological issues. It was necessary to raise the question about change resulting from socialization rather than personality development because this seems central to the study of the impact of the liberal arts college. While we were able to place our results in some perspective by introducing this issue, we are far from being able to draw any clear distinctions between attitudes derived from long-standing personality dispositions and attitudes reflecting a particular social climate. Although mean score changes are helpful to us in theorizing about the relative impact of socialization or development, this level of generality is useful only for clarifying certain conceptual problems.

At the level of analysis concerned with variability in the direction of change, important questions come into sharper focus.[10] We observed that more than half the individuals who had high Impulse Expression scores at freshmen had lower scores as seniors. While there was an overall mean increase in the IE score, it would be misleading to extrapolate from this and make assumptions about the change experienced by all individuals. The issues become more complex when we begin to look at the internal structure of the scales. Here we touch on fundamental questions concerning how to conceptualize personality and how to measure the constructs that make up personality theory. An examination of the psychological complexity of the scales led us to consider several questions which otherwise might have been missed. Given the finding that the personality scales could be broken down into a variety of empirical clusters, we were forced to consider whether there was a differential amount of change from cluster to cluster. In doing so, we found that in the SM Scale, the clusters with items touching on social standards and mores changed more than the clusters dealing with intellectual dispositions. When we see a mean change score for Social Maturity, we tend to think about its central defining characteristics according to the OPI Manual: "High scorers are not authoritarian, and they are flexible, tolerant and realistic in their thinking." The data we have presented sug-

---

[10] It should be pointed out that the analysis of mean scores can be useful when one is dealing with a group that is homogeneous with respect to some important criterion, as well as when one is trying to evaluate the homogeneity of a group.

gest that it is possible to have a large mean score change without much change in the items that most directly reflect these central defining characteristics.

The complexity of the Impulse Expression Scale also led to questions about the nature of the observed change. Although the authors of the test recognized that there were at least two major aspects of impulse expression built into the scale, this is seldom taken into account in the interpretation of mean scores or mean score changes. The application of cluster analysis and the examination of the differential changes in frequency of response have revealed additional details for the interpreter. There is evidence of a marked increase in those items dealing with the spontaneous, though conventional, aspects of impulse expression, and changes with respect to the defensive aspects. We see evidence for a shifting around of the modes of expression, but the continued presence of a good deal of psychological discomfort throughout the college years.

It must be evident to the reader that our purpose is to encourage caution in the use of personality scales, while at the same time attempting to interpret and understand our own results. This somewhat contradictory position reflects the dilemma of the researcher who deals with complex human problems. There is an urgent need for answers, and policy decisions cannot wait until the researcher is satisfied with his means for providing answers. Nevertheless, a host of complex methodological issues have yet to be solved.[11] It is necessary to act on the basis of what we know, but it is just as necessary to continue to broaden and define the basis for our actions.

---

[11] In addition to the four areas focused on here—the interpretation of mean score changes for large heterogeneous groups, variability in direction and magnitude of change for individuals with different initial scores, the internal structure of the scales, and different patterns of change in item frequencies—there are other problem areas in the measurement of psychological change. Harris, Charles. *Problems in Measuring Change*. Madison: University of Wisconsin Press, 1963, provides an excellent introduction to many of these problems. Several of the chapters start with assumptions about the importance of a coherent theory of measurement in the social sciences, then go on to describe the difficulties involved in formulating such a theory. Many illustrations are given of the statistical and methodological pitfalls that plague the researcher studying change.

PART TWO

From Curriculum to Career

❧ 4 ❧

DIFFERENCES IN STUDENT
RESPONSE TO THE
CURRICULUM

Harold A. Korn

There is a general
lack of agreement between professors, college administrators, and
state legislators about the goals of higher education. More im-
portantly, there is a general tendency to overlook the fact that
students have goals and aspirations of their own. Even in those
rare institutions where curriculum and philosophy of education
are clearly integrated, there is little regard for the differing agendas of the students; and in the more typical college, the problems
of the students are further complicated by the diversity of goals
among the faculty. The curriculum is seldom an integrated whole
designed to encourage intellectual development; instead, it is a

patchwork made up of what numerous specialists feel is vital to an understanding of their own particular disciplines. Under such conditions, any hope that the student will be afforded an opportunity to fruitfully work through a set of integrating experiences is faint indeed.

Let us explore one aspect of this complex issue by examining the ways in which students differ in their reactions to the curriculum. From this perspective, the goals of higher education can be discussed more realistically. Both college students and those who study their behavior agree that there are different types of students. This recognition of types is based upon an observation of recurring patterns of individual differences. It is but a step from such observation to the formation of stereotypes; yet we all need the efficiency and the insight potential of meaningful classifications. What is more, we need a conceptual schema that will permit us to understand the differences between students and thus allow us to be more effective in teaching them. Our task, then, is to select a basis for classification with sufficient conceptual richness to raise it above the commonplace. At the same time we must examine the validity of our schema, in order to avoid the danger of finding only what we expect to find. Our goal must be to work toward the development of a meaningful classification of student orientation to the curriculum, so that college teaching may eventually be made more meaningful to more students. Our argument centers on the inutility of teaching all students in the same way. It is wasteful of the teacher's effort, and it is wasteful of the student's potential.

Of the men and women in our Student Development Study at Stanford and Berkeley who were freshmen in 1961, approximately 60 per cent of those registered as seniors in 1965 filled out a Senior Questionnaire. These four groups—Stanford men, Stanford women, Berkeley men, and Berkeley women—provided the samples for our study of student types, and their responses to one of the questions in this questionnaire provided the initial basis for our classification. In addition, since a wide variety of other data were available for each of the four groups, we were able to examine the corollaries of our classification schema. Each of the four groups (Stanford men, Stanford women, Berkeley men, and Berkeley women) was handled separately under a threefold classification system reflective of basic student attitudes toward the curriculum—(1) grades, (2) career preparation, and (3) intellectual interest. We placed emphasis upon the psychological and behavioral characteristics of each of the three classes. Analysis was carried out for all four groups; for reasons of space, we give only the results for the Stanford men here.

In Table 21 we summarize the frequencies (*f*) of student responses to the following question: *"In general, when you consider most of the courses you have taken, how would you rank all the following in their order of importance to you?"* Table 21 contains the frequencies for all those students who ranked the category as first in importance.

TABLE 21

FREQUENCY OF RESPONSES TO THE QUESTIONNAIRE ITEMS
USED AS A BASIS OF CLASSIFICATION

Stanford				Questionnaire Item	Berkeley			
Men		Women			Men		Women	
f	Per cent	*f*	Per cent		*f*	Per cent	*f*	Per cent
49	18	9	4	A. Getting good grades	62	24	31	12
70	26	35	17	B. Useful for your career	92	35	55	22
144	54	162	76	C. Intellectual interest	100	38	153	61
1	< 1	2	1	D. Getting to know professor in class	3	1	4	2
1	< 1	2	1	E. Getting to know professor outside class	0	0	1	1
3	1	3	1	F. Getting recognition from professor	4	2	1	1
268		213			261		245	

We used Groups A, B, and C as the initial basis for our classification schema because these three groups had adequate numbers of students represented in each category. In light of all the recent discussion about a "sense of community" on campus, it is of interest to note that categories D, E, and F account for under 5 per cent of the first-ranked categories. For many reasons, students do not turn to the faculty for meaningful personal or intellectual associations.

When we examine Table 21 in greater detail, several significant camparisons emerge. As might be expected, more men than women indicated that their course work was of importance to their careers, and more women than men indicated the importance of intellectual interest in their evaluation of course work. When we consider the differences between Stanford and Berkeley, we see that a larger percentage of Berkeley students than Stanford students were career- and grade-oriented.

The reasons why a student ranks one category higher than another are very complex. Yet it is a fact that students do differ in this respect; and we have taken this fact as a starting point for building a classification scheme. Our long-range goal is the development of a typology that will carry with it information relevant to the process of teaching and learning. Starting from our phenomenologically based classification, we move to another level of analysis to discover whether the typology also has meaning there. We have scores on six Omnibus Personality Inventory (OPI) scales for each of the four samples.[1] The students took this inventory both as entering freshmen and as graduating seniors.

One of the principal statistical tools used in the analysis of these data is the discriminant analysis. This multivariate statistical technique, developed by R. A. Fisher to answer questions about the existence of class membership among a group of individuals, is well suited to our needs. We begin by testing the meaningfulness of classification based on self-description for other realms of data. In this instance, we start with scores on the Omnibus Personality Inventory. The discriminant analysis takes into account the variability of group means (Groups A, B, and C) on the n variables (six OPI scales), variation of individuals about group means on the n variables, and the interrelationships of the n variables.

Since we have both freshman and senior test results for each of our four groups, we have eight separate discriminant analyses to consider. In Tables 22 to 26, we show the standard score means

---

[1] See Chapter 3, for a brief definition of the Omnibus Personality Inventory Scales.

for three classes (A, B, and C) for each of the four separate groups (men and women at both Stanford and Berkeley). (We present the classification matrix for the Stanford men only; the matrices for the other three groups were similar.) If our variables allowed for perfect discrimination, all the cases would appear in the diagonal row of the classification matrix. While the overall level of significance tells us whether or not we can have confidence in our findings, the classification table tells us how practical our findings would be in actually classifying individuals.

TABLE 22

FRESHMAN MEAN SCORES ON SIX OPI SCALES FOR STANFORD MEN [a]
AND BERKELEY MEN [b]

First column gives scores for Stanford men (S);
second column gives scores for Berkeley men (B)

		Grades		Career		Intellectual Interest	
		(N = 41)	(N = 62)	(N = 59)	(N = 85)	(N = 130)	(N = 97)
		(S)	(B)	(S)	(B)	(S)	(B)
SM	(Social Maturity)	44	48	48	46	53	55
IE	(Impulse Expression)	47	51	46	47	49	52
SF	(Schizoid Functioning)	48	52	49	49	50	51
MF	(Masculinity-Femininity)	51	51	52	51	48	47
Es	(Estheticism)	45	48	48	47	52	55
DS	(Developmental Status)	46	50	48	46	51	53

[a] Generalized Mahalanobis $D^2 = 37$; with 12 degrees of freedom, $p < .001$.
[b] Generalized Mahalanobis $D^2 = 63.1$; with 12 degrees of freedom, $p < .001$.

For each of the eight analyses (four groups, freshman and senior) we have found the students within the three classes A, B, and C to be significantly different from each other. It is important to remember when the first OPI was given and when the Senior Questionnaire was administered. Our classification is based on the responses made by students when they were seniors. The evidence suggests that the psychological characteristics that lead to differences in student responses to the curriculum are present when the student arrives on campus.

For all four freshman groups, the SM scores were highest for those choosing intellectual interest. Moreover, all but one of the freshman groups choosing intellectual interest had the highest scores on the Developmental Status (DS) Scale. (The exceptions were the Stanford women, who appear to have been atypical in many respects.) We find that the same pattern of relationship held in the results of the senior testing. For all four senior groups, the SM Scale was highest for those choosing intellectual interest. Again, among all but the Stanford women, the DS Scale was highest for those choosing intellectual interest. While these same relative positions were maintained for the SM and DS Scales, there was a general shift upward in the standard scores on SM and DS for all four groups as they moved from freshman to senior standing. (There is a paradox here, for on the one hand, we see evidence that the absolute scores of SM and DS do seem associated with the different classes we have described, while on the other, we note that all three classes have significant increases in their scores. In other words, the mean SM score for the freshman intellectual interest group is practically identical with the mean SM score of the senior grade group.)

TABLE 23

CLASSIFICATION MATRIX FOR STANFORD MEN ON SIX OPI SCALES
AS FRESHMEN AND SENIORS

Function Group	*Freshmen*			*Seniors*		
	1	2	3	1	2	3
Grades	26	4	11	17	6	5
Career	19	19	21	15	16	12
Intellectual Interest	33	30	67	11	13	52

While we find an impressive array of consistent differences in these scores, there is also evidence of much heterogeneity within the groups and across the groups. One way of quickly ascertaining the extent of this heterogeneity is to examine the classification tables. Here we find evidence that, although large numbers of students within a single class were alike on the OPI variables, others were more like students in one of the other classes. For example, some students who placed themselves in the "Intellectual

Interest" group on the Senior Questionnaire had OPI scores more similar to the "Career" group than other members of "Intellectual Interest" groups did; therefore, they do not appear in the diagonal column of our classification matrix. The "Function" group is the "ideal" classification based on the statistical analysis; the other grouping is based on our empirical grouping. (Only two of the eight classification tables for the discriminant analyses are presented here; however, all the tables portrayed a similar heterogeneity within groups.)

TABLE 24

SENIOR MEAN SCORES ON SIX OPI SCALES FOR STANFORD MEN [a]
AND BERKELEY MEN [b]

First column gives scores for Stanford men (S);
second column gives scores for Berkeley men (B)

	Grades		Career		Intellectual Interest	
	(N = 28)	(N = 63)	(N = 43)	(N = 85)	(N = 76)	(N = 97)
	(S)	(B)	(S)	(B)	(S)	(B)
SM	52	54	54	53	62	62
IE	48	55	50	48	52	54
SF	46	51	46	44	45	46
MF	49	49	50	49	48	45
Es	47	49	48	47	56	57
DS	54	58	56	54	61	60

[a] Generalized Mahalanobis $D^2 = 41.3$; with 12 degrees of freedom, $p < .001$.
[b] Generalized Mahalanobis $D^2 = 28.6$; with 12 degrees of freedom, $p < .001$.

When we consider the IE scores (Table 22), we see that it is highest for the "Intellectual Interest" group for Stanford men, but not for the Berkeley men. The magnitude of change is also far less between freshman and senior year for the IE Scale than it was for the SM and DS Scales. Similar complexities and inconsistencies exist for the other scales. This means that there is evidence suggesting that the phenomenologically based classification system has some reality in the context of personality scales. At the same time, we have a good deal of evidence that these types are far from pure, and that they differ from sample to sample.

Another way to ascertain the meaningfulness of this classification system is to examine some other realm of behavior and determine how the different classes of students perform. We have data on the cumulative grade-point average and on the Scholastic Aptitude Tests for our students. For each of our four samples, we can determine whether there are differences in the mean cumulative GPA, mean verbal aptitude score, and mean mathematical aptitude scores. Tables 27 and 28 contain the relevant information for these variables for the four groups. (When we examined the personality realm corresponding to our classification system, we found consistent differences across our four samples; however, this is not the case with this particular set of variables.)

TABLE 25

FRESHMAN MEAN SCORES ON SIX OPI SCALES FOR STANFORD WOMEN [a]
AND BERKELEY WOMEN [b]

First column gives scores for Stanford women (S);
second column gives scores for Berkeley women (B)

	Grades		Career		Intellectual Interest	
	(N = 7) (S)	(N = 8) (B)	(N = 31) (S)	(N = 23) (B)	(N = 155) (S)	(N = 146) (B)
SM	48	46	46	46	50	53
IE	57	50	49	46	50	49
SF	54	51	52	47	50	49
MF	53	50	51	53	49	49
Es	45	45	48	45	50	52
DS	56	49	46	46	50	51

[a] Generalized Mahalanobis $D^2 = 21.1$; with 12 degrees of freedom, $p < .05$.
[b] Generalized Mahalanobis $D^2 = 48$; with 12 degrees of freedom, $p < .001$.

In Table 27 we find that the career group of Stanford men had significantly lower GPA's than both the grade and the intellectual interest groups. For the Stanford women and the Berkeley men and women, we do not find significant differences in GPA among the members of the different classes. This is further evidence for the complexity of the psychological bases of the grade-point average, and points up the need to search for the reasons why students achieve certain grades. When we examine the verbal aptitude scores, we find some interesting differences. In Table 28, we see that among the Stanford men, the grade group had significantly lower scores than the intellectual interest group. Yet we have just observed that the grade groups had the highest cumulative GPA. It should also be noted that there are no significant differences for math aptitude among various groups of Stanford men.

TABLE 26

SENIOR MEAN SCORES ON SIX OPI SCALES FOR STANFORD WOMEN [a]
AND BERKELEY WOMEN [b]

First column gives scores for Stanford women (S);
second column gives scores for Berkeley women (B)

| | Grades | | Career | | Intellectual Interest | |
	(N = 8) (S)	(N = 34) (B)	(N = 23) (S)	(N = 51) (B)	(N = 98) (S)	(N = 146) (B)
SM	55	55	52	54	59	61
IE	54	52	51	48	55	53
SF	46	46	46	44	46	47
MF	50	47	51	51	47	48
Es	46	48	48	47	53	55
DS	64	58	55	55	62	61

[a] Generalized Mahalanobis $D^2 = 25.9$; with 12 degrees of freedom, $p < .02$.
[b] Generalized Mahalanobis $D^2 = 47$; with 12 degrees of freedom, $p < .001$.

The Berkeley women are the only ones showing differences among the three classes on aptitude variables. Here we find that the women who ranked intellectual interest first had the highest verbal aptitude scores. Those who ranked career first had the highest math aptitude scores. We noted that although the intellectual interest group had the highest GPA, there were no significant differences in the cumulative GPA for the Berkeley women.

TABLE 27

MEANS, STANDARD DEVIATIONS, AND t TESTS FOR
CUMULATIVE GPA (STANFORD MEN)

	N	$\overline{X}$	SD	t test A	B	C
A. Getting good grades	28	3.00	.50	x	**	x
B. Useful for your career	42	2.72	.42		x	**
C. Intellectual Interest	76	2.91	.39			x

** $\leq .01$ level.

TABLE 28

MEANS, STANDARD DEVIATIONS, AND DIFFERENCES IN
SAT APTITUDE SCORES (STANFORD MEN)

| | *Verbal* | | | | *t* test | |
	N	X̄	SD	A	B	C
A. Good grades	28	606	74	x	x	**
B. Career	42	613	72		x	**
C. Intellectual Interest	76	644	62			x

| | *Math* | | | | *t* test | |
	N	X̄	SD	A	B	C
A. Good grades	28	654	79	x	x	x
B. Career	43	662	69		x	x
C. Intellectual Interest	76	672	72			x

** $\leq$ .01 level.

The Stanford men not only have personality scores consistent with the classification system, but they also have consistent
GPA's and verbal aptitude scores. Along with the Omnibus Personality Inventory, the freshmen at Stanford were also given the
California Psychological Inventory. In Table 29, we can see the

TABLE 29

FRESHMAN MEAN SCORES ON 18 CPI SCALES [a]
(STANFORD MEN)

	DO	CS	SY	SP	SA	WB	RE	SO	SC	TO	GI	CM	AC	AI	PY	FX	FE[b]
Grades (N = 30)	53	52	51	53	59	45	47	52	43	48	45	47	49	55	53	51	50
Career (N = 60)	56	56	54	57	61	51	53	54	46	52	48	52	53	59	55	54	49
Intellectual Interest (N = 142)	56	56	52	56	60	49	53	52	46	52	48	49	51	59	56	58	52

[a] Generalized Mahalanobis D^2 = 57.7; with 36 degrees of freedom, p < .001.
[b] See page 206 for definitions of these abbreviations.

results of the discriminant analysis for our three classes. There
are significant differences between these classes, and the results
are in the direction we would expect in view of the OPI analysis.
What emerges from this analysis is evidence of the relative dis-

comfort the grade group experienced in interpersonal relationships. They have lower scores than the other two groups on all
scales of the first quadrant. In contrast, the career group appears
quite comfortable with itself, able to accept contemporary social
mores, and interested in seeking out interpersonal relationships.
The intellectual interest group scored higher than the other two
groups on the Flexibility and Femininity scales.

TABLE 30

CLASSIFICATION MATRIX FOR STANFORD MEN ON
18 FRESHMAN CPI SCALES

Function Group	1	2	3	Total
Grades	18	7	5	30
Career	11	35	14	60
Intellectual Interest	25	40	77	142

Another way in which to enlarge our conceptual picture of
what these three groups are like is to examine their career plans.
We compared information regarding their graduating major with
our classification scheme. Only those majors involving nine or
more students were chosen. In Table 31, we have the chi-square
matrix, with both the observed and expected frequencies (the chi-

TABLE 31

CROSS-TABULATION OF SELECTED MAJORS BY THE
THREE-WAY CLASSIFICATION [a]

	Grades		Career		Intellectual Interest		
	Ob-served	Ex-pected	Ob-served	Ex-pected	Ob-served	Ex-pected	Total
Engineering	11	7	16	10	8	18	35
Mathematics	0	2	2	3	9	6	11
Chemistry	1	2	4	3	4	5	9
Biology	5	3	4	4	6	8	15
Economics	5	5	9	8	13	14	27
Political Science	8	6	10	9	12	16	30
History	4	8	5	11	31	21	40
Psychology	2	4	3	6	16	11	21
							188

[a] $X^2 = 36.1$, p $< .001$.

square was significant at the .001 level). Some interesting patterns are apparent.

As might be expected, the engineering students are under-represented in the intellectual interest group, while the history majors are very much over-represented. Even though some of our expectations are confirmed, there are also a number of surprises. In every major except mathematics (N = 11), there are some students who say grades are the most important thing to them; and for every major represented here, there are some students who indicate that the required courses were important for their careers.

As we move from one perspective to another according to the data being examined, we find that our typology is both supported and challenged. The SM Scale provides us with the most powerful and consistent differences across our several groups. In Table 32, the range of item content and some of the shifts in frequency of response between the freshman and senior year are illustrated. The frequency of true responses by each of our three classification groups of Stanford men is also shown. Fifteen representative items are grouped together on the basis of the apparent meaning of the content. Thus, the first eight items deal with attitudes toward the use of intellect. The intellectual group endorsed items indicating pleasure and satisfaction in the use of intellect much more than the other two groups did. Facts had an appeal for the grade and career groups, whereas ideas had more appeal for the intellectual group. It is once again evident that we are talking about group trends, and that there is some overlap between all classes.

Certain shifts in endorsement frequency that occurred between the freshman and senior years pose some important questions for developmental theory. In Item 4, we find a dramatic shift on the part of the grade group in the direction of endorsing the intellectual and critical aspect of the statement, whereas the career group is seen as maintaining a practical approach to life. In order to understand this shift by the grade group, we must consider their responses to other items. The content of Item 8 deals with the need for clarity and the tolerance for complexity. Here we once again see the career group moving toward a greater need for the practical. The grade group, on the other hand, is the least tolerant of ambiguity; and this does not change over the four years. We see the grade group expressing more enthusiasm about ideas, but there is also evidence that they are the most rigid of the three groups. It is our expectation that the grade group's shift in the intellectual direction carries with it a very different set of attitudes and feelings toward ideas than we would find in the intellectual group. This difference can be understood in the context of items dealing with attitudes toward family and self. For example, the grade group's response to Item 11 reveals a certain pessimism and lack of confidence. We find clues to the causes of this rigidity and cynicism in response to those items related to the importance of parental approach and close family ties, where we find that the grade group shows much more immaturity and parental attachment than the other groups do. In contrast, the intellectual group is relatively free, perhaps even alienated, from the family. The career group falls somewhere between these extremes.

TABLE 32

ITEMS FROM THE SM SCALE [a]

| | Percentages | | |
	Intellectual Interest (N = 142)	Career (N = 60)	Grades (N = 30)
1. I enjoy reading essays on serious subjects. (T) [b]	74–76	64–50	50–54
2. There is too much emphasis in school on intellectual and theoretical topics—not enough on practical matters. (T)	11–9	29–24	21–21
3. I would rather be a brilliant but unstable worker than a steady and dependable one. (T)	41–63	26–36	11–29
4. Facts appeal to me more than ideas. (F)	14–11	33–36	54–25
5. It is not the duty of a citizen to support his country right or wrong. (T)	46–72	36–55	18–64
6. People ought to pay more attention to new ideas, even if they seem to go against the American way of life. (T)	76–93	76–90	75–82
7. Nowadays more and more people are prying into matters that should remain personal and private. (F)	41–25	52–45	57–36

TABLE 32—Continued

ITEMS FROM THE SM SCALE [a]

	Percentages		
	Intellectual Interest (N = 142)	Career (N = 60)	Grades (N = 30)
8. I don't like to work on a problem unless there is the possibility of coming out with a clear-cut and unambiguous answer. (F)	17–18	29–36	43–46
9. It is a pretty callous person who does not feel love and gratitude toward his parents. (F)	63–51	81–64	82–68
10. One of my aims in life is to accomplish something that would make my mother proud of me. (F)	49–39	60–48	75–54
11. It is better never to expect much; in that way you are rarely disappointed. (F)	20–21	17–19	39–36
12. My conversations with friends usually deal with such subjects as mutual acquaintances and social activities. (F)	39–28	43–43	54–46
13. I have had more than my share of things to worry about. (F)	14–17	12–29	32–11
14. I have been quite independent and free from family rule. (T)	45–66	57–76	64–64
15. Nothing in life is worth the sacrifice of losing contact with your family. (F)	22–12	24–24	32–46

[a] Figures are percentages of those answering "True." The first figure is percentage in freshman year; the second is percentage in senior year.

[b] "T" and "F" in parentheses indicate the direction for obtaining one point in the scale.

In our journey through this maze of data we have moved from the analysis of differences among several OPI scales to the analysis of the meanings of individual items. Along the way we have examined the relationships of our classification system to grades, aptitudes, and college majors. Now it is time to bring the implications of all these data together and evaluate their relevance for college teaching and student learning. The needs of society and the happiness of individuals require that optimal use be made of human talent. If this is to be accomplished, we must recognize that there are profound differences in the ways students learn and in their underlying patterns of motivation for learning. Our findings with regard to student attitudes invite interpretation in several ways. From one perspective, we see clear differences; from another, complex interactions.

Generally speaking, the career groups seem comfortable in their relationships with others and with themselves.[2] This comfort is perhaps bought at the expense of not seeing and feeling many of the subtle shadings of human experience. The implication is not that these men are defensively shutting out conflict and unknown impulses, but that they are more attuned to an external system of rewards than to an intrinsic set of human values. These men find the well-defined pathways to success interesting and rewarding. The suggestion that there are other paths or other criteria of success is at best met with tolerant disbelief; at worst, with angry rebuke. These men are ready to take positions of responsibility in a man's world. Practicality is their credo. They are skilled in using their intelligence as long as they feel they are using it to accomplish an end that fits their value system; but they reject any commitment to an evaluation of their underlying value system. The result of this absence of commitment is a loss of creativity and potential for instituting fundamental change.

The men in the intellectual interest group differ from those in the career group particularly in this last respect. They are more flexible, and a questioning attitude toward many of the "givens" in our society is apparent in some important areas of their thinking. The paths they choose must be personally meaningful to them. Although the members of the career group feel that their personal worth is enhanced by conventional signs of success, students in the intellectual interest group are searching for something beyond the conventional. The differences in what these two groups find rewarding seem to be a key to understanding variations in their behavior and attitudes.

A clue to some of the causative factors operating here may be found in the conflicts that intellectually motivated students

---

[2] These composite pictures of the various groups are based on extrapolation from the data. The reader who wishes to examine these ideas more clearly is referred to the California Psychological Inventory results and the endorsement frequencies of the items on the SM Scale.

characteristically encounter in their family relationships. These conflicts may result in not only a nagging dissatisfaction with self but also in a continuing need to right the wrongs of the world. The usual rewards are not enough to overcome this need. One could speculate that the career group we examined did not encounter such profound dislocations in the family, and thus were able to acquire more conventional patterns of self-reinforcement.

It should be made clear that here we are describing the characteristics of the hard-core intellectual, though not all the students in our intellectual interest group fall into this category. Further clarification of the relationship between familial discord and involvement with ideas *qua* ideas would be the next step necessary for a more precise categorization. At this point it is not clear which is the essential ingredient: freedom to experience dissent in the family, or profound familial discord. In addition, further research should be done with regard to the differences between men and women in respect to the development of intellectual orientation.

We have said that in general, members of the intellectual group use their intelligence to work through personally meaningful agendas. The attitude of the grade group toward course work is in many ways similar, but appears to differ essentially in the need for repetition rather than growth. Not only do grade-oriented students work hard at mastering course material, but they seem to work equally hard to avoid integrating this material into other areas of their personality. The grade-seeking group is further removed from both other groups in several respects. They express greater concern about their interpersonal relationships and more dissatisfaction with them; and they apparently perceive their college years as a battle to survive. If the other groups are conceived of as following divergent paths to success, the grade-oriented group might be said to be on a circular path. For them, success is defined in terms of excelling in the immediate task; as soon as it is completed, they are back where they started. Self-respect is not accumulated, but is only temporarily and haltingly renewed.

Despite the general trend of the evidence, which indicates the validity of our overall classification system, there are several points at which the evidence must be viewed as inconclusive or ambiguous. One problem is misclassification of individuals; the other is lack of consistent findings across our four groups. Although our findings for the personality scale differences among the three classification groups were consistently statistically significant, there was some misclassification. The ambiguity inherent in the original questionnaire responses, and the many possible sources of error in the measuring devices, could account for a large part of this misclassification. With respect to differences of response to the curriculum, the problem of imperfect classifications is less important than the inconsistent findings across groups. We find that while there are consistent differences in personality characteristics associated with different attitudes towards the curriculum, this does not necessarily result in significantly different grade-point averages.

Why should personality characteristics be related to grade-point average for the men at Stanford and not at Berkeley? Why is the relationship between grade-point averages and personality characteristics not apparent for either group of women? When we examine the classification of grade-point averages for the Berkeley men, we find that the grade group is once again the highest. This was also the finding for Stanford. The range between the three groups is so small, however, that significant differences do not appear. The finding that the Berkeley men who classified themselves as having intellectual interests achieved the lowest grade-point averages further confounds our results. We are encountering unknown factors, not only in the grading practices of the two institutions, but also in the ethos of the students. Could it be that the "intellectuals" at Berkeley have other things on their agenda than working for grades? Our data do not provide any clear answers to this, but it does seem evident that the educational climate of an institution can interact with the personality characteristics of its students and affect their behavior to a significant degree.

Cutting across and interacting with institutional differences are the culturally defined differences between men and women with regard to their use of intellect. Among Stanford men, response to the demands of the classroom is affected by differences in underlying attitudes and personality characteristics. Among Stanford and Berkeley women, profound differences in underlying attitudes toward the required course work do not clearly affect their behavior. It may be that women are early taught to separate their inner life (personality) from their behavior in school. College women, no matter how hard they work in school, are usually faced with the prospect of a future in which they will be forced by marriage and family obligations to abruptly give up their academic pursuits. The anticipation of this outcome may encourage women to isolate their "academic selves" from the major segments of the rest of their personality.

Despite our emphasis on the personality differences that exist among students, we know that the total educational climate must be taken into account when trying to understand student behavior. With this in mind, we return to an examination of the implications of our findings for college teaching. In order to set some limits, we direct our attention to the teaching of those courses intended to have a "liberalizing" effect upon the student; and we accept as given the fact that the typical curriculum is segmented into finite units and courses that have little or no relationship to each other.

The aim of a liberal education is to teach students how to think critically about a wide variety of human experiences, and how to express these thoughts clearly. When we contrast this goal with the differing personal goals of the students, we begin to see some of the problems facing college teachers. Consider the responses to Item 8, Table 32, from the Social Maturity Scale: "I don't like to work on a problem unless there is the possibility of coming out with a clear-cut and unambiguous answer." Here we find that only 17 per cent of the intellectual interest group endorsed this item, while 43 per cent of the grade group and 29 per cent of the career group endorsed it. Unless such differences in student orientation are made explicit, both the students and the instructor will end up working at cross-purposes. Once they are made explicit, the important question is what should and can be done to help the student and teacher work toward a common goal. Suppose that one of the lessons of history is that for many problems, clear-cut and unambiguous answers do not exist. How is the instructor to respond to those students who cannot tolerate this perspective, and therefore in some fashion disengage themselves from the learning process? The usual response of the instructor is to ignore the student's view, to show his displeasure, or to attempt to demonstrate on some rational basis why the student is not seeing things clearly. Often one of these responses is helpful and appropriate, but if it becomes the teacher's inevitable response, individual growth ceases to be a possibility, and rote learning is substituted.

The necessary element in a response to a student who is thinking in logic-tight, oversimplified terms about a complex issue is some understanding of why it is necessary for the student to take that position. Here the descriptions of the three groups presented earlier may prove helpful. We noted that the grade group differed from the other two groups in that so much of their motivation seemed to be based on fear of failure. This kind of student requires some kind of reassurance that he will become able to encounter more and more of the world's complexity without becoming overwhelmed. The very fact that Student A has found it necessary to develop a simplified view of the world suggests that certain kinds of complexity are frightening to him. In contrast, Student B, from the career group, may be uninterested in some facet of the complexity of the world simply because it does not seem relevant to his particular plans. It is easy to see how the needs of both these students differ from those of Student C, an intellectual who eagerly reaches out for the world's complexity.

Although Student A and Student B may work equally hard to keep themselves disengaged from certain kinds of learning, their motives in doing so may be quite different. Nevertheless, no learning situation can help effect the aim of liberalization unless it engages some fundamental characteristic of the student's psychological makeup. This poses a dilemma for the individual instructor and for educators in general. If the instructor does, in fact, try to make his course effective as a liberalizing experience, then it will be necessary for him to involve himself in a struggle with the students who have a powerful resistance to this kind of experience. We have seen that in a single classroom the instructor can be faced with at least three different orientations to learning. Even a very sensitive and sophisticated observer of human behavior must find the task of the instructor in the usual course a formidable one. Higher education has long avoided facing up to this reality. The tremendous pressure to have a college degree and the enormous demands of our society for trained people have created an environment in which the commitment to the goals of liberal education is often reduced to rhetoric. In the last few years, the students themselves have demanded some explanation for the discrepancy between what colleges promise and what they actually accomplish. No easy answers are available, but some answer should be sought.

Note

California Psychological Inventory Scale names: Do = Dominance, CS = Capacity for Status, Sy = Sociability, Sp = Social Pressure, Sa = Self-acceptance, Wb = Well-being, Re = Responsibility, So = Socialization, Sc = Self-control, To = Tolerance, Gi = Good Impression, Cm = Communality, Ac = Achievement via Conformity, Ai = Achievement via Independence, Ie = Intellectual Efficiency, Py = Psychological-mindedness, Fx = Flexibility, Fe = Femininity.

❧ 5 ❧

CAREERS: CHOICE, CHANCE, OR INERTIA?

Harold A. Korn

It is part of the American dream, and a main goal of higher education, that each individual be encouraged to develop his unique potentialities. The underlying assumption is that he will then choose an intrinsically satisfying and maximally rewarding career plan. Most college students are given only a year or two in which to find both themselves and a vocational plan for their lives; and too often during this short period, while they are being offered encouragement to explore, their daily academic tasks are at odds with their goals. The student's hour-to-hour work involves courses of a highly specialized nature that are intended to prepare him for a psychologically distant future. Even the broad range of introductory and general studies courses are most often taught by men trained to be specialists. Students, in turn, are willing to engage in specialized discourse. Much of the structure of higher education encourages them to put aside questions of personal relevance in favor of mastering a complexity of academic subject matter.

Our main purpose is to show that today's college students are confronted with a system that has not even openly acknowledged these contradictions. We will look first at the academic plans and career aspirations of an entire college class, from freshman year through the first year after graduation, focusing upon presentation of facts and certain relationships between these facts; and then discuss some of the forces operating in society that confront the student with contradictory and often unfair alternatives. By studying the progress of an entire class with respect to plans and actual achievement, we can bring into focus the play of these social forces on the lives of individuals. In contemporary society, the career an individual settles into not only determines to a great extent the content of his working hours, but has a powerful effect on the remainder of his life as well. Adolescents are keenly aware of this. They see a career choice as an invisible lifeline connecting them to the adult world. It can be a gentle pull toward full development, a strangling conception of what the adult world demands, or a broken line of communication that leaves the young person with a sense of isolation and desperation.

In 1961, the members of the entering freshman class at Stanford were administered a variety of psychological tests, including the Strong Vocational Interest Blank. In addition, the entering freshmen were asked to complete an information blank prepared by the National Merit Scholarship Corporation. This questionnaire asked that they indicate their anticipated career choice and probable college major. The instructions were: "Be as specific as you can. List *mechanical engineering* (not *engineering*), *teaching high school* (rather than *teaching*), etc. If you are not sure what field you wish to enter, you may write *undecided.*"

In the spring of 1966, we tried to obtain follow-up information for all students entering in 1961 and graduating in June, 1965 (not all 1961 freshmen had graduated). All students in the class of '65 were mailed a questionnaire concerning their current status. In addition to the data collected at the beginning and end of their undergraduate years, we also obtained complete data on their grade-point averages and aptitudes. (Although we were dealing with a single large group—860 male and 425 female students—there were many instances in which the subgroups we selected for detailed study differed in size. This was because we were collecting data at different times over the five-year period, and at various times some subjects were not available for testing, did not respond to questionnaires, or omitted data. Each table given here states the size of the group that is being described.)

Let us begin by providing an overview of the stated career expectations of the freshmen, and then briefly describe what many of these men were doing approximately nine months after graduation. After presenting this overview, we shall describe three groups of men who as freshmen expressed an interest in either medicine, law, or engineering, and then examine some of the characteristics of both the men who actually went on to graduate or professional school and those who changed their plans. We have selected these three professional groups for illustrative purposes. Our intent is to question how well the educational system is working to fulfill both the needs of society and those of the individual. Are changes in career plans usually made after rational consideration of the alternatives, or are chance and irrational factors allowed to influence vital decisions? What of the student who stays with a decision reached in early life and never subjects it to critical examination?

Table 33 shows a breakdown of the men in our sample by probable future occupation. In addition to a breakdown of the total number who expressed an occupational choice, there is a further breakdown by expected probable major. This cross-tabulation makes it clear that freshmen see many different academic paths to the same career. Conversely, students in any given major are likely to be headed for many different careers. The data in Table 33 will be viewed differently by different readers. Those who feel, for example, that society is not encouraging enough young people to become artists will find it alarming that not a single male in our sample considered art as a probable future career. Those who feel that we must continually replenish and expand the pool of lawyers will be encouraged to see that nearly 13 per cent of the entering freshmen planned to go to law school.

None of the following occupations were chosen by any student in the sample: accountant; advertising man; anthropologist; artist; clergyman; clerk (business). The following occupations were chosen by ten or less students in the sample: actor; architect; biological scientist; businessman-salesman; chemist; college professor-scientist; dentist; farmer; aide in government service; engineer-sales executive; interpreter; journalist; military career officer; missionary; pharmacist; psychologist.

TABLE 33

PROBABLE FUTURE OCCUPATION BY PROBABLE MAJOR FIELD OF STUDY
(Men [N = 695])

	Frequency		*Frequency*
Businessman and		College Professor	
Business Executive		or Teacher	
Social Sciences,		Chemistry, Mathematics,	
Psychology	9	Physics	13
Business Administration	7	Humanities	11
Economics	5	Political Science,	
Engineering	3	Sociology	3
Language	2	Education	2
Natural Sciences	2	Engineering	2
Mixed majors	4	Mixed majors	2
Undecided	3	No response	8
No response	8		—
	—		41
	43		
		Physicist	
		Physics	25
Engineer		Natural Sciences,	
Engineering	47	Mathematics	3
Natural Sciences,		No response	2
Mathematics	5		—
Mixed majors	2		30
No response	14		
	—	Other Occupations	
	68	(including double	
		choices)	
Foreign Service		Social Sciences,	
Political Science	15	Psychology	17
Social Sciences	4	Natural Sciences,	
Humanities	2	Mathematics	9
Mathematics	1	Humanities	8
No response	1	Engineering	5
	—		—
	23		39

TABLE 33—Continued

PROBABLE FUTURE OCCUPATION BY PROBABLE MAJOR FIELD OF STUDY
(Men [N = 695])

	Frequency		*Frequency*
Lawyer		Undecided About	
Political Science	18	Occupation	
Humanities	15	Social Sciences	13
Pre-law	11	Natural Sciences,	
Economics	5	Mathematics	11
Engineering	5	Engineering	6
Other Social Sciences	4	Speech	1
Mixed majors	5	Mixed majors	7
Undecided	5	Undecided	53
No response	13	No response	10
	—		—
	81		101
Mathematician		No Response	
Mathematics	16	Natural Sciences,	
Engineering	1	Mathematics	20
No response	2	Engineering	16
	—	Social Sciences,	
	19	Psychology	16
		Humanities	10
Physician		Premed	6
Premed	43	Mixed majors	5
Natural Sciences	23	Undecided	16
Psychology	4	No response	31
Language, Philosophy	3		—
Economics	1		120
Mixed majors	1		
Undecided	1		
No response	17		
	—		
	93		

Considering the pressure that our society brings to bear on the individual to make a decision, it is interesting to note that 13 per cent of the freshman men explicitly stated that they were undecided. In addition, another 13 per cent did not answer this question. This category of "No Response" is ambiguous, but one would expect that a large segment of the 13 per cent were also undecided. When one considers the large proportion of students who shift from one career commitment to another during their undergraduate years, one realizes that the ranks of the undecided are probably much larger than they appear to be at first glance.

What happened to these men after graduation? Table 34 presents the data organized according to the undergraduate college from which each student graduated, and lists seven different alternative activities the student might be expected to engage in after graduation. Although the percentages vary slightly for the several undergraduate colleges, on the average, about 65 per cent of the sample were in graduate school when they filled out the questionnaire.

TABLE 34

SCHOOL LAST REGISTERED IN AS UNDERGRADUATE AND
PRESENT ACTIVITY
(Men [N = 502])

	Frequency	Per cent
School of Humanities and Sciences (N = 420)		
Graduate School	281	67
Job	51	12
Military Service	38	9
Other—unclassified	34	8
Peace Corps	11	3
Other Volunteer Work	4	1
Seeking Employment	1	0
School of Engineering (N = 58)		
Graduate School	37	64
Job	9	15
Other—unclassified	8	14
Military Service	4	7
Did Not Indicate School (N = 24)		
Other—unclassified	9	38
Graduate School	8	33
Job	5	21
Military Service	2	8

We are now in a position to bring together our two sets of data: freshman career expectations and postgraduate status. In Table 35, we have listed the postgraduate status of students who started as freshmen with similar occupational choices. There is a varying relationship between the freshman career preference and the likelihood that a student will go on to graduate school. We would expect this, because it requires a different kind of commitment to say, "I am going to be a physician," than it does to say, "I plan to be a lawyer." The future physician is tacitly saying that he is willing to go along a well-defined path during his undergraduate years, in addition to enduring the rigors of medical school. The future lawyer has much more freedom in course selection during his undergraduate years, as well as in the type of occupation the law degree will enable him to enter. There is some evidence in our data (and in the data of cognitive dissonance studies) suggesting that decisions requiring more psychological commitment from the very beginning also carry with them the likelihood of greater perseverance.

TABLE 35

FRESHMAN OCCUPATIONAL CHOICE AND POSTGRADUATE STATUS
(Men [N = 337])

	Frequency	Per cent
Business Executive (N = 8)		
Graduate School	5	
Military Service	2	
Job	1	
Businessman (N = 12)		
Graduate School	7	
Job	3	
Military Service	2	
Engineer (N = 32)		
Graduate School	15	47
Job	7	22
Military Service	4	13
Other Work	4	13
Other Volunteer Work	1	3
Unknown	1	3
Lawyer (N = 62)		
Graduate School	37	59
Other Work	8	13
Job	7	11
Military Service	4	7
Peace Corps	3	5
Other Volunteer Work	1	2
Unknown	2	4
Mathematician (N = 11)		
Graduate School	9	
Unknown	2	

TABLE 35—Continued

FRESHMAN OCCUPATIONAL CHOICE AND POSTGRADUATE STATUS
(Men [N = 337])

	Frequency	*Per cent*
Physician (N = 53)		
Graduate School	42	79
Other Work	4	8
Job	3	6
Military Service	1	2
Peace Corps	1	2
Other Volunteer Work	1	2
Unknown	1	2
Physicist (N = 21)		
Graduate School	17	81
Other Volunteer Work	1	5
Unknown	3	15
Undecided (N = 71)		
Graduate School	37	52
Job	12	17
Military Service	8	11
Peace Corps	3	4
Unknown	11	15
No Response (N = 67)		
Graduate School	42	63
Other Work	7	10
Job	6	9
Military Service	3	5
Peace Corps	2	3
Unknown	7	10

Of those freshmen who expressed an interest in becoming a physician, 79 per cent were in medical school or in some graduate program at the time of our follow-up study, whereas 59 per cent of those who had expressed an interest in law as freshmen were in law school or in some graduate program. About half of those who were undecided or did not indicate a career direction were also in graduate school during the first year after graduation. In keeping with our expectations, these percentages are smaller than for some of the groups with explicit career directions. Nevertheless, they suggest that freshman indecision cannot be taken as an index of lack of motivation for graduate study.

In order to focus attention on the complexity of the process of career selection, it is necessary to point out an exception to our generalization concerning degree of commitment and perseverance. Undergraduate engineers would seem to be making a commitment to a definite undergraduate program, yet we find a large percentage of these students engaged in something other than engineering after graduation. Through interviews with these students, we were able to look more deeply into their motives, and discovered that many viewed engineering as a stepping-stone to some other career. This suggests the importance to the investigator of assigning a carefully defined meaning to "commitment."

We can now return to an examination of the extent to which the freshman's choice of a future occupation is congruent with what he is doing in graduate school. The definitions of congruence must be made clear. We shall, as we go along, offer several different operational meanings. One definition is particularly obvious: a counting of the number of students who are pursuing postgraduate careers with some apparent direct relationship to freshman career choice.

In Table 36, we trace the graduate and professional school choices of men who had expressed different career expectations as freshmen. For example, we see from Table 35 that 62 men who expressed interest in law as freshmen returned follow-up questionnaires. Table 35 also indicates that 37 of these men were in graduate school. From Table 36 we see that of those 37 men,

TABLE 36

FRESHMAN OCCUPATIONAL CHOICE AND PRESENT
GRADUATE SCHOOL PROGRAM
(Men [N = 198])

	Frequency	Per cent
Business Executive (N = 5)		
School of Business	3	
Psychology	1	
School of Law	1	
Businessmen (N = 7)		
School of Business	3	
History	2	
School of Law	2	
Engineer (N = 15)		
School of Business	9	60
Engineering	3	20
Architecture	1	7

TABLE 36—Continued

FRESHMAN OCCUPATIONAL CHOICE AND PRESENT
GRADUATE SCHOOL PROGRAM
(Men [N = 198])

	Frequency	Per cent
Divinity School	1	7
School of Medicine	1	7
Lawyer (N = 36)		
School of Law	25	69
English, History	4	11
Political Science	2	6
School of Business	2	6
Advertising	1	3
General Studies	1	3
School of Medicine	1	3
Mathematician (N = 9)		
School of Business	2	
Accounting	1	
Computer Science	1	
Divinity School	1	
Economics	1	
History	1	
Operations Research	1	
Psychology	1	
Physician (N = 42)		
School of Medicine	28	67
Natural Sciences	5	12
English, History	3	7
School of Law	3	7
School of Business	2	5
Counseling	1	2
Physicist (N = 14)		
Physics	5	36
Other Natural Sciences	5	36
School of Business	2	14
Psychology	1	7
School of Education	1	7
Undecided as a Freshman (N = 28)		
Humanities	8	28
School of Business	5	18
Natural Sciences, Mathematics	4	14
School of Education	3	11
Economics, Psychology	2	7
School of Medicine	2	7
Divinity School	1	4
Government Work	1	4
Industrial Relations	1	4
Veterinary School	1	4

TABLE 36—Continued

FRESHMAN OCCUPATIONAL CHOICE AND PRESENT
GRADUATE SCHOOL PROGRAM
(Men [N = 198])

	Frequency	Per cent
No Response as a Freshman (N = 42)		
Humanities	9	21
Natural Sciences, Mathematics	8	19
Social Sciences, Psychology	8	19
School of Law	7	17
School of Business	5	12
School of Medicine	4	10
Dentistry	1	2

25 were in law school at the time of the follow-up study, and the others were in a variety of other fields. Upon examining the results for the 32 freshman men who indicated a preference for engineering, we note from Table 35 that 15 were in graduate school one year after graduation. Table 36 indicates that of those 15 men, only 3 were in graduate programs in engineering, whereas 9 were enrolled in a graduate school of business. The remaining 3 students were enrolled in schools of architecture, divinity, and medicine.

We are interested in evaluating these findings both from the perspective of the degree of satisfaction the individual will obtain from his choice and from that of optimal utilization of talent in a society that has strong need for well-trained individuals. It is significant that 65 per cent of the class attended graduate school immediately following graduation. From the perspective of the production of men with degrees, the educational system is clearly working. Whether or not it is working to produce the quality of talent needed in our society cannot, of course, be answered by the data thus far presented; nor have we determined whether or not the system is helping each individual make the most satisfying choice. In order to come even partially to grips with these questions, we must examine other kinds of data. This examination will also serve to further our analysis of congruence between freshman choice and eventual decision.

The first factor to be considered is how the students we have been describing differ from one another with respect to certain standard academic measures. Here we are interested in both the student's overall aptitude for traditional academic work and his actual academic performance. Table 37 lists the cumulative grade-point averages (GPA) and the Scholastic Aptitude Test (SAT) scores for eight different groups of students. Most of the differences in academic performance between these eight groups are accounted for in three categories: graduate business students, engineering graduates who are employed, and humanities and science graduates who are employed. It is the last two groups that account for most of the differences in the verbal scale of the SAT.

TABLE 37

FOLLOW-UP QUESTIONNAIRE STATUS DURING THE 1966–67 YEAR [a]
(Men)

Senior Cumulative Grade Point Average

	N	X	SD	1	2	3	4	5	6	7	8
Graduate School—Engineering	22	3.09	.37							*	*
Graduate School—History	20	3.07	.42							*	*
Graduate School—Science	16	2.93	.41								*
School of Business	44	2.74	.35	*	*		*	*			
School of Law	56	2.98	.41							*	*
School of Medicine	35	2.96	.29							*	*
Engineering Graduate w/job	6	2.62	.29								
Humanities/Science Graduate w/job	48	2.63	.37								

Verbal SAT

	N	X	SD	1	2	3	4	5	6	7	8
Graduate School—Engineering	21	632	61							*	
Graduate School—History	22	638	63							*	*
Graduate School—Science	18	642	58							*	*
School of Business	47	609	63						*		
School of Law	63	647	57							*	*
School of Medicine	41	624	61						*	*	
Engineering Graduate w/job	6	570	53								
Humanities/Science Graduate w/job	48	605	65								

Math SAT

	N	X	SD	1	2	3	4	5	6	7	8
Graduate School—Engineering	21	692	58					*	*		*
Graduate School—History	22	631	62								
Graduate School—Science	18	721	62						*	*	
School of Business	47	668	68					*			
School of Law	63	658	70								*
School of Medicine	41	669	55					*	*		
Engineering Graduate w/job	6	668	42								
Humanities/Science Graduate w/job	48	655	76								

[a] t tests were made between all pairs, and those significant at the .05 level are indicated by an asterisk (*) in the matrix of results.

We might make the cautious generalization that men who find positions immediately after graduation from Stanford tend to have relatively low GPA's and low verbal aptitude scores. We find, however, that in mathematical aptitude scores, these three groups do not differ radically from the others. Given this evidence that the employed group possess a high aptitude for quantitative reasoning and have relatively low cumulative grade-point averages, we can formulate the hypothesis that these men have a certain constellation of aptitudes that are not rewarded as much as others at Stanford. This is not to suggest that the whole undergraduate curriculum should be made more quantitative in emphasis for the good of this subgroup of students. It does, however, raise some questions about the use of different styles of teaching and the breadth of our concept of academic learning. Considering the need in our society for men with skills of quantitative reasoning, it is incumbent upon educators to search for ways to make the entire curriculum meaningful to students whose patterns of aptitudes and skills differ widely.

A more traditional view of this evidence might be that these students were simply not motivated to work very hard. Whether the institution has failed these students, or whether the students have failed themselves, or some complex interaction has occurred, cannot be answered by our data. Still, the fact remains that by some of the prevailing standards of our society, these students are not fulfilling themselves; and since graduate education is becoming the new national standard of achievement, this situation may result in a loss of self-esteem for the student as well as a loss of talent for society.

With regard to the optimal development of individual talents, our concern should not be limited to those students who lack such an obvious sign of success as acceptance by a graduate school. Moreover, our data raise significant questions about those who do go on to graduate school. Much of the data in Table 37 suggest that students entering widely diverse fields may have remarkably similar patterns of aptitudes and levels of academic performance. (A notable exception are the science students, who have an extremely high level of aptitude for quantitative reasoning.) A superficial view of these data would suggest that the careers men pursue are interchangeable. Yet a large literature in the social sciences suggests that a career choice is a very personal expression of the complex human personality.[1] If work is to be a continuing source of intrinsic satisfaction, it must involve significant segments of the individual's system of needs, wishes, and aspirations. In order to deal with this question, we must turn to our next level of analysis and examine the variables that tap these complex human motivations. Here congruence between freshman choice and eventual decision is considered from a psychologically more sophisticated point of view.

The traditional approach to a discussion of the appropriateness of an individual's career choice places great emphasis on his measured interests. One of the most widely used measures in this field is the Strong Vocational Interest Blank. The essential goal of this instrument is to compare the interests of an individual with those of men in general, and with those of men employed in particular occupations. Approximately fifty different occupations are represented in the Strong inventory, and for purposes of ease of conceptualization, these are often reduced to seven "families" of occupations. These seven groups are organized on the basis of the intercorrelation between scales, and thus represent a distillation or focusing of different kinds of interests. For each of these seven families of interest, a scale is given representing the degree of interest. A primary pattern indicating the greatest degree of interest represents a majority of A or B+ scores on the occupational scales in a family of occupations. A secondary pattern, the next level of interest, represents a majority of B+ or B scores on the occupational scales in a family of occupations. At the other extreme, if the student shows a less-than-average amount of interest, he has a "reject" pattern, with all scores below C. Scores not in these categories are referred to as "other" patterns.

We have complete information for 55 men who expressed interest as freshmen in a future law career. Table 38 gives the Strong interest patterns for these men according to their postgraduate status. The lawyer scale appears in the verbal-linguistic family of occupations, and we would expect students expressing an interest in law as a career to have high scores in this area. Of

[1] Borow, Henry, *Man in a World of Work* (Boston: Houghton-Mifflin, 1964), gives an integrated view of this literature.

those entering the School of Law, 13 had either a primary or secondary pattern in the area, and 12 had an "other" pattern. Of those entering graduate school, four had either a primary or a secondary pattern, and three had an "other" pattern. Of those engaged in secondary activities, eight had primary or secondary patterns, and 15 had "other" patterns. The same variability in matching measured interests and career choice is reflected in the data for physicians and engineers. Using a primary or secondary pattern as an index of appropriateness of interest, we find that approximately half the men in law and medicine had an appropriate constellation of interests.

TABLE 38

STRONG PATTERN ANALYSIS FOR STUDENTS WHOSE
FRESHMAN CAREER CHOICE WAS LAW
(Men [N = 55])

	1 (Prim)	2 (Sec)	5 (Other)	9 (Reject)
Attending School of Law (N = 25)				
Biological Science		2 (8%)	21 (84%)	2 (8%)
Business Detail	4 (16%)	3 (12%)	18 (72%)	
Physical Science			20 (80%)	5 (20%)
Sales	6 (24%)	6 (24%)	13 (52%)	
Social Service	3 (12%)	6 (24%)	14 (56%)	2 (8%)
Technical		1 (4%)	23 (92%)	1 (4%)
Verbal	5 (20%)	8 (32%)	12 (48%)	
Attending Other Graduate Schools (N = 7)				
Biological Science			5 (71%)	2 (28%)
Business Detail	3 (43%)	4 (57%)		
Physical Science			4 (57%)	3 (42%)
Sales	3 (43%)	1 (14%)	3 (43%)	
Social Service	1 (14%)		6 (86%)	
Technical		1 (14%)	6 (86%)	
Verbal	2 (29%)	2 (29%)	3 (43%)	
Other Plans (N = 23)				
Biological Science			16 (70%)	7 (30%)
Business Detail	6 (26%)	4 (17%)	13 (57%)	
Physical Science		1 (4%)	17 (74%)	5 (22%)
Sales	6 (26%)	7 (30%)	10 (43%)	
Social Service	4 (17%)	4 (17%)	14 (61%)	1 (4%)
Technical		2 (9%)	20 (87%)	1 (4%)
Verbal	3 (13%)	5 (22%)	15 (65%)	

In Table 39, results are given for the respective occupational scales of the three groups: lawyer, physician, and engineer. Using the B+ category as a minimum criterion for judging appropriateness of career choice, we can examine what happened to the men in the three career groups. Only half the men attending a school of law shared the interests of other lawyers, whereas 80 per cent of the men attending a school of medicine had interests in common with other physicians. (It is of interest to note that men who had a professional career in mind as freshmen, and are now attending other graduate schools in pursuit of other paths to a career, had a higher proportion of B+ or higher scores than those entering the field represented by the scale.)

TABLE 39

FRESHMAN CAREER CHOICE PHYSICIANS AND
STRONG PHYSICIAN SCALE
(Men [N = 141])

	C−	C	C+	B	B+	A	(N)
In Medical School		3		3	2	20	(28)
Other Graduate Schools			1	2	2	9	(14)
Not in Graduate School	1			1		8	(10)
				$\chi^2 = 8$		N.S.	

FRESHMAN CAREER CHOICE ENGINEERS AND
STRONG ENGINEERING SCALE

	C−	C	C+	B	B+	A	(N)
In Graduate Engineering					2		(2)
Other Graduate Schools	2	1	3	2		4	(12)
Not in Graduate School		1	2	3	3	7	(16)
				$\chi^2 = 17$		N.S.	

FRESHMAN CAREER CHOICE LAWYERS AND
STRONG LAWYER SCALE

	C−	C	C+	B	B+	A	(N)
In Law School		2	2	8	6	7	(25)
Other Graduate Schools				4	3	4	(11)
Not in Graduate School	1	4	4	6	1	7	(23)
				$\chi^2 = 12$		N.S.	

When we examine the results of the Strong in the light of what happened to the career plans of our students, questions arise concerning the permanence and stability of interests during the college years. Traditionally, interests were thought to be fairly stable, but we see evidence in our data of a good deal of shifting. Therefore, the Strong results for a freshman may not be an accurate representation of the same student's interests as a senior. Furthermore, just as there is evidence that interests may not be as stable as we once thought, there is also evidence that occupations are in a state of transition. If this is so, how appropriate are the original occupational criterion groups used in the construction of the Strong? The most obvious example of change is the field of engineering, which has been transformed in the last twenty years; but other occupations and professions, too, are undergoing similar revolutions.

In view of this evidence, our next move must be to question the use of the Strong Vocational Interest Blank in counseling and guidance. To the extent that the counselor sees his job as that of helping the individual match his interests with a specific career, he must be careful to take into account both the evolving nature of the individual's interests and the evolving nature of occupations. It would seem appropriate, therefore, to encourage the college student to think of himself as continually developing. Students should be encouraged to assess their interests when they enter as freshmen, again at the end of their sophomore year, and again when they are seniors. If the present structure of college majors were modified to allow such a plan to become a practical reality, students would be free to experiment, rather than being forced to arbitrarily choose a major.

Thus far, our intent has been to present a detailed description of the career aspirations and the first step of career realization for a group of talented men. We have focused our attention on several groups of men who, as freshmen, expressed an interest in professional careers, because this permitted us to illustrate several trends representative of the entire class. Most obvious of these trends is the shift in career direction for large numbers of men between the freshman year and the year following graduation (see Table 36). In itself, this is not at all surprising, given the tentativeness of the freshman commitment and the four years of intervening experience. Trends that are less obvious, but are nevertheless of central concern, have to do with factors contributing to an individual's decision whether to stay with an early career commitment or to change. Following an analysis of data for women in this same class, we will turn to a more general discussion of factors influencing the career selection process among the students in our sample.

Freshman women's responses to questions concerning probable major field of study and probable future occupation are cross-tabulated in Table 40. The single largest category among future occupations is teaching at other than the college level, which accounts for 14 per cent of the students. Consideration of the probable major field of these potential teachers reveals a broad range of interests, in which "language" is the largest single category.

TABLE 40

PROBABLE MAJOR FIELD OF STUDY BY PROBABLE FUTURE OCCUPATION
(Women [N = 362])

	Frequency		Frequency
Artist		Journalist	
Fine Arts	4	Humanities	4
History	1	Journalism	3
	—	Social Science	2
	5	Mixed Major	1
		No response	1
Biological Scientist			—
Biology	5		11
Other Natural Sciences	5		
	—	Mathematician	
	10	Mathematics	9
			—
Chemist			9
Chemistry	7		
Other Natural Sciences	1	Physician	
No response	1	Premed	8
	—	Natural Sciences	3
	9	Undecided	1
		No response	1
College Professor			—
Humanities	8		13
Mathematics	2		
Political Science	1	Physicist	
Mixed Major	1	Physics	4
Undecided	1	No response	1
	—		—
	13		5

TABLE 40—Continued

PROBABLE MAJOR FIELD OF STUDY BY PROBABLE FUTURE OCCUPATION
(Women [N = 362])

	Frequency		Frequency
Foreign Service Aide		Psychologist	
Political Science	13	Psychology	7
Language	7	No response	1
History	2		—
Other Social Sciences	2		8
Mixed Major	1		
No response	6	Social Worker	
	—	Sociology	3
	31	Social Sciences	2
Housewife			—
Humanities	4		5
Fine Arts	1	Teacher	
Mixed Major	1	Other Humanities	21
Undecided	3	Languages	12
No response	1	Education	8
	—	Mathematics	6
	10	Biochemistry	1
Housewife with Job		Psychology	1
Natural Sciences	3	Mixed Major	2
Humanities	2	Undecided	2
Social Sciences	2	No response	4
	—		—
	7		57
Interpreter		No Response	
Language	5	Humanities	10
Mathematics	1	Natural Sciences,	
	—	Mathematics	8
	6	Social Sciences,	
Other		Psychology	4
Natural Sciences,		Mixed Major	7
Mathematics	10	Undecided	8
Humanities	8	No response	16
Social Sciences	4		—
Mixed Major	7		53
Undecided	1		
No response	6		
	—		
	36		
Undecided			
Humanities	11		
Social Sciences	8		
Natural Sciences,			
Mathematics	3		
Mixed Major	4		
Undecided	38		
No response	10		
	—		
	74		

It is noteworthy that only about 5 per cent of the freshman women indicated "housewife" as a future occupation. It is apparent that many others planned to marry, but at this point in their lives did not define being a housewife as an occupation. Among all the women, the largest single category for probable future occupation was "undecided." This accounted for approximately 20 per cent of the women. Another 12 per cent did not respond to the question concerning future occupation. Five or fewer women chose the following occupations: advertising executive; architect; businesswoman; clerk (business); engineer; government aide; laboratory technician; lawyer; musician; nurse; speech therapist.

Moving five years ahead in the lives of these students, we can examine the outcome of their early statements of choice. Follow-up data for the women are summarized in Table 41 which shows the status of these women approximately nine months after graduation. Some 35 per cent of our sample were attending graduate school in some capacity, although only 28 per cent were full-time graduate students. The two other largest categories are made up of (1) women who were employed and (2) women who were married. Each of these categories accounted for approximately a third of the group.

TABLE 41

SCHOOL LAST REGISTERED IN AS AN UNDERGRADUATE AND
PRESENT ACTIVITY
(Women [N = 301])

	Frequency	Per cent
School of Humanities and Science (N = 279)		
Job	89	32
Housewife	77	28
With Job (37)		
Attending Graduate School (24)		
Housewife Only (10)		
Other (6)		
Graduate School	73	26
Graduate School and Job	19	7
Other Work	9	3
Seeking Employment	6	2
Peace Corps	3	1
Other Volunteer Work	2	1
Travel	1	1

TABLE 41—Continued

SCHOOL LAST REGISTERED IN AS AN UNDERGRADUATE AND
PRESENT ACTIVITY
(Women [N = 301])

	Frequency	Per cent
School of Education (N = 9)		
Graduate School	7	
Housewife	1	
Travel	1	
School of Engineering (N = 2)		
Graduate School	1	
Job	1	
Did Not Indicate Undergraduate School (N = 11)		
Graduate School	4	
Housewife	3	
Peace Corps	2	
Other Work	2	

The various graduate fields entered by these women are presented in Table 42. The largest single group was in a school of education. While this cannot necessarily be equated with preparation for teaching, it does bear some relationship to the freshman figures regarding an early interest in teaching.

TABLE 42

SCHOOL LAST REGISTERED IN AS AN UNDERGRADUATE AND
PRESENT GRADUATE FIELD OF STUDY
(Women [N = 77])

	Frequency	Per cent
School of Earth Science (N = 1)		
Chemistry	1	
School of Education (N = 7)		
Education	7	
School of Engineering (N = 1)		
Education	1	
School of Humanities and Science (N = 68)		
Humanities	20	29
School of Education	17	25
Social Sciences, Psychology	10	15
School of Medicine	7	10
Natural Sciences	4	6
Library Science	2	3
Physical Therapy	2	3
School of Business	2	3
School of Law	2	3
Other	2	3

When we categorize these Stanford women on the basis of what they were doing nine months after graduation, their respective grade-point averages and aptitude scores reveal some interesting patterns. It becomes clear that the women who were full-time graduate students had the highest undergraduate GPA's. Many of the differences between groups on GPA are small, however, and are not statistically significant. The greatest difference occurred between full-time graduate students and those who were employed full time. An examination of differences between these groups on their verbal aptitude scores reveals results similar to those of the men. Again, the largest difference occurred between full-time graduate students and women employed full time. It is of interest to note that women who were both married and attending graduate school had the highest mean aptitude scores. Quantitative aptitude scores revealed no significant difference among groups.

Why do some women go on to graduate school while others do not? Both GPA and aptitude differences between the several groups are so slight that very little of the variance is accounted for by them. It is natural, therefore, to consider interest and motivation as bases for understanding the differences among these women. Responses to the Strong Vocational Interest Blank administered at the time of their entrance to college were studied in an effort to discover why some women chose to continue their educations and others did not. Since the greatest disparity on other counts existed between those women who chose to attend graduate school full time and those who had taken full-time jobs, it seemed desirable to examine the scores of these two groups on each of the 25 scales of the Strong inventory. Results of the four scales on which significant differences occurred are presented in Table 43. It is important to note that there was remarkably little difference between these two groups, whose goals appeared to be so far apart—a finding in keeping with the unimpressive differences in other variables.

Results of the four scales do suggest some trends. The job-only group had more high scores on the Office Worker scale. Conversely, the graduate-school-only group had more high scores on the Social Worker, Music Teacher, and Occupational Therapist scales. At first glance, it would seem that the graduate school

TABLE 43

INDIVIDUAL STRONG SCALE SCORES FOR WOMEN ENTERING
GRADUATE SCHOOL AND OTHER OCCUPATIONS

	C	C+	B−	B	B+	A	(N)
Music Teacher							
Graduate School	30		18		8		(56)
Job Only	61		12		6		(79)
					$\chi^2 = 6.90$	.05	
Occupational Therapist							
Graduate School	11		22		23		(56)
Job Only	57		6		6		(69)
					$\chi^2 = 39$	.01	
Office Worker							
Graduate School	36		7		3		(46)
Job Only	30		33		16		(79)
					$\chi^2 = 10.96$	.01	
Social Worker							
Graduate School	4	5	12	10	12	11	(54)
Job Only	24	8	17	16	5	9	(79)
					$\chi^2 = 13.29$	.05	

women exhibited something that might be called a professional social service interest. Nevertheless, in view of the many "professional" scales for which there was no significant difference, this kind of designation must be offered tentatively. One of the non-significant differences deserves special attention because it tends to contradict some popular misconceptions: the graduate-school women were not significantly different from the employed women on the Masculinity-Femininity scale. The most striking fact revealed by the data is that slightly less than half as many women as men are now in graduate school. Given the high level of ability represented by this group of women, a sure loss of academically trained talent is evident. If there were evidence that the decision to continue or not to continue had been made on the basis of measured interests, this finding would be less alarming. Yet no strong evidence is revealed of differences between the group of women going to graduate school and those choosing other alternatives.

In order to put these results into context, let us briefly cite some of the overall results of our four-year study reported in

Chapter 1. Our data suggest that students are moving on to important career choices without a careful evaluation of what they most want for themselves. Does this mean that most seniors are actively dissatisfied? On the Senior Questionnaire they were asked, "How sure are you that your present choice of career or occupation is the most appropriate for you?" Approximately 70 per cent of the men and women said that they were very sure or moderately sure. Clearly there was no widespread anxiety on this point. Yet when they were asked at the same time, "To what extent has your planning for your life's work involved you in a struggle of conflicting thoughts and feelings?" about 80 per cent of the men and women answered, "Very much," or "Moderately." Does this indicate that the conflict had been resolved, and that the students were as sure of the appropriateness of their choices as they indicated? It is impossible to draw any firm conclusions. The data do suggest, however, that large numbers of very talented students appear to be choosing careers on some other basis than that of their measured interests. It is not our intent to use measured interests as an ultimate criterion of the wisdom of an individual's career choice. Rather, we are simply using the Strong Vocational Interest Blank as a crude mirror to help reflect some aspects of an extremely complex process.

The very complexity of this process demands that we go beyond that which is easily quantifiable. One kind of analysis that adds clarity is the study of individual cases. In Chapters 2 and 6 of this report, case studies are presented that serve to illuminate the process of career choice. But in spite of the fact that case studies can reveal the variety and subtlety of the psychological forces that bear on the individual, they cannot pinpoint the many social forces that also affect him. Let us now outline some of these social forces, and describe briefly the impact they have on the lives of students.

There is a beguiling ease and orderliness to the process by which college seniors become graduate students, employees, or members of the military services. Every year the sorting takes place and the economy prospers. The whole structure of higher education is designed to produce external signs of success, and to focus only rarely on the needs of the individual. But only if the needs of the individual are fulfilled can orderliness become a symptom and the conventional analysis of success be seen as a criterion of wastefulness and inefficiency.

A prevailing opinion in both the home and the school is that the young person should decide for himself what direction to take toward a future career. The pressure to decide is often so great that the individual begins to feel there is no time for a genuine exploration of career possibilities. This all starts very innocently—when, for example, we jokingly encourage or discourage the child's wish to be a fireman when he grows up. The humor disappears, however, when the adolescent begins to feel the pressures on him to amass the grade-point average that will allow him to enter a "prestige" college. We say very piously to the high school student that we want him to develop his individual talents, and to eventually pursue a career that will be maximally fulfilling. At the same time, the secondary school and the student's parents are so committed to helping him achieve college entrance that they focus their primary attention on the achievement itself. While the student is told that he has freedom of choice, it is made clear to him that this freedom has to be earned by achievement. This emphasis in our society upon achievement as a vehicle for the attainment of something else is both pervasive and pernicious.

Students are expected to work hard in high school in order to gain admittance to college. Once admitted, they must work hard in college so that they will gain admittance to graduate or professional school. Finally, they are told that they must work hard in graduate school in order to start out well in the "real world," which is much akin to the student's world in its emphasis on scholastic achievement as a vehicle. The rewards of the game are different, however, with financial gain replacing cumulative grade-point average as a goal. If the student begins to doubt the value of the system that determines so much of his behavior, he is forced to deal with a wide variety of consequences arising from not playing the game. The system of rewards and punishments that are part of the outside world is brought home to the student in a variety of ways: the disgrace of the hard-working high school senior who fails to gain acceptance by the college of his choice; the ever-increasing escalation of educational requirements for nearly all the most desirable positions; the discovery in later life that he has been passed over for a promotion in lieu of someone with more impressive academic credentials. It is easy to imagine the price paid by those students who, for one reason or another, cannot play the game as defined by the system. What is harder to see, but is perhaps of even greater consequence to our society, is the price paid by those who do play the game. Dropping into place can be fully as disastrous as dropping out of school.

The plight of the adolescent caught between his personal sense of urgency about immediate concerns and the vast array of constraints he feels are put in his way, is grave indeed. The adolescent is particularly sensitive to the contradiction we have been describing. He is told that his life is his own; yet he is expected to follow a certain preordained pattern in his daily behavior. "Postponement" is the password offered; if he can accept this, doors will be opened to him later. It is before college that this contradiction is most clearly visible. For twelve years, the student is encouraged to think—or at least to do work requiring intelligence—in order to meet an external set of demands and expectations. Inherent in the emphasis on achievement as a vehicle and postponement as a rationale is an unavoidable danger that the sense of meaningful participation we ask him to postpone will in fact be lost to him.

The freshness of approach and passionate involvement of the adolescent are qualities we search for in many segments of the adult world. That such characteristics are hard to find is evident; and it would appear that they are hard to find because many of our educational procedures systematically train individuals to deny them. It is not that this is planned in the program; rather, it is an inevitable result of the emphasis on achievement as a vehicle. Adolescents want answers to their questions. When they discover that the formal requirements of school do not provide such answers, they remove themselves psychologically from their studies. The capacity to do this permits adolescents to work hard at school tasks while pursuing their own inquiries in their own fashion; but as they enter college, many of them still entertain the great hope of integrating the several parts of their lives.

For the adolescent, preparation, postponement, and paternal constraints are all worth putting up with because they carry with them the promise of the unknown but sought-after college experience. The entering college freshman is remarkable in his willingness to try out new ideas and modes of behavior. This is not to deny the great impact of his previous twelve years of schooling upon his capacity for independent thinking, nor to deny the effects of eighteen years of socialization—an experience perceived by parents as a gift they themselves bestow upon their children. But the intellectual atmosphere of a liberal arts college, the heightened influence and emotional impact of the peer-group, and the anxiety associated with the challenge of a new adventure all combine to form the ingredients for growth and change.

Although the entering freshman may be ready scholastically to engage in higher education, a wide variety of factors combine to thwart this desire. Long before he began to think seriously about going to college, higher education was confronting him with a series of inescapable requirements. College preparatory courses were taken, not as a matter of conscious decision but rather as a mandate from the system. He was probably not strongly encouraged to develop his intellectual skills in order to have a better chance of understanding himself and the world around him. Instead, hard work was justified to him on the grounds that it would lead to high scores on college board examinations. Thus, the freshman's eagerness is restricted by his having been conditioned to accept the inevitable demands of the system. The freshman year itself is a curious introduction to the contradictions inherent in the liberal arts curriculum. It contains many of the same elements of emphasis upon preparation and absence of choice that the student experienced in high school. Yet it contains elements of a learning experience that can set the student free. Many will come in contact with teachers, other students, or books that will have a profound impact on their thinking about themselves and the world around them. Whether a student builds on such an experience will depend on a host of factors in his past. The student's history will, in many ways, condition his response to fresh stimuli and new ideas.

The typical liberal arts college discourages the student from pursuing the avowed goals of a liberal education. Time is needed to follow a thought and its ramifications through to some satisfactory stopping point; but when the student does get caught up in his work, he can go only so far with it because the demands of the curriculum require that his intellectual energies be directed elsewhere. Yet students continue to accept the frustration inherent in this system. The explanation has already been suggested in part: their whole school experience has trained them to trade something that may not be meaningful now for the promise of something better in the future. Just as the academic experience in high school prepares the student to accept the early contradictions inherent in the liberal arts curriculum, so does the early emphasis on career selection prepare him for contradictions at the college level. Is the liberal arts program designed to prepare for a career, or to encourage development of individual talent? From the time he fills out his first application form, the student is asked what his interests are, what major he plans to elect, and what career he hopes to pursue. While he is assured that he is not honor-bound to stay with his major, and that he may even elect a General Studies program for the first two years of college, he is nevertheless forced to make at least a token decision based on an eventual career—in other words, on the demands of a graduate school or a future employer.

Insofar as the operational definition of goals is concerned, many prestige universities suffer from a disorder akin to schizophrenia. The aims of education should be twofold: to provide a liberal education, and to make available the best in specialized study. The prestige college is caught in the same crossfire as the adolescent, because it defines its goals in light of the demands of the society that supports it. For various complex reasons, whether these goals are compatible or even necessary is not raised as a serious question. We single out one of these reasons because it is central to the main theme of this chapter.

The faculties of prestige colleges are made up of outstanding specialists who are deeply committed to their professions. These men are in the forefront of their own areas of knowledge, and as a consequence are often far removed from the level of understanding of the undergraduate. Not only does specialization become a way of life for the faculty member, but it produces certain psychological consequences for others also. One of these consequences is commitment to the value of specialized knowledge. Some faculty members secretly scorn the goals of a broad liberal education. Many introductory courses taught by specialists become reviews of past and present frontiers of knowledge in which the need to equip the student for his own intellectual explorations is quite forgotten. Courses purportedly designed to enlarge the intellectual skills of the student and to encourage new perspectives often become effective barriers to independent thought. In addition to failing to contribute to the student's intellectual development, these courses also reinforce in his mind the value placed on specialized thought and the importance of developing some specialized skills of his own. For many undergraduates, experience with the curriculum becomes a source of great disappointment, because they find it no more meaningful in their lives than their high school curriculum was. Nevertheless, they are pressured from every side to fix upon a major and a career. How are they to arrive at an appropriate decision?

In an ideal sense, a college is organized to encourage the student to search for intellectual understanding. This kind of personal search, however, is often thwarted by the student's need to satisfy other demands that he feels are more important to him. Intellectual understanding takes second place to the student's need for acceptance and security. He becomes involved in a search for the personal satisfaction inherent in private goals and immediate rewards. Freshmen arrive at college with widely divergent concepts of themselves, their talents, and their goals. Common to all is the hope of gaining an answer to the question of how to give meaning to their lives, and how to pursue an orderly path through a maze of contradictory pressures. Some students find meaning and order by narrowly defining what they want in terms of training for a career. Others are so diffuse in their goals, and have such complex problems of personal meaning to resolve, that their academic work is virtually isolated from their real lives. In both instances, there are extremes of response that would be difficult for any college to handle adequately.

For the vast number of students who have the openness to consider actively the potential richness of the curriculum and the personal soundness to be responsive to new experiences, college life could offer unparalleled opportunities for personal growth and intellectual development. Most college students could be encouraged to use these four years as an opportunity for the personal search that is the cornerstone of the liberal education; but at the present time, the average curriculum is so lacking in articulation, and the course emphasis is so specialized, that most students are forced to seek personal and private sources of meaning. This search takes them away from academic pursuits into the realms of the extracurricular. Consequently much of the passion and curiosity of the college student is spent on friends, causes, and activities.

There has always been a tacit recognition by educators and students alike of the existence of two cultures: the academic culture, defined by the classroom, and the multiform student culture. The importance of the academic culture is continually stressed in terms of career goals. This robs the student of satisfaction in his day-to-day endeavors in proportion to his inability to sense the relevance of present work to future plans. Only the most resilient succeed in playing the academic game and in pursuing the more meaningful side of their lives as well.

It is true that colleges do make some effort to help students integrate their undergraduate experiences. There is some realization that students vary tremendously in their degree of independence and need for guidance. In many colleges, the underlying reason for providing faculty advisors is an attempt to change the search for the personal into a personal search. Implicit in this system is a recognition of the fundamental importance of human relationships to individual growth and development.

The significance of a meaningful relationship between student and advisor is emphasized by the discrepancy between the goals of the university and those of the student. For the student, the real world consists of questions about himself and his place in society, and how his education can be related to his long-term goals. For the faculty, it consists in a commitment to specialized knowledge, with a high degree of involvement in the specific work. The advisor must find a way of integrating the two worlds for the student. His methods may vary from what one might expect from the clerk at an information booth in the department store of knowledge to the services performed by a well-informed museum guide who knows and loves all he describes. In the first instance, it is incumbent upon the student to ask the right questions; in the second, he must learn to be a receptive listener, and somehow develop a desire to share the advisor's enthusiasms. When it becomes clear that most students have neither this kind of enthusiasm nor well-articulated questions about the curriculum, the potential for a meaningful human relationship may often disappear, and the barren exchange of signatures begin. The relationship between advisor and student is often a source of great frustration for both. If the advisor is at all seriously concerned with the student, he cannot understand why all the virtues of the educational system are not quickly seen and embraced. The student, for his part, soon perceives that although he is in a face-to-face encounter with his advisor, their relationship is still essentially a formal exercise between teacher and student.

At most universities, there are other individuals with whom a personal relationship is possible for the student. These people are found in residence halls, the offices of deans, and counseling centers. Broadly speaking, professionals in student personnel services have little or no relationship to the academic life of the student. Their lack of connection with the main currents of the university reinforces the student's conviction that there are two cultures on campus. Some students may, in fact, find their most meaningful adult relationship in this sector of the university, but such relationships seldom help them integrate the world of classroom learning with that of other student concerns.

Our data have provided us with a segment of the life history of one college class. The fact that 65 per cent of the men are pursuing advanced degrees should be a source of satisfaction; but this satisfaction can be enjoyed only in the abstract, for a deeper examination reveals that the student's choices are not so much an indication of wise planning as they are the result of the need to keep up with a demanding timetable. The high level of talent represented in the entire class brings into sharper focus the loss occasioned by the failure of even one individual to pursue a direction intrinsically meaningful to him. The loss is most obvious with regard to those men and women who have failed by the standards of the system. There is, however, an equal loss to the "successful" student whose decision proves to have been inappropriate for him.

In an effort to place these data in context, we have outlined some of the conflicting forces operating on the student. In a way, it is inevitable that large numbers of our students will not have had adequate opportunity to examine their career plans critically, because nowhere are they encouraged to do so. Their experience is filled with mixed messages. So many different, equally powerful, often contradictory positions are presented to the student that efforts to help him as an individual tend to be remedial, temporary, and time-consuming. The pressures to conform are too great for many individuals to resist successfully. If widespread changes are to be effected, all segments of the educational institution must be genuinely committed to the task of encouraging the individual student to explore and to grow.

❧ 6 ❧

INCOMPLETE LIBERATION:
TWO PREMEDICAL
STUDENTS

Harold A. Korn

Despite the obvious success of our educational system, some fundamental questions about its methods and goals remain unanswered. Abstractly conceived, these questions are concerned with how men can live the good life. It is the avowed goal of a liberal education to confront the student with man's long struggle to make life meaningful and survival possible. With regard to professional education, these questions are more difficult to formulate. Traditionally, professional education has been the training ground of the competent specialist. But the fantastic increase in the rate of knowledge production and the growing complexity of professional problems have forced a new kind of orientation on those who educate future professionals. Paradoxically, the creation of a technologically specialized society has increased the need for broadly educated men. Many decisions made by professionals profoundly affect the daily lives of large numbers of people. Now, more than ever before, wisdom is an indispensable adjunct of technical competence.

Aware of this need, some professional schools and organizations are putting more emphasis on the value of a meaningful undergraduate education. They no longer confine their interest to the student who merely demonstrates academic proficiency, but make the extra effort to search out students with the emotional potential necessary to handle the responsibilities of professional life in the coming decades. It seems that the increasing complexity of our society has forced upon us the need to reexamine our basic value system. Liberal arts education, which has long been considered a "frill" by many, must become a meaningful part of education for all professionals, for the sake of their own personal development, and for the sake of competent professional functioning. Sadly enough, the present structure of the average liberal arts curriculum is not equal to this task.

The cases that follow afford us an opportunity to examine in detail the impact of undergraduate education on two men who were accepted into a prestigious medical school. These particular men were selected for analysis here for several reasons. First, by the criteria of the established educational system, they are very "successful"; second, they illustrate a variety of questions with which the system fails to come to grips; and finally, the pattern of similarities and differences in the personalities of these two men raises a variety of important theoretical issues for the psychology of assessment.

These men were among the nearly two hundred students whom we interviewed intensively twice a year for each of their four undergraduate years.[1] In their first senior year interview,

---

[1] The quotations used here are the men's replies to questions that appeared in the interview schedules. The interviewer's questions appear in italics.

our two students, Warren and Steve, were asked: *"What has been the impact of formal education upon you as a person?"* Warren answered: "Very little. I don't feel I've learned a great deal. It's kind of disappointing. If I had spent four years marking time, I would have learned as much. The chemistry degree won't give me any happiness in the future." Steve's answer was: "Well, I think I've got a lot more knowledge than I had before I came to the university . . . I can think a little more analytically and critically about problems. I had a lot of science courses, so certainly I can attack physics, chemistry, biological, and mathematical problems better than I could before. But I also think about problems much more easily, more deeply, than I could. And I suppose that in taking all the general studies courses, I've become more well-rounded."

Remarks like these raise some interesting issues about our data. Some would argue that all we can reliably accept is what we can objectively measure. In such terms, Steve and Warren are remarkably similar. Both have been admitted to a prestigious medical school after graduating from a respected college. Both have worked to earn high grade-point averages (3.29 and 3.11, respectively). In terms of their measured aptitudes, both men have demonstrated a very high level of ability. The College Board scores for Warren are: verbal, 650; mathematical, 700. For Steve, the scores are: verbal, 620; mathematical, 750. (By contrast, the scores for Stanford men are: mean verbal, 617; mean mathematical, 652.) But the men's answers suggest that their subjective experiences at the university have been quite different. It is in the subjective realm that the good life is either found, ignored, or desperately sought. Furthermore, success or failure in this realm makes an important difference in one's professional life. There is increasing concern with the discrepancy between the physician's technical competence and his ability to view his patient's condition broadly and sympathetically. Unless our future physicians come to terms with their own inner lives, they will be unable to respond to the inner needs of their patients.

Looking below the surface of success, we tried to establish more firmly some of the differences and similarities that characterized Steve and Warren. During their junior year, both were asked to describe the impact of the first two years of college: *"Apart from your courses, what has been happening in your life during the past two years that has been of great importance to you?"* This is Warren's reply:

> It's difficult to take it out of the academic sphere. The most important thing is a feeling of marking time until I go out into the world. I realize the thinness of the intellectual façade I've been fabricating. Undoubtedly I will not use nine-tenths of the course information gotten here at the university. I probably will not use any of it if I go into dentistry or medicine. Of course, it'll be a different story if I go into biochemistry. There's a difference between one's intellectual and one's academic life. In the past few years, I feel I've been taking courses that have little impact on what I do, and that are not fruitful intellectually—or I haven't perceived that they are. These two years have not meant a great deal, yet I can't imagine myself in any other situation. I'm where I belong: I have no doubt about it.

In answer to the question, *"Would you have felt differently if you had been able to spend more time in the humanities and social sciences?"* Warren replied: "Perhaps, but even this I feel is quite sterile. The only worthwhile thing you could hope to do is to renounce yourself and help others, or renounce others and help yourself totally. This probably shocks you or startles you— but in doing this, in renouncing others, you'd be able to devote your entire energy to attaining a plateau."

It is difficult to understand the meaning of this last answer completely. Warren seems to be struggling with the question of why he finds the curriculum so sterile. At first glance, his reply seems to be a non sequitur, but the intensity of feeling suggests that it is a very personal statement of an emotional conflict that plagues his intellectual life. Somehow Warren cannot allow himself to align his concern for other people with his motivation for achievement. The curriculum becomes a battleground for intense personal conflict with origins in the distant past. Steve's response to the same question was: "It's a gradual thing, considering what I want to do with my life, so when I get through I can say it's been meaningful. I think about that more and more."

The evidence presented so far would lead one to characterize Warren as disappointed, dissatisfied, and self-critical. He writes off his academic success as an "intellectual façade." He's unable to integrate what he has learned into something meaningful and satisfying. Steve, on the other hand, comes across as someone who is searching for the meaningful. For reasons we shall examine later, he's been able to extract from essentially the same science curriculum as Warren's some sense of discipline and purpose. There is an element of the philosopher in Steve.

In their sophomore year, Warren and Steve were asked to describe how their convictions had changed. Warren said:

> The search for something of value in life is becoming important. Perhaps this is life itself. I feel that I must live life instead of passively accepting it. Unfortunately, I don't quite know how to do this. Many things that I consider worthwhile in this vein are ruled out by economic considerations. This consideration immediately prompts the consideration that they are not worthwhile.

In answer to the same question, Steve responded:

> Certainly I'm far more future-oriented now than ever before. I look to the future as a reward for the tedium of college life. I've been giving a lot of thought recently to the problem of whether it is best to say whatever you think. My friends say, "Play it cool"—but I don't know how to "play it cool."

This information both confirms and complicates our characterizations. Steve engages the world in a far less abstract manner than Warren. Should he say what he thinks? How does one restrain oneself? These are the mundane but interpersonally vital questions that he wants to answer. Now it is Warren who poses the question about the meaning of life and Steve who reacts to the tedium of college life. Despite the similarity in the content of the struggle reported by these two men, there are sharp differences in their underlying attitudes. Warren can admit to yearning for the good life, but he sees it as inaccessible. He struggles with the issue in logic-tight compartments of renunciation and economic necessity. Warren feels caught, wants to fight, but doesn't know how. His detachment from his feelings gives him some of the "coolness" that Steve's friends have advised Steve to develop.

The dimension of detachment versus meaningful involvement is of great importance to an understanding of these two men. On the basis of many objective criteria, these two men are very similar, and on our psychological measures of self-control and impulse expression, their scores are nearly identical. Nevertheless, in the realm of subjective experience, they handle feelings and make decisions in different ways. More evidence of their emotional dissimilarity is revealed in their patterns of career choice. Steve started out as a mathematics major, but found that he was not as good in mathematics as he had thought. He had a need to excel and couldn't live up to his own expectations. In addition, he found his courses in the history of Western civilization and the humanities so fascinating that he considered dropping his mathematics major in favor of gaining a broader range of knowledge in the liberal arts. Warren chose to major in chemistry when he entered the university. He had worked as a laboratory assistant in a chemical plant during the previous summer, and he had also been a semi-finalist in a national science contest. During his first interview, he expressed some interest in pursuing philosophy as a minor. From the day they registered for their first college courses, Steve expressed a restless curiosity and Warren exhibited a staid and steadfast career orientation. Steve enrolled in an upper-division world literature course, but subsequently found that he could not compete with the sophistication of the other students. He reported that he learned a great deal, but also suffered a severe blow to his self-confidence. Warren took a traditional academic load and came up with a very respectable grade-point average.

In their junior year, both students were asked how their interests had changed since high school. Steve replied:

In high school, English and literature courses didn't appeal to me; I was always in science courses. I'm getting tired of science courses now. I seek relief in English courses. Before college, I never gave any thought to teaching at the high school level, but now it interests me. It seems an interesting and rewarding and quiet life. This, of course, is from the perspective of the pressures of college life. I'm not sure if I really care for pediatrics. In teaching, your life is your own. Also the idea of having a lot of little kids' lives in my hands [in working as a pediatrician] is not very appealing. The pressures here are increasing. Looking back on high school, it was fun. If I didn't think it was chicken, I'd go into teaching right away. But I'm afraid I'd just be avoiding the pressures of medical school. Also I have to convince myself that it would be respectable to teach.

Warren was asked the same question. He said his interests had not really changed; but he added that for want of time, he had given up pursuing his musical interests.

Despite expanded awareness, Steve was moving cautiously in his change of major from mathematics to physics to chemistry. What prevented him from using his undergraduate years to explore the alternatives to his previously chosen career? A partial answer came during the seventh interview, in response to the question, *"What kinds of things annoy you?"* Steve answered:

The system at Stanford, as far as grades go. That people are so grade-conscious—as I was for a year or two—that annoys me. And I don't think that things are conducive academically—that there is a conducive environment in which to learn. I've talked to professors about this, and they don't seem to know any other way, so I guess there will always be grades given in the undergraduate universities. But I think without grades I could have done a lot more in school than I did, just taking more courses without worrying about how I was doing. It's a funny thing, but you have to decide whether you're going to play the game—if you want to go to medical school, for instance. Even if I decided it was silly to study for grades and all, I'd still have to play the game and get good

grades, or else my application would come in with another guy's whose grades were a little better, and he
would be taken instead of me, and then I sure won't get
to my goals, so I am sort of being forced into playing a
game, which I was not sure I really liked. In fact, I know
that I didn't want to play; that is, fighting it out for
grades in premedical courses.

This is revealing, because it is stated as an example of something
that really annoys Steve. Why does he continue to "play the game"
—to submit to such a personally unsatisfactory situation? At least
Steve feels he is a victim of an impersonal and unsympathetic system, is annoyed by it, and does what he can to circumvent it.
Warren seems to accept the system stoically.

What factors in the psychological backgrounds of the two
men could possibly account for their reactions to pressure and responses to the curriculum? And how might the curriculum have
been modified to encourage these men to be more receptive? We
have available for these men several measures that were given
when they were entering freshmen and when they were graduating
seniors. In many respects, these measures reflect the pattern
of similarities and differences we have seen at the phenomenologi-
cal and behavioral levels. To begin with, we shall consider some
of the similarities. On the Ominbus Personality Inventory (OPI),
Steve and Warren have very similar scores on SM (Social Maturity)
and IE (Impulse Expression); both are very close to the mean of
the distribution. On the California Psychological Inventory (CPI),
the Sc, or Self-control Scale score, is very similar for both, and
appears in the bottom quarter of the distribution (the correlation
between Sc and IE is $r = .48$). The two men are also very similar
on the Re (Responsibility) and Wb (Well-being) scales.

With regard to the differences between the two men, two
clear dimensions emerge. One is a general tendency to be dominant
and assertive. Warren is considerably higher than Steve on the
following scales: Dominance, Capacity for Status, Sociability, Social Presence, and Self-Acceptance. Further support for this assertiveness comes from Warren's MF (Masculinity-Femininity)
scores, which are representative of more "masculine" attitudes and

interests than Steve's are. The other dimension can be described as a general tendency to rigidity in thought and action. Here we find Warren high on the Authoritarianism Scale and low on the Flexibility Scale. While Steve has a relatively high score on the Flexibility Scale, he also has a high score on the Communality Scale, which suggests a certain conventionality in his thinking. Still another important difference between these two men shows up on the Socialization Scale. Warren's very high score suggests an internalization of society's standards to such a degree that his own freedom of action is seriously impaired.

The Senior Questionnaire, which both men filled out during their senior year, gives us additional information about their psychological makeup. Both described themselves as largely dissatisfied with themselves as freshmen; Steve described himself as reasonably satisfied as a senior, while Warren said he was moderately dissatisfied with himself as a senior. Warren stated that important decisions at home were usually made by his father, while Steve said his mother was the decision-maker. According to Warren, his mother was overly dependent on her husband for her happiness, and seldom differed with him, while Steve stated that differences between his parents were frequently and strongly expressed. They were both asked: *"Which of your parents do you resemble more in your emotional makeup?"* Warren checked "Mother" and Steve checked "Father."

Further information about the psychological background of these two men was obtained during interviews, when each was asked to characterize his parents. Steve described his father as depressive; unwilling to make decisions; anxious lest his wishes conflict with those of others; frugal with regard to his own needs; opinionated, but socially shy; and quiet, but given to occasional outbursts of temper. Steve felt he had many of these traits also. He described his mother as a very dominant person, active as a leader in the PTA, who controlled the life of the family. According to Steve, she would often make the father take her out, instead of letting him "brood" at home; the father would then cheer up and have a good time.

In Warren's description, there are hints of an ambivalent relationship with a father "who felt he knew everything." However, he is described as a devoted father, who wanted his son to have everything he himself did not have. There also is some discussion of the father as having been socially retiring during his adolescence. The mother is described as being very intelligent. She characterizes herself as "manic-depressive," but Warren disagrees, though he thinks she is somewhat moody. He finds himself more like her than his father, but denies that he is moody.

We can look for further clues about Steve and Warren in their descriptions of the emotional climate of their childhood experiences. Warren was never exposed to open parental arguments, while Steve found them a part of everyday life. Warren's father was aloof, and made all the decisions. His mother was overly dependent on his strong father, and seemed a victim of very strong feelings that could only be manifested in depression and moodiness. For reasons we can only speculate about, Warren found it necessary to identify with his mother in terms of emotional makeup. Strong feelings were there, but they were never openly identified. In Steve's home we find the mirror-image of the dynamics in Warren's. Steve's father is weak and moody. The mother is strong and assertive. Again we do not know all the reasons, but the weak parent is chosen for identification. Steve finds that he is like his father. The striking difference in the emotional tone of these two families is revealed by the strident note of open conflict in Steve's family. Of even greater significance, perhaps, is the reversal of the culturally acceptable pattern in which the father is the head of the household.

As a child, Warren saw only that he was a member of a very successful family. His father was clearly in charge, as a father should be, and his mother idealized her relationship with the father. Given this surface appearance of family success and the evidence of Warren's strong sense of guilt, we can infer the following conclusion on Warren's part: if he felt troubled, it must be his own fault. How then did he come to terms with the many strong and conflicting feelings that lay beneath the surface in his family? It seems evident that the rigid control we see reflected in the psychometric data was an almost inevitable solution. We see evidence during the college years that Warren was aware of a struggle within himself, but was not free to examine its content or causes.

Indeed, much of the time he worked hard to deny the existence of the struggle.

For Steve, there was a wide variety of evidence that things were not as they should be at home. It was clear from the way his parents interacted. It was also clear from the way his family structure differed from the "typical" family structure. His only "choice" was to blame himself, but he did it in a different manner from Warren. He viewed the world in such a way that change was deemed possible, though hazardous. In some respects, we can say that change was more of a necessity for Steve because he did not have Warren's method of protecting himself from uncomfortable feelings. Warren essentially was operating within a closed system. His thinking consisted of many logic-tight components that permitted avoidance of serious conflicts. Thus we can see that for reasons grounded in their psychological makeup, Warren and Steve reacted differently on the subjective level to the stimuli they encountered in college life.

Most college catalogues promise to provide a liberal education and to make available the best in specialized study. Students expect that their undergraduate education will help them come to terms with both the daily task of understanding their experience of the world and their long-term career aspirations. Upon hearing the rhetoric of higher education and reading the college catalogue, students are encouraged to believe that the curriculum will provide the structure for fulfilling their expectations. One reason why contemporary higher education is facing so much upheaval and confusion is that this promise is not adequately fulfilled.

Steve and Warren have provided us with an illustration of why the promise is so difficult to fulfill. In studying their cases, we can see the basic dilemma facing higher education. While there is a great expenditure of effort on the part of both faculty and student, undergraduate education fails to make itself relevant to the student's basic concerns. Both Steve and Warren wanted more from the liberal arts curriculum than they were getting, but neither could escape the partly coercive and partly seductive call of specialized study. At one time or another, both men expressed a vital concern for the meaningful in life. In the abstract, they wanted what the liberal arts curriculum is said to provide. Despite their ability to recognize this quest, each in a different way found it easier to avoid coming to grips with the issue. We have outlined some of the reasons why Warren's and Steve's past experiences caused them to be so ambivalent about using their undergraduate years to search for enlightened understanding.

A liberal education has the potentiality of confronting the individual with the need to examine the feelings, attitudes, and beliefs that he has uncritically acquired during his lifetime. The process of self-examination is at best painful, and at worst a catastrophe of disintegration. The interplay between a desire to search for understanding and the often unrecognized need to avoid searching is a phenomenon that is always present, but it has a special intensity during late adolescence. This fundamental ambivalence toward growth and learning is both the hope and the bane of those who are committed to the implementation of the ideals of liberal education. The dynamic play between wanting to know and being afraid to know could provide the motivation necessary for the difficult task of becoming an educated person. A great deal of motivation is needed to maintain the discipline necessary to continue the effort that is involved in critical evaluation and to put up with the pain of self-evaluation. The potential for this kind of motivation is present in nearly all adolescents. We have observed how Steve and Warren flirted with their quest to understand more, but turned away at critical choice points. Something more was needed to encourage them to persevere in their search.

Just as the forces of constraint operate in students, they operate in the faculty also. While many faculty members may subscribe to the ideals of a liberal education, they often fail to implement these goals in the classroom. Again, these forces of constraint must be examined in terms of both internal and external determinants. We can only mention these in passing, as they bear on our understanding of Warren and Steve. If some faculty member teaching one of the "liberalizing" courses for these two men wanted his course material to become relevant, it would be necessary for him to tolerate the potential stress or genuine excitement created by such an experience. The quality of learning that is at the heart of a liberal education necessarily involves the student in some kind of crisis or, at minimum, some high pitch of feeling. The student's response to his own intense feelings will necessarily be communicated to his teacher in one form or another. If the teacher intends to encourage further learning at that particular point, he must be prepared to respond appropriately to the student's feelings. The whole approach of the typical college professor to "anti-intellectual" phenomena makes this kind of relationship highly unlikely. This is one part of the dilemma facing higher education. Unless the relationship between learning and the emotional response to learning is taken into account in the teaching of the liberal arts, learning will tend to remain an absorption of facts, and education will be an impersonal game. The sources of resistance that come from within are powerful. Environmental pressures can either work to strengthen them or to encourage a genuine climate for learning and teaching. For both the faculty and the student, the commitment of the present-day university curriculum to specialized study makes true education an almost impossible task.

We have suggested throughout that the forces of constraint within individuals are so great that genuine learning is at best a very difficult undertaking. When this "natural" obstacle is combined with institutional barriers to understanding and critical evaluation, frustration is inevitable. For Steve and Warren, both the reality of and their perception of the entire pattern of medical school recruitment worked against the intended impact of the liberal arts curriculum. Because of their need for the structure of the science curriculum and the security of a future career in medicine, they tacitly accepted and perhaps even welcomed a long series of ready-made decisions about their future courses of action. It is not accidental that this commitment to the future greatly diminished their need to search for personal meaningfulness. The issue here is not whether these two men should have chosen medical careers. Rather, it is more paradoxical: because one arm of the medical profession is searching for broadly educated men while another arm of the profession encourages undergraduates to be narrowly career-minded and grade-oriented, the pursuit of a career in medicine encouraged in Steve and Warren patterns of behavior inimical to their development as wise and compassionate physicians.

PART THREE

Student Life and
Its Problems

❦ 7 ❧

RESIDENTIAL GROUPS
AND INDIVIDUAL
DEVELOPMENT

Marjorie M. Lozoff

The residential milieu
has a strong effect on the undergraduate student. It may either
aid or retard his social, academic, and emotional development. In
this chapter we will describe the living conditions and reactions
to them of several groups of undergraduate men. The description
is based primarily on information given to us by our interview
sample—42 men who were interviewed twice a year during their
four undergraduate years—and on the test scores and responses
of our questionnaire sample—271 men who attended Stanford
University from 1961 to 1965, and who responded to the Senior
Questionnaire. Additional information was obtained from inter-

views with other undergraduates, graduate students, resident advisors, and faculty, as well as from class observations and meetings with groups of students.

Each student in the interview sample was seen by more than one interviewer. Frequent staff discussions enabled us to pool our observations and maintain an overall impression of the interview sample. With the consent of the forty-two men, written descriptions of the them were obtained from their friends. We also have freshman and senior psychological test responses, self-ratings, and written material, ratings by interviewers and friends, aptitude scores, and academic transcripts for these men.

Out of a total of 281 men who responded to the Senior Questionnaire, we selected all those who had clearly defined residence histories (N = 236). This sample was divided as follows: fraternity men who lived on campus (N = 69); fraternity men who lived off campus (N = 44); unaffiliated men who lived in off-campus apartments (N = 44); dormitory men (N = 42); and eating-club men (N = 37). This sample represents about a third of the men in the senior class.

Most of the students we studied had postponed many of the social and developmental tasks of adolescence until their college years. During high school, many of them had concentrated on proving their competence as students in order to gain admittance to the university. Some students had postponed development in the social area regretfully and others, because of feelings of inadequacy, had utilized the reality of the difficulty of college entrance as a rationalization for limiting social involvement. In any case, most of them looked forward to an improvement in their social relations at college, where they hoped to find themselves among peers of comparable ambitions and intellectual capacities.

As we interviewed students, we were impressed by the importance they placed on their social development. Some students handled this area with painful avoidance or denial, but most appeared to be deeply involved in trying to understand themselves and their relations with other people. This absorbed their energies and affected their academic and intellectual activities. The university as an institution showed relatively little interest in facilitating their social development. The challenge of aiding youth in developing academic, intellectual, and vocational skills was its area of competence, and the problem of supplying housing, social facilities, and proper personal guidance was seen as a peripheral task. The students related to each other in ways that were both constructive and destructive. By trial and error, they developed varying degrees of social skill and responsibility. In spite of egocentric involvement with their own pressing personal developmental tasks, they offered various kinds of guidance to each other. Receptivity to peer pressures varied with the anxiety of the recipient, his stage of separation from his parents, his sense of autonomy, and innumerable other factors, including identification with charismatic fellow students.

Important developmental tasks of late adolescence seemed to depend upon the support of peers for solution. These tasks included evaluating oneself as a person separate from one's family, and clarifying certain aspects of one's sexual role and career goals. As students face the actuality of the separateness of their existence and the need to seek out and adapt to peers for gratification of their emotional needs, painful emotional adjustments often ensue. These tasks have a particular urgency, and cannot be postponed because of academic demands. Often membership in an affiliation group, or, conversely, inability to become part of a group, have meaningful effects on this process. In either instance, sharing experiences and values with one or several friends influences the tempo of the separation process and provides experiences that the students utilize in clarifying their self-concepts and goals. As Joseph Katz has commented: "Most students have relatively narrow ranges of friendship associations. To be stressed is the fact that these groups make very specific demands on such matters as when and how alcohol is consumed, what kinds of people of the same or opposite sex one should associate with, and even what kinds of views are at the fringe but acceptable, and which are purely beyond the fringe. The peer pressures receive added force from the fact that they are usually derivative from and parallel to the views held in the student's own home situation. Therefore, deviation imperils not just one's association with the group, but even one's deeper ties with one's upbringing." Our purpose is to describe the influence of family values, housing-affiliation groups, and peers on individual development.

All entering students as Stanford are required to live in

dormitories. The bulk of the men live in a complex of houses exclusively reserved for freshmen. The assumption that young people, accustomed to homes, will adjust easily to the challenge of living in a multi-purpose room with a stranger is an unrealistic one. Their introduction to dormitory living occurs at a time when they are feeling insecure and at a loss for familiar cues. Within the freshman dorms, personality types who consciously avoid each other are sometimes thrown together. As roommates, they are placed in little box-like rooms where privacy is not possible. Many of our students reacted to the freshman experience by intensification of dislike of those who were very different from themselves in backgrounds, values, or personalities, and became determined to choose future housing arrangements that would protect them from such differences.

After their freshman year, the men at Stanford are free to choose fraternities or dormitories as their residence, or to move off campus. During the period studied, approximately fifty per cent of the men students belonged to fraternities, and about the same percentage was reflected in our interview sample. Besides their numerical superiority over other groups in our study, the fraternity men were objects of comparison, reluctant admiration, or angry disapproval to other men and women. The fraternity system seemed, at its best, to actively encourage a sense of loyalty and security for the in-group; and at its worst, to permissively allow regressive and undemocratic behavior. The fraternity men, on the whole, differed from other groups in their appearance, interests, and attitudes toward group activities. The general impression made by most of the fraternity men on the interviewers was one of self-confidence, physical grace, and attractiveness. This was true regardless of their social class, or the quality of the fraternity in which they had membership. This appearance was not accidental; it was the result of several factors in the men's precollege experiences. First, most of them came from sociable families. Second, during their high school careers, many of the fraternity men had been in the limelight by virtue of positions as cheerleaders, athletes, or student body officers. Most of these men were not characterized by outstanding intellectual or artistic interests, but they had acquired a certain social know-how: they drank alcoholic beverages, had considerable experience in dating girls, and considered themselves superior to their high school class-mates in the area of group participation and social activity.

The average verbal and mathematical aptitudes of the fraternity men were lower than those of men in the other groups. This was particularly true with regard to verbal aptitudes.[1] On the other hand, if they had been tested and rated on the basis of aptitude in physical activities or group participation, the fraternity men probably would have been on top. In general, these students enjoy the company of other men and want security and response from their peers. As a freshman, the son of a professor from a large university explained his interest in group and social activities thus: "A lot of people like to be by themselves—to just know one or two people really well—and aren't interested in group activities. I'm not like this, so I better join a fraternity. It's hard for independent freshmen to get dates; there's an awful lot of upperclassmen who don't have girls, and they reach down to the freshman girls. A lot of girls come to college and are interested in fraternity parties, but they aren't much interested in freshman men."

Another student, at the university on a scholarship and from a small-town, low-income family, gave this reason for joining a fraternity: "Joining a fraternity is a unique experience, because although it is selective, and the selection process isn't always fair, you still find—after rush is done—that you are living with people with whom you have common interests—people with whom you can get going in one direction easier than if you were in a dorm. Consequently you'll have a unity you might not achieve elsewhere. You can organize things and get them going."

Their differences in scholastic aptitude were a source of guidance for these men in planning their futures, and in their behavior during their college careers. From data based on a questionnaire mailed to graduates of the class of 1965 in January, 1966, it appeared that a large proportion of fraternity men were planning careers that involved business or legal training. It was apparent that many of them aimed for managerial and administrative

[1] The freshman mean scores for the verbal part of the Scholastic Aptitude Test indicate that students who later become fraternity men (N = 324) scored about twenty points below the off-campus men (N = 122) and clubmen (N = 88), and about forty points below the dormitory men (N = 66).

positions rather than professional or artistic careers (see Table 44). The fraternity men appeared to be interested in a model that

TABLE 44

POSTGRADUATE STATUS OF SENIOR MEN ONE YEAR
AFTER GRADUATION [a]
(IN PER CENT)

	Eating Club (N = 44)	Frat/On (N = 93)	Frat/Off (N = 55)	Off-Campus (N = 51)	Dorm (N = 37)
Business School	20	22	16	4	3
Prof. Schools					
Engineer	16	5	4	12	8
Law	7	28	25	18	16
Medicine	7	9	15	14	16
Graduate Schools Science and					
Mathematics	14	9	9	8	19
Humanities	11	5	7	16	16
Social Science [b]	22	14	24	18	14
Education	0	4	0	6	5
Other	3	4	0	6	4

[a] The five living groups were compared by an χ^2 test to check differences in representation among the graduate fields, excluding "Education" and "Other." The test yielded p < .02.

[b] The fraternity off-campus students were in international relations, economics, and political science (none were in psychology, sociology or anthropology).

would be appropriate for potential leaders of men, persuaders of men, and decision-makers. Their physical vigor and the relatively limited emphasis they placed on their verbal skills may have contributed to their tendency to make quick and easy decisions, and to avoid introspection and complexity.

In the Senior Questionnaire, the men indicated the activities they had participated in during their college years (see Table 45). The fraternity men were significantly different from the other groups of students in their interest in sports, social activities, and parties. This is not surprising, in light of their skills and future life goals. On the other hand, they reported less activity than the other groups did in activities involving cultural interests and services to less fortunate people. Life within the fraternity en-

TABLE 45

ACTIVITIES: PERCENTAGE OF SUBJECTS IN EACH TYPE OF
LIVING GROUP WHO PARTICIPATED FREQUENTLY [a]

	Frat/On (N = 69)	Frat/Off (N = 44)	Eating Club (N = 37)	Off-Campus (N = 44)	Dorm (N = 42)	p
Reading						
Non-fiction	45	50	62	52	62	
Fiction	30	39	41	39	26	
Cultural and Service						
Lectures	19	16	30	23	15	
Student committes	19	16	19	15	5	
Service activities	7	7	16	0	7	
Creative expression	10	14	16	23	17	
Museums, drama, symphony	6	7	16	13	19	*
Political Activities						
Campus	12	7	14	5	7	
National and community	1	0	14	0	5	
Civil Rights	0	5	3	2	5	*
Social Activities						
Social activities, parties	71	80	46	34	12	***
Seeking out off-beat people and places	4	9	5	7	2	**
Travel	43	45	30	45	21	***
Movies	19	25	32	41	20	**
Church	20	9	16	9	21	
Athletics						
Spectators sports	75	57	43	39	24	***
Participant sports	65	57	35	27	9	***
Hiking	13	9	8	7	2	

* $p < .05$.
** $p < .01$.
*** $p < .001$.

[a] In the Questionnaire, the students were asked whether they had participated in each activity frequently, occasionally, or never. Where the frequency in the "frequently" or "never" categories was extremely small, they were combined with the "occasionally" category, resulting in 2 x 5 contingency tables with 4 df.

hanced the interests that the men had prior to college entrance. On the positive side, this included a willingness to assume responsibility for group activities, and to offer loyalty and a sense of belonging to a chosen group of fellow students. On the negative side, this often led to an intensification of a high school model of masculinity, including admiration of heavy drinking and conquest of women, contempt for individuals who were less attractive, strong, or adventurous, and a condoning of aggressive behavior toward individuals who were not in the in-group. Although most men at Stanford drank frequently during their college years, the fraternity men were more apt to take "getting drunk" for granted as acceptable and anticipated behavior. Two-thirds of the fraternity men and the unaffiliated men who lived off campus described themselves as being drunk more than once during the senior year, in contrast to 43 per cent of the clubmen, and 21 per cent of the dormitory men. However, most of the men drank more heavily during their sophomore year, when they first entered the fraternity, than they did in later years. Individuals who were not able to control their heavy drinking had difficulty surviving at the university.

Regardless of social class, the fraternity men tended to come from families where the parents were younger than those of unaffiliated men. On the average, they were more likely to have brothers; and less likely to have sisters, or to be only children. From our interview sample of twenty-two fraternity men, we derived the impression that although each of the fraternities had a number of members from minority or low-income groups, the pace-setters in the fraternities were men who came from "white Anglo-Saxon" families where the parents had positions of affluence and influence within their communities. We will refer to these fraternity men as "inheritors."

Of the thirteen "inheritors" whom we interviewed for a four-year period, six came from prep schools, and the others came from public schools in upper-middle-class suburbs. Since the successful families of the "inheritors" represent models that appealed to most of the fraternity men regardless of their class background, a description of these parents is worthy of special note. The "inheritors" viewed their fathers with evident admiration. In some instances, the fathers were respected as leaders in their communities, and sometimes they had national or international reputations. These fathers were often above the layer of management where conformity and depersonalization is evident, and their strengths seemed to lie in a capacity to understand different points of view, and to make and assume responsibility for clear-cut decisions. The sons were aware of this. They indicated respect for their fathers, but also some distance from them. The fathers had often been away from home, but the homes they had been away from reflected the power, wealth, and status of the father. When the fathers had been home, they had been interested in the sons' athletic, social, and academic achievements. Not infrequently, a father would express nostalgia for his carefree college days. Many of these fathers drank heavily, and belonged to elite country clubs.

As Nevitt Sanford says, "inheritor" fraternity men are not "Momma's boys." In fact, some of the contradictions in their attitudes about women resulted from their parental situation. The mothers were younger than the fathers, and had few occupational or intellectual interests, although most of them had college educations. Home and community activities, mainly social or esthetic, occupied their days. References to the mothers by their sons were often affectionate but condescending. The sons discounted the ability of their mothers to have objective and balanced opinions. The mothers appeared to their sons to be less well-informed than the fathers, and to be more opinionated and less tolerant regarding political and social matters. The mothers were described as attractive women, devoted to their families and friends; but the fathers were described as logical, clear-thinking achievers.

The actual existence of diversity within the fraternity is often questioned by outsiders; yet the fraternity men we interviewed frequently stressed this as one of the main advantages of fraternity membership. The outsider may be impressed by the fraternity man's self-confidence, physical attractiveness, and interest in masculine gregarious activities. If the outsider is hostile to fraternities, he may stress the fraternity members' bias against "non-fraternity" types, lack of judgment or control with regard to drinking and pranks, and general anti-intellectual and anti-introspective attitude. Fraternity men, taking for granted their common interest in social and athletic activities, are impressed by the variations within fraternity membership of geographic areas of origin, social class background, and choice of majors. In most of the fraternities that we studied, the core group was social, athletic, and interested in managerial positions or the professions; few students were interested in the arts, pure science, or college teaching.

Differences do exist between fraternities and within each fraternity. One difference is the quality of autonomy. Almost half of the fraternity men lived in off-campus apartments. These students appeared to differ somewhat in interests, relationships, self-concepts, and possibly development from those of their brothers who preferred to live on campus. The men who lived off campus appeared to be less interested in sports and more interested in parties, travel, and "off-beat" places. They were more inclined to read fiction and to participate in civil rights activities. Both groups of fraternity men were relatively disinterested in visiting museums, or attending plays or symphonies. The off-campus fraternity men appeared to have more complex relationships with others than their on-campus brothers did: more than twice as many off-campus as on-campus fraternity men described family problems and crises in relationships as stimulants for change.

Although both groups of fraternity men dated more frequently during the four years of college than other groups of men did, the off-campus fraternity men felt that they had deeper relationships with women, and 43 per cent of them, in contrast to 20 per cent of the on-campus fraternity men, indicated that they frequently had enjoyed a high degree of intimacy with women. In addition, the off-campus fraternity men attributed changes regarding attitudes and behavior to the influence of women with greater frequency than the fraternity men who lived on campus did. This might indicate that the off-campus men were at a stage in their heterosexual development in which closeness to women had more significance than masculine gregariousness did.

Only 18 per cent of the off-campus fraternity men described being away from home as an important factor causing change; whereas 40 per cent of the fraternity men who chose to live on campus attributed changes to this adjustment. The on-compus fraternity men gave interviewers the impression of being more conservative and conforming. They showed considerable interest in social activities connected with churches, were very active in athletics, and appeared to enjoy participation in student committees and campus politics. The fraternity men who lived off campus showed little interest in affairs connected with churches or in campus politics. These differences suggest that the two groups of men differed in a feeling of independence and in the timing of their developmental tasks. Possibly the off-campus men had moved more quickly away from their homes and toward hetero-sexual involvements.

A question dealing with feelings of self-satisfaction indi-cated that of all the groups, the fraternity men had the greatest feeling of self-satisfaction upon matriculation. When the fraternity men first arrived on campus, the social education they had received at home stood them in good stead in making new friends. Besides that, they had experienced the advantage of being recognized leaders in their high-school communities. Many of them also had known the satisfaction of having parents who were prominent and well-educated. The freshmen who were sons of alumni here or at other prestigious universities may have had a greater sense of familiarity and belonging than students who were the first of their families to attend this type of institution did. Except with regard to academic achievement, most fraternity men felt relative-ly "self-satisfied" as freshmen. Within the fraternity group, how-ever, the off-campus men were less self-satisfied upon entrance. Over the four years, the fraternity men as a group moved in the direction of feeling more dissatisfied with themselves, with the on-campus fraternity men indicating the greatest dissatisfaction.

Let us describe these students who were representative of the "inheritor" subgroup:

(1) A task-oriented, pleasant, rather tense young man from a military background who joined a "straight-arrow" (conserva-tive) fraternity was described as follows: "His fraternity brothers admired his sincerity but found him too conservative in his sense of duty, which restrained him from joining others in impromptu seeking of new experiences." Although he liked his fraternity brothers, and said he chose them because he wanted to be with people like himself, he also felt that they were only "out for a good time." His own attitude was: "I have long-range plans and have to work for them." By his senior year, however, his fraternity brothers had helped him ease up, and he was enjoying an occa-sional "evening on the town."

(2) A wealthy West Coast student, whose intellectual and esthetic development during his college years was more impressive than his academic achievements, as a senior commented: "I came to college thinking I had to go to college, and I didn't think any more about it. I never thought about a career or why I was here. Both of my brothers had gone here, but I never had a serious discussion with them or my parents. I had a lot of fun, basically. I had a car; I went to the city a lot; went out with a lot of different girls. I have always dated Stanford girls exclusively. . . . Sometimes I surprise myself by how immature I am, and then sometimes I feel like an adult. I don't know, but I think I've achieved a very high level of education—much higher than I thought I would—in personal matters as well as in broad education. I like people much more than I used to, and I have a great deal more awareness of what makes a democracy run. I have more latitude in speaking about world situations, and I have more freedom to express my beliefs. I can stand up in social situations and be myself more than I used to be. I think I have more courage to speak out."

(3) A third student, who came from a well-established and prominent family in the East, joined a fraternity composed of students deeply interested in international affairs and government. (One perceptive woman student said of these men: "Their rebellion seems to be directed into fairly constructive channels. It's not so much a personal rebellion against the world; their way of dealing with rebellion is organizing things to deal with it.") He described his experiences thus: "Our House is divided into two groups—the group I'm with, who spend a lot of time drinking and having a good time, and the other group, which studies a great deal. We profit from this. In prep school, there was a general awareness that was confined to understanding people and social things—this is true here, but it extends to books and subjects. My House places value on 'eccentricity'—we have a larger proportion of interesting people in my fraternity than in the university as a whole—the university attempts to achieve a norm of personality. I viewed the freshman year as a year for prodigality, which would be followed by years of work. For as I observed, and as appeared logical, life is most productive when lived to the extreme—no matter what the extreme may be." After a year of poor grades, heavy drinking, and gregarious activities and pranks, this student

was able to settle down to serious academic and intellectual achievements and to move toward close personal relationships.

None of the "inheritors" just described were at Stanford on academic or athletic scholarships. None of them were driven to maintain a high grade-point average, nor to devote long hours to sports practice. In general, if any of the "inheritors" worked, they did so voluntarily, to bolster their self-esteem or sociability, or to test their ability to get along with other social groups. None of them participated in major athletics, although they were all enthusiastic supporters of varsity and professional athletics. They enjoyed intramural sports, and liked to keep fit and to compete physically on an informal level. Academically, a number of them did well enough to gain admission to outstanding graduate schools, but three of them were within the lowest 10 per cent of their graduating class.

These men accepted their academic inferiority at the university with a grace that might have been difficult for those with less assurance of superiority. Although fraternities disapprove of poor academic achievement, a member is not ostracized or condemned for it. Once one is a member, he has a certain security within the group. However, the general tone of the fraternity prescribes playing down the time and effort required for academic excellence. It is all right to get good grades, but not to appear greedy for them, boast of them, or sacrifice friendliness or loyalty in pursuit of them.

The nine "non-inheritors" in our interview sample fell into two groups. The first group of six consisted of sons of small-town public school administrators and successful men in West Coast suburbs who lacked college educations. The other three were at the university on scholarships, came from low-income households, were not of Anglo-Saxon descent, and had been forced to cope with the problems of serious illness or domestic difficulties. These three were among the hardest-working students on campus. Prior to college, most of the "non-inheritors" had enjoyed active and flattering social lives and the adulation that accompanies success in high-school athletic endeavors. Because their scholarships covered tuition and little else, most of them worked at part-time jobs to pay for their other expenses. Most "non-inheritors" had two other burdens as well. One was that they were involved in a dramatic separation process from their own families. The closer they moved in their social activities toward an acceptance of upper-middle-class suburban values and patterns, and toward professional life, the further they removed themselves from the values and way of life of their former friends and family. During college, some of these men found themselves in a social no-man's land. It was no longer possible psychologically for them to return to the ways of their parents, but they had not yet grasped the nuances and subtleties of upper-middle-class social life. As a result, they were often depressed. They rarely dated Stanford coeds until their senior year at college, and their pride prevented them from exposing themselves to situations in which they would appear gauche. On the other hand, their relationships with women who were less well-educated and socially self-confident no longer satisfied them. To add to their difficulties their high schools had generally not prepared them for college with the same skill and proficiency with which the upper-middle-class suburban high schools or prep schools had prepared the "inheritors," and as a result, many of the "non-inheritors" had a much harder time academically than their fraternity peers did. Providing for their financial needs, competing academically in spite of inadequate preparation, adapting to a new set of social patterns and values, and contending with the emotional pain involved in separation from their former environments were sources of stress for these men. At the end of four years, most of the "non-inheritors" in our study complained of feeling exhausted and depleted. Some of these men described feelings of depression; others, difficulty in controlling their anger. However, most of them were well on their way to higher socioeconomic status and an enriched awareness of intellectual and cultural matters.

The cost of upward mobility seemed to increase in relation to the number of steps up the social ladder to be made by the students. For example, one of the "non-inheritors," whose father lacked college training, had grown up in an upper-middle-class suburb and had enjoyed a social life at home comparable to that of the "inheritors." He was under less strain than most of the other "non-inheritors." By contrast, the son of a Spanish-American construction foreman, who had been educated at a small Catholic school, and whose moral and religious values were challenged by his contact with the questioning attitude he found in the university, experienced much pain in his upward progress.

Students from blue-collar families and those of foreign parentage were a small minority within most of the fraternities, but their presence gave the fraternity men an opportunity to know at least one or two individuals from very different backgrounds who were attempting to achieve upper-middle-class status. Each fraternity had one or two members of minority groups. These exceptions did not noticeably disturb the homogeneity of the fraternities, for two reasons. First, their number was very small; and second, minority-group members pledged by fraternities appeared to have somewhat the same qualities that distinguished the fraternity men in general—self-confidence in social matters, attractive appearance, physical energy, and good physical coordination.

In addition to differences in autonomy and socioeconomic status within each fraternity, there usually appeared to be a wide difference in orientation. Some members were very much interested in campus activities; some were primarily interested in getting good grades; others were distinguished by being favorite escorts in the "deb" circuits. Some members were recognized as hard drinkers, and were capable of wild, destructive behavior; while others were interested in intellectual matters. Although almost all these types were represented within each fraternity, some fraternities had a preponderance of one or two types of individuals. Two extreme groups will serve as illustrations. One was described as a "straight-arrow house." Here the men were apt to be churchgoers; to limit their drinking; to be interested in achieving good grades; and to prefer masculine company, with occasional forays into the world of women. At the opposite extreme was a house of the sort known as a "wild-animal house," in which the members seemed to try to outdo one another in exploits of heavy drinking, and freely showed contempt for students interested in esthetic, artistic, or political matters. They delighted in aggressive behavior toward women and in dangerous or destructive activities. The truth of the claim of the fraternity men that there is diversity within the fraternity lies in the fact that men do join fraternities from a variety of socioeconomic backgrounds, aspire to a variety of careers and occupations, and exhibit a variety of behavior styles and values.

Interviews over the four years with twenty-two fraternity men indicated some of the areas where the fraternity system, as it existed, impeded the personal development of the members and encouraged resistance to the intellectual and cultural values of the university. Some of the students found the continuous round of social and athletic events burdensome. For others, socializing provided a tempting escape from the discouraging task of academic competition. Simulating lightheartedness—adopting a "hang-loose" attitude—was less disturbing to their self-esteem than admitting their inability to compete successfully. Gregariousness within the fraternity often encouraged superficiality in relationships and values and a blunting of perceptions. In the interest of group solidarity, fraternity men were expected to act in a friendly and loyal way toward the 40 to 60 others with whom they had daily association. To maintain good-natured acceptance of a large number of individuals with varying patterns of behavior requires self-discipline, and some students experienced considerable strain as a result of inhibiting their critical or hostile reactions. Provisions existed within the fraternity way of life for relief of tensions through athletics, heavy drinking, and pranks. Outbursts against a brother for tabooed behavior occasionally occurred, but a more frequent displacement of aggressive feelings was made through disparaging remarks and occasional attacks on those in the "outgroups."

Although the majority of the fraternity men in our interview sample never or rarely participated in antisocial behavior, they often acquiesced by non-interference. The interviewees whose behavior had been most aggressive were students with considerable anxiety about survival in the university community. These students experienced difficulty in controlling their impulses; often their fate at the university appeared to them to presage rejection by their homes and communities. The puppy-like exuberance of a group of vigorous males looking for fun would often stimulate them to overstep the limits of appropriate behavior. Discussing such behavior, one "non-inheritor" remarked: "I enjoy going to fraternity parties. You could say that this is for letting off steam, as well as for gaining experience in what parties are like. Our parties aren't wild to the point of maliciousness—there isn't as much destructiveness in our fraternity as in others. I have destructive problems to deal with about once a month [he was president of his fraternity]. Gross behavior with girls isn't much of a problem in our House. We have our parties and date girls and get our pleasures, but we don't make a big thing out of what is called 'grossing' a girl—people in our fraternity agree that this is childish." An "inheritor" had this to say: "I don't like to get raucous and out of hand at parties. I don't like to make a fool out of myself. Destructiveness turns me off. So does obtrusiveness. The trouble with the two Houses nearby that I consider 'animal houses' is just this. We had $1,500 damage done to us this year—BB guns were shot through our windows twice; somebody threw a tire pump through the window; exotic plants were uprooted; skis were stolen and destroyed. This is unforgivable. I would like to see these guys sent to the penitentiary. I don't care if the guy is a straight 'A' student and has the world's greatest girl friend—I don't give a damn. I'd like to send him up."

Another student described a not unusual fraternity phenomenon that defies common concepts of manners and includes a waste of time and money. A graduate student living in one House had expressed contempt for some of the brothers, and they felt that he should be paid back for it: "We had a food fight in his honor—we put him against a door and just smashed food at him. We don't have food fights too often—just every now and then, when it's appropriate. This guy had said that he was amazed at some of the things we did—that they clashed with his idea of society." One can only speculate why intelligent young men from privileged backgrounds and with potentialities for success would need to actively or passively engage in such violent inhibitional releases. Speculation is necessary, because capacity for thoughtful introspection and communication about complicated motivations was not one of the characteristics of most of the fraternity men we interviewed. Some of them learned this complicated skill gradually throughout their college years, first by discussing values with their men friends, and later by trying to explain their feelings to their women friends. At first, many of our students resisted discussing motivations, or openly indicated that they disliked the process of analyzing their behavior or that of others.

One factor in wasteful behavior may be a permissive attitude on the part of parents, some women friends, and even some university authorities. Pranks that go beyond reason may reflect feelings of anxiety over inadequacies, and the tendency to "act out" rather than "think through" periods of discomfort and lowered self-esteem. The traditions of the "Wild West," and the men's physical energy may also play a part. Rebelliousness may be another factor. The men in our sample came primarily from ambitious, hard-working, sometimes fundamentalist families, and they anticipated leading responsible and circumspect lives. College provided them with a brief interlude free from feminine restraints and adult responsibilities. Some students seemed to want to collect and store away incidents of gaiety and abandon for future remembrance.

The fraternity men were more interested in quickly establishing homes of their own than the non-fraternity men were. Whereas all the fraternity men hoped to be married by age 28, 11 per cent to 14 per cent of the men in other groups did not expect to be married by that time. When asked about fourteen important postgraduate values, the fraternity men rated "future family" and "love and affection" as among the first three most important factors more frequently than the other men did. It is as if these men, having conformed to familial demands in the past, and expecting to accept responsibilities as heads of households and community leaders in the future, were seizing at college a fleeting opportunity to rebel against care of property and concern for community approval.

The self-esteem of many of the fraternity men proved to be higher upon entrance into college than that of men in the other groups. They had been the heroes of an earlier stage in adolescence. Some of them had an elitist self-image because of their physical prowess and good looks. In addition, some felt their own superiority enhanced by the affluence and social position of their families. A socially ambitious "non-inheritor" from a wealthy family commented: "I could admittedly lead a terribly double-faced life—what I do and what I want somebody else to do are not at all the same. Anything I'm involved in, I can condone." (A friend of his, to whom we sent a questionnaire, commented: "He tends to be overcritical of people who don't look 'cool,' and over-impressed by those who do. Perhaps one could say he is a conformist, determined to be in the 'ingroup' whatever the cost to values.") At another time, the student said: "My parents want me to get good grades, but they would rather see me having a good time and not getting good grades than getting all A's and not enjoying myself. They keep impressing on me that these are the most 'fun' years, and that I should mix—and that half of college is who you meet and how you get along with people."

Although many of the fraternity men may have entered the university with high self-esteem based on a feeling of natural superiority, two elements in the university environment, the faculty and some women students, tended to discount wealth, good looks, and athletic prowess. The faculty admired and rewarded skills in abstract thinking and communication, and men in other groups appeared to excel in these areas. The practice of admitting two to three times as many men as women brought into the university community women students who were often superior to the men in areas of academic and social competence. They were in a favorable position in regard to the laws of supply and demand, and frequently made it clear that they wanted men who were not only outgoing and fun-loving, but also intellectual enough to discuss ideas, esthetic enough to share cultural interests, and introspective enough to discuss and understand their own personalities and those of the girls. Some of the fraternity men found themselves working harder than formerly at academic tasks and getting less recognition, and at the same time, having difficulty obtaining feminine approval. Thus, their feelings of adequacy as men and their feelings of self-respect as achievers were challenged by the university environment. Some men had the resources to develop the new skills valued by the university environment, but others only became more anxious and reacted by acting-out. Some of them bolstered their self-esteem by depreciating other people, including those who appeared to them to be less manly, less physically courageous, and less loyal to traditional leaders and ways of doing things than they themselves were. A few students escaped into hard drinking, destruction of property, fast driving, or sexual exploits, all of which they exhibited for the amusement or attention of other fraternity men. Frequently, these poorly adapted men failed to survive at the university, but their activities served to provide ammunition for those who had borne the brunt of the fraternity men's elitist attitude, or who envied them their solidity and ability to enjoy leisure pursuits.

Some fraternity members expressed strong aggressive feelings toward students who dressed unconventionally or took liberal or radical stands. The more violent expressions appeared to come from students who were having a great struggle controlling their impulses in general. One "inheritor" remarked: "The people who are banning fall-out shelters are asinine. People who wear 'Peace' on their lapels are the dregs of society. They think they are 'cool'; they think they are modern; they think they are beatnik. I don't want to know them. Fall-out shelters on campus were thought out seriously by the University." This student did not survive at Stanford. Neither did one of the others, who said with regard to the peace-button wearers: "This brings to mind the business that is going on in Berkeley. I think every one of those guys should be kicked out of school. I think education is not a right, but a privilege. Students ought to be able to get the education they came for. I think the administration at Berkeley didn't know what they were doing [in dealing leniently with protestors]. The students weren't in the right, but the University kind of kissed it off." It should be remembered that these comments came from men who were failing to adjust to college life. An "inheritor" who barely survived the academic competition commented: "I think the Free Speech Movement is disgusting. I don't mind sit-ins, walk-ins, strike-ins—I would do it myself. But when it interferes with the lives of other people, there is recourse to law and it should be used. Anyone who takes the law into his own hands is creating havoc."

Most of the fraternity men we interviewed were conservative, but attempted to be tolerant in their opinions and controlled in their behavior. They indicated an openness to new and liberal ideas if presented to them in a rational and convincing manner. Because of their respect for authority and their reliance on interpersonal contacts rather than on reading and introspection, they were influenced by professorial comments. Many of the fraternity men indicated that the four years of college led to important changes and taught them to be more liberal. Higher scores on scales of psychological tests dealing with social maturity and developmental status, and lower scores on the Ethnocentrism and Authoritarianism scales seem to confirm their self-evaluation. Nevertheless, few of them felt obliged to restrain the minority of fraternity members who tended to "scapegoat" liberal or unconventionally dressed individuals. Possibly the tendency toward uncritical acceptance of the behavior of others within the "in-group" and their own latent hostilities toward less traditional individuals prevented them from helping the more hostile brothers control their aggressive feelings.

These same factors may have prevented them from interfering in incidents of offensive behavior toward women. The men's ambivalent attitude toward women evidenced itself in many ways. The main interest of the men, especially early in their college careers, appeared to be in establishing themselves as accepted members of a male group. They tended to view women partly as potential sources of restraint and partly as "trophies"— proofs of their attractiveness and manliness. Women were admired if they were pretty, fun-loving, and non-judgmental. Later in their development, some of the men, through the efforts of specific women, became more comfortable with their masculinity and with their women friends' femininity, and were able to enjoy intimate and close relationships based on mutual acceptance as individuals. For others of the men, difficulty in getting dates, overt disapproval by women of their aggressive behavior, and impersonal treatment led to resentment. These men reacted by engaging in derogatory gossip about women students. They viewed at a distance and discussed as sexual objects the women whom they were not able to date, or they boasted about actual or imagined exploits with those they did date. Occasionally the unpleasant phenomenon of "grossing" a girl took place. This infrequent occurrence, which involved treating apparently masochistic or intoxicated girls in a dehumanizing or degrading fashion, was apparently indulged in by the participants in order to show their willingness to degrade women and themselves.

Drinking appeared to be a frequent activity among Stanford men, and Stanford fraternity and off-campus men described themselves as getting drunk more frequently than the men in the dorms and eating clubs did. Some students said they drank to "get high," to relax, or to add enjoyment to dates and special occasions. Others found in it a way of relieving tensions and coping with bad moods. Interviewees and other informants indicated that they were less involved in exhibitionistic drinking in their senior year than during the first two years of college. For some men in all fraternities, drinking was an activity integrated into their personalities. Some of them enjoyed a beer or two "with the boys" and a couple of drinks at parties; and some were heavy but controlled drinkers. Although the fraternity culture encouraged drinking, students who did not care to drink heavily were free to follow their own value systems. There even existed small clusters of abstainers. A woman student, in commenting about her fiance's choice of fraternity, said: "John's first choice of fraternity wouldn't take him because he doesn't drink. We think it's silly to have something to drink when you don't enjoy it. John explained this to another fraternity that interested him, and they kept inviting him back, and he joined. It has worked out well. There are a few others in the fraternity who don't drink." Another student was an occasional drinker. When he joined his fraternity, he felt that there was no pressure on him to drink. He enjoyed a drink or two at a party, but otherwise abstained. By his junior year, he felt that his fraternity brothers would "notice" if he didn't have an occasional beer after studying, and had no reluctance in complying with this pressure. However, when they demanded, on the occasion of his twenty-first birthday that he down twenty-one beers at a sitting, he rebelled: "A couple of times I've drunk too much beer, but never that much. If I feel like doing it, I'll do it. But I'm not just going to do it because I have to."

For other students, drinking was an escape or necessity. One student remarked: "I drink because I enjoy it. I've never gotten so drunk that I couldn't control myself. I have never had to be driven home. I remember being depressed about a girl, or school, and going out and tying a good one on. Generally, it loses its attraction once you start drinking—at least it does for me." Although this man seems to have been able to cope with his desire to "drink and forget," another was not so well controlled. His background included family and academic problems, as well as the fear of becoming an alcoholic. He noted that whenever he was displeased with something, he got "smashed." He had had two accidents while driving, and knew that he drank too much. In discussing excessive drinking, he commented: "The problem stems mostly from fellows just seeking an escape. It's a question of how disturbed you are. A lot of people, if they work for something and then don't quite get it, get very disturbed—it takes time for something like that to wear off. When you get smashed, the feelings don't wear off, but your interests change and you don't think about it."

TABLE 46

DRINKING PATTERNS OF MEN STUDENTS
(IN PER CENT)

	Off-Campus (N = 44)	Frat/On (N = 69)	Frat/Off (N = 44)	Eating Club (N = 37)	Dorm (N = 42)
Beer "frequently" a	68	64	68	32	26
Wine "frequently"	27	11	14	6	5
Hard liquor "frequently"	39	28	36	16	10
Beer "never"	7	4	2	11	26
Wine "never"	11	10	0	5	29
Hard liquor "never"	16	6	5	3	40

a "Frequently" was defined as daily or once or twice weekly. Differences between residential groups regarding consumption of each of the alcoholic beverages are significant beyond the .001 level. Omitted are per cents of students indicating that they drank specific beverages occasionally.

Whether they drank lightly or heavily, most of the fraternity men did not consider drinking a problem. However, if a person were in danger of becoming a problem drinker, the pressure of fraternity life for frequent masculine conviviality, the easy availability of liquor, and the round of parties and dates provide more than the usual opportunity for him to overindulge.

Although fraternity life creates definite problems for its participants, we found that it also facilitates some of the developmental tasks of the students. The information obtained from our twenty-two interviewees led us to infer that their fraternity par-

ticipation may have aided them in the separation process by helping them to make the transition from home living. In contrast to
the impersonal environment of the freshman dorm, the fraternity
house offers the students a sense of belonging to an ingroup, a
feeling of security, and a housing arrangement that affords more
continuity with their previous experiences than the dormitory
does. The functional aspects of the fraternities appeared to these
students to provide a continuity of experience in group activities,
and to be helpful in enabling them to move emotionally from
their home community to the university community. The comments of a student from a small town summarize the reasons given
by many other students for joining a fraternity: "I joined a fraternity mainly because it's a chance to get to know more people
better. In the dorms, I went around with a clique; there doesn't
seem to be the great desire to get out and build friendships that
there is in a fraternity. My two close friends joined the fraternity
with me. They're interested in someone else and not themselves
all the time. They like to have a good time, and they're interested
in school, too."

Many future fraternity men react to the universal freshman
dormitory experience by quickly becoming part of an informal,
friendly clique; by assuming positions such as social chairman or
athletic chairman for their house in the dormitory; and by trying
to get dates in spite of the difficuities freshman men have in dating
Stanford girls. By the time of "rush," most fraternity men in our
study had spent considerable time finding friends who enjoyed
athletics, camaraderie, dating, or drinking. Their behavior in the
dormitories prior to rushing and their behavior during the rushing experience indicated that they wanted the advantages of being
part of a well-defined group, and that they were willing to pay a
price for this opportunity. They were willing to redirect some of
their aggressive and individualistic tendencies in ways prescribed
by the fraternity. In many houses, special opportunities were provided for the new brothers to get to know a number of men well.
Fraternity living also provided opportunities for them to get to
know upperclassmen and thus "learn the ropes."

Earlier we discussed some of the problems arising out of
a lack of critical attitude among fraternity members. There is
another side to that coin. When the individual fraternity member

contracted to be friendly and loyal to his "brothers," he could expect this to be reciprocated. This sort of arrangement sometimes provided protective insurance against factors in the university environment that tended to make students feel insecure and unworthy. Although relationships between fraternity men were often more reserved than intimate, they did give a certain sense of security. With the exception of those who were moving rapidly up or down the social ladder, fraternity men rarely complained of feelings of alienation or diffusion. This may have been because they experimented so infrequently with new ideas or new experiences. The security and group identity provided by the fraternity may have provided a support for their self-esteem that enabled them to proceed with their educational tasks. Dr. Helene Deutsch speaks of group participation among younger adolescents as providing an opportunity for peer-approved regressive behavior in the service of slowing growth, so that disintegration can be avoided and progress eventually abetted.[2] Thus, even some of the regressive aspects of fraternity living may have functional value for students who need relief from the anxiety of moving too rapidly toward independence, or who are unready for heterosexual mutuality, or for confrontation with differences of values, ideas, and behavior in their classmates.

The task of relating to women in a voluntary and independent way is one that causes considerable anxiety for men students. Among the students in our samples, this was true even for men who had much experience in dating during high school. Asking for dates and venturing toward physical contact was an anxiety-laden experience for many of these men. Such movement is fraught with potentialities for confrontation with ambivalent feelings, mutual dependency, and commitment, and therefore for rejection and lowered self-esteem. As we have indicated, the self-esteem of most freshman and sophomore students is not very sturdy. With the support of fraternity brothers and the aid of planned social events, the task of making arrangements for social life with girls was facilitated. In light of the men's fear of rejection and actual experiences of rejection, some of their less desir-

[2] Deutsch, Helene, *Selected Problems of Adolescence.* New York: International Universities Press, 1967.

able behavior toward women becomes more understandable. But in spite of their anxieties, most of the men were successful in moving away from isolation or exclusively same-sex relationships toward comfortable and pleasant group activities or casual relationships with women. Other men were able to move toward closer and more mature relationships.

Another advantage the fraternity provided was the opportunity for non-competitive or mildly competitive physical activities. The fraternity men, more than others, appeared to be physically vigorous and energetic. College athletics are too time-consuming or too competitive for many students, and the informal and easily available athletic activities connected with the fraternities provide an important outlet. The fraternity is one of the few institutions on campus that seriously concerns itself with the need of young people for fun and relaxation. This is important, in light of the many demands made of students to question their values and goals and to compete in a demanding academic and social environment.

Descriptions of life within the fraternities provided some of the few examples given by men of commitment and helpfulness to others. By joining a fraternity, these men had indicated a willingness to be depended upon and to depend upon others. The fraternity man was expected to offer and to receive friendliness and helpfulness. Because of continuity and propinquity, a fraternity man had the opportunity to perceive pain and pleasure in a variety of other persons, and to have his own pain and pleasure perceived by them. When illness or some other mishap occurred to a fraternity man, he could count on help from his brothers. Most fraternity houses provided study tables to aid students who were failing; one acceptable excuse for non-participation in group activities was academic failure or problems. One student, in commenting on the help he got from fraternity brothers, noted: "They help me out as far as grades go. We just kind of made an agreement—I told them that my grades had to come first, and they agreed, and are doing all they can to help me. I think this will help a lot too, because now I get all my English papers graded once before I turn them in and then I rewrite them. They help me with my math and anything that I have problems with. In general, I can go to the House and find an expert in just about anything." This student had come to the university from a small town, and had encountered many problems in adjusting to the more sophisticated and intellectual college milieu. In addition, his athletic scholarship required long hours of practice. He attributed his survival at the university to the comfort and help he received from his fraternity brothers. (In common with some other athletes and fraternity men, he expressed feelings resembling those of being persecuted when he described the way he experienced criticism of athletes and fraternity men.)

Another functional aspect of the fraternity is that it offers informal training in leadership. We found individual fraternity members who aspired to varying levels and types of leadership. These students did not want lives detached from other people, and they did not necessarily need to restrict their friendships to one or two close friends. They wanted, and appeared to be able to accept, a variety of encounters every day and many times a day; and they seemed able to play as well as work with the people around them. They aspired to more-than-casual contact with many individuals and groups throughout their lives, and accepted the fact that such aspirations involve the mastering of complex skills. The fraternities seem to have tried to cope with the complexity of teaching these skills by developing certain rituals and definitions of appropriate behavior, and by offering opportunities for taking on tasks involving varying degrees of leadership. Innumerable comments made by fraternity men indicated either a willingness or a desire to lead others, or respect for "brothers" whom they considered leaders.

In every fraternity, the necessity for cooperation in managing the household and planning social and athletic events requires the assistance of all the members at various times. Participation in such activities gave our students an opportunity to learn how much responsibility they were willing and able to take for group activities, and what some of the costs and rewards of leadership were. Experience in enlisting cooperation and loyalty and in avoiding group tensions were valuable training experiences for those students who were interested in management or politics.

What of those male students who, either through chance or election, did not join fraternities? This segment of the male student population was divided into those who joined eating clubs, and those unaffiliated men who lived either in dormitories or in off-campus apartments. These men differed in their attitudes toward group membership and autonomy. The fraternity men, with their interest in leading and manipulating others, were willing to adapt to group demands and to rely on the group for status and support. Often their needs and preferences as individuals were subordinated to group patterns. Eating-club men described themselves as more individualistic and less socially sophisticated than fraternity men. However, belonging to a personally selected and formally organized group of men appealed to them, and may have represented an effort on their part to move toward more active participation with peer groups than they had enjoyed in high school. The dormitory men, with their shyness and emotional investment in themselves as workers, appeared to desire minimal response from other men, individually or in groups. The off-campus men appeared to choose a few people as close friends, and to avoid living with large groups of men—either because of their desire for independence, or because they were perceived by others as not easily adaptable to group living.

An "eating club" is an organization composed of a group of from 30 to 60 men who live either in off-campus apartments or in dormitories that do not provide meals. As their name indicates, eating clubs provide facilities for a congenial group of men to meet for meals. In addition, they provide for social, athletic, cultural, and service activities. Although eating clubs have existed on the Stanford campus for about sixty years, only in the last fifteen years have they had permanent housing—a one-story L-shaped building that contains kitchens and all-purpose dining rooms. Together the clubs share an athletic field, picnic grounds, and a common game room. The clubs are open 24 hours a day, and provide a place for studying, goofing off, and "raiding the icebox." They are far from glamorous in appearance, but are functional and easy to maintain. The clubs boast a diversity of membership. One club, with a large proportion of members interested in drama, art, and creative writing, could be described as having an atmosphere of great casualness. There are about a third as many eating clubs at Stanford as there are fraternities, and they have about a third as many members.

The men in our interview sample who joined eating clubs often came from modest backgrounds, and they lacked the self-confidence in social matters that characterized the fraternity men. A number of them had been "good boys" during high school, occupied with academic challenges and less involved or skilled in athletic and group activities than the fraternity men were. Having felt themselves part of a small, intellectual minority during high school, they looked forward to a more active social life at college, where they anticipated finding a larger number of students with their own values and interests.

The freshman year proved to be a great disappointment to these men, and the process of separation from home was made more difficult by their discouragement with regard to social life at the university. Three groups in the freshman dormitories contributed to this feeling. First there was a small but active group of students whose pranksterism and anti-intellectual attitudes served to dampen any tendency on the part of others to exhibit an interest in intellectual or cultural matters. Second, there were the potential fraternity members, who were locating each other and grouping together in anticipation of the rushing experience. They tended to exclude students who did not make a "cool" impression, because they were reluctant to be thought of as the friends of those who would not be pledged. Third, there were the students who were isolated or "booked" all the time. The problem of exhaustive academic demands and the danger of low grades further dampened the hopes of the eating-club men for a pleasant social life. In answering the Senior Questionnaire, almost half the eating-club men said they had been very dissatisfied with themselves as freshmen, and that this was largely because of their disappointment with the social milieu. By their senior year, the social environment seemed more in harmony with their high-school expectations, and they had adapted well to academic demands. In many cases, for many of them, their experiences at the university began poorly, but ended happily.[3]

[3] Forty-six per cent of the club men described themselves as being "quite" or "very" dissatisfied with themselves as freshmen, whereas 24 per cent of them so described themselves as seniors. Of the five subgroups—fraternity men living on campus, fraternity men living off campus, eating club men, dormitory men, and non-fraternity off-campus men—they had been the most dissatisfied as freshmen and least dissatisfied as seniors.

The nine club men in our interview sample appeared to be more different from one another than the fraternity men were. There were three thoughtful small-town students who had been outstanding for academic skills and leadership in small-town communities. They appeared to be more intellectual, less athletic, and less social than the fraternity men who had come from small communities. Perception of the superiority of students educated in urban, suburban, or "prep" schools was described by one of the three in this way: "In high school I was a big man. I kind of came here with the thought that there would be no problem in college and that I had a pretty good background. When I got here, I found that that wasn't true. From the first, I ran into people who had definite ideas about politics and I hardly knew who they were talking about. It didn't seem as if I knew very much. Mainly I realized how much I had missed by coming from a small community."

Three of the nine students had grown up in large communities and came from families with strong ethical convictions. Two of these families were from minority groups.[4] The majority of the eating-club men in our interview sample viewed both parents as individuals with strengths and weaknesses, and attempted to understand them as they were attempting to understand themselves. Sometimes this involved confrontations and conflicts leading to greater understanding. The mothers of these men appeared to be active in professions or community affairs, and to communicate freely with their sons. The remaining three students had eccentricities and problems that made it difficult for them to adapt to group demands, but they found certain benefits in the easygoing environment of the clubs. For example, one student with professional aspirations joined a club partly out of awareness of his ineptitude in dealing with people; he hoped to gain more skills in this area through his club associations.

The clubmen typically lacked the social self-confidence of the fraternity men. Many of them had been interested in academic

---

[4] Another student could be described as having "minority status," in the sense of the uniqueness of his being from a family with high-income status and a history of many generations of intellectual and social prestige. He chose to remain "out" of the fraternity culture, and disdained many of its values as materialistic and anti-intellectual.

matters and good citizenship in high school and had been among the students who delighted teachers and adults with their interest in the problems of the adult world. A graduate student informant summarized some of the outstanding qualities of the clubmen as follows: "In eating clubs, you get compliant, nice, small-town, easygoing, not-too-talkative boys. If you get to know them, you find they're interesting. A familiar quality of the men is quietness. These guys don't go out of their way to slap you on the back, but they do have opinions. A lot of these guys were tops in high school: top athlete and top leader. They got here, and they had difficulties when they were freshmen—they weren't socially oriented. They don't date much.[5] They get into clubs, but they don't get active on the campus. When they do, they get involved with the radio station or the drama groups."

The quality of professionalism was more evident in our interview sample of clubmen than in the fraternity group. Of our nine students, the majority came from homes where the fathers were professional men who practiced their professions and were recognized for specific competencies based on education; usually they were not in managerial or leadership positions per se. Three were lawyers, two were teachers, one was an artist, the seventh was a physician interested in teaching and research, the eighth a small businessman, and the ninth, a white-collar worker with a Master's degree. Four of the mothers were employed part-time or full-time as teachers; one was a social worker, and another a bookkeeper. Of the nine clubmen, four wanted to be physicians, and three of these were interested in research or teaching. Two aspired to be writers, and another to be a psychologist—and these three also included university teaching as a possibility. Of the two eating-club men who were atypical of the interview group, one aspired to business administration and the other to engineering.

Our interview sample ($N = 7$) differed from the questionnaire sample ($N = 37$) in its greater representation of premedical

---

[5] We interviewed the students intensively about interpersonal and sexual relationships at the end of the junior year. Of the forty-two men in our interview sample, none of the dormitory men and about a third of the "inheritor" fraternity men and the eating-club men had had sexual relations. About two-thirds of the "non-inheritors" and the men who lived in off-campus apartments had had sexual relations.

students and smaller representation of business and engineering students. In a follow-up study indicating the graduate school the students are attending, the eating-club men had a large number of students in business, engineering, and fields that generally lead to college teaching or research. The large number of students preparing for business and engineering as well as for possible academic careers suggests the existence of considerable diversity in the eating clubs. (The absence of students entering law may be connected with the "quietness" suggested earlier as a characteristic of the eating-club men: see Table 44.)

Many of the clubmen lacked the "coolness," that is, the smooth, outgoing, apparent self-confidence, that characterized many of the fraternity men. The clubmen had not belonged to the most popular crowds in high school, although some had held formal student offices. They were not like the white Protestant males from upper-middle-class suburbs we described as the pace-setters for the fraternities, although they may have had one or more of these characteristics. The fraternity men appeared to some of the clubmen like college models for magazine ads, and the girls they were seen with seemed attractive and superficially desirable. Many of the clubmen felt inferior to the able and attractive men in the fraternity groups, and envied them their group solidarity, manliness, and ability to have fun. Although moving toward masculine gregariousness and fun, the clubmen often were far from carefree. In other ways, the clubmen felt indifferent or superior to the fraternity men, whom they perceived as lacking idealism and understanding of themselves and the world.

A few words about some of the clubmen in our interview sample may serve to illustrate their lack of "coolness." Three of them were serious premedical students with interests either in research or in serving others directly. They yearned for more social grace and ease than they felt they possessed. Two of the three were from minority groups, and suffered from self-consciousness in this regard. Two others were potential creative writers, and shared a detached and watchful attitude toward everything they experienced. They were sharp observers, skilled in translating into words the impressions they received. The appearance of the first three men was overly neat and conventional for the campus, whereas the second two dressed carelessly, even unconventionally.

Their hair was a little long, and one of the students, the son of a distinguished and wealthy family, usually wore clean but shabby jeans and tennis shoes. The other potential writer was from a small town, and lacked urbanity and sophistication. Possibly because of a lack of interest, or of finances, or of the knowledge of what was most fashionable and attractive, these men were not as well-groomed as the fraternity men. One serious and long-haired student from a minority group was deeply involved in applying his elementary knowledge of depth psychology to understanding his own motivations and those of people around him. Another clubman, a Negro, had not made a good social adjustment in his own home community, and appeared to be bewildered by the college environment.

In general, the clubmen appeared to be more introspective than most of the fraternity and dormitory men. They showed more facility in discussing their behavior and relationships with others and their opinions about the validity of ideals and philosophies. The writers-to-be, the psychologist-to-be, and two of the potential doctors were intensely involved in trying to understand and evaluate what they experienced, and to develop their own personal philosophies. They were concerned about questions of integrity and individual responsibility. They often were critical of the adult world, but were not rebellious. They took seriously their responsibility to determine their own values. Their relationships with other students involved discussions of personal problems and clarification of values and feelings. Although career interests and graduate school were important to them, they were also involved with the world of ideas. In spite of their academic and career interests, the clubmen were more outgoing than the dormitory men, and were more interested in a variety of relationships with others.

A large proportion of the eating-club men in our interview sample had felt "different" prior to college, because they had adhered to adult-approved behavior while many of their high school peers behaved in a more peer-approved way. Most of the clubmen had been serious, hard-working, future-oriented, controlled students; but in contrast to the dormitory men, they now had more desire for fun and popularity. Looking back on his college years, one clubman commented: "Until recently, 'doing my duty' and 'being a good boy' were my main goals. Although I still want to be a competent doctor and do significant research, I also want to go to parties, drink with my friends, and have some fun while at college. As a result of getting to know more friends, I feel that I have moved from being self-centered to being more interested in others. I am less enthusiastic about knowledge for the sake of knowledge alone; I have moved toward wanting to work with people and do something for them." This student was an unusually competent person interested in medical teaching or research. He was aware that his relationships with others were characterized by formality and distance, and commented that absence of conflict with others might reflect his reluctance to risk intimacy.

The tendency to value intellectual gratifications more highly than emotional relationships was suggested by the students' answers regarding activities and interests they considered of importance after graduation. The fraternity men were more interested in careers than the clubmen were; twice as many clubmen, dormitory men, and off-campus men expected intellectual and artistic matters to be of primary importance. Almost twice as many fraternity men as clubmen expected activities with their future families to be of major importance. The latter showed considerable interest in helping others, but, as one student suggested, they seemed more inclined to love "mankind" than to love "men."

The self-evaluation of the students in our samples and the results of psychological test scores seem to indicate that the students in the eating clubs were relatively open to change as a result of the college experience. More than students in the other subgroups, the clubmen described themselves as having changed regarding moral, political, and religious values, and as having enhanced their academic skills and intellectual interests. They may have found enough pleasing factors in the university environment to provide gratifications, yet sufficient displeasing aspects to stimulate independent and critical thinking; or they may have come to this specific university because of a readiness to change in the direction of greater social sophistication or increased intellectual interests. Then, too, their capacity for introspection and communication may have enabled them to utilize relationships in the service of personal modification. When asked about the reasons for changes that occurred, the clubmen indicated ten out of a possible sixteen reasons with greater frequency than men in the other housing groups did. More clubmen indicated emotional readjustments connected with their homes as being factors of importance. Our interview data indicate some reasons why being away from home may have had the importance it did for some of these men. Many of them had ventured far from home either geographically, or in cultural patterns, or both. Our interview sample included a Boston Brahmin, several students from New York City, several students from small towns, a Negro student, a Japanese student, and two Jewish students. For many of these students, living among a population of predominantly white, Protestant suburbanites, in a Western atmosphere, stimulated them to evaluate their familiar values from a different point of view. More clubmen than others indicated problems in their families as reasons for changes that had occurred. This may have indicated either more family problems or greater interest and perception on the part of the students. Table 47 suggests many interesting variations in the perceptions of men in the different housing-affiliation groups. Many of the clubmen had enjoyed closer relationships with other men during college than they had previously experienced. They spoke with enthusiasm, as the men in other housing groups did, of long, serious discussion dealing with religion, politics, and morality. However, they, more than men in other housing affiliation groups, indicated that changes had occurred in these areas. Change was perceived by them as being most noticeable in the area of moral values. This is in harmony with the impression given by our interviewees that a segment of the clubmen had been "good boys" in high school, and were eager to become more venturesome and independent as they moved into young adulthood.

The eating-club members we interviewed indicated to us some of the advantages and disadvantages of the clubs. Like the fraternities, the clubs provided a group that was small enough for closeness, yet large enough for diversity, and which promised continuity for several years. Moreover, the clubs offered group activities for students who were more social and athletic than the dormitory students, but less self-confident and experienced in

TABLE 47

STUDENT SELF-EVALUATION OF CAUSES OF CHANGE DURING COLLEGE
(PER CENT WHO SAID THE FOLLOWING HAD "GREAT
INFLUENCE" DURING COLLEGE)

	Eating Club (N = 37)	Frat/On (N = 69)	Frat/Off (N = 44)	Off-Campus (N = 44)	Dorm (N = 42)	p
Factors within self						
Problems in self	51	45	45	45	50	NS
Gaining self-understanding	65	58	45	55	45	NS
Peers						
Closeness to opposite sex peers	43	43	57	39	21	*
Closeness to same sex peers	43	42	34	34	30	NS
Crises in relationships	27	10	20	20	19	< .10
Problems in others	30	19	20	20	12	NS
Family						
Being away from home	57	40	18	32	40	**
Problems in own family	24	4	11	11	7	*
Ideational						
Living group	27	61	50	7	21	***
Ideas from teachers and courses	35	20	30	16	26	NS
Ideas in books	24	12	14	23	36	**
Close relations with teachers and adults	16	10	14	14	12	NS
Involvement with social, political improvement	19	9	5	0	14	*

* p < .05
** p < .01
*** p < .001

these matters than the fraternity men.[6] For young men with limited incomes and many academic responsibilities, it was convenient to have access to inexpensive and regular social activities. "The main advantage of the eating club is, of course, meals and eating together—social life is pretty good. We pay $20 a quarter for social fees, which isn't too high. Every two weeks or so there's a party of some kind to go to. 'Thank God it's Friday' parties are generally stag parties where you drink beer, sing, and talk—sort of an unloosening at the end of the week. In addition, there are dances; and there is always a group that you can go with to the various things around campus—a bunch of boys will get together and go see a movie or something like that. Most of my dating is for club functions." Another student, nostalgic about his hometown crowd, commented: "I enjoy going to parties at the eating club because I like to dance and I enjoy drinking. I like the sense of being with a crowd. But I don't have the sense of being at home —I'm being at the parties without real contact. I say 'hello,' and things like that, but I don't have a meaningful relationship with the people at the party."

There appeared to be greater encouragement of individuality and less emphasis on conformity in the clubs than in the fraternities. One student commented: "I suppose the main thing that I can say about my friends being helpful during college has been presenting different points of view. In the eating club, you get a large number of people together, and consequently you get varying opinions on things. I wasn't just getting an athlete's view all the time, or a scientist's, or something like that. There have been fellows who have been exceptionally able to have insights into my problems and see things that I was overlooking."

Intellectual, cultural, and service activities were regarded with open acceptance and approval by more clubmen than fraternity members. More of the clubmen we interviewed gave time to university service, tutoring underprivileged children, visiting mental hospitals, and so on, than men in the other groups did. Because of their interest in getting good grades for admission to graduate schools, the clubmen were often unable to satisfy their

[6] See Table 45.

former interests in reading and cultural matters; our interviewees indicated resentment because of lack of time for these activities. In their free time, many of the students in all the groups interviewed felt the need for relaxation, and for relief from exercising control in the interests of achievement and development.

As described by the interview sample, the main disadvantages of eating clubs were as follows: first, the housing arrangements of the eating clubs were not as attractive as those of the fraternity men; second, the position of the eating clubs in the university community was perceived by many of the members as having lower status than the fraternities; third, a "group image" analogous to the "fraternity man" image was lacking among clubmen, and they somehow resented this; fourth, although the eating clubs had a history of many years on campus, they lacked the traditional sense of continuity and cohesion that characterized many of the fraternities; and finally, the conflict between individual independence and group needs resulted in an indifference that showed itself in lack of participation in group activities and lack of responsibility for club affairs. This indifference directs our attention to the interesting question of ingroup solidarity. Some criticisms of fraternities deal with the scapegoating of outsiders, and with the pressures on fraternity members to conform and to participate in fraternity-sponsored affairs. Loyalty to a group appears to involve renunciation of some individual preferences. It would be interesting to try to ascertain the point at which an excess of either individuality or diversity leads to the deterioration of a group.

The next two major student groups we will describe—the dormitory men and the non-fraternity off-campus men—defined themselves by their choice of living arrangements as being either uninterested in or unacceptable to a defined social group. The two groups of men differed dramatically in terms of conventionality and independence. Many of the dormitory men were quite dependent and conventional within a limited circle of relationships. The men who lived in off-campus apartments were often resistant to attempts to limit their freedom to live as they wished. Most of them were in protest against the restrictions of conventionality, and were open to a variety of new experiences. Another group preferred off-campus living because of its economy and relative privacy.

With regard to the off-campus men, there is obviously no clearly defined single milieu in which they existed. Except in a few unusual circumstances, three or four men would move into one of the many apartment houses available in the area, and share the expense and work involved in housekeeping. They cooked, shopped, and lived like members of the non-university community—coming and going as they wished, eating and drinking at will, and spending whatever they could afford. Of the nine off-campus men in our interview sample, two physicists-to-be resembled the dormitory men in their task-orientedness and desire for minimal relations. They had been reasonably content with dormitory living, but had moved to off-campus apartments for reasons of economy, because of friends who made similar decisions, or because of annoyance with dormitory efforts to involve them in social life. "They are trying to turn the dorm into a fraternity," one of them complained.

Three other men gave an impression of "rootlessness." These men appeared to be constantly excited and restless, and had difficulty finding a comfortable place for themselves in the university environment. Their fathers had been well-educated and successful, but the families seemed never to have taken root in their communities. In two instances, the mothers had died during the early adolescence of the sons, and this probably had contributed to the son's confusion. These three had all been "rushed," and one of them had actually joined a fraternity. The son of an international diplomat, he said he would not have considered an "ordinary fraternity," but required one that had "proof of suitable measures of social independence and academic excellence." After three months, he moved out of the fraternity house, maintaining that he liked the house and the men, but didn't like "to get up at nine on Saturday and rake the lawn, fix meals, and so on." He maintained a tangential relationship to the fraternity, as did a second student. They enjoyed attending occasional parties at the fraternities, but felt that beyond that, they did not wish to participate in cooperative efforts or group living. The second student, a Scandinavian, had felt "out of it" in the Italian neighborhood of his high-school days. He deeply resented being classified by others at the university according to where he lived. He had exhausted himself as a freshman in trying to remove the "dorm stigma." [7] He and his roommate chose an old house to live in. They rented their house to on-campus groups for beer parties. This enabled the student to enjoy gratification from arranging for men and women to come together and be congenial—a need of his that had an almost compulsive quality to it.

The third "rootless" student became a heavy drinker. His choice of housing reflected his attitude toward school: "All I have to do with school is going to classes and eating lunch there. Other than that, I live completely out of it." He and his circle of friends were described by an acquaintance as "individuals." "They're all bright; they're all different; somebody from the group is drinking every night." According to another student: "This group achieved almost legendary status for its incredible parties, feats of drinking, sexual promiscuity, and other irresponsible acts. The goal was to seek new thrills and experience—new sensations. However, as in the case of most thrill-seekers, the desire for thrills became an insatiable hunger. As the group slipped more and more into a life without meaning, it became defensively exclusive, barring from its ranks people who wouldn't or couldn't condone its actions. At the same time, the group desperately sought appreciation and acceptance. Their increasing social defaults and increasing rejections began a period of misery from which they couldn't extricate themselves."

The remaining four off-campus men in our sample were energetic and eager. They came from low-income families, and their parents had not had college educations. The men, by virtue of their abilities and energies, were pioneering into a new and exciting world. As freshmen, they appeared self-confident and pleased with the impression that they felt they were making in their new environment. But egocentrism and naïveté led them to evaluate their situation more optimistically than reality warranted. Although most of them would have liked to join organized groups, they were not accepted. In the main, they moved to off-

[7] This refers to the reputation the dormitory men had for being socially inept, especially in their behavior with women.

campus apartments either because they disliked regulations, or because they wished to avoid being identified with the dormitory students. Said one: "I didn't enjoy life in the dorms. It was noisy, and I hate regulations of any sort whatsoever—the dorms have certain rules, such as no women, no liquor, and so forth. There were record players going at all hours, screaming and howling, all sorts of animalistic activities. I can't see standing in line and having food dumped on me, either. I decided that possibly my place was not in the dorm."

Their inexperience in social affairs, egocentric verbalizations, and nonconformity may have prevented the off-campus men from achieving the sort of social life they desired. By the end of their four years, they had gained an awareness of how their comments might have jarred others in a group situation. They had benefited from being at overseas campuses, or from forming close relationships, and had learned to show recognition of the needs of others to express their ideas and interests. If rushing had occurred in the senior year, these men might have been able to join a fraternity group, and to benefit from further knowledge of social skills.

Most of the off-campus men were characterized by the interviewers as critical, verbally skilled, energetic, troubled, impulsive, and interested in intellectual matters. They seemed to relate to family and friends in ways that were intense and often involved conflict or alienation. One of the students was distinguished by his interest in Christian ethics, which was not that of a constricted and judgmental person, but that of a strongly impulsive person who felt that he could understand pulls toward indulgent or immoral behavior in others and could help them and himself through applying and teaching the principles of his church. In one way or another, the off-campus men in our interview sample stood out as being and perceiving themselves to be "different" from most of the students on campus. Accompanying their feeling of "difference" was a sense of being more intellectual and creative than most of the other students. They showed less interest in social and athletic activities than did men in the affiliated groups. One of their favorite recreational activities was attending movies, which they did more often than men in the other groups. Attendance at movies provided a relatively inexpensive form of recreation and one that did not necessitate much planning ahead or group involvement. (This interest may also have reflected their concern with emotional problems.) The eating-club men shared their interest in movies and attending lectures. However, the clubmen appeared to have been interested in service to others and in political activities, and this interest was not evident among the off-campus men.[8] Their greatest involvement was possibly in clarifying their own goals and values. Many were deeply concerned with the meaning of life and with their own identities. Some of them were actively rebelling against their home backgrounds and attempting to find new answers, whereas others came from professional and intellectual families, and were following a family pattern of criticism and dissent.

Many of the off-campus men yearned for something, but found it difficult to define what it was that they actually wanted. One troubled student commented: "There are so many people I've met in different societies, and different things I've seen, and each one hurts me in some way. I've got to read a lot and find out for myself. Everything I see has something wrong with it. I can laugh at everything, but with kind of a sadistic laugh, not a humorous one. In my reading and writing, I'm trying to piece it all together—because then I don't feel so unreal, so lost." He was representative of those off-campus men who came from intellectual and cosmopolitan families, but were thrown early in life upon their own emotional resources. Others of the men had more protective emotional backgrounds, but lacked intellectual stimulation. As these students were very well endowed with intelligence, they were attracted to and stimulated by many of the ideas and opportunities available to them on campus. Their problem lay in choosing among a variety of interests, and in integrating their new experiences into their personalities and life goals. Integrating forces such as identification with an intellectual friend or relative or clear-cut professional aspirations helped some of the students avoid feeling overwhelmed or diffused.

Questionnaire answers indicated that about 45 per cent of the off-campus men shared with the fraternity men an interest in traveling. Of our nine men, three traveled as part of the overseas

[8] See Table 45.

program, and three as a result of personal restlessness and discontent with their environment. Four of the men interrupted their college careers because of adventurousness, or because they were suspended, and traveled during this period. Traveling may have symbolized their restless attempts to define themselves or to find a place for themselves where they could feel that they belonged. While at the university, they often moved from place to place, or among different groups, critically appraising each situation and finding that it fell short of their expectations. One student, for example, unsuccessful in joining an eating club, became part of a group of students, mostly from the East Coast, who joined an off-campus cooperative whose members were "existentialist" and highly critical of Stanford and the West. "Way-out" ideas were seriously considered and evaluated. Dissatisfied, the student, a Protestant, left this group and joined a Catholic eating cooperative. Later on, he continued to try to clarify his thoughts and values, first attending an overseas campus, then doing service work in an underprivileged community.

The off-campus men's feelings of alienation may result from the turbulence of the separation process from their families, from the rebuffs they receive in the university community, or from feelings of superiority because of their perception of their intellectual and creative capacities. In any event, these students seem more inclined than students in the other subgroups to feel that their college years are not particularly happy ones, to complain of frequent feelings of depression, and to express the wish that they had gone to other universities.[9]

Their independence and sense of confidence in their cognitive skills may have influenced the choice of occupation of the off-campus men: many of them were interested in entering the professions of medicine, law, or engineering, which allow for independent action. This may have resulted from their identification with professional parents, since 28 per cent of the off-campus students had professional parents, in contrast with 15 per cent to

---

[9] Only a fourth of the off-campus men indicated that the years from 17–21 were among the three happiest, in contrast to half of the fraternity men. In a write-in question, 16 per cent of the off-campus men (N = 44) indicated the wish that they had gone to other colleges, in contrast to 5 per cent of most of the other subgroups.

19 per cent of the students in the other residence groups. On the other hand, many of the fathers of the off-campus men had not had college educations; for these students, the professions seemed to promise an opportunity for upward mobility. The fact that only a small number of off-campus and dormitory men were interested in business may reflect a disinclination toward the type of adaptation to large groups of people that is often required for success in the business world.

There are many reasons why individuals have a desire for independence. These reasons include such diverse factors as distrust of others, confidence in one's own capacities, identification with independent persons, and fearfulness of accepting dependency need and obligations. All these reasons appeared in one or another of our students' case histories. Another possible factor is ordinal position. In our interview sample, all but one of the nine men were oldest children. Assuming that dormitory living provides the most dependent and institutionalized form of living, and that off-campus housing is the least institutionalized and provides the greatest independence, it is interesting to note that the proportion of oldest sons in our interview sample increased as the students chose housing in harmony with the above assumption. From our data, it appears that being oldest may coincide with desiring independence in living arrangements. More than twice as many off-campus men as fraternity men came from families with sisters only. Perhaps having sisters and no brothers may be associated with an unwillingness to live with a large group of men. There were more only children among the least gregarious group in our sample—the dormitory men—than in the other groups. Men with brothers only were more apt to join fraternities and eating clubs, while the off-campus men—or those unwilling to live with large groups of men—were least likely to have brothers. Since our interview sample was relatively small, these observations are far from conclusive, and should be considered only as offering suggestions regarding motivations for choosing housing-affiliation groups, and as a basis for further explorations.

The fraternity men who lived in off-campus apartments shared with the off-campus men an interest in seeking out off-beat places and people. Although only a small proportion of men noted this as a "frequent" activity, fewer of the off-campus men "never" engaged in this sort of activity than the men in other housing groups did. All those who lived in off-campus apartments appeared to be the least religious of those we interviewed. They were less inclined to participate in church-connected activities, and were least likely to pray.

While the fraternity men, who respected authority figures, felt that they had changed as a result of ideas presented in courses or by teachers, the off-campus men were less inclined to acknowledge such influence. This was in harmony with their argumentative and rebellious attitude toward figures of authority. Members of this group were very critical about the Stanford administration. One student commented: "The right of the student is to satisfy his intellectual curiosity without interference from the administration, whose sole activities should be housekeeping, getting funds, and so forth. Conflicts between departments should be handled by the Academic Council. I think students are treated like employees in a company with no rights. They can be thrown out for some action that has absolutely nothing to do with the academic environment. Students have the right to indicate what type of courses should be offered. Another thing, the whole idea of a major is a ridiculous thing. From my point of view, there were a lot of courses I wanted to take but couldn't, as a result of the requirements for my major. With most people going into graduate school nowadays, I think the student's ends could be better served if he could pick out his own courses as an undergraduate according to his own interests. A major is important only in terms of an occupation. If you plan to go on to graduate school, the *raison d'être* of a major disappears."

Regarding a controversial issue involving the administration, he remarked: "I am delighted with the present problem. The students now psychologically have the advantage over the administration. The administration is defensive. They are just looking for a way out right now. Now they have been found out to have a scandal among their own administrators—this has undermined the prestige or image of the administrators. Now they cannot say, 'We are the administration, and we run the school, and the rest of you are peons.'" With reference to regulations, he said: "I am against overnight regulations—you can't regulate morality. My attitude is, if the administration approves of something, why not oppose it? I feel that the administration uses student groups as catspaws—so it looks as if students have enforced something when it is the Deans of Men and Women who are actually at the back of it." Predictably, this student had evidenced prior to college a spirit of independence and a desire to challenge authority and to institute what he perceived as necessary changes and reforms.

A clue to this attitude toward authority may be found in the relationship of some of the off-campus men with their parents, especially their fathers. The fathers of the physicists-to-be resembled those of the "dorm men," with their emphasis on hard work and tendency toward minimal communication with family members. The rootless ones felt that their fathers were distant from them, and had given them a freedom that verged on indifference. "My father is a walking encyclopedia. He will condemn me if he feels that I have done something wrong, but he won't stop me. I think he puts a certain amount of trust in me, which in some cases I've justified and in others I've not. I was very intolerant of Mother's worrying and nagging. I resemble my father in that we both want to do things. He does a lot of traveling, and whatever strikes his fancy, he will do. I didn't go to my parents with my problems. I don't think there was much need to go to them—whatever interests me is OK with them. They don't care. They figure it's up to me." A hard-drinking student commented: "My father has always said: Do what the strength of your convictions—your intuition—tells you to do. He's brilliant, intellectual, fond of the finer things in life. He knows many people from different areas and classes. I haven't seen much of him—I was at prep school or traveling, and when I'm home, he commutes." A third student, who, like the one just quoted, had lost his mother during preadolescence, commented: "My dad was a yeller and a screamer, and he still is. I don't have much trouble with him; I know how to handle him pretty well. He is very intelligent, and if you get him reasoning, he won't yell and scream. But once he blows, it's all over." Other comments about fathers by the off-campus interviewees seem to indicate considerable ambivalence. In some instances, the fathers had experienced failure, and the students were placed in the threatening position of feeling destined to surpass their fathers, whose lives had been a disappointment to themselves and their wives. Sometimes the men were openly critical of their fathers, while at other times they were strongly defensive of them.

The upwardly mobile students among the off-campus men were often critical of their families. "My father is dependent, childish. He tries to be fair, and a good person, but he never puts all the facts at his command together like I do. He doesn't worry until a crisis occurs," one remarked. On the other hand, some were defensive about their fathers' lack of material success: "I'm like my father in that I'm stubborn. My father has had a lot of influence on me—the idea that I should work hard and be successful. I get my literary ability from him; he would have been a top-notch writer or teacher if he hadn't married before he finished college. He loves his family very much, but he has a bad temper. He pays his bills first and then enjoys spending money on racing and gambling. I am like my mother. We are both easily hurt." These four students were intense, ambitious, and had intellectual aspirations. For a variety of reasons, they had been dissatisfied with their former environment, and self-confident that they could design a better life for themselves. At the university, their critical attitude, ambition, and restlessness continued. One remarked, with regard to his laboring class parents: "My parents don't read at all, so I can't talk to them. Their interests are in things I don't care for. My younger brothers aren't intellectual. There are almost no intellectual adults in my small town."

The freedom with which the off-campus men were able to evaluate others was shared by only two of the nine dormitory men in our interview sample. These two, whom we dubbed "genius-isolates" were very critical of their fathers, whom they felt to be strong-willed and stubborn, and with whom communication and cooperation seemed impossible. However, even these two students were not as free to criticize others as the off-campus men were. Although they had hostile and aggressive feelings, their psychic structures were such that the expression of these feelings was blocked. They threw their tremendous talents and energies into creative work in the sciences. They were convinced of their genius, and the day did not have sufficient hours for them to devote to their work. They were stimulated by abstract or theoretical ideas in fields such as philosophy and political science. People, however, seemed to make them anxious, and they tended to be isolated. These two students differed from the majority of the dormitory students, although socially their behavior had many similarities. They were more global and adventurous in their thinking, and occasionally behaved in a rather impulsive way, with manifestations of hostility or creativity. The other dormitory men in our sample tended to be conservative, hard-working, reliable, and over-controlled. All nine were shy, distrustful of others, and work-oriented. They kept to themselves, and limited their social, athletic, and recreational activities. They were interested in completing each academic assignment in an irreproachable manner and obtaining the highest possible grade. Only the two scientists were inclined toward rebellious and non-conforming behavior, but even they were usually too busy with their work and theoretical preoccupations to get seriously involved in other matters.

Of all groups in our sample, the dormitory men seemed to have remained the most constant in regard to the aspect of self-evaluation. The dormitory group contained the largest percentage of men who drank lightly or were abstainers. In their occupational interests, very few of the dormitory men were interested in business, but a large percentage were interested in fields that might involve college teaching or research. The dormitory men shared with the off-campus fraternity men and the off-campus men in general an interest in the professions. Like the relatively intellectual men in the eating clubs, the dormitory men were quite low in their interest in future family and love and affection, and high in their interest in intellectual and artistic matters. One way that they differed from the clubmen was that their postgraduate values did not include a great interest in helping others.

The dormitory men indicated that they had not changed much over the college years. They changed less than men in other groups regarding intellectual interest, freedom to express feelings, and kinds of friends. In regard to reasons for change, they indicated that problems in their families, and the problems of others had little to do with the changes that took place. The same was true for involvement in matters that dealt with social and political improvements. What had influenced them more than other groups of students were ideas from books read on their own and the discovering of new capacities in themselves. About a fifth (N = 42) of the dormitory men and a fourth of the clubmen listed the living group as a great influence in changes that occurred to them during college. This is significantly less than was true for the fraternity men (61 per cent of the on-campus fraternity men and 50 per cent of the off-campus fraternity men ascribed great influence to the living group), but considerably more than was true for the off-campus men who belonged to no fraternity. Only 2 of the 45 men said that their living group had greatly influenced them to change.

A reason for change given by a relatively large number of the dormitory men was involvement with student organizations. This is worthy of further comment. Some of the shy, small-town, constricted young men in our interview sample had lived in the same dormitory, and often in the same house within the dormitory, for four years. By their senior year, some of them had been asked to take offices and responsibilities in the houses where they lived, and they had been deeply pleased by this opportunity and had attempted to rise to it. Their new positions involved working with other people toward common goals in a relatively narrow area; but for these constricted young men, it was an opportunity to venture out of their own personal lives in a way that was not frightening or overwhelming. This may suggest to the educator a way to help such shy and reserved young men.[10]

We observed that dormitory men tended to avoid off-beat places and people, and participated less frequently than other men in most recreational activities. They were significantly less inclined to be involved frequently in activities of a social and athletic nature. The activities that involved them most frequently were social events connected with churches, attendance at symphonies and the theatre, and visits to museums. Although a segment of the dormitory men were involved in religious commitment and church-sponsored social events, there also appeared to be a large group in the dormitories who were indifferent or even anti-religious.

[10] More than twice as often as men in other residential groups, dormitory men reported participation in student organizations and committees as causing changes in themselves; 24 per cent of the dormitory men attributed change to such activities in contrast to 2 per cent of the unaffiliated off-campus men.

Responses from the larger questionnaire sample have indicated that the dormitories tended to attract as four-year residents the students who were most isolated and constricted. The dormitory men in our interview sample came from families where the parents had been relatively unsociable, and somewhat older than the parents of men in the other groups. The larger questionnaire sample supported the impression the nine interviewees gave of being serious, hard-working men who wanted a limited amount of personal interaction with other people. For some, this reflected feelings of personal inadequacy and fear of criticism or of experiencing closeness. These men seemed to think of themselves as workers rather than as changing, developing, and interacting individuals. They tended to treat the university as a vocational experience. They were often conservative in their behavior and views, and preferred to live within a narrow and limited life-space. The description given by a steady girlfriend of one of these students could apply to most of the men in this group: "He generally keeps to himself, and talks little except with his family, or unless the subject is engineering or physics. He spends much of his free time on engineering or in sleeping. He enjoys picnicking, camping, going to the mountains or beach. He is a conscientious worker outside of school, and finishes what he starts. He doesn't participate in normal 'fun' activities, but is well-liked and respected by his co-workers. He is content with himself as he is—pleased that he is competent where others aren't. Sometimes I wish he would appear to enjoy life more by some show of excitement or enthusiasm over something I could understand, but I think he would rather enjoy life in his own way—and who but he can say which way is better for him?" This student, along with several others in our interview sample, treated Stanford as a place of training, and consciously determined to avoid social and emotional involvements while in school. Two men who were drifting toward marriage had chosen high school friends who, prior to college, were "like members of the family." Some dormitory men seemed to prefer the familiar and predictable in social relations, and others kept themselves relatively isolated.

The dormitory men's reserve was combined with a cheerful, distant type of friendliness for the majority. Comments like "the folks and I went everywhere together" were common in descriptions of their high school days. In some instances, the sons were following their fathers' vocational interests; others were attempting to achieve professional status with the encouragement of fathers who had had no opportunity for formal education beyond high school.

The fathers, as described by the boys, were quiet, hard-working, thrifty, conscientious, often stubborn, men with whom it was difficult to converse or argue. The mothers frequently were involved in church work, were careful housekeepers, frugal, quiet, hard-working, perfectionistic, and more outgoing than the fathers. The families had been isolated geographically, or had limited their social contacts to a few relatives or old friends. They had moved about very little, and with a few exceptions, had been characterized by stability. The students themselves were often described by friends as very stable. This stability was sometimes accompanied by passivity and avoidance of change. They had depended on other family members for services and physical presence. If their home situation had satisfied them, they were content to retain their emotional attachments to it. They chose as friends one or two men who were hard-working and disinterested in personal involvement. If the home situation had been unsatisfactory, the student hoped to depend as much as possible on his own resources or on impersonal sources for gratification of his needs. In either case, most of these students lived in the dormitories for four years and were content as long as their physical needs were cared for with a minimal demand of time and money.

Although most of the dormitory men we interviewed were courteous, industrious men who tended to deny their hostile feelings or to control all feelings to the point where intimacy was sacrificed, a few were more passionate, and seemed fearful about the aggression of others and their own anger. In their descriptions of their homes, they often portrayed a father who was quiet and amiable until crossed, and then stubborn and irritable. Since the father usually was a devoted family man, the son and mother often combined forces to avoid situations that would disturb his equanimity. However, in most cases, the mother seemed unable to protect the man from his fears of the father, from his own anger, and from the father's wrath, although it is hard to say definitely, since some of the students who were particularly isolated and wary of others responded to our questions about their families with reticence or contradictions. Interviews with these men sometimes elicited inappropriate comments regarding hostility, or expressions of fear about their inability to control their own rage.

Many dormitory men had committed themselves to a vocation and way of life prior to college. Of the nine students in this group, two were engineers, two were premedical students, and the others were in a variety of fields. All these students had placed themselves in situations that required long hours of hard work. Excellent grades in demanding courses were necessary for the maintenance of scholarships or for entrance into graduate schools. The young men viewed themselves mainly as workers, and had recognition of their worth from their academic departments and from future employers. An interviewer commented about one of these students: "Although his whole orientation is to work and productivity, he does seem to obtain real satisfaction out of it. The trouble is, he seems unable to have fun in any other way. He is indeed machine-oriented, and may be something like a machine himself."

Most of these students had moral, political, and religious values that emphasized individual initiative. For the most part, they wanted institutions that either let the individual alone, or supported such characteristics as hard work, thrift, and virtue. They were not rebellious, or inclined to break rules, or to go in for heavy drinking. Regarding religion, they either were traditionalists, or had become confirmed agnostics after a period of soul-searching while in high school. Politically, they, like most Stanford men at the time of our study, tended to adopt a passive attitude toward political issues, but their preference was for a conservative approach to economics and politics.

All the dormitory men in our interview sample were concerned in one way or another with the value of money, the value of time, and the importance of orderliness. Although most of them were content to anticipate modest but hard-earned incomes, two were conspicuously eager for great wealth. Because of either shyness, low family income, or of family patterns of thrift, the dormitory men spent little money on dates, parties, or trips to San Francisco: cultural activities that they could attend alone or with another man seemed to them a more justifiable expenditure of time and money. They considered drinking a waste of both.

Most of them were prompt and reliable about time. One student commented about a friend he liked: "I don't know about his negative traits; I always try to think in positive terms. A lot of times he's late. This has always been one of my pet peeves. It was part of my bringing up. My parents think there is something radically wrong if you can't be on time. We live a hundred miles from nowhere, and yet we get places on time." And time enters into a later comment by the same student in talking about the wish that his friendships had been closer: "I would like all my friends to be closer. Perhaps lack of time to discuss things prevented this." Another student commented at the end of four years that he regretted his lack of time for lectures, participation in the university community, and getting to know the faculty. Regarding the last, he added that he didn't have any questions to ask them, and didn't like to take up their time for nothing.

With one exception, the dormitory men were fastidious in their appearance. Their rooms were orderly, and they expressed resentment of slovenliness in others. Regarding a freshman roommate, a student commented: "We have our little differences. We have common interests, but since we come from two completely different backgrounds, we once in a while have our little clashes in personalities. We have no real outbursts, but I come from a home where everything is always neat, and so naturally, I keep my side of the room neat. My roommate tends to scatter papers all over the room, and his bed is usually unmade. Shoes on the floor and all that kind of thing irritate me a little bit, but I try to overlook it. Mother is very neat and orderly, and likes things run on schedule, and so do I." Three years later, the same student commented: "I had this roommate all year, although we didn't get along very well. I gained a lot from this. We kept up a surface friendliness. I think it was very important that I learned to tolerate this and control my emotions, and not break out and shout at him. I tried not to care about it. Many times his friends would come in at one or two o'clock, and I would be in bed, but I never let anyone in the dorm know that I was angry. I let off steam by writing home." Only one man, a scientist, was conspicuously dis-

orderly. According to a friend, "he kept his room in an unbelievable state—an absolute shambles—with bed never made, sheets
seldom changed, desk stacked high with books, and closet crammed
with junk."

As indicated by the students we interviewed and the answers the men gave on the Senior Questionnaire, many of the
dormitory men had limited social lives. They usually had only
a few men friends and were reserved in their relationships with
them. They either dated infrequently, or moved from their parental homes to early marriages with girls from their home towns
whom they had known prior to college. In regard to most activities that involved social life or recreation, the dormitory men were
more isolated than the other men.

The "genius-isolates" dealt with their lack of involvement
with others by openly acknowledging to the interviewers their
anxiety in this area, and indicating that creative efforts in their
chosen field provided a gratifying sublimation for their feelings
of inadequacy as social beings. One of these students found himself less interested in social contact and personal involvement at
the end of his undergraduate years than he had felt as a freshman.
A brilliant young man with a long history of being a "loner," he
had been thrown on his own resources at an early age, and had
been humiliated by a penurious and rejecting father. His academic success made him feel free to avoid human contact, and to
relinquish the humanitarian attitudes that had characterized him
earlier in his academic career: "When I entered Stanford, I didn't
really mind meeting people and doing and seeing things, but I
do now. For one thing, I don't have as much in common with
others as I did when I first entered, because now I'm not interested in anything that isn't in my field. I'm an introvert most of
the time. I've always been terribly shy—the trouble is that I don't
want to work on it. I'm sure I would have moved more at another
college. When you have a lot of inhibitions and lots of inertia,
you just don't want to get over that barrier. I won't even place
myself in a situation where I can work on it. I used to laugh at
almost everything, anytime, anywhere, but now, if it's not intellectual enough, I just give a surface laugh. I get a kick out of
things that are subtly humorous—that have some ingenuity behind them. I like solving problems. I like delving into problems.

When my intellect is resting or isn't constantly searching, then I'm bored and dissatisfied." When asked if he felt that his feeling of alienation was undesirable, he responded: "No, I'm not really sorry. I feel that it is a bit of a loss, but it is something I don't want to correct. I suppose I could have taken some positive steps somewhere along the line."

The friendships of almost all the students in this group were characterized by a lack of personal involvement. One student, in discussing his roommate and closest friend during college, gave an extreme example of this phenomenon: "I don't really know Joe very well—we just go fishing together." (What do you talk about in your room?) "Fishing." (Not about yourselves?) "Hardly at all. We don't talk about backgrounds. Just incidentally. I kid him about being a country boy and he kids me about coming from the city. We don't talk much about our work. We don't understand each other's fields. I don't think if either of us had a personal problem we would go to the other one. When we fish together, we talk about how we would rather fish than get back to the books, or we talk about different types of bait, or fishing trips. I don't like anyone who's bossy and wants his own way. He's been my roommate for three years, and we get along fine. He does what he wants to do and I do what I want to do. I get along with most people, although I don't like to be around a lot of people. I don't have a lot of real close friends, but I don't have any enemies either."

An attitude of acceptance of their inability or lack of desire to cope with problems in interpersonal relations was characteristic of some of the students, and may have been a reflection of a generally passive attitude. Many of the students were content to adapt to dormitory conditions they found unsatisfactory, or to academic demands that oppressed them, or to other displeasing situations, rather than actively attempting to make more satisfactory modifications. In some instances, the student's initiative and independent spirit may have been stifled at an early age. In other instances, his behavior reflected identifications with parents or relatives who behaved in a passive or constricted way.

One dormitory man who was attempting to cope with his inertia in social matters described the process for us: "I had to work at it more than other people—that is, to force myself to be with others. Left to myself, I wanted to be more by myself. But I forced myself to participate in debate and in intramural sports. It takes a little bit more effort to meet people. It is much easier to be introverted; then there is no danger from the world—no danger of being criticized. We would all like to be star football players, but we can't—not all of us. What I really like to do is to enjoy a lemonade, a good book, and soft hi-fi music." He indicated dissatisfaction with his relationships and a determination to work on them even though his extra time was limited. His academic abilities were rather mediocre for the university and for his professional aspirations. He described his mother as lively and flexible—a contrast and stimulus to him in avoiding the rigidities, reticence, and social awkwardness of his father. Because of his idiosyncrasies, he must have met rebuffs as he cheerfully attempted to mix with others, but eventually he developed some social skill, if not greater empathy for others. This grew with his self-confidence, and was a product of hard work and determination. His comments reveal attitudes about a much earlier struggle. As a child he was physically inept and had a speech defect, but was determined to overcome these handicaps. Although far from being a warm, empathic, and spontaneous person, he was moving in that direction. Admission to professional school was the signal that he could relax a little, and he commented that he wished that this had been possible earlier. As a senior, he admitted indulging in the luxury of occasionally coming to class a few minutes late—an indulgence that he could not have allowed himself as a freshman.

Although the dormitory men liked the company of women, most of them were shy and hesitant about asking for dates. When questioned during the senior year, 26 per cent of the dormitory men reported that they had had no dates at all during the senior year. In contrast, 16 per cent of the off-campus men, and 1 per cent to 5 per cent of the men in the fraternities and eating clubs reported a no-dating status during the senior year. From our interview sample, we gained the impression that the dormitory men were in need of guidance and education in social interactions and in gaining respect for themselves as persons. The stress that they seemed able to face was that of occasional feelings of loneliness or boredom. The stress that they were more reluctant to bring into awareness was that connected with their feelings of inadequacy as people and their difficulties in coping with anger or sexuality in themselves and others. A difficulty that they shared with the fraternity men involved limited skills in communication and avoidance of introspection. In general, the dormitory men were not at ease in social situations, nor could they verbalize their needs as well as others. These handicaps served to make their isolation that much deeper.

In conclusion, what are some of the things that the university expects of the student in addition to the many compartmentalized and loosely integrated tasks demanded by his courses? Possibly, the university hopes to produce an individual who thinks in a certain way. This individual might be expected to look at himself, society, and history in a way that is based on knowledge and welded together by a balanced and integrated attitude; he should have a receptivity for a broad variety of ideas and yet be capable at any time of taking a stand and committing himself to action. Ideally, this commitment would be harmonious with the sum total of his integrated knowledge at a specific time, and not be a sort of cemented commitment that resembles rigidity. It is obvious that these goals cannot be achieved during the few hours a week that the student is in the classroom; and that the extracurricular experiences of the student are relevant to both his developmental and his educational goals.

We did not start out with a specific interest in residential arrangements, but the importance of this aspect of college life to the students forced itself upon us. In the light of the information we have gathered, we offer several observations and recommendations. First, the relationship between the social environment of the students and intellectual receptivity and emotional well-being was frequently noted by students and interviewers over the four years. In the interviews, most of the students indicated that a great deal of their mental and psychic energy was involved in developing a sense of their own separateness and uniqueness, and in modifying their behavior so that they could relate to others in a gratifying and meaningful way. The residence groups to which they belonged played an important part in defining the patterns of adaptation. Second, although generalizations about subgroups may not prove true of all individuals within each group, a difference can be discerned between groups in regard to certain values, interests, and behavior. Unless a university's admission policy is such that a small homogeneous group is admitted, there probably will be considerable variation among students in their social development and in their perception of their social needs. With this in mind, we recommend diversity in housing arrangements and flexibility over the college years in allowing students to move from one group to another. Third, our experience sug· gests that ascertaining the characteristics of subgroups within a college is a worthwhile research project for the university to undertake. Research into the experiences of individuals should precede suggestions for change. What might be helpful for individuals in one group might be unnecessary, irrelevant, or even harmful for another group. Such research should be undertaken at fairly frequent intervals, since the college social scene seems to be in a state of rapid change.

How could the students themselves be encouraged to ameliorate their adjustment difficulties? The clubmen in our study believed that they had experienced beneficial changes and an increased sense of self-esteem over the college years. With their relatively greater interest in service to others and in social and political improvement, they possibly could further contribute to the university community and their own education by administering a service center comparable to the Phillips Brooks House at Harvard. Such a suggestion is made with full awareness of the excellent work already done at Stanford by a number of service-oriented organizations. However, apparently there is still room for a greater variety of students to participate more fully in such activities if opportunities are made available. This sort of activity might enhance the self-esteem of the clubmen and their status among their fellow students. Improvement of their physical plants would also be of benefit to them.

The fraternity men could be encouraged to follow in the footsteps of adult fraternal groups and offer more services to others. For example, their aid could be enlisted in providing publicity and financial assistance for a service center and in participating in a variety of service activities. Out of this sort of experence, they might gain more empathy and understanding of individuals different from themselves. Many fraternity men have athletic knowledge and skills that could be transmitted to young people from less privileged backgrounds. (Some of the fraternity men had held summer jobs in the recreational field, and had experience in encouraging others to enjoy leisure time activities.) Teaching others their own skills could conceivably enhance the fraternity men's feeling of usefulness and give them a better understanding of the problems faced by the upward mobile young person. Modification in the intellectual level of the fraternities could possibly be achieved in an evolutionary fashion by a revision of the rushing procedure that would give the seniors more weight than other fraternity men in the process of selecting pledges. Test scores show that fraternity seniors tested higher on scales such as Social Maturity, and lower in Authoritarianism than fraternity men did as entering freshmen. (Their rate of change was about the same as that of other men in our total sample.) Since such changes seem to indicate a greater capacity to view social and psychological factors in a more complex open-minded manner, the seniors might be able to evaluate potential pledges in a way that would bring into the fraternities students less inclined toward elitism and masculine bravado. Our interview experience has shown that the fraternity underclassmen we saw were more prone to drink heavily, disparage academic involvement, and display disregard for community approval than the upperclassmen were. A group like the Inter-fraternity Council might offer to provide a setting and professional services for group discussions modeled after group psychotherapy. Such groups might have more attraction for fraternity members than more individualized guidance services do, and might have preventive as well as curative functions. In addition to helping individual students with personal problems, such groups might add to the general information about ingroup tensions. This information could provide for modification of fraternity life and also have implications for other groups dependent upon ingroup solidarity for achievement of common goals.

Given the characteristics of the dormitory men in our interview sample, it seems probable that one way to increase their social capacities lies in increasing their social experiences. Greater encouragement of on-campus and off-campus organizations serving the needs of the students would be helpful: we described the function of church groups in this regard. We reported that some dormitory men, especially in their last year or two as undergraduates, discovered that they had the ability to work with other men on committees within their houses in the dormitories; their participation in this work should be encouraged. Another way to assist the dormitory men lies in enlisting the cooperation of the student employment services. If these men could be placed in positions that involved working with others, they might develop more ease in social contacts. Dealing with unfamiliar people in work situations helped some of our interviewees. If students as reserved and shy as some of our dormitory men were given jobs as waiters or desk clerks in libraries, for example, it might be more helpful to them than to have jobs in which they had little contact with other people.

The off-campus men could benefit from the type of plan that attempts to introduce into the housing units more of the intellectual and cultural aspects of the university community. Certain members of other groups, especially the "genius-isolates" of the dormitories, might enjoy a social milieu that stressed a sharing of abstract ideas rather than camaraderie or mutual dependence and empathy. The off-campus men who often complain about a lack of intellectuality in the dormitories could possibly relate more easily to others on this kind of basis. Establishment of small housing units for those with special interests (designated as "drama houses," "creative writing houses," "political problem houses," and the like) with faculty members as residents might have special interest for these students. Residence in such houses might provide these students with a sense of belonging to the university and aid them in overcoming their feelings of dissatisfaction or alienation.

Such "special interest" houses suggest a possibility for helping freshmen. As freshmen, many of our students felt that the university was very demanding academically but not sufficiently rewarding intellectually. They often came from accelerated high-school classes and were enthusiastic about intellectual ideas. Their feeling of intellectual let-down might be alleviated if they were able to choose houses within the freshman dormitories on the basis of their special interests, skills, or curiosities. At a time when all is unfamiliar, it might be helpful to find new friends with shared meaningful interests. It would hasten their acceptance of the university as an intellectual and cultural community, and might affect the nature of housing groups that would be formed later. After such an introduction to the university community, freshmen who later joined fraternities might bring to the fraternity subculture a more open acceptance of esthetic and intellectual interests. These few suggestions are offered in support of our contention that knowledge of the college careers of men in various groups could lead to recommendations beneficial to the needs and values of the individual.

Finally, regardless of their place of residence, almost all the men benefited in their social development from attendance at our overseas campuses. Here, regardless of interests, they were placed in relatively homogeneous groups in unfamiliar environments. This necessitated their being helpful to each other. Because of the novelty of being abroad for a limited period, enjoyment of new experiences and pleasure was approved and expected. This was a particularly valuable experience for the dormitory men. Competition was less fierce overseas than on the home campus because of the nature of the curriculum, the special selection of students, and the even numbers of men and women. The students tended to explore the surrounding areas in groups rather than as couples, and the emphasis on coquetry and sexual competitiveness was replaced by a more leisurely opportunity to get to know members of the opposite sex as individuals and friends. In our interview sample, we saw dormitory men delighted with themselves for having been able to enjoy feminine companionship and group fun; we saw fraternity men expressing interest in artistic and cultural matters without feeling that this was inappropriate masculine behavior; and we saw off-campus men learning, through inescapable group involvement, that they could modify some of their behavior in the interests of getting along with others.

We recommend that attempts to modify the various living milieus be the products of joint efforts on the part of students and administration. The administration, besides having professional skills, provides a continuity of experiences that is lacking among the constantly changing student population. On the other hand, the students may be more responsive to the urgency of their developmental tasks and the effect of the many rapid changes that are occurring at the universities on their personal and social lives. They usually are better informed than anyone else about what goes on in their residences. Research into the nature of student populations should be repeated at appropriate intervals in order to ascertain changing conditions and to avoid self-perpetuating but inappropriate regulations.

As we look back critically, it seems to us that none of the existing housing arrangements for the men are ideal for meeting the developmental needs of the students and the goals of the university. Possibly the universities tend to overemphasize intellectual capacities and tasks. However, since man is a unitary creature, when his physical and social needs are disregarded or minimized the whole man suffers. It is likely that such neglect will interfere with the intellectual process itself. Often it appears that housing arrangements—the circumstances under which the students spend a great proportion of their time—have been more or less left to chance, to matters of economic efficiency, or to artistic design, and have not been thought through in terms of the developmental and intellectual needs of the students.

The developmental tasks of the individual are many and difficult, and require years beyond college for fulfillment. Some of the tasks that occupied the students we interviewed included searching for autonomy, evaluating oneself as a separate individual, and achieving a loosening of symbiotic attachment to the parental home. Other tasks involved developing the capacity to formulate and move toward the sort of life one can create out of the multitude of opportunities in the environment and the great variety of personal potentialities.

For his security and growth, the student needs to find ways to meet both his needs for autonomy and his social needs. The latter requires the capacity to give and to receive, to laugh and have fun, to be refreshed and recreated by the stimulus of other personalities and patterns of motivation, and to move toward adult assumption of responsibility and commitment in interpersonal relations. To achieve these social ends, the student must develop skills and patterns of adaptation that may not have been demanded of him as a younger person in his family and home community. It is our belief that proper residential and social facilities based on an understanding of the special needs of the members of subgroups can substantially aid the individual student in this difficult but essential and rewarding process.

❦ 8 ❧

STUDENTS WHO SEEK
PSYCHIATRIC HELP

Ving Ellis

Of the 3,474
students who entered the University of California at Berkeley in
the fall of 1961 as undergraduate freshmen, 493, or about 14 per
cent, availed themselves of the services of the psychiatric clinic
at the student health service, Cowell Memorial Hospital, during
the four undergraduate years ending in June, 1965.

The psychiatric clinic, which is essentially restricted to the
use of students, and is financed by a share of the student's incidental fee, is housed in one wing of Cowell, which has a capacity
of approximately 130 beds. The clinic is adequately staffed with
psychiatrists, psychologists, and psychiatric social workers, who
treat students mainly on an outpatient basis. All psychiatric care
is voluntary, that is, it is given only at the request of the student.

The Cowell psychiatric clinic has been practicing an "open
door" policy for many years. Would-be patients are seen promptly

instead of being put on a waiting list, and scheduling of interviews is flexible. Students continue with their initial interviewer as therapist, unless there is a specific reason for transfer to another psychotherapist. Although the Cowell therapists are of many schools, they all tend toward an ego-oriented psychotherapy focused on adaptation and integration rather than on adjustment and conformity to the expectations of others.

When a student applies to the Cowell psychiatric clinic for help, he fills out an application form consisting of a face sheet for family and personal information and an attached sheet on which he is asked to respond to the following questions: *(1) What prompts you to come to the clinic at this time? Describe problems. (2) Describe recent upsetting occurrences.*

Data from this application were utilized in an analysis of the total sample of 493 students presented here. Twenty-two of these students took part in our interviews. We have data for 265 of these students (120 males and 145 females), obtained from the battery of psychological tests we administered when they entered as freshmen in 1961. For 91 students (46 males and 45 females), there are test data on entry in 1961, and on departure in 1965.

Entering students learn about the Cowell psychiatric clinic in a variety of ways. There is a brief mention of the service in the general catalogue, and an article about the clinic and its services is usually run in the student newspaper at the beginning of the semester. It is probable that most students hear about the clinic by word of mouth. A breakdown of the total sample of the 493 students over the four years indicates the following distribution of sources of referral:

TABLE 48

DISTRIBUTION OF SOURCES OF REFERRAL
(N = 493)

Source	Number	Per cent
Self-referred	335	68
Student Health Service	43	9
Counselors and advisors (academic)	32	6
Deans	27	5
Other students	22	4
Parents and other relatives	12	3
Other	22	4

A distribution of students by sex indicates that 252 men and 241 women used the psychiatric services. Although in absolute numbers more men than women used the services of the clinic (252 to 241), the percentage of women who used the clinic was greater, since 43 per cent of the students of this class were women and 57 per cent were men. Nineteen-year-olds constituted the largest percentage of clinic patients (31 per cent), with eighteen-year-olds (27 per cent) and twenty-year-olds (18 per cent) next.

TABLE 49

NUMBER OF SIBLINGS

Patients		Number of	Berkeley Students Number Per cent	
Number	Per cent	Siblings [a]	(Senior Questionnaire Samples)	
80	16	0	57	10
197	40	1	186	34
136	28	2	148	27
46	9	3	87	16
32	8	4 or more	60	11
Not reporting				
2	1		17	3
493			555	

[a] In comparing students with no siblings, with one sibling, and with two or more siblings, $p < .01$.

There have been many hypotheses about the effects of siblings and their rivalries and positions on the growth, development, and intelligence of children. Among the students who came to the clinic, the greatest number were only children or children with only one sibling. We also computed ordinal position, and found that in the patient sample, 63 per cent of the men and 64 per cent of the women, including only children, were first-born, while only 57 per cent of the men and women in our Senior Questionnaire sample were first-born. This difference is statistically significant ($p < .05$). Studies summarized by William D. Altus indicate that first-born are present in greater proportions in the brighter segments of the population.[1] These children seem more achievement-oriented than others, and have a greater "conscience" development.[2]

[1] Altus, William D. "Birth Order and Its Sequelae." *Science*, 1966, *151*, 44–49.

[2] See Note 4 below, page 321.

Sixty-six different majors were listed by the students in our study (N = 493). On the whole, each major seemed to contribute its appropriate share of patients. Our figures seem to counter the commonly held belief that students in the natural sciences utilize psychiatric clinics less than students in the humanities. Engineering students did use the clinic in lesser proportions. On the other hand, the number of social science majors making use of the clinic was not disproportionate to their numbers in the population. Business administration and history majors seemed to underuse the clinic. Grade-point averages reported by the students upon application to the clinic were as follows:

TABLE 50

DISTRIBUTION BY GRADE-POINT AVERAGE

Grade-point Average	Number	Per cent
Not reporting	104	21
1.9 or below	52	11
2.9 to 2.0	233	47
4.0 to 3.0	104	21

The notion that the students who use psychiatric clinics are those who excel *academically* does not seem to be borne out here.[3] At the same time, their performance is not lower than that of their peers. In aptitude and intelligence, however, the patients were superior. Their verbal and mathematical Scholastic Aptitude Test scores were significantly higher ($p < .01$) than those of their peers.[4] Moreover, the patients obtained significantly higher scores than non-patients on cognitive and other personality scales (see Tables 54 through 57). One hundred and thirty-seven of the students (or 31.85 per cent) reported previous counseling; and 83 students, or 16.84 per cent, reported previous psychotherapy.

[3] The cumulative senior GPA for patients on the basis of the Registrar's records were: Men patients 2.62 (N = 125), women patients 2.65 (N = 122). In two random senior samples from the whole class, the GPA for the men was 2.64 (N = 400); for the women, 2.65 (N = 400).

[4]

SAT SCORES—BERKELEY

	Male Patients (N = 220)	Male Students (N = 1857)	Female Patients (N = 211)	Female Students (N = 1494)
Verbal	584 (91)	548 (93)	577 (86)	544 (86)
Mathematical	662 (84)	606 (88)	545 (85)	519 (88)

Of the 493 students who came to the psychiatric clinic, 321 later dropped out of school. In a separate study of dropouts, using Student Development Study data, it was found that during the four-year period following initial admission to the university, a total of approximately 59 per cent of the class interrupted their stay at Berkeley.[5] Of these, 9 per cent subsequently returned, leaving about 50 per cent of the original group still registered at the end of the fourth year.

In the present sample of 493 students, of the 321 who interrupted their stay at Berkeley, 77, or about 24 per cent, returned to the Berkeley campus. In comparing the sample with the whole class, it might be said that although more people who come to the psychiatric clinic tend to drop out of school (65 per cent, as opposed to 59 per cent), the proportion of returnees is considerably greater among them than among students who do not come to the clinic. It must be stressed that very few students in either group leave as a result of academic failure. This has been true during all the years that records have been kept at Berkeley.

Why do students come to the clinic for help? Their responses to the question, What prompted you to come to the clinic at this time? fall into at least fifty-one distinct categories. In some instances, students complain of difficulties in two or more categories. The distribution of frequency of categories of complaints among our sample was as follows:

TABLE 51

ENTERING COMPLAINTS

Reason for Entering	Number	Per cent
Depression	91	18
Inability to do schoolwork	80	16
Family problems	32	6
Nervousness, tenseness	31	6
Too personal to state	16	3
Confusion	15	3
Psychosomatic problems	14	3
Strong anxiety	13	3
Not stated	22	4

[5] Suczek, Robert F., and Alfert, Elizabeth. *Personality Characteristics of College Dropouts*. Berkeley: Department of Psychiatry, Student Health Service, University of California, 1966.

One hundred and twelve students were seen for a second series of therapy interviews; thirty for a third; five for a fourth; and one for a fifth. The most common complaints, usually stated together, were depression and inability to do schoolwork (18 and 16 per cent respectively). The next most frequent complaint was that of family problems. During the four years 1961–65, forty-one students from our group were admitted to the inpatient service. Of these, twenty-one were hospitalized for three days or less.

All studies dealing with emotional disturbances and their treatment must come to terms with the notion of improvement, or "cure." For the purposes of our study, we used the following as the criteria of improvement: if the rater, following a careful examination of the student's record, decided that the student or the psychotherapist felt that the interaction was of some benefit to the student, the outcome was considered positive and the student was rated as improved. If there was no such evidence, the outcome was considered negative. (In the latter case, there is always the possibility that the student may have benefited by the encounter in ways not recorded by the therapist.) In addition to the author of this chapter, who rated every record, two other psychotherapists with even longer histories of experience with college students in psychotherapy rated every tenth patient record (N = 50) in order to establish reliability of the criteria of ratings. Reliability was found to be very high.[6]

In all five therapy series taken together, 43 per cent of the patients were benefited and 57 per cent were not. Students who were seen for only one hour benefited the least. In the first series, only 7 per cent of the men and 3 per cent of the women seen for one hour were judged to have benefited. If all contacts that were terminated after one hour are omitted from the calculations, the percentage of students benefited goes up from 42 per cent to 58 per cent for the first series.

Why students come for only one hour and then stop is a matter of conjecture. Some probably get what they came for in

[6] The author's judgments agreed with those of the other two raters in (1) 82 per cent and (2) 86 per cent of the cases. The other two agreed with each other in 80 per cent of the judgments. All three agreed in 74 per cent of the judgments.

that period of time. In most cases, however, the student makes a second appointment, but either does not keep it or calls in to cancel it. In some cases, it is clear from the records that the student feels he has made a mistake in coming to the clinic, and does not wish to continue.[7] The figures in Table 52 indicate that students who put in from three to ten hours appear to have the best possibilities of benefit from psychotherapy at the clinic.

TABLE 52

NUMBER OF HOURS SEEN DURING FIRST ADMISSION SERIES
(Males, N = 252) (Females, N = 241)

Hours Seen	Benefited:		Not Benefited:	
	Males Per cent	Females Per cent	Males Per cent	Females Per cent
1	7	3	47	48
2	16	12	25	19
3	15	20	7	6
4	11	11	8	5
5–10	40	42	11	15
11 or more	12	13	2	7

If one examines a breakdown of diagnoses for these students, it is apparent that the highest frequency of undiagnosed students was among those seen for the least number of hours. Among unbenefited males, 49 per cent were given a "deferred" diagnosis. Of the unbenefited females, 48 per cent received a "deferred" diagnosis—an almost identical percentage as that among students seen for only one hour.

It is of interest to note that 34 per cent of the complaints that students make on entry to the clinic fall into the category of "depression" and "inability to do schoolwork," while the diagnosis "depressive reaction" makes up only 22 per cent of all diagnoses. This may be because in this age group, depression tends to come and go relatively quickly and may not be part of the clinical picture seen by the psychotherapist. The statement that 34 per cent of all intake complaints fall in the categories of

---

[7] Another service available to students at Berkeley is the Counseling Center. Of the 160 students followed in the Student Development Study, 60 were seen by the Counseling Center and 22 by the psychiatric clinic—a ratio of almost three to one.

depression or inability to do schoolwork does not convey the desperate flavor of the verbatim complaints. Two examples illustrate the poignancy and despair that characterize these presenting problems.

TABLE 53

DISTRIBUTION OF DIAGNOSES

Diagnostic Classification	Frequency: Males (N = 252)		Frequency: Females (N = 241)	
	Benefited Per cent	Not Benefited Per cent	Benefited Per cent	Not Benefited Per cent
Deferred	14	49	13	48
Anxiety reaction	9	3	5	4
Conversion reaction				2
Obsessive-compulsive reaction	4	1	1	2
Depressive reaction	8	3	7	4
Schizoid personality	8	6		6
Passive-aggressive personality	17	13	18	5
Compulsive personality	8	3	3	1
Adjustment reaction of adolescence	26	13	38	20
Other	6	9	13	8

(1) Can't study, or at least when I think I am studying, all I am doing is putting in time. I want to think about doing nothing. Just plain tired of school, yet don't want to stop. Difficulty in getting to sleep. Have been recently using drugs to sleep. Usually in the latter part of the week. A general feeling of uselessness—that what I am doing nobody cares about, and I am just about to quit caring. . . . I just can't go on like this. I feel miserable, and I am getting very disagreeable and upset at the most insignificant incidents. Anything in the way of quizzes or tests usually upsets me for the whole day. Probably the whole idea of my being here is upsetting. I don't know, or for that matter care, but then I do care in a way.

(2) I have a lack of interest in school, life, etc. I seem to be a spectator to everything. Because of this lack of interest, I find it very difficult to force myself to study. Whenever an important decision comes up, I really have

a tough time knowing what to do, and many times I am
dissatisfied with the decisions taken. I have periods of
extreme depression. Some days I feel fine, and other days
I feel like everything goes wrong and nothing will ever
get better.

Virtually none of the students who complain in this manner are
failing in their academic tasks, and very few ask for a medical
excuse to drop out of school. Each is struggling in his own way
to cope with these problems, and is seeking psychotherapeutic
help to continue doing so.

People who ask the help of the psychiatric service seem to
be different from the rest of the student population (Tables 54
through 57). Benefited and unbenefited patients alike are different from their peers both at the start and at the end of their
college careers. The users of the psychiatric service score significantly higher as freshmen on scales measuring such personality
characteristics as flexibility, autonomy, imaginativeness, and
esthetic responsiveness, and they score lower on authoritarianism.
Interestingly enough, there is no significant difference in their
scores on the Schizoid Functioning Scale, which measures bizarreness of thinking and social alienation, except among the unbenefited women students, for whom as freshmen there is a difference at
the .10 level of confidence. The differences between patients and
non-patients persist into their senior year.

One may interpret the differences in the freshman and
senior scores to mean that people who seek out the psychiatric
service possess a higher degree of psychological awareness and
flexibility than their peers; they seem more able to admit that
they have problems and to face up to them. (Some and perhaps
many of the non-patients may be characterized not so much by
the absence of trouble as by the tendency to deny problems, or to
leave them unchallenged and unexamined at the price of greater
rigidity and emotional flatness.)

The sources of the information we have been examining
were real students struggling to adjust to a specific university
environment. In order to give a human dimension to our data,
let us examine two case histories—those of Mr. A and Miss Z—
which may serve to illustrate the problems faced in some form or

TABLE 54

PERSONALITY INVENTORY SCORES OF BERKELEY FRESHMEN AND OF BERKELEY PATIENTS AS FRESHMEN

(Males)

	I Berkeley Freshmen (N = 1026) Mean (SD)		II Patients Benefited Freshmen (N = 51) Mean (SD)		III Patients Not Benefited Freshmen (N = 71) Mean (SD)		t tests comparing the difference between the means of the following groups: I & II	I & III	II & III
Social Maturity	50	(10)	54	(11)	56	(9)	**	**	n.s.
Impulse Expression	50	(10)	53	(10)	54	(9)	*	**	n.s.
Schizoid Functioning	50	(10)	52	(11)	52	(10)	n.s.	n.s.	n.s.
Masculinity-Femininity	50	(10)	47	(11)	45	(12)	*	**	n.s.
Estheticism	50	(10)	54	(11)	57	(10)	**	**	n.s.
Developmental Status	50	(10)	56	(11)	55	(10)	**	**	n.s.
Authoritarianism	116	(26)	108	(26)	105	(28)	*	**	n.s.
Ethnocentrism	56	(21)	54	(21)	52	(22)	n.s.	n.s.	n.s.

** Significant at the .01 level.
* Significant at the .05 level.
† Significant at the .10 level.

TABLE 55

PERSONALITY INVENTORY SCORES OF BERKELEY FRESHMEN AND
OF BERKELEY PATIENTS AS FRESHMEN
(Females)

	I Berkeley Freshmen (N = 852)		II Patients Benefited Freshmen (N = 58)		III Patients Not Benefited Freshmen (N = 83)		t tests comparing the difference between the means of the following groups:		
	Mean	(SD)	Mean	(SD)	Mean	(SD)	I & II	I & III	II & III
Social Maturity	50	(10)	54	(8)	56	(10)	**	**	n.s.
Impulse Expression	50	(10)	53	(8)	55	(9)	*	**	n.s.
Schizoid Functioning	50	(10)	52	(9)	52	(10)	n.s.	†	n.s.
Masculinity-Femininity	50	(10)	49	(11)	49	(10)	n.s.	n.s.	n.s.
Estheticism	50	(10)	53	(10)	55	(10)	*	**	**
Developmental Status	50	(10)	54	(10)	56	(10)	**	**	n.s.
Authoritarianism	113	(27)	108	(25)	97	(28)	n.s.	**	*
Ethnocentrism	50	(18)	51	(22)	42	(19)	n.s.	**	*

** Significant at the .01 level.
* Significant at the .05 level.
† Significant at the .10 level.

Table 56

PERSONALITY INVENTORY SCORES OF BERKELEY SENIORS AND OF BERKELEY PATIENTS AS FRESHMEN AND SENIORS
(Males)

	I Berkeley Seniors (N = 286)		II Patients Benefited Freshmen (N = 18) a, b		III Patients Benefited Seniors (N = 18) b		IV Patients Not Benefited Freshmen (N = 24) a		V Patients Not Benefited Seniors (N = 24)		t tests comparing the difference between the means of the following groups: I & III	I & V	III & V
	Mean	(SD)	Mean	(SD)	Mean	(SD)	Mean	(SD)	Mean	(SD)			
Social Maturity	57	(11)	55	(12)	63	(8)	54	(11)	61	(11)	*	†	n.s.
Impulse Expression	52	(11)	51	(11)	56	(12)	52	(9)	57	(11)	n.s.	n.s.	n.s.
Schizoid Functioning	47	(11)	52	(11)	50	(10)	52	(11)	49	(12)	n.s.	n.s.	n.s.
Masculinity-Femininity	47	(13)	50	(9)	43	(10)	45	(10)	40	(13)	n.s.	*	n.s.
Estheticism	52	(12)	56	(11)	58	(11)	57	(11)	59	(12)	†	**	n.s.
Developmental Status	58	(11)	54	(11)	64	(9)	53	(11)	62	(10)	*	†	n.s.
Authoritarianism	96	(26)	108	(29)	83	(21)	108	(31)	96	(32)	*	n.s.	n.s.
Ethnocentrism	44	(18)	52	(22)	36	(14)	51	(23)	47	(22)	†	n.s.	†

** Significant at the .01 level.
* Significant at the .05 level.
† Significant at the .10 level.

a These are the students for whom we have both freshman and senior scores.

b For the Authoritarianism and Ethnocentrism scores of the benefited patients, N = 21.

329

TABLE 57

PERSONALITY INVENTORY SCORES OF BERKELEY SENIORS AND
OF BERKELEY PATIENTS AS FRESHMEN AND SENIORS
(Females)

	I Berkeley Seniors (N = 265) Mean (SD)	II Patients Benefited Freshmen (N = 16)[a] Mean (SD)	III Patients Benefited Seniors (N = 16) Mean (SD)	IV Patients Not Benefited Freshmen (N = 30)[a] Mean (SD)	V Patients Not Benefited Seniors (N = 30) Mean (SD)	I & III	I & V	III & V
Social Maturity	58 (10)	57 (7)	67 (5)	57 (11)	62 (11)	**	*	n.s.
Impulse Expression	52 (11)	53 (8)	59 (7)	55 (7)	58 (9)	*	**	n.s.
Schizoid Functioning	46 (11)	51 (8)	48 (7)	53 (7)	50 (11)	n.s.	†	n.s.
Masculinity-Femininity	48 (10)	48 (11)	49 (6)	47 (9)	44 (12)	n.s.	*	n.s.
Estheticism	53 (10)	54 (9)	59 (8)	54 (10)	59 (9)	*	**	n.s.
Developmental Status	59 (11)	56 (8)	69 (6)	56 (9)	65 (11)	**	**	n.s.
Authoritarianism	89 (26)	101 (21)	70 (16)	97 (29)	78 (29)	*	*	n.s.
Ethnocentrism	39 (16)	47 (18)	30 (10)	40 (14)	35 (16)	*	n.s.	n.s.

t tests comparing the difference between the means of the following groups: I & III, I & V, III & V

[a] These are the students for whom we have both freshman and senior scores.

** Significant at the .01 level.
* Significant at the .05 level.
† Significant at the .10 level.

another by the 493 unique individuals who came to the clinic from 1961 to 1965.

Mr. A was eighteen years old when he came to the university. He is a blond, well-built young man with a short haircut and a deep tan. He never smiles, but almost always scowls, moves slowly, and appears depressed. When he talks, he holds his hand over his mouth and turns his head away slightly. He came to Berkeley from a small California city, where he had been living with both parents and a younger brother. Both his mother and father had completed high school, but had gone no further with their education. A's father works in a factory, and his mother works as a medical assistant.

A feels that his early life was not particularly happy. His father was a severe disciplinarian with a "tremendous need to be right almost all the time." Because of his mother's interference and restrictiveness with regard to his dating during his last two years of high school, A had suffered a severe depression requiring psychiatric care. He had come to the university on an athletic scholarship. During his first semester, he lived in a rooming house, made very few friends, and did practically no dating. In his second semester, he joined a fraternity and began to participate in much of the social activity around the house. Sports and fraternity events took up most of his free time. In addition to the scholarship funds, A received money from his parents, and planned to work during summer vacations for extra money.

It was difficult to know what A's self-perception was during the first year. His research interviewer during that time saw him as pessimistic, bitter, covert, frightened, not very outgoing or giving, and markedly conservative. He seemed strongly resentful of being bossed, unless it was by someone with high status or prestige, in which case he would become extremely compliant. Other liabilities included a restricted childhood, overdependence on parents, a "jealous" mother (where girlfriends were concerned), and an authoritarian father.

When A was first seen by his research interviewer, he was felt to be a good candidate for long-term psychotherapy because he seemed so depressed. However, shortly after he pledged a fraternity, he began to go out with girls a little, had more interaction with members of his own sex, and made some adjustment to the

academic side of school, although still handicapped by poor reading skills. During his second semester, A seemed more self-assured
—less anxious and less depressed. He attributed his improvement
to having joined the fraternity.

Following his return to school from summer vacation, he
again felt depressed. This was thought to be related to his summer
job, which had apparently been a very difficult one. He seemed
genuinely pleased to get back to school, if for no other reason than
to get away from his job situation. A had entered school hoping to
earn a law degree. By the beginning of the second year, he had
decided he was going to become a sociologist, although he sounded
unsure about it. His interviewer had real doubts at this time about
whether A was even going to make it through school, mainly because there was so much anger in him, and a great reluctance to
do academic work. The interviewer felt, however, that A could
probably benefit considerably from some kind of long-term investigation of himself.

A's second interviewer, who saw him in the fourth semester,
felt that he was "somewhat phoney about his renunciation of the
past." This interviewer felt that A was deceiving himself—that
he was as socially withdrawn and self-centered as ever. "He spoke
more as if he were in a trance than wide awake. His view of
morality and sex expressed conservatism and restraint, and was
further evidence of domination by rather than emancipation from
his past."

Mr. A first came to the psychiatric clinic for help in December, 1961, between his first and second research interviews. His
entering complaint was: "Lack of adjustment and good mental
health, becoming cynical, becoming sacrilegious, periods of elation
and depression, and sensitivity to the actions of others." For "recent upsetting occurrences" he wrote: "A trip home during
Thanksgiving vacation and a realization of how I have changed,
linked with memories I would do well to forget."

The admission note by the psychotherapist stated:

> An eighteen-year-old boy who is not too interested ma-
> joring in social sciences. He has been a rather isolated
> and not too involved person, who in his last year of high
> school became infatuated with what seemed to him to
> be his ideal girl. After going with him for a year, she

dropped him. Since that time, he has lacked any zest in his life, and has not been able to pick up the threads in his life that were enjoyable to him before. He has spent a good deal of time mulling over his loss of her and comparing her with all the other girls he sees. Actually, this has passed its peak, and he now begins to find his voluntarily increased isolation unsatisfactory. A good number of his questions seem to be around whether he should try and engage more actively in life again. There seemed to be little need for any continuing therapy at this time and I told him so, as well as reassuring him about his tentative efforts to pick up the pieces.

The psychotherapist felt that A had somehow expected college life to change his isolation and give him social poise. He had been isolated and ill at ease in high school also.

This young-appearing boy seems to have been greatly hurt and depressed by seeming rejection of first love, since she had become the guiding light in his beginning adult adaptation and identity formation. College is incidental to this, but he seems to be recovering and beginning to be ready to make use of the college environment. Above adult adaptation and identify formation appears delayed in this boy. There was no treatment at this time.

In 1962, Mr. A was seen twice at the Counseling Center—in September and in October. He was described as "verbalizing easily with a considerable number of slang expressions; rather adolescent, rebellious tone of voice, slightly effeminate." He came in specifically to take tests because he was thinking of going into law, and wanted to see if this was an appropriate choice. He said that the only thing he was good in was social science, with the exception of psychology or economics, which he had "tried" and not done well in. Political science was "out," because he did not like current events. He felt that he could make "a great living in either sociology or anthropology," though he really wondered about his choice. He knew he could not work in a social science because he would not want to teach. He also said, "I know I do not want to help people." Physical sciences were completely out because he could not understand math; and he could not consider the humanities, because he was "not a good writer," though he did like English and history. He said that he himself wrote poetry, and that he did not understand why so many people were "against poetry." He had never had anything published. He had never been able to write stories, because he could not develop a whole plot.

Because of outside commitments, A's grades had dropped perceptibly prior to his coming to the Counseling Center (he worked in the athletic department five hours a week). The fraternity house did not please him any longer, so he depledged and moved to an apartment with two other men— a student in physics and a student in engineering—who had also depledged from the fraternity. He asserted when discussing his roommates that practically everyone he met whom he liked was either in science or in engineering. He did not "cotton" to the few people he had met who were in the humanities or social sciences, because they seemed to be "beatniks." The counselor's impression was that A was a great deal more interested in the fine arts than he recognized or would admit. He had done some painting in the past, and said that this was the only thing he had really been able to ge involved in. He had taken one art course in high school, but had dropped out of it because he did not like the teacher. It had never occurred to him to take another one.

In the second interview at the Counseling Center, Mr. A admitted that he had thought of taking an art course but had decided against it, feeling that 17 units would be too much for that semester. There was some discussion about his writing. He recalled that he had been in a class for gifted children in high school, and that many of the other children could write so easily that he had always felt stupid by comparison. He imagined that people who went into the humanities had "enormous" backgrounds in literature, art, and music. He seemed to have a strong need for achievement, and spent some time talking about how "law" appealed to him because of the high regard in which it is held by society. He also admitted that he missed the social life of the fraternity. He had not dated recently. He disliked all his teachers, but had been working hard on his courses, and hoped to get at least a 3.0 average.

At the end of his second year, Mr. A left the Berkeley campus and registered at another University of California campus.

After leaving Berkeley, Mr. A answered three questionnaires for the Student Development Study. In the first questionnaire, in 1963, he asserted that the new campus offered a more relaxed, socially easy atmosphere than Berkeley did. There was, he said, more friendliness on the part of fellow students and a more pleasant classroom atmosphere. In response to the question: "If you were required to take only one-half of your courses, but were given full credit, what would you do with the half-time so freed?," he wrote: "(1) Socialize, drink, party, lay as many girls as possible; (2) read and listen to music." In response to the question: "Have your interests changed since high school? To what do you attribute these changes?" he wrote: "I like sports, movies, TV, and kissing less [than I did then]. I like reading, music, women, people, plays, drinking, and smoking more, with studying about the same as before." He attributed the change to an increase in maturity, to widening experience, and to age. He said that he had come to realize that "working for the grade and considering the knowledge gained as only secondary is an attitude that may not be very academic, but it is practical, especially in a cutthroat multiversity."

He now wanted to achieve "prestige, social stature, money, and a feeling of accomplishment" after graduation. If he had all the money he wanted, he said, he would become a "playboy," and would completely anesthetize his senses with physical and mental pleasures. "I realize I do not possess a great enough mind to leave any noticeable footprints in the sand. I also realize that 'when you're dead, you're dead, so live for the present.' " He stated that the first two college years had had absolutely no impact on him, apart from his courses; he had switched to sociology because it was an easier major.

Mr. A's answers to the next two questionnaires reflected his deep confusion. His jovial extroversion contrasted sharply with such statements as "There is intense loneliness underlying my conscious existence, realized most strongly when I am alone, particularly at night with only the ocean's rushing." To the question, "What do you do when you are alone?" he responded:

I long for feminine companionship, become restless, spend hours writing poetry and an occasional short story, always romantic, or I listen to music, particularly

Wagner, and lapse into technicolor reveries of what I
imagine the music represents, becoming so emotionally
enthralled that I weep and am wafted from the pinnacle
of joy to the abyss of depression by the flowing notes and
chords. I always feel lonely; it is suppressed only by
study or feminine companionship or carousing. Daytime
loneliness is ameliorated by talking to someone, but frequently it is incurable. Nighttime loneliness is cured by
going to bed or increased by reveling in a poem I have
written or am writing at the time. A Saturday night
alone is horrible, and I greatly envy persons at parties.
During intense periods of loneliness, the entire world of
social convention seems shallow as a puddle of rain-
water, and I am in the depths of despair.

Mr. A planned to get married after he got his degree; and
he listed some of the requirements an ideal wife should possess.
His girl must be very feminine, have polished nails, pretty hair,
be effervescent, affectionate, and sensitive. She must cry as much
when reading Fitzgerald's *Tender is the Night* as she would at a
tragic opera. Above all, she must be submissive and dependent on
him: "A union with a masculine, aggressive, unsensitive, or non-
delicate girl would be as impossible for me as would one with a
woman who was stupid, or who liked rock and roll music, or had
majored in anything but the liberal arts."

In December 1964, he again responded to a questionnaire.
At that time, he was living with a graduate student in an apartment near the campus. He was working toward a B.A. degree in
a humanities subject, and planned to go on from there to acquire
a teacher's credential, a law degree, or an advanced degree in
history. He planned to stay away from his family. He felt he had
acquired a large degree of stability during the semester just past,
and also felt that his career plans were not as nebulous as they
once had been. He described himself as follows: "I have been an
eternal Shelleyesque idealist with aspirations transcending my
mental potentialities. I shall always wallow in poetry, music, and
art, but I realize the necessity of trying to support myself in this
Protestant-ethic practical world. I still hold certain values that I
shall not permit to be thwarted. There is an inherent value in
the arts. Men pass on, but the footprints they leave behind are
forever fossilized in the sand. Footprints are more important than

corporations." Now "a hundred-per-cent independent," he was financially his own boss, and was paying for his own education. He claimed to feel no inferiority in comparison to his peers. To the question, "How often do you get depressed; what is it like; how do you handle it?" he responded: "I get depressed several times a week, usually when I have nothing with which to occupy my mind, or when I am alone, or when I receive a bad grade. I feel like immersing myself in a mist of forgetfulness. I go to bed."

Mr. A had had an unhappy childhood with a severe father and a jealous mother, but it is not clear why he came to the psychiatric clinic. Perhaps it was suggested to him by the research interviewers, or by a memory of previous psychiatric help. It is fairly clear from the record that he got no benefit from his visit to the psychiatric clinic; but he did seem to accept some of his more feminine impulses after interviews at the Counseling Center. Social deprivation seemed central to this young man's difficulties, although there was more than a hint of severe authority problems lurking in the background. From the last contacts with him, it seemed that his life had not changed much; and it is felt that he probably will have to seek help in the future, when acute crises related to authority conflicts or loneliness confront him.

Our second student, Miss Z, was described by her research interviewer as a slender blonde with braces on her teeth. When first interviewed, she was lightly made up and was wearing a becoming dress. Miss Z's father was a school administrator; her mother stayed home and kept house. Miss Z herself stated that she wanted to become a doctor, mainly because a doctor had done a great deal for her mother when she was suffering from an emotional problem. At the time, the interviewer was impressed with the student's apparent commitment, and noted that she sounded persevering. Miss Z also asserted that she wanted to get married, and hoped that she would be able to combine marriage and a career successfully. She felt that her father had little faith in her ability to succeed, but she herself seemed to have gained confidence and independence since she had been in school. She had been self-conscious and shy when she started at the university, but had become less so. She continued to be dependent on her family financially as well as emotionally, but also seemed to be dependent on her immediate friends. Essentially, she conformed to what was expected of her, trying to adapt herself to the group with whom she lived.

The research interviewer described her as friendly and honest, with good verbal facility and an openness to learning. He also saw her as intelligent, esthetic, and capable of emotion and close relationships, but overly dependent. He felt that the student was open to change, but feared that "she would be reluctant to let herself go—to indulge her impulses." Throughout the research interviews, Miss Z continued to persevere in her career goals. She did not feel that her moral convictions had changed since coming to school, except that she had become more tolerant of the opinions of others. She did not feel that her own opinions had changed much. She was politically apathetic, but was aware of the contradiction between her apathy and her belief in a democratic form of government.

The interviewer's summary stated that Miss Z impressed him as morally conventional, with a growing tolerance for others and a good chance for self-development. He doubted that her political indifference would change during her college years. She appeared to get some comfort from her religion, but did not seem to depend on it excessively. Much of her general lack of involvement struck him as the result of her determination to reach her career goal, medicine. There was a good possibility that she might enlarge her ideological world when she had enough time to give it some thought, and that she might be forced to make the time when she came into contact with the countless human problems a doctor must face.

After Miss Z's first interview during the junior year, her interviewer stated: "Z is bright, but is not intellectually engaged. She has one goal to accomplish, which is to become a doctor. She has only now discovered that she feels 'uncultured,' but she has no time at the moment to do much about it except to recognize it and let her boyfriend influence her. There are vast areas she will have time for only after she is through with medical school." The interviewer felt that acquiring a steady boyfriend was one of the more important things that had happened to Z, and that what was hindering her personal development most was her strong desire to enter medical school, which seemed to inhibit her vision of anything else. He felt that Miss Z appeared less attractive but happier since she had found a boyfriend. She had acquired other new friends, and appeared more at ease and secure. She had developed a genuine liking for music, art, and literature, but still felt obliged to become more cultured.

During her second interview in her junior year, Miss Z seemed to be even more self-confident and happy with her steady boyfriend. Her interpersonal life had been limited, and she had only one close friend other than her boyfriend. She felt that interpersonal relations would have to take second place to her goal of becoming a doctor. She was not very optimistic that marriage to her boyfriend would work out. She was looking forward to entering medical school the following year. At that time, her relationship with her boyfriend was close, but stopped short of intercourse, which she felt she would reserve for the man she wanted to marry (a sexual experience that had taken place in high school now seemed to her to have been "all wrong").

After Miss Z had been in medical school for a year, she was seen again by her interviewer. He felt that changes in her were taking place at a fairly rapid rate. Miss Z felt that she had developed greater independence, social ease, and a capacity for enjoyment. She was one of the few girls in her class of medical students, and was enjoying her studies. She hoped to marry eventually, but planned to go into practice before having children. At this interview, Miss Z looked more sophisticated, was attractively dressed, seemed sure of herself, was at ease, and appeared happy. She had lost some of her dependence and need for security, and did not seem as narrowly focused on career as she had been previously. She felt she had become less self-conscious, and gave credit for this to the psychotherapist she had seen at Cowell Hospital. She said that she now felt more free, and had intimate friendships with her fellow medical students. She was attracted to one of the male students, and had been having sexual intercourse with him, but was not "going steady." She had been able to take her studies much less seriously, was satisfied with B's and C's, and spent more time going to art shows and symphony concerts. Her interests had widened, and so had her external involvement in them. Her behavior seemed more flexible. The interviewer felt that Miss Z was one of the few students he had seen who had changed greatly while going to school: there had been so much healthy development that he felt sure that she could take care of her remaining conflicts, and eventually would be able to combine career, family, and other interests successfully.

Miss Z had been seen by two psychotherapists in the psychiatric clinic while she was an undergraduate. The first psychotherapist, who saw Miss Z four times, summarized the entering complaint as follows:

> Patient came in because her mother felt she should. Patient's mother had been upset by a letter the patient had written home. The substance of the letter was that the patient was not experiencing the hoped-for expansion of dating activities. During therapy, the patient focused primarily on the troubles of her parents. The mother had recently resolved a severe emotional problem, and was in therapy. The father had responded by becoming emotionally disturbed himself, and the patient somehow felt responsible for this. She was also missing her role of mediator between her parents. Very prominent was her overevaluation of psychiatry and her mother's psychotherapist, with much emphasis on how he had helped her mother—not apparently noting the influence on father. Patient expected to resolve dating problem. Had gone steady in high school, had broken up with her boyfriend as a senior, and did no dating thereafter. She expected new environment to change this. When it didn't happen, she complained to mother, who suggested therapy, and hinted at her expectation that the patient would act out sexually. The patient was infuriated at this.

Miss Z's responses to a questionnaire she answered after entering medical school fill out the picture. To the question, "How would you describe yourself, giving an uncensored and uninhibited picture of yourself?" she responded: "That is a task: physically attractive when I take care of myself, and I consistently do. Socially capable of handling any situation. If I handle it awkwardly, even that is charming, and usually is laughed at. Mentally capable of handling a large amount of mental exercise—probably more than I do. Since I have finally learned to be myself at all times and to love myself for what I am, I have some people who like me for what I am, and some who don't like me, and everyone is happy."

To the question, "How were you different when you entered college in 1961, and what accounts for this difference?" she replied: "If you look back in my records, you'll see a tremendous change. In 1961, I felt I was extremely homely and plain; that I was socially completely incompetent; and that I wasn't intelligent. How can I give any facts to account for the difference—three years of growing, longing to be myself, proving my capabilities? I could say finding 'the answer to life' if there is one, and I know there isn't—[learning] to be completely and consistently honest about the ugliness and sorrows of life as well as the beauties. When I was a sophomore, I talked several times with a psychotherapist at Cowell Hospital who pointed me in the right direction. My mother went through psychotherapy after an emotional breakdown in 1959, which may have helped too." To the question, "What changes have there been in the principles or rules by which you guide your conduct?" she answered: "I have discovered there are no right or wrong rules or principles. The only principles I hold are these: (1) True things are good things. (2) The most important aspect of life is communication with my fellow man. (3) I must always be myself no matter who wants me to be how." She summed it up by stating that she felt she had changed a great deal, but slowly.

Her second psychotherapist's description of her, taken from his notes after the first interview, said:

Nineteen-year-old sophomore, slender, pretty features, braces on teeth, somewhat apologetic about coming, feared the therapist would feel she was wasting his time. Mother encouraged her to come, said patient didn't need to have as much trouble in college as she had. Mother is a real mother now, and easy to talk to since her psychiatric treatments. Mother says patient hasn't even shown anger toward her, and she thinks she should. Patient does feel some resentment now that her mother is more ambitious for her than she is for herself. Mother hoped she would be accepted at a prestigious private college, but the patient didn't care. Mother wanted her to join a sorority, though she told patient she was free to choose. Patient didn't, mother said O.K., but patient felt she was disappointed. Father is quiet, doesn't go in for small talk. His staff loves him. Student feels unable to communicate with him. Nothing she has to say feels quite as good as it should be. Unhappy that she isn't dating more.

A summary of the treatment by her therapist concludes: "Better able to know, reveal, and accept her own feelings. Happy relationship with new boyfriend. Aware of and critical of tendency to be scornful of the fact that his grades were lower than hers. She now wants to be in a service profession, as her father is. At end of semester, somewhat fearful of falling into the old patterns when she returns home, but feels she has some choice. May return for a few interviews in the fall."

At the final interview, Miss Z felt that she had benefited from her psychotherapeutic experience, and was subsequently less isolated, lonely, and depressed. Can it be this simple? Can a few hours with a psychotherapist have such a profound effect, when there is continual doubt in the literature that any psychotherapy, no matter how prolonged, has any effect? Some who have practiced college psychiatry for many years in such a setting as the one at Cowell Hospital are convinced that mutual exploration of difficulties at the appropriate time can change the direction of lives for the better very quickly.

But what of those troubled students who avail themselves neither of the psychiatric clinic nor of the Counseling Center? How do they handle their problems? In partial answer to that question, let us consider brief summaries of the careers of two non-patients, B and C.

B, a young man of eighteen, serious, attractive, well-dressed, and looking older than his years, came to the university from a small rural community. He hoped to become a teacher, and perhaps eventually a writer. He lived alone in an apartment, attended classes regularly, and did acceptable scholastic work. He had few acquaintances and no friends, and was frequently lonely and depressed.

When B was four years old, he left a toy on the basement stairs. His mother tripped on it, fell down the darkened stairs, and injured her back. She had been a chronic invalid ever since. No one in the family ever blamed B openly for the accident, but he received constant reassurances from the other members of the family that he would be "forgiven" by God if he remained a good boy henceforth. The mood of the family, a striving, hopeful, and rather happy one, changed from the day B's mother fell. The father and older brother manifested ill-concealed bitterness, and the mother became a whining complainer. Everyone felt deprived. The family had been moderately religious before, but following the accident, the church and God became almost compulsive solutions to even the most trivial of life's daily problems.

B was intelligent. During his early years, he complied unquestioningly with the family practices of home prayer and regular church attendance. He also read a great deal, mostly for solace and escape from an ever-present feeling that he had committed some great crime. By the age of eleven, he had carefully considered and firmly rejected all belief in God, but he continued to go through the motions with the family, fearful of their severe disapproval if he disclosed his secret convictions.

He finished high school successfully and came to the university in order to get as far away from his family as possible without leaving the country. His parents supported him in school, but he felt sure that they would withdraw their financial support if they knew he no longer attended church and was an unbeliever. He remained a "good boy" in the traditional family sense. He had very little social experience with members of either sex, and no sexual experience except for occasional masturbation, which made him feel guilty and somewhat of a failure. At the end of his second year in college, he left school and did not return.

C, a young man of the same age, serious, attractive, and colorfully but tastefully dressed, came to the university from a large city. He was shy, soft-spoken, and somewhat self-depreciating. He was not sure about what he would like to become, but had some vague ideas about going into television newscasting or acting. More secretly and fancifully, he dreamed of becoming a writer. His mother and father were both dead; they had lived apart since he was five years old. His father had gone to another state following the separation, but had returned to the home from time to time during the student's childhood. When the student was fourteen years old, he witnessed his mother's murder by one of her lovers. His father died about six months later, following an alcoholic spree.

The student had been an excellent scholar in grammar school and high school. He attributed this to his mother's example and exhortations. She had worked as a housemaid during the day, and had gone to night school to complete her high school education. She had hung her diploma on the living room wall for all to see. The student was sure that he was the first member of his family ever to have attended college.

In high school, he had been successful in all scholastic, social, and athletic endeavors. He had been elected student body president in his senior year. When he came to the university, he felt like an outsider. He attended classes, but made no friends and participated in no school activities. If it had not been for some of his old high school friends, who still hung on, he would have been virtually alone. He had dissociated himself from his "family," none of whom were very interested in his activities.

After the first year of college, C got a job in the bookstore. He began to feel a little more comfortable in the university surroundings, although he still had no friends, and participated in no school activities. By the beginning of the second undergraduate year, he had married his high school girlfriend. This helped assuage his loneliness. He did remarkably well scholastically throughout his four years, graduated at the head of his class, and received a coveted award and a number of scholarships to prestigious graduate schools.

Neither B nor C sought any professional help, although it was available and they could both have benefited from talking with someone. C admitted that he had thought of doing so from time to time, but had decided that psychiatric help would be useless because the doctor could not possibly understand a person of his social and cultural background. The first student refrained from seeking help mainly because he felt that no one could straighten out the real problems of his family relations or the bitterness of his childhood following his mother's accident, for which he still irrationally felt guilty. Like B and C, each student in our research study had his own "story." It is not at all clear why some came to the clinic and others did not. Yet it is amply clear that many who did not come needed help as much or more than those who did.

By the time a student reaches college, he is usually chronologically and physiologically an adult. It is primarily in his psychological and social growth that he is considered an adolescent or in transition to adulthood. Many writers in the educational and psychological fields have recently been listing the numerous tasks that college students must master if they are to be considered successful in their maturation: for example, achieving independence, dealing with authority, handling ambiguity, developing with regard to sexual matters, attaining prestige, and developing value systems.[8]

When something goes wrong and students seek help, they or their families are often held responsible for the difficulties, both by themselves and by others. One of the major presenting problems that students talk about with psychotherapists and counselors concerns a marked to moderate depression and an inability to do schoolwork. Of the 493 students in the class of 1965 who sought help, 34 per cent were struggling with this syndrome. Almost all explanations of depression and apathy point to them as ways of handling unacceptable aggression. The aggression is often described as a hangover from past family resentments, transferred to present situations. What ails these people? They seem to be achieving academically, but they are desperately unhappy. They complain about depression, and yet to an experienced psychotherapist, most of them do not seem pathologically depressed. Diagnoses of "depressive reaction" are much lower among them than complaints about depression. They have been called "the voluntarily compliant." They conceal from themselves that they are doing what they do not want to do. In the university environ-

---

[8] Dana Farnsworth, in his recent book, *Psychiatry, Education, and the Young Adult* (Springfield, Illinois: Charles C Thomas, 1966), devotes his third chapter to an analysis of the developmental tasks of college students. He describes what, "ideally," college officials should strive for: "an environment in which students may learn how to acquire mature habits of thought and behavior, develop potential creativity, and learn to be independent without being unnecessarily offensive to those who may not agree with them." He asserts (and we wholeheartedly agree) that "to apply sanctions in a punitive manner at this period of development only perpetuates the [undesirable] behavior and makes the rebellion more intense, more painful, and more prolonged. Punitive action seems to justify the young person's resentment, and to postpone or prevent the acquisition of self-control."

ment, with its diversity of values, their need for the approval of their peers, their desire for status and self-esteem, and their fears of loneliness force them into conformity against their best interests and their own basic values. Clara Thompson differentiates them from the obviously "neurotic"—from those who suffer from a failure to adapt—and calls them the victims of "an anonymous cultural tyranny which subtly exacts submission as the price of success." [9] Erich Fromm writes about them extensively when he writes of the "marketing" orientation.[10] These students, like many older people, seem to suffer from the compromises they have made in order to adapt.

In order to understand how psychotherapists can help such students, one must examine some of the underlying differences between the goals and methods of traditional education and that education or reeducation in self-knowledge and self-values called psychotherapy. In psychotherapy, there are no lectures. It is a one-to-one relationship in which a dialogue is expected and a human relationship is established. Much learning is by example, from a person who is trained and, in some cases, gifted in human living. Admission to the "course" is not based on previous "standards" of performance. Routine tests are not given, and there are no grades. No scholarships are available or necessary; no diplomas are conferred. Humiliations, indignities, blame, and other subtle or crude forms of punishment form no part of the modern psychiatric armamentarium. Advice is not given. Students are neither implored nor compelled to take this path rather than that, and psychotherapists do not appeal to force. For a majority of the students, this is probably the first time in their lives that they are able to talk about their problems with skilled professional adults who have no special self-interest, no axes to grind.

In a relatively short time, their potentialities are freed, and choices become possible again. For many, "What do you want to do?" becomes a meaningful question for the first time. In some of these cases, the students desire to take a leave from school after

[9] Thompson, Clara M. *Interpersonal Psychoanalysis*. New York: Basic Books, 1964. This problem is discussed in the chapter called "An Introduction to Minor Maladjustments."

[10] Fromm, Erich. *Escape From Freedom*. New York: Farrar and Rinehart, 1941, and *The Sane Society*. New York: Rinehart and Company, 1955.

completing the semester. The pejorative term for such students is "dropouts." Others discover for the first time that they do not know whether they wanted to go to college at all, or were just trying to please parents, or at least not disappoint them badly. Others decide that another institution would better suit their needs. Some, of course, return after a certain time away.

In an article in the *Saturday Review*, October 16, 1965, entitled "Why Teachers Fail," B. F. Skinner briefly reviews the history of punishments, crude and subtle, in education. Professor Skinner feels that aversive control "is perhaps an achievement, but it is offset by an extraordinary list of unwanted byproducts traceable to the basic practice. . . . One of the easiest forms of escape is simply to forget all one has learned; and no one has discovered a form of control to prevent this ultimate break for freedom." He continues: "In college and graduate schools, the aversive pattern survives in the now almost universal system of 'assign and test.' The teacher does not teach: he simply holds the student responsible for learning." Knowledge of the objective world has indeed been the concern of our educational systems, but there has been insufficient interest in or concern with the teaching of knowledge of self and the relation of self to its human and non-human environment. Counselors and psychiatrists have done their share, but the teaching of self-knowledge is too important to be left solely to a small minority. It should permeate the entire educational process.

❧ 9 ❧

DRINKING AND
PERSONALITY

Nevitt Sanford and Susan Singer

The investigation reported here was directed to the hypothesis that there are observable ways of drinking and abstaining, as well as attitudes, beliefs, and values with respect to drinking that are characteristic of the individual and can be ascribed to persistent dispositions of his personality. If this hypothesis is true, then we should expect changes in personality over the college years to be accompanied by changes in alcohol-related behavior. It does not follow, however, that changes in alcohol-related behavior can be attributed to change in personality; this is quite possible, to be sure, but as we shall see, such behavior is heavily influenced by social factors.

348

From a practical viewpoint, our major hypothesis is not easy to demonstrate. Common sense and everyday observation tell us that on the part of non-problem drinkers, drinking is heavily determined by the situation of the moment. Little or nothing can be made of a single episode of drinking or abstaining, unless it is extraordinary in its social impact or is known to be very unusual for the individual. There is little reason for even asking about the ways in which personality factors are involved until some consistency of behavior over time has been observed; but even this would not be strongly indicative of personality involvement for, as Verden and other sociologists have shown, consistency of alchol-related behavior is often the result of the persistence of the social situation in which the individual lives, chiefly his membership in social groups within which he conforms.[1]

Still, there are considerations that lend plausibility to our "personality hypothesis." For one thing, there are large individual differences between drinkers. Whatever the drinking patterns of a group, it is always possible to discover various differences among its members. When subjects are administered alcohol in situations where an effort is made to control sources of variation, the researcher often becomes aware of large individual differences that have intervened to attenuate experimental effects. It seems reasonable to suppose that some of the differences in readiness for response that people bring to group drinking situations or to psychological experiments originate in relatively durable personality characteristics. Again, even people with alcoholism differ markedly in respect to when, where, what, and how they drink, and in their behavior during or following their drinking.[2] There is no evidence that persons whose drinking patterns are not problem-induced or problem-causing are categorically different from those who have problems.

Finally, there is the argument from anthropological studies that alcohol is used in radically different ways in different cultures, and has radically different meanings and symbolic values; and that

[1] Verden, Paul. "Alcohol in Contemporary American Society," in Nevitt Sanford (Ed.). *Alcohol Problems and Public Policy*. New York: Oxford University Press, 1968 (in press).

[2] Levin, Max. "The Nature of Problem Drinking." In Nevitt, Sanford (Ed.). *Alcohol Problems and Public Policy*.

these phenomena can be understood as expressions of the shared needs of the people in a given culture. An individual, no less than a culture, is capable of using alcohol in the service of his needs, however little or much these needs may be shared with other people. And he, no less than a culture, is capable of assigning meanings to alcohol; of using it to symbolize other objects or ideas; and of concocting fantasies and beliefs about it that accord with his way of looking at the world. Indeed, we may imagine that cultural patterns, like contemporary fads and fashions, begin in the brains of particular individuals who are trying to think of some way to make their lives more satisfying. Such patterns are no less unique for having been produced by a number of different individuals in similar circumstances at about the same time. Once such patterns have proved their usefulness in a community and have become integral parts of its structure and functioning, they are, of course, adhered to by many individuals whose motives are quite different from those of the innovators. However, those members of the culture with similar personality structures would presumably find similar meanings in drinking.

The study of drinking behavior does not confront the student of personality with unique problems. That all observable behavior is in part determined by the situation of the moment, a situation that includes the individual's various group memberships, is a truism of personality theory. But it is also a truism that individuals manage to put their own stamp upon what they do, to express something of themselves in their behavior—so that an investigator, given a sufficiently broad sample of an individual's behavior, can make reasonably accurate inferences about his enduring characteristics.

To judge by the literature, the personality hypothesis seems not to have held much interest for psychologists in the past. Most of what we know about non-problem drinking we owe to sociologists and anthropologists who, incidental to their studies of the social and cultural determinants of drinking practices, have contributed observations on individuals. Some of these writers have gone so far as to delineate types of drinkers, differentiated primarily on the basis of consistent motivational trends. In a major theoretical paper, Jellinek gave considerable attention to how individual patterns of drinking or abstaining might be expressive of different personality needs.[3] But the great emphasis in all the studies reported is on the social situation, and on factors in the drinker's social background. Instead of relating observed drinking behavior or inferred motives for drinking to dispositions or other attributes of personality, and thereby increasing our understanding of the meaning of drinking to individuals, the authors focus on correlations between alcohol-related phenomena and a wide range of social factors, contemporary and historical.

In much psychological and social scientific work in recent years, personality tends to fall, as it were, between two chairs. Either it is fragmented, as in those experimental studies that focus on two or three variables, or else it is lost in a surround of supra-individual social processes, as in social-psychological studies of drinking behavior. In this light, it seems ironical that psychologists who are primarily interested in personality, and who have carried out intensive and comprehensive studies of personality, have neglected to inquire into the drinking behavior of their subjects. For example, in the Office of Strategic Services assessment studies published in 1948,[4] and in studies largely modeled after them that were carried out at the Institute for Personality Assessment and Research at Berkeley, a "drinking party" was included among the procedures, but the interest was mainly in whether there were problem drinkers among the assessees, and in whether there was anything to the idea of *in vino veritas*. There was no systematic inquiry into the details of the subjects' drinking practices, into the phenomenology of their drinking, or into their beliefs, attitudes, and values with regard to alcohol-related phenomena. The same is true of other assessment studies. One might say that even in a comprehensive three-day assessment study, the investigators cannot attend to everything. Probably a number of important areas of behavior were left out of account. Yet when one considers the enormously wide range of phenomena that were somehow covered, in questionnaires and in interviews, one is left with some suspicion that students of personality have participated in a conspiracy of silence about alcohol.

[3] Jellinek, E. M. "The Problem of Alcohol." In *Alcohol, Science, and Society*. New Haven: *Quarterly Journal of Studies on Alcoholism*, 1945.

[4] Office of Strategic Services Assessment Staff. *Assessment of Men*. New York: Holt, 1948.

In order to add to our understanding of drinking in the context of personality, an investigator must be interested in both personality and non-problem drinking.[5] This seems to be a rare combination of interests; we have been able to find it in only two investigators. Emery (1960) suggests that beverage preferences may reveal dispositions of personality.[6] One hypothesis, which is presumed to hold in the absence of pathology, is "that preferences for sweetness in an alcoholic drink reflects a desire to seek an infantile kind of pleasure, and by implication, escape, in that respect at least, from reality." Preference for bitterness in a drink reflects a greater willingness to face up to reality and to meet it on its own terms. When these opposite taste preferences are combined with other qualities of the drink, three types of drinkers are hypothecated: the indulgent, the social (impulsive, acting-out), and the reparative. The last adjective describes a drinker who is steady, hard-working, reality-oriented, and desirous of putting back by means of his alcoholic beverage at the end of the working day what he gives out in his duty relations. The author concludes that "if the correspondence can be verified [between types of drinkers and their preferences in drink], the theory should offer a valuable means of exploring and predicting many other things about the drinkers of different drinks."

[5] There are, of course, many studies that have found differences in personality between problem drinkers and other people; for example, Button, A. D. "A Study of Alcoholics with the MMPI." *Quarterly Journal of Studies on Alcohol*, 1956, *17*, 263–81; McCord, W., and McCord, Joan. *Origins of Alcoholism*. Stanford: Stanford University Press, 1960; Rosen, A. C. "A Comparative Study of Alcoholics and Psychiatric Patients with the MMPI." *Quarterly Journal of Studies on Alcohol*, 1960, *21*, 253–66; and Singer, E., Blane, H., and Rasschau, R. "Alcoholism and Social Isolation." *Journal of Abnormal and Social Psychology*, 1964, *69*, 681–89. Most such studies leave open the question of whether personality factors predispose to problem drinking or are, rather, effects of it. The McCords' study, however, using data on adolescent boys, some of whom later became alcoholic, produced evidence that personality problems, for example, a struggle with dependence, had a role in the etiology of alcoholism. Such evidence is in line with what has been suggested by numerous clinical studies, for example, Hanfmann, Eugenia. "The Life History of an Ex-Alcoholic, with an Evaluation of Factors Involved in Causation and Rehabilitation." *Quarterly Journal of Studies on Alcohol*, 1951, *12*, 405–43.

[6] Emery, F. *Characteristics of Guiness Drinkers*. London, England: Tavistock Institute of Human Relations, 1960. Document No. 567 (mimeo).

Closer to our own work is that of Mary Jones, who, like Emery, set out to determine whether variations in drinking practices were associated with characteristics of personality.[7] The subjects were 66 men, members of the Oakland Growth Study, who had been studied intensively for seven years beginning in their tenth year, and who had taken part in follow-up studies at ages 33, 38, and 43. In the follow-up interviews at age 43, in 1964, Jones questioned the subjects carefully about their drinking, and on the basis of the information they gave, classified them according to the following amount-frequency scheme: (1) problem drinkers, (2) heavy drinkers, (3) moderate drinkers, (4) light drinkers, and (5) non-drinkers-abstainers. The California Q-sort was used for obtaining measures of personality attributes. The basis for the Q-sorts was a series of intensive interviews, averaging 12 hours overall, conducted when the subjects were age 38.[8] Ratings were made from the judgments of two psychologists. Numerous differences among problem drinkers, moderate drinkers, and abstainers were found. Concerning the moderate drinkers, Jones writes: "On the whole, ratings for being controlled, consistent, objective, moralistic, and ethical, with a high aspiration level, are above average for this group of men; but their position is midway between the problem drinkers in one direction and the non-drinkers in the other."[9]

In another part of the study, Jones shows that the differences in personality among her three groups of drinkers were already beginning to show when the subjects were in junior high school. During the early years of the Oakland Growth Study, when the subjects were ten-and-a-half to seventeen-and-a-half years old, they were given numerous tests of abilities, attitudes, and interests; they were interviewed, observed in various natural settings, and rated on personality characteristics. Parents contributed information on family background and home life, teachers reported on classroom behavior, and classmates gave their impressions. On the basis of this material, three psychologists

[7] Jones, Mary. "Personality Correlates and Antecedents of Drinking Patterns in Adult Males." *Journal of Consulting Psychology,* 1968 (in press).
[8] Block, J. *The Q-sort Method of Personality Assessment and Psychiatric Research.* Springfield, Ill.: Charles C Thomas, 1961.
[9] Jones. "Personality Correlates."

sorted for each subject the 100 items in the California Q-sort: once for the junior high school period, and once for the senior high school period. It was found that 53 per cent of the 36 items that differentiated among the men in the three drinking categories in adulthood were also differentiating at the junior high school level, and 44 per cent were differentiating at the senior high school level. This is evidence that personality factors may predispose not only to problem drinking, as the work of the McCords indicated, but to other forms of alcohol-related behavior as well.[10]

Our study of the relationship of drinking to personality among college students began in the summer of 1961, when the Institute for the Study of Human Problems was also beginning an intensive study of alcohol problems for the Cooperative Commission on the Study of Alcoholism. Accordingly, when plans were being made to administer a battery of tests to the entering freshman classes at Stanford and at Berkeley, it was natural to include items pertaining to alcohol. Fifty-four such items, written by Max Levin and Mary C. Jones, were included among the personality and attitude scales being used.

Fred and Zelda Strassburger used these 54 items in developing two 10-item attitude scales, one (Scale I) measuring favorableness of attitude toward social drinking, and the other (Scale II) tolerance or enlightenment of view with respect to "alchoholism and the alcoholic." [11] Examples of the items in Scale I are: "All things considered, drinking does people more good than harm" (True), and "It is best not to go around with people who drink" (False). In Scale II, "An alcoholic is an ill person" (True), and "A drunk makes me feel disgusted" (False). The scales had adequate internal consistency, and were validated by comparison with ratings of attitudes and drinking behavior made on the basis of freshman interviews with 92 Stanford freshmen and 102 Berkeley freshmen. The major findings of the Strassburger study were that freshmen who are favorably disposed toward the use of alcohol and have enlightened views on alco-

---

[10] McCord and McCord. *Origins of Alcoholism.*

[11] Strassburger, Fred, and Strassburger, Zelda. "Measurement of Attitudes Toward Alcohol and Their Relation to Personality Variables." *Journal of Consulting Psychology,* 1965, *29,* 440–45.

holism score higher than others on the Social Maturity and Impulse Expression Scales.

The basic data of this study were obtained from 271 senior men and 213 senior women students at Stanford. These students filled out the Senior Questionnaire, which contained enough questions about drinking so that is was possible to classify the students according to a scheme that combined frequency of drinking hard liquor with frequency of being drunk.

Group 1. Abstainers: never drink, never drunk.

Group 2. Drinks, but doesn't get drunk: drinks daily, once or twice a week, or once or twice a month, but has not been drunk in the past year.

Group 3. Drinks seldom, but gets drunk: drinks once or twice a month, or once to twice a year, but has been drunk more than once in the past year.

Group 4. Drinks frequently, and gets drunk: drinks daily, or once or twice a week, and has been drunk more than once in the past year.

For most of these students, scores on the following instruments were available: The Strassburger Scales I and II, for both freshman and senior years; the Omnibus Personality Inventory, six scales, for both freshman and senior years; the Ethnocentrism (E) Scale, for both freshman and senior years; the Authoritarianism (F) Scale, for both freshman and senior years; the California Psychological Inventory (CPI), for the freshman year; and selected items from the Senior Questionnaire.

We are thus in a position to relate scores on the Strassburger scales with various personality measures, and to compare subjects in the various categories of drinking behavior in terms of their Strassburger Scale scores as well as in terms of their scores on the personality measures. Because sex differences of some importance appear in the data, it seemed best to carry out separate analyses for the men and for the women. Correlations between scores on the Strassburger Scales and scores on the OPI, E, and F Scales are shown in Table 58. Also shown are the correlations found in the groups of freshman and senior men and women between Scale I and Scale II. Despite the fact that the scales have three items in common, and that one of these items scores in the opposite direction in the two instances, these correlations are not very high. This suggests that the scales actually measure somewhat different attitudes—an interpretation that is consistent with the fact that in some cases, their correlations with the personality measures are strikingly different.

TABLE 58

CORRELATIONS BETWEEN STRASSBURGER SCALES (S I AND S II) AND
OPI, E AND F SCALES
STANFORD

	Freshman Women (N = 380)		Freshman Men (N = 773)		Senior Women (N = 123)		Senior Men (N = 162)	
	S I	S II	S I	S II	S I	S II	S I	S II
SM	.16 *	.39 *	.18 *	.38 *	.28 *	.44 *	.15	.35 *
IE	.25 *	.26 *	.34 *	.29 *	.28 *	.23 *	.30 *	.27 *
SF	.02	—.06	.10 *	.02	.05	—.01	.04	—.06
MF	—.06	—.03	—.04	—.08	.02	—.07	—.08	—.08
ES	—.02	.12	.04	.15 *	.20	.27 *	.04	.10
DS	.29 *	.43 *	.35 *	.46 *	.26 *	.41 *	.30 *	.47 *
F	—.10	—.30 *	—.13 *	—.33 *	.12	.11	.02	—.31 *
E	—.04	—.17 *	—.01	—.13 *	—.09	—.16	.08	—.20 *
S I		.44 *		.55 *		.35 *		.48 *
S II	.44 *		.55 *		.35 *		.48 *	

* Significant at the .05 level.

We may note first a confirmation of the Strassburgers' major finding: favorable attitudes toward drinking and nonpunitive attitudes toward alcoholics go with higher scores on the Social Maturity (SM) and Impulse Expression (IE) Scales. Positive correlations of approximately the same order are found in all four groups of subjects. These findings are consistent with, and are to some extent bolstered by, the positive correlations between the alcohol scales and the Developmental Status Scale (DS), a scale correlated with SM and IE that measures maturity, flexibility, sophistication, tolerance, and acceptance of impulses.

In all the groups of students, Social Maturity correlates more highly with Scale II than with Scale I. The SM Scale was derived from the F Scale, which, in all the groups but one, is correlated significantly with Scale II, but is in no group correlated with Scale I. It may be suggested that in a drinking culture (the Strassburgers have reported that in their sample of Stanford freshmen, 78 per cent of the men and 77 per cent of the women were users of alcohol), we should not expect to find much opposition to drinking on the part of authoritarian subjects, but that with regard to alcoholics—a group that is deviant or "different," a group that might be blamed for their condition—the authoritarian tendencies toward stereotyped thinking, rigid moralism, and punitiveness might be expected to come to the fore.

Mean scores on Scales I and II of freshman and senior men and women grouped according to drinking pattern are shown in Table 59. First to be noted here is a sex difference in the way the subjects are distributed among the drinking categories. For men, the modal pattern is to drink and to get drunk occasionally, whereas for the women, the modal pattern is to drink but not to get drunk. Comparatively few of the women either abstain or drink frequently and get drunk.

The Strassburgers suggest, on the basis of studies of interview protocols, that many women swim with the tide on questions of social drinking, allowing their drinking behavior to be determined by the climate of opinion or by the particular occasion. It is as if alcohol did not mean as much to them personally as it does to men. That so small a proportion of the women abstain is not surprising, when considered in the light of the survey made by Straus and Bacon, who found that although only 46 per cent of the females and 69 per cent of the males in their large sample of students in various colleges were users of alcohol, the proportions were approximately the same at private, nonsectarian schools like Stanford.[12] Also, there is evidence that there has been more drinking among young people during the 1960's than there was in 1953, when Straus and Bacon conducted their survey.

The data in Table 59 also show that the reported drinking behavior of our subjects was consistent with their attitudes toward drinking and alcoholism. For senior men and women, scores on both Scale I and Scale II increase directly with frequency of reported drinking and drunkenness; the same tendency was also found in freshmen. In freshmen as well as in seniors, men and women abstainers were significantly less sympathetic toward drink-

12 Straus, R. and Bacon, S. *Drinking in College.* New Haven, Conn.: Yale University Press, 1953.

Table 59

SCORES ON STRASSBURGER SCALES I[a] AND II[b] FOR STANFORD MEN AND WOMEN AS FRESHMEN (1961) AND SENIORS (1965)

STANFORD MEN

	Abstain		Drink—never drunk		Drink occasionally—drunk more than once		Drink frequently—drunk more than ten times		Significant difference between groups (p < .05)
	Mean	SD	Mean	SD	Mean	SD	Mean	SD	
1961									
S I	(N = 33) 2.67	1.49	(N = 31) 4.77	1.73	(N = 70) 4.56	1.98	(N = 48) 5.48	1.97	I-II, I-III, I-IV, III-IV
S II	4.21	1.58	6.58	2.00	6.79	1.78	7.06	1.98	I-II, I-III, I-IV
1965									
S I	(N = 2) 3.86	1.70	(N = 17) 5.76	1.09	(N = 44) 6.64	1.22	(N = 30) 6.80	1.24	I-II, I-III, I-IV, II-III, II-IV
S II	5.82	2.04	7.76	1.30	8.30	1.22	8.57	1.30	I-II, I-III, I-IV, II-IV

STANFORD WOMEN

	Abstain		Drink—never drunk		Drink occasionally—drunk more than once		Drink frequently—drunk more than ten times		Significant difference between groups (p < .05)
1961									
S I	(N = 6) 3.50	0.55	(N = 58) 4.28	1.68	(N = 34) 4.94	1.56	(N = 13) 4.15	1.63	I-III
S II	5.33	1.86	6.76	1.81	7.64	1.86	6.61	1.85	I-III
1965									
S I	(N = 6) 4.00	1.10	(N = 34) 5.94	1.46	(N = 23) 6.04	1.22	(N = 10) 6.60	1.26	I-II, I-III, I-IV
S II	7.00	1.67	7.85	1.40	8.17	1.30	8.20	0.63	I-IV

[a] Attitude toward social drinking (high score means favorable).

358

ing and toward alcoholics than students reporting various patterns of drinking were. In all groups of abstainers and drinkers, the mean scores of seniors on the Strassburger scales are higher than those of the freshmen.

The mean personality scale scores—OPI, F, and E—of subjects in the four drinking categories are given in Table 60. What first strikes the eye here is the fact that abstainers are a very distinctive group. Male and female abstainers, both as freshmen and as seniors, score lower than drinkers on Social Maturity, Impulse Expression, and Developmental Status; these groups of abstainers are also higher on Authoritarianism, though it is only in the female group that the differences are statistically significant. These results are consistent with those involving the Strassburger scales, and serve to give a picture of the abstainer as relatively moralistic, constricted, and unsophisticated. This picture is similar to that which emerged when Jones applied the Q-sort technique to the adult abstainers in her study: they were distinguished from problem drinkers and moderate drinkers by being more overcontrolled, emotionally bland, fastidious, introspective, moralistic, considerate, and giving.[13]

Among the drinking groups, we find, as might be expected, that men who drink frequently and get drunk are higher on Impulse Expression than men who drink but are never drunk. But here the women veer off in a different direction. Both as freshmen and as seniors, women who drink occasionally and get drunk not only score higher on Impulse Expression and Developmental Status than those who drink without getting drunk—a finding not inconsistent with the findings for men—but they score higher than those who drink frequently and get drunk do. One clue to the meaning of this finding may be found in the fact that women who drink occasionally and get drunk score highest on Schizoid Functioning; this suggests that they are conflicted, and have difficulty both in accepting and in controlling their impulses. Another interpretation is suggested by what was said earlier about women swimming with the tide: women who drink frequently may simply be the most "social," in the sense that they have many dates and often find themselves in situations where drinking is the order

[13] Jones. "Personality Correlates."

TABLE 60

PERSONALITY SCALE SCORES OF STANFORD MEN AND WOMEN STUDENTS IN FOUR DRINKING GROUPS

STANFORD MEN

	I Abstainers (N=36) Mean	SD	II Drink—never drunk (N=33) Mean	SD	III Drink occasionally—drunk more than once (N=73) Mean	SD	IV Drink frequently—drunk more than 10 times (N=52) Mean	SD	t ratios between I-II	I-III	I-IV	II-IV	III-IV
Freshmen [a]													
SM [b]	46	12	52	8	50	9	50	11	2.37*	2.04*			
IE	44	9	47	10	50	9	51	10		2.91**	3.51***		
SF	50	9	48	11	49	10	50	10					
MF	53	11	47	11	49	10	50	10					
Es	52	11	52	9	49	10	49	11					
DS	44	11	48	7	51	10	51	10		3.56***	3.40**		
F	116	28	110	20	110	22	109	21					
E	53	18	50	17	53	17	55	19					
Seniors	(N=24)		(N=20)		(N=46)		(N=31)		I-III	I-IV	II-IV	III-IV	
SM	52	12	58	8	59	9	59	9	2.65*	2.64*			
IE	46	10	50	9	52	9	57	9	2.85*	4.37***	2.81**	2.34*	
SF	46	10	44	10	45	9	49	9					
MF	49	13	50	10	47	9	45	12					
Es	52	13	53	11	53	10	52	10					
DS	51	12	56	9	60	9	64	9	3.51***	4.50***	3.13**		
F	98	29	98	28	96	23	88	28					
E	43	16	46	19	45	14	42	18					

* p < .05   ** p < .01   *** p < .001

[a] Scores were also computed for those freshmen for whom we have both freshmen and senior responses (Men N = 118, Women = 78). Their scores are nearly the same as the scores of students reported here (Men N = 194, Women = 121), about a third of whom did not respond to the senior test.

TABLE 60—Continued

PERSONALITY SCALE SCORES OF STANFORD MEN AND WOMEN STUDENTS IN FOUR DRINKING GROUPS

STANFORD WOMEN

Freshmen [a]

	I Abstainers (N = 7) Mean	SD	II Drink—never drunk (N = 61) Mean	SD	III Drink occasionally—drunk more than once (N = 36) Mean	SD	IV Drink frequently—drunk more than 10 times (N = 14) Mean	SD	t ratios between I-II	I-III	II-III	III-IV
SM [b]	45	8	52	10	50	12	50	6	2.14			
IE	49	6	48	9	56	8	49	7			3.98 ***	2.71 **
SF	54	5	49	9	55	8	49	9			2.95 **	1.96
MF	49	10	49	10	50	12	50	11				
Es	54	8	51	10	47	12	51	10			1.98	
DS	43	7	49	11	55	9	47	5		3.18 **	2.38 *	2.84 **
F	120	22	101	22	104	25	109	14				
E	51	19	49	14	45	16	45	15				

Seniors

	I Abstainers (N = 6) Mean	SD	II Drink—never drunk (N = 37) Mean	SD	III Drink occasionally—drunk more than once (N = 25) Mean	SD	IV Drink frequently—drunk more than 10 times (N = 10) Mean	SD	t ratios between I-II	I-III	I-IV	II-III
SM	50	8	59	10	58	11	58	8	2.24 *		2.09 *	
SF	44	7	44	8	52	10	57	10		4.21 ***	3.10 **	3.58 ***
IE	43	5	51	9	61	10	48	12	2.60 **	3.64 ***	2.59 *	2.26 *
MF	49	9	49	10	48	11	52	11				
Es	49	6	54	9	50	13	53	11				
DS	50	6	60	10	67	10	62	9	2.27 *			3.10 **
F	112	22	89	25	91	27	89	22				
E	50	14	39	15	44	20	39	14	2.13 *			

* p < .05   ** p < .01   *** p < .001

a See Note a, preceding page.
b See Note b, preceding page.

of the day. This is conventional behavior for Stanford women; it may well be that those who drink only occasionally but get drunk find more pleasure and meaning in their drinking—drink more like men, we might say—in which case, we should expect them to be more "impulse-expressive" and sophisticated.

Mean California Psychological Inventory (CPI) scores were calculated for freshmen in the various drinking groups. In the case of males, abstainers scored lower than drinkers on dominance, capacity for status, sociability, social presence, self-acceptance, and flexibility, and higher on responsibility, socialization, self-control, and femininity. Here again the abstainers stand out as being shy, retiring, socially uncomfortable, controlled in behavior, and rather rigid in their thinking. Among the three drinking groups, those who did not get drunk scored higher than those who did on measures of responsibility, socialization, capacity to make a good impression, and achievement through conformance, which suggests that this group drinks when it seems appropriate, but with much caution.

Female abstainers scored significantly lower than the drinking groups on social presence, achievement through independence, and flexibility, which indicates that they tend to lack social poise and are conforming and rigid in their thinking. The most deviant group on the CPI (as on the OPI) was the group of women who drink infrequently but do get drunk. Compared to the large group of women who drink often but do not get drunk, this group is significantly lower in dominance, sociability, sense of well-being, responsibility, socialization, communality (responding to items as the majority of subjects do), achievement through conformance, independence, intellectual efficiency, and femininity. Compared to the women who drink frequently and get drunk, these infrequent drinkers who get drunk scored lower on sociability, socialization, self-control, good impression, and achievement through conformance. These data substantiate the hypothesis suggested by the OPI results, that the women who drink seldom but do get drunk are a troubled, conflicted group, not quite in control of themselves, and also perhaps ashamed of behavior that they feel they ought to control. The large group of women who drink often but do not get drunk seem to be following an expected and acceptable pattern that enables them to adapt smoothly to social demands. The women who drink often and get drunk now and then do not seem to feel troubled or conflicted about their behavior. As we have suggested, they seem to be acting well within the limits of conventional behavior at Stanford.

The four drinking groups differed in their responses to a number of the Senior Questionnaire items. Usually the abstainers, or the abstainers and those who drink without getting drunk, differed from the groups who drink and get drunk. The important dimension here seems to be strength of impulse and degree of control: the heavier drinkers have more fun; the non-drinkers are somewhat constrained. In general, senior men who drank and got drunk were more social, more influenced by peers, more permissive about sex, had more intimate sexual relationships, more physical complaints, and more periods of depression than non-drinkers. Abstainers (and, to some extent, controlled drinkers) were less sociable, less influenced by peers, less permissive about sex, more inhibited in sexual behavior, and more religious. The three groups of drinkers differed in some of their reasons for drinking. Those who got drunk said more often that drinking relaxed them and made them feel confident, and that they especially liked to "get high" and to drink on dates. Those who did not get drunk attributed less importance to these reasons for drinking.

In the case of women, abstainers indicated the least amount of participation in social activities, the greatest involvement in church activities, the greatest frequency of prayer, and the least change in moral values during college. Compared with women drinkers, they indicated that they had more frequent conflict with girlfriends and less conflict with adults in authority. They were more opposed to premarital sexual relationships, and had a lower degree of sexual intimacy than those who drank.

The women who reported drinking seldom but getting drunk devoted the least time to church activities and were the least inclined to pray. They were the most affected during their college years by problems in their own families and by problems and conflicts in themselves: 17 per cent had drinking problems in their immediate families, in contrast to 6 per cent for the group who drank without getting drunk, and none for the abstainers and frequent drinkers. Of the four groups, they indicated the most frequent conflict with adults in authority. They were the most permissive regarding premarital sexual relationships; they had the greatest amount of sexual intimacy, but also the greatest conflict over sexual impulses. More often than the other women, they said that drinking helped them feel more confident. In general, the questionnaire data support the impression gained from the personality measures that the women in this group were troubled and conflicted—unable to accept or to suppress their impulses. Perhaps they were in a period of flux, when their values and self-concepts were changing.

The women who reported drinking frequently and getting drunk were characterized by much social activity, early physical development, and fairly high sexual intimacy attended by some conflict. They said they drank on dates, on special occasions, and for relaxation. Many of them (93 per cent) knew someone with a drinking problem, but none had a drinking problem in her immediate family. This is probably a sociable, fun-loving group of young women who grew up earlier than their peers.

In summary, our data indicate that drinking behavior, crudely described in terms of frequency and amount, as well as attitudes toward drinking and toward alcoholism, are related to personality characteristics. Where drinking is the norm, abstainers —both male and female—stand out as a relatively rigid, intolerant, and immature group. For men students, the modal pattern is to drink and get drunk, and the students who follow this pattern tend to be the most self-accepting, tolerant, and socially mature group. Among women, however, the modal pattern is to drink often but not to get drunk—to go along with the group, but to maintain self-control. There is a rather small group of sociable, self-accepting young women who drink often and do get drunk, but there is a larger group of troubled and conflicted women who drink seldom and get drunk. Control seems to be a more important issue for women than for men, with the women less able to permit and enjoy expression of impulse.

In all groups of male and female drinkers and abstainers, seniors score higher than freshmen on the two Strassburger scales. Differences on particular items show something of the contrasting frames of mind of entering and graduating students. In the following examples, figures in the columns indicate the percentage of students answering "Yes."

TABLE 61

STRASSBURGER SCALE ITEMS
(FIGURES INDICATE PERCENTAGES OF STUDENTS ANSWERING "YES")

	Men		Women	
Item	Freshmen	Seniors	Freshmen	Seniors
(3) On a date, it is up to the girl to set the standards in regard to drinking behavior	19	16	76	47
(5) Most people drink because of personal problems	38	15	32	19
(6) All things considered, drinking does people more good than harm	15	32	9	19
(7) I resent people who preach the evils of drink	45	57	45	66
(12) People with a purpose in life have no need for alcohol	63	30	51	16
(13) People with adequate morals cannot become problem drinkers	31	11	26	8
(19) It is best not to go around with people who drink	44	13	41	9
(26) Most teenagers drink merely to defy authority	69	65	76	74
(34) Only people with weak characters drink to excess	37	17	28	7
(36) The law should permit serving liquor to eighteen-year-olds	42	69	34	70
(38) I have gotten away with buying a drink when I was under the legal age limit	32	71	28	76
(49) College students should be allowed to drink as often and as much as they like	28	68	20	66
(52) An alcoholic is an ill person	88	92	93	92

Not only are seniors more favorable toward drinking in general (Items 6, 36, 38, and 49 particularly) and toward freedom of choice for the individual (Items 7, 36, and 49), but they are more straightforward in reporting their own drinking behavior (Item 38) and less given to moral rigidity (Items 12, 13, 19, and 34). They are more confident of their ability to control themselves (Item 3, women particularly), and generally more knowledgeable and sophisticated (Items 5, 12, 34). Although freshmen as well as seniors think of alcoholism as an illness (Item 52), the former are much more likely, nonetheless, to see it as a moral failure. This is by no means the only instance of inconsistency in the thinking of freshmen. Very few believe that drinking does more good than harm, but there is nonetheless relatively strong resentment of people who preach its evils. Freshmen rather overwhelmingly believe that most teenagers drink merely to defy authority, but relatively few of them believe that college students should be allowed to drink as they please. Revealed here, it seems, is an important aspect of the freshman's developmental status: he has conflicts about authority, not being quite able to do with it or to do without it; while striving for independence, he nevertheless wants authority to be there in case he needs it. Seniors are not altogether free of this conflict, but they are more consistent: their opposition to authority is even stronger than that of the freshmen, and they expect teenagers to defy it; but they do not ask for external controls of their behavior in college.

It was possible to categorize the reported frequency of drinking of Berkeley seniors according to a scheme that is essentially equivalent to that used in the Strassburger ratings. Here is a comparison in these terms of Berkeley freshmen and Berkeley seniors. Men and women are treated separately.

TABLE 62

DRINKING HABITS OF BERKELEY MEN AND WOMEN

| | Men | | | | Women | | | |
| | Freshmen | | Seniors | | Freshmen | | Seniors | |
	N	Per cent	N	Per cent	N	Per cent	N	Per cent
Abstain	25	39	18	6	17	32	21	9
Drink occasionally or infrequently	24	38	37	15	22	41	49	22
Drink moderately	14	22	98	39	14	26	106	47
Drink heavily or frequently	1	2	97	39	0	0	51	22

In the case of one category, abstaining, the data may be supplemented by data from Stanford. The Strassburgers reported that 78 per cent of the Stanford men and 77 per cent of the Stanford women were users of alcohol. Taking these figures in conjunction with the Senior Questionnaire, we find that the percentages of abstainers in the freshman and senior samples of men are 22 and 19 respectively; in the samples of women, 23 and 8 respectively. These data make sense and are generally in accord with what might be expected. Let us consider first the case of abstainers. At Berkeley, a relatively high proportion of the men, 39 per cent, arrive at college without having begun to drink. Most of them are introduced to alcohol at some time during their college careers. The same trend is to be observed in the case of the women, though there are fewer abstainers among them at the beginning of college. This is what we might expect: young people of conservative or religious backgrounds with more or less protected upbringings become "liberated" at college, or at least adapt themselves to the prevailing standards of the college community. It has often been noted by observers at Berkeley that the men students come from more varied socioeconomic backgrounds than the women do, a fact which may well explain the sex differences in rates of abstainers.

But what about Stanford, where the proportion of abstainers is almost as great among senior men as among freshman men? Here it is suggested that since the great mass of these students comes from families of relatively high socioeconomic status, those who are going to drink begin to do so while they are still in high school. The persistent abstainers are therefore a distinctive group, as their personality test scores have indicated. To explain the differences between Berkeley and Stanford men, we may make use of the distinction drawn by the Strassburgers between "militant" and "tolerant" abstainers. Of the twenty-five abstainers in the Berkeley freshman sample, only three were classified as militant. At Stanford, on the other hand, clinical evidence indicates that the great majority of the freshman abstainers were militant, and that they stuck to their guns throughout their college careers. Typically, these young men came from homes in which there were religious scruples against drinking; they had apparently accepted their family values fully, and they remained oriented toward their families throughout the four college years. They had their minds made up about their future careers when they arrived at college, and they focused upon their work, allowing themselves to be influenced little by their peers or by the general culture of the college. Their relatively high scores on F (Authoritarianism) and E (Ethnocentrism) and their relatively low scores on SM (Social Maturity), IE (Impulse Expression), and DS (Developmental Status) changed little during college.

With women, on the other hand, the story is different. There were no more militant abstainers at Stanford than there were at Berkeley. Indeed, it is extremely rare to find among women at either of these institutions exhibiting such grim, family-supported, achievement orientation as that just described in the case of men. Drinking is not as much of an issue with them as it is with the men. Some arrive at college without having begun to drink, having been brought up, we may imagine, in abstinent homes or otherwise protected environments, but most of them soon adapt themselves to the culture of the college, and drink enough to meet the demands of conformity, but not enough to find in drinking an important means for the release of impulses.

Concerning the categories of drinkers, we find in both men and women a change in the general direction of greater frequency of drinking: fewer subjects drink occasionally and infrequently, more drink moderately or frequently. This result is consistent with our findings concerning the personality correlates of attitudes and practices respecting alcohol. Greater frequency of drinking, like more liberal attitudes toward drinking and alcoholics, is associated with higher scores on Social Maturity, Impulse Expression, and Developmental Status; these personality variables increase during the college years, and so does the frequency of drinking. Both of these kinds of changes are, we may suppose, indications of the liberating effects of the college experience.

Here it must be noted that the changes that take place in students during the college years are rarely very radical, and generally they are congruent with the students' precollege personalities. We have noted that in freshmen as well as in seniors, personality variables are correlated within attitudes and practices respecting alcohol, and that the attitudes and practices of seniors are correlated with personality variables measured when they were freshmen. This is consistent with Jones's finding that the personality dispositions associated with particular drinking practices in adults are continuous with dispositions observed when these subjects were in junior high school.[14] The general rule seems to be that subjects change in their absolute scores on personality measures, but still tend to retain their positions relative to other subjects. Our senior abstainers, who are high on the F Scale as freshmen, are not quite so high as seniors, but they are still higher than most other subjects. Again, students who are high on the Impulse Expression Scale as freshmen are likely to be drinking with some frequency, and during college both their IE scores and the frequency of their drinking are likely to increase— hence there is a correlation between IE and frequency of drinking in seniors as well as in freshmen.

Let us now consider the implications for action of findings such as those we have reported. What should teenagers be told about drinking and alcoholism? What should the position of the college administration be with regard to drinking among its students? There are wide differences of opinion in our society concerning these relatively simple questions; and discussion of them is troublesome, because we as a society have not worked out any generally agreed-upon standards governing the use of alcohol. What is needed is an evaluative scheme based on the various contexts and meanings of drinking and abstaining, and on their implications for long-range social and individual developmental goals.

The results of our study could become the basis for some first steps toward the development of such a scheme. But merely to raise the question of action is to expose the deficiencies of the work we have reported. For one thing, our categories for describing behavior with respect to alcohol, though far from being meaningless, lack sensitivity and subtlety. Abstaining, for example, appears to have different meanings and different implications for action in different cases. It is correlated with authoritarianism, and authoritarianism is generally considered to be a mark of failure, or at least of delay, in personality development. Should we then regard abstaining as something that college students should get over as soon as possible? Hardly, for one can easily find abstainers who are not authoritarian. Presumably, such an abstainer would be less

14 Jones. "Personality Correlates."

"militant" and perhaps freer of inner conflicts about the question of drinking than his more authoritarian counterpart. It is much the same for the several categories of drinking: "heavy" drinking, for example, is associated with higher scores in Impulse Expression, a variable that generally increases as students go through college, and is usually taken as a sign of progress toward maturity; but as we all know, heavy drinking sometimes turns into problem drinking. We are left with the important practical question of how to judge the significance of particular patterns of heavy drinking.

To gain an indication of how far we still have to go, we need only consider what has been reported from clinical investigations of individuals with drinking problems. The psychoanalytic literature contains many reports in which alcohol-related behavior is shown to be dependent upon underlying personality needs and conflicts: one man's problem drinking is said to be an expression of an unconscious fantasy of being reunited with the mother of his infancy; another man becomes intoxicated in order to make possible the indulgence of homosexual needs; another uses the same device in order to express hostility toward his restricting mother-wife; a woman's problem drinking is an acting out of her unconscious identification with her alcoholic or delinquent father; and so on. If these psychoanalytic formulations are valid, they are of considerable significance, for we cannot believe that the personality functioning of problem drinkers is categorically different from that of ordinary drinkers.

When people who are not problem drinkers are studied carefully, as in the course of psychotherapy undertaken because of symptoms or complaints apparently unrelated to drinking, it is possible to see that personality processes and drinking practices are related in ways not unlike those found in problem drinkers. One of us treated, in psychoanalysis and in psychoanalytic psychotherapy over a period of nearly three years, a young woman social worker who presented at the beginning a variety of symptoms including frigidity, but who drank abstemiously and only occasionally. During the course of the psychotherapeutic work, she developed a pattern of dependence on beer and coffee, switching from one to the other and arranging her life so that during her waking hours she was never without the felt effects of one or the other substance. This pattern, it seemed, was expressive of her deepest conflict. On the one hand, she wanted to tear off, devour, possess totally, some source of life and power, be it her mother's breast or a man's penis; and on the other hand, she wanted to be sweet and good, full of love and loved fully, free of all aggressive impulses. Beer enabled her to achieve something of this latter state; it allowed her to feel for a time warm, comfortable, and loved (another effort in the same direction was her restricting herself to soft foods; biting or chewing made her unbearably anxious). If the drinking continued, these good feelings began to give way to feelings of helplessness, stupidity, and passivity, which meant for her giving up her masculine strivings and all hope of success and power. She needed coffee to make her snap out of it. Coffee could for a time make her feel alert and ambitious, and she could then do some work, but pretty soon the destructive impulses would be aroused, anxiety would begin to well up, and she would go back to beer. One can see how beer served her purposes better than wine or spirits; it gave the needed sense of fullness, and permitted her to prolong the feeling of goodness.

It is safe to say that the meaning of beer-drinking for this young woman was quite different from that found in other cases. But there would appear to be nothing unique or pathological about her capacity and inclination to assign personal meaning to drinking—to give it symbolic value and thus to use it as a means of expressing personality needs. This seems to be a general human tendency. The pathology in her case did not lie in the fact that infantile needs were expressed in drinking behavior. Rather, it was involved with the intensity of our patient's conflicts, and with the fact that they led to rigidity of personality—a state of affairs in which major strivings were unconscious, or were not in communication with the conscious ego. One might say that her way of managing her conflicts was not the worst that could have been contrived. She might have acted out her aggressive impulses and her dependence in overt behavior, with painful or highly annoying consequences for other people, and serious consequences for herself.

Clinical studies of individuals in trouble, though they have so far been the major source of our knowledge about the relations of drinking to infantile needs and the unconscious process, are certainly not the only source of understanding of the place of drinking in the overall functioning. Much can be found out from research interviews that are focused on drinking and guided by theory. The following cases of two brothers, taken from Jones, show how different in meaning and implications "heavy" drinking may be.[15]

They [the drinkers, who happened to be brothers] were raised in an immigrant household, in an Italian section of a large city. The parents, born in Italy, spoke little English, and clung to their Italian customs, including the drinking of wine with meals and on social occasions. The older of these boys conformed to the family background. He went from high school into a traditional Italian family business, and continues at age 45 to live next door to his parents. He married late, has two children still in grade school, and does not mention college among the goals he wishes for these children. The younger boy was brighter, more ambitious, and more aware of the differences between his background and that of his schoolmates. Eventually he rejected his background. He went to college, became an entrepreneur, married before his older brother, moved from the Italian community of his origin, and after several subsequent moves, each time to better neighborhoods, is now established in a superior residential section of a suburb. His children are preparing for college in private schools.

The older man, like his parents, drinks wine on most occasions, though liquor is consumed in fair amounts. He says drinking makes him "more lively." He enjoys drinking, likes the taste and doesn't "drink for effect." The younger brother drinks "to be sociable" or "because others are drinking," while the older brother drinks "to make social occasions more enjoyable." The latter expresses pleasure in the situation; the former lacks this emotional involvement. In addition, the younger brother says that he drinks "when tense and nervous," and feels "relaxed" rather than lively after drinking.

The older brother drank "fairly often" at home as a child, and had liquor before graduation from high school. The younger brother hated wine as a child. Even the smell of it made him sick, so that when the family

[15] Jones, Mary C. *Drinking and the Life Cycle* (in preparation).

cleaned up after a party, he was excused from helping. Both men recalled this experience in their separate interviews—the older with humor, the younger with some repugnance.

The older brother reports that his children have had wine with water at their grandparents' homes since an early age, and that he believes that young people should be allowed to take a drink with friends before age 21. The younger man thinks that youths should postpone drinking until they have come of age, although his teenagers now have a cocktail at home occasionally with the family. Neither of these men is likely to drink unrestrainedly, but the reasons which keep them in balance are quite different. The older man's drinking pattern, like that of his overall behavior, is integrated with his family role. He likes to drink for the taste and for the enjoyment it lends to a social occasion. There is no ambivalence about drinking or not drinking, no self-consciousness about . . . the amount or frequency, no concern about an occasional display of uninhibited impulse. He is tolerant with regard to young people drinking, especially groups of friends in their late teens.

The younger brother shuns wine as the symbol of a background that marked him as "different" from his classmates and presented some handicaps to his educational and occupational ambitions. On the other hand, his drinking of beer and cocktails is symbolic of the higher social status he has achieved—he drinks because it is the thing to do in the circles to which he aspired and into which he has been admitted. But in addition, he drinks because he needs to when he is tense and nervous in the new cultural milieu to which he has climbed, and in the occupational roles that accompany his high income. But he is successful; he has "made the grade"; he knows how to control whim, pleasure, relaxation, and escapist tendencies. Drinking is a form of behavior engaged in without pleasure to display social status and, with discretion, to escape anxieties. This use of alcohol facilitates his social mobility, and provides limited release from the tensions created by this social striving.

It has been stressed that the same drinking pattern, as described in terms of frequency and amount, may have different meanings for different people. Nevertheless, it seems clear that drinking is meaningfully related to personality functioning. One of us has elsewhere outlined such a typology, according to which the drinking of a group or of an individual can be classified as primarily *escapist, facilitative,* or *integrative*.[16] Integrative drinking is illustrated by the case of the older brother just described. The key notion is that integrative drinking has a place among ongoing personality processes and is therefore not only satisfying in itself, but is also helpful in the attainment of the drinker's larger purposes. It is not a necessity, does not interfere seriously with the satisfaction of other needs, has a place in the conscious self, is not engaged in automatically or against the will, and is not followed by regret. Facilitative drinking is illustrated by the case of the younger brother. This is drinking that facilitates the non-destructive purposes of the individual without impeding integration of the personality. Escapist drinking, as the term implies, is the kind typically done to avoid the pains of frustration, anxiety, or emotional stress, and to gain by a short cut the gratification of impulses that cannot be admitted into the conscious ego. Patterns of abstaining may be classified in the same way.

This scheme is frankly normative, and is intended to meet the requirement stated above for a plan that can supply a basis for action. What is desirable is the integration of behavior and personality, both in those who abstain and in those who drink. This should be the basic aim of national alcohol policy and of alcohol education in schools and colleges. It is our belief that such integration of behavior and personality occurs, in the normal course of events, during the college years. Seniors who abstain, although they do not change greatly, are lower on Authoritarianism and higher on Impulse Expression, Social Maturity, and Developmental Status than freshman abstainers; and we would say on the basis of clinical impressions, that their abstinence is less militant and more integrative. Seniors, on the whole, drink more than freshmen, but there is no evidence that their drinking is more problem-determined or problem-generating. On the contrary, we judge from their higher scores on Social Maturity, Impulse Expression, and Developmental Status, and their lower scores on Authoritarianism, that they have made progress toward the inte-

---

[16] Sanford, Nevitt. *Where Colleges Fail.* San Francisco: Jossey-Bass, 1967.

gration of their personalities and that their drinking is thus more integrative. This is also what clinical impressions suggest. If, as has been suggested at various places in this book, the college experience can be made to favor even more progress toward personality integration than has been observed in our subjects, we may look forward to a time when alcohol-related problems among college students will have become rare or mild.

❧ 10 ❧

CHANGES IN
AUTHORITARIANISM

Max M. Levin

The term "authoritarianism" refers to a cluster of personality traits that predispose a person to be submissive to authority, dogmatic, and punitively moralistic; to deny some of his own impulses and needs, particularly dependence, weakness, and sexual urges; and to project unacceptable characteristics of his own nature onto outgroups against which he is prejudiced.[1]

[1] This brief formulation does not do justice to the complexity of the authoritarian character structure. The interested reader should consult the major report of the fundamental study: Adorno, T. W., Frenkel-Brunswick, E., Levinson, D. J., and Sanford, Nevitt. *The Authoritarian Personality*. New York: Harper and Row, 1950.

Some argue that authoritarianism is primarily a sociological phenomenon: the traits of the authoritarian cohere simply because they are the norms of people with little education and low socio-economic status.[2] If that were true, authoritarianism would be rare among the college population. Students who qualify for admission to such institutions as Stanford and Berkeley have had more than a little education. Furthermore, if despite their education at these institutions, their authoritarianism persists, we are dealing with something other than educational or sociocultural deprivation. More likely such authoritarianism involves some relatively enduring personality characteristics.

In recent years, both Sanford and Loevinger have suggested that adolescence may be an authoritarian phase.[3] At least some youths adopt overly conforming, rigid, and dogmatic defenses to cope with conflicts deriving from emerging impulses and their control, as well as other dilemmas concerning the self, beliefs, and values. These views suggest that with the gradual decline of such conflicts during late adolescence and early adult years, authoritarianism should decline, at least in those individuals who are making normal developmental progress in managing and satisfying their impulses, especially impulses involving sexual behavior and autonomy, and are adapting adequately to social reality as well as to internal needs. This developmental model implies, of course, that such changes might well occur quite independently of college attendance, since developmental changes in personality can certainly occur in the absence of a college education. The findings of Plant,[4] and of Plant and Telford,[5] show that a decline in authoritarianism, dogmatism, and ethnocentrism (all interrelated charac-

2 Brown, R. *Social Psychology.* New York: Free Press, 1965.

3 Sanford, Nevitt. "Developmental Status of the Freshman." In Sanford, Nevitt (Ed.). *American College.* New York: Wiley, 1962. Loevinger, J. "The Meaning and Measurement of Ego Development." *American Psychologist,* 1966, *21,* 195–206.

4 Plant, W. T. "Longitudinal Changes in Intolerance and Authoritarianism for Subjects Differing in Amount of College Education of Four Years." *Genetic Psychology Monographs,* 1965, *72,* 247–87.

5 Plant, W. T., and Telford, C. W. "Changes in Personality for Groups Completing Different Amounts of College Over Two Years." *Genetic Psychology Monographs,* 1966, *74,* 3–36.

teristics) in young adults does occur in the absence of a college education.[6]

A developmental view of authoritarianism raises some interesting new theoretical issues, particularly with regard to whether certain aspects or components of authoritarianism undergo developmental changes while others do not. Moreover, the developmental issue needs to be viewed in the light of a typology of authoritarianism. It is conceivable that the developmental processes affect some types of authoritarianism, or some components of some types, but not others. The personality data and other information collected in the Student Development Study provide answers to some of these questions.

In the light of numerous reports (including the results of our study) that authoritarianism declines during the college years, change seems most likely among those whose authoritarianism as freshmen is relatively high. Further, it can be assumed that the authoritarian characteristics of a number of this group would be likely to change in varying degrees. The standard measures of authoritarianism are various forms of the Authoritarianism Scale (F) developed by Adorno and his associates.[7] We utilized a 32-item scale adapted from their Form 40, which has very high reliabilities. F-scale means for the Berkeley and Stanford freshmen who were also retested as seniors were 115 and 110 respectively, with standard deviations of approximately 26 and 24; these means were not significantly different from those of a random sample of the students who were tested only as freshmen at Berkeley and Stanford. Subjects whose scores were approximately one standard deviation or more above the group means were selected for study. The cutoff was relatively high: 139 (item mean, 4.34). This yielded a total of 68 students with usable freshman and senior F-scales.

Over the college years, the senior scores of two-thirds of these students declined by at least 25 points, while the remaining third changed much less. We referred to those who changed by 25

[6] For findings that lead to a contrary conclusion, see Trent, James W. and Medsker, Leland L. *Beyond High School*. San Francisco: Jossey-Bass, 1968, Ch. 6.

[7] Sanford, Nevitt, Adorno, T. W., Frenkel-Brunswick, E., and Levinson, D. J. "The Measurement of Implicit Antidemocratic Trends." In Adorno, et al. *The Authoritarian Personality*.

points or more as the LC (Large Change) group and those who changed by less than 25 points as the SC (Small Change) group. This division resulted in an LC group of 45 students, with an average F-scale score of 149 as freshmen, which declined to an average of 104.5 during the senior year; and an SC group of 23 students, whose average F-scale scores were 146 and 133.7 for the freshman and senior years respectively.

Because of the range in freshman F-scale scores, there was some overlap in senior F-scale scores between the LC and SC groups. Thus, even some in the LC group who had changed considerably were still relatively high as seniors, while some in the SC group, who changed less, had lower F-scale scores as seniors than some of the LC seniors. This illustrates one of the difficulties encountered in studying change, the problem of the initial level. To circumvent this problem, another change group was developed, consisting of 17 subjects whose F-scale scores as seniors did not overlap with any of the senior scores in the SC group. This "purified" LC group, which we designated as PC, provided us with a group that not only had changed relatively—that is, with respect to their authoritarianism as freshmen—but in addition, had reached a relatively low level of authoritarianism.

Our research strategy called for a comparison of the Large Change and Small Change groups of students in order to unravel the factors associated with varying amounts of change in authoritarianism, including family background, and curricular and extracurricular college experiences. We also examined personal characteristics other than authoritarianism to see if these suggested other factors to explain the differences in susceptibility to change in authoritarianism. Finally, we attempted to determine whether the nature of authoritarianism differed initially among students who showed varying amounts of change during the college years.

We first asked whether there were any background characteristics that differentiated our various groups.[8] A student's sociocultural background may be inferred crudely from his father's occupation. Students whose fathers were in business were more

---

[8] In this presentation of the results, differences will be designated only where they reach adequate statistical levels of confidence, minimally p values of .05. Most positive findings were, in fact, significant at considerably smaller p values.

numerous in the SC group than in the LC group (71 per cent and 47 per cent respectively), while students whose fathers were professional men, white-collar workers, or skilled workers, were more numerous in the LC group.[9]

In our samples of students, academic aptitude and performance was not associated with amount of change in authoritarianism. That authoritarianism is associated with intellectul and educational levels in broad samples of the population is well established; but apparently in the case of our students, either factors other than academic aptitude were associated with change in authoritarianism, or their range of academic aptitude was too narrow (on a very high level) for a relationship to become manifest.

To determine whose authoritarianism is more and whose is less apt to change developmentally, we turned to the various scales of the Omnibus Personality Inventory, described in Chapter 3. As freshmen, the LC group scored significantly higher than the SC group on the Social Maturity (SM) and Estheticism (Es) Scales. Most of the items in the SM Scale that significantly differentiate LC and SC subjects are in the intellectual and esthetic domains. A sample of 23 students in the LC group was compared with the 23 students comprising the SC group on 120 items of the SM Scale. The items that showed statistically significant differences were the following: "Trends toward abstractionism and the distortion of reality have corrupted much art in recent years" (LC, 8; SC, 14); "I like to listen to primitive music" (LC, 11; SC, 4); "I like to discuss philosophical problems" (LC, 13; SC, 7); "I like to read about artistic or literary achievements" (LC, 11; SC, 4); "Nothing about fascism is any good" (LC, 12; SC, 3); and "It's better to stick by what you have than to try new things you don't actually know about" (LC, 9; SC, 14).

When comparing two groups on 120 items, one may, of course, expect to find some differences to be significant as a result of sampling errors alone. But there is a consistency in the content of these items that suggests that we may be dealing with more than sampling errors. For example, the SC group seems to be slightly more ideological (politically authoritarian) than the LC group.

---

[9] This particular finding did not reach statistical significance and hence is suggestive only.

The responses also suggest that students in the LC group are higher in intellectual-esthetic interests and values even as entering freshmen. We can assume that such students are more likely to be influenced by an environment or by an institution that emphasizes such values than students without such preexisting values are. (As entering freshmen, the PC group was even higher in Social Maturity and Estheticism than the LC group.) It is possible that the relatively high F-scale scores of the larger change groups reflect conventional beliefs in family and social background. With increasing autonomy and cognitive development in a more sophisticated environment, authoritarianism often lessens.

We obtained information about many aspects of student life from the Senior Questionnaire. Only two questions out of seventy yielded significant differences between the LC and SC groups. Students in the LC group tended to evaluate their courses on the basis of how useful they would be to their careers, while the SC group was grade-oriented. A significantly larger segment of the LC group attributed the changes they underwent in college to ideas they had encountered in independent reading. Since these two differences show some coherence, and are in line with the higher intellectual disposition of the LC group, they may constitute more than a chance finding. Again, greater differences are found when we compare the PC and SC groups.

When asked to rank in order some fourteen interests and activities for the relative degree of importance they expect them to have in their future lives, the PC and SC groups showed some noteworthy differences as well as some striking similarities. The PC group gave top ranking to career or occupation, future family, and intellectual or artistic activities, in that order. The SC group also ranked career or occupation first and future family second, but set love and affection third. The least valued activities for the PC group were civic participation, sports or athletics, and religious beliefs and activities. For the SC group, the least valued were participation in activities directed toward national or international betterment, intellectual and artistic activities, and civic participation. Again the greater intellectual disposition of the PC group is apparent.

The type of residence lived in during the college years might well be expected to exert considerable influence on the amount of change in authoritarianism. In an earlier study made at Stanford, Siegel and Siegel did, in fact, find that F-scale scores of female undergraduates changed in the direction of the prevailing attitudes of their particular housing group.[10] But we found no differences traceable to college residence among our various groups. Plant, too, has recently reported no differences in amount of change in F-scale scores over a two-year period between sorority and non-sorority members.[11]

What impact do different aspects of the curriculum have on the student's basic beliefs and cognitive disposition? We found that the PC, LC, and SC groups differed much in the proportion of natural science majors they contained. Twenty-four per cent of the LC and 50 per cent of the PC groups majored in the natural sciences, in contrast to 10 per cent of the SC group. Thirty-five per cent of the SC group majored in the humanities and social sciences. What are we to make of these findings? One can readily postulate that the very essence of science is anti-authoritarian. Students exposed to critical, analytic thinking cannot long cling to reliance on authority, conventionalism, and dogmatism. There is also the possibility that the relatively greater precision and structure of the natural sciences are more effective in inducing change than the more ambiguous, relativistic concepts and the less certain findings of the social sciences and humanities. On the other hand, an authoritarian student exposed to the humanities might well find the relative absence of structure and the ambiguity quite intolerable. Further, the direct questioning of conventional and traditional social views and values that commonly occurs in the humanities and social sciences would immediately put him on guard.

We now turn to the question of whether differences in the nature or type of authoritarianism are the critical factors in varying degrees of change in authoritarianism. To find answers to this question, the author developed special subscales from among the

[10] Siegel, A. E., and Siegel, S. "Reference Groups, Membership Group, and Attitude Change." *Journal of Abnormal Social Psychology*, 1957, *55*, 360–64.

[11] Plant, W. T. "Changes in Intolerance and Authoritarianism for Sorority and Non-Sorority Women Enrolled in College for Two Years." *Journal of Social Psychology*, 1966, *68*, 79–83.

many items in the Omnibus Personality Inventory. Ten subscales with varying numbers of items were developed. Since they are rational scales, no claim can be made for their homogeneity without empirical evidence. These subscales were designed to obtain scores on the following components of authoritarianism: conventionalism, authoritarian submission, primitive sexual moralism, dogmatism, anti-intellectualism, anti-ambiguity, religious fundamentalism, distrust and cynicism, power and toughness, and punitive moralism.

For the Large Change group, the changes were general, extending over all the dimensions of authoritarianism represented in our subscales. But this did not obtain for the SC group, which manifested change along some dimensions, but not others. This group changed significantly with regard to authoritarian submission, power and toughness, primitive sexual moralism, and punitive moralism. It is not unreasonable to assume that changes in these components of authoritarianism are probably developmental in nature. In achieving greater independence and autonomy from parents and parental surrogates, even the authoritarian adolescent can be expected to become less submissive. Similarly, with greater maturity, the grosser aspects of authoritarianism become modulated, and hence power and toughness also decline. Perhaps the development of a somewhat more mature sexual identity reduces the need to express cruel or sadistic tendencies. The decline in punitive moralism is a commonly reported phenomenon of the college years—a lowered judgmental attitude toward the deviant behavior of others, including sexual behavior. Thus, it would appear that even the SC group underwent significant change in some aspects of superego functioning, in the direction of a somewhat less harsh superego and somewhat more impulse freedom.

Equally significant, however, are the authoritarian dimensions along which the SC group manifested little or no change. It showed little change in cognitive content, that is, particular beliefs and attitudes, and in cognitive controls and styles. To us, this finding is unexpected and challenging. Those very dimensions of authoritarianism that might be expected to change more readily as a result of college education are precisely the dimensions that appear to have changed least in students whose F-scale scores remained elevated. On the other hand, the dimensions of authoritarianism that might be presumed to be more closely linked to superego and impulses are the dimensions that appear even in this group, to have changed more. Authoritarian aggression and submission, power and toughness—dimensions that might, on theoretical grounds, be assumed to be more centrally linked to the basic drive structures of the individual and thus be more resistant to change—are precisely the ones that showed more change in all our authoritarian subjects.

If we view these findings developmentally, they may seem less paradoxical. Late adolescence is that phase of the life cycle during which many impulses and defenses are reorganized. The achievement of greater autonomy and a clearer ego identity, the development of more integration, and control of the impulses are major developmental tasks achieved in varying degrees during this period. Our data suggest that even students who remain relatively high in authoritarianism progress in these directions, although somewhat less, to be sure, than others do. What has been referred to as the external superego can thus be said to become weaker during the college years, even for those whose authoritarianism otherwise changes relatively little; while the cognitive attitudes change less.

We suggest a congruence hypothesis with important implications for educators. Students with initially higher intellectual disposition are more likely to be receptive to influence from intellectual-esthetic sources because they value these more initially. By contrast, the less intellectual student might avoid or resist such influence because of his initially low valuation of intellectual activity. Thus, the impact of college on different students varies with the congruence or fit between the student's initial values and perspectives and those values evidenced by various components of the college culture. You cannot easily fit students who have low intellectual interest into an intellectual environment. More authoritarian students may prefer clear-cut structure, order, and precision to ambiguity, vagueness, and relativism. When they find congruent styles in the curriculum, they are more susceptible to the influence of the content and values of those courses.

Some form of challenge is commonly assumed to be an effective mode of educating and inducing change in students. But challenges that go too sharply against the student's cognitive grain may be precisely the techniques to be avoided. In the case of authoritarian students, well-organized, structured content and course style may be more effective in inducing change than the more general, less concrete, and more ambiguous, which they are apt to resist and reject strongly. So long as their authoritarianism persists, the liberalization and humanization of such students may more likely occur within more highly structured college environments, disciplines, and instructional approaches, rather than less highly structured ones.

It seems apparent that there cannot be one ideal curriculum suitable for all students. Yet we see little evidence that the need for diverse educational approaches is given sufficient consideration in higher education. In fact, we hardly have sufficient knowledge at present to provide a basis for differentiated higher education. Our findings indicate the need for experimental educational efforts. Authoritarian and otherwise anti-intellectual students present a considerable challenge, for their well-being may require educational methods distinctly different from those effective with other types of students. They must be led gradually, by means adapted to their particular life-style.

❧ 11 ❧

THE ACTIVIST

REVOLUTION OF 1964

Joseph Katz

On September 14, 1964, a series of directives issued by the administration of the University of California at Berkeley set in motion a chain of events that led eventually to the mass student protest, or sit-in, of December.[1] On September 14, the Dean of Students announced that

---

[1] There is a large literature on the Berkeley events. Three anthologies bring together some of the literature. They are Lipset, S. M. and Wolin, S. S. (Eds.). *The Berkeley Student Revolt.* Garden City, N. Y.: Anchor Books, 1965; Miller, M. V. and Gilmore, S. (Eds.). *Revolution at Berkeley.* New York: Dell, 1965; Katope, C. G. and Zolbrod, P. G. (Eds.). *Beyond Berkeley.* Cleveland: World, 1966. See also Draper, Hal. *Berkeley: The New Student Revolt.* New York: Grove, 1965; Lipset, S. M. and Altbach, P. G. "Student Politics and Higher Education in the United States." *Comparative Education Review,* 1966,

the sidewalk in front of the campus could no longer be used by the students for setting up tables, fund-raising, electioneering or recruiting, or giving speeches in support of off-campus political and social action.[2] Leaders of 18 campus organizations, including political groups ranging from the far right to the far left, met with the Dean of Students to discuss the prohibition. This resulted in some concessions, but students were still forbidden to advocate off-campus political or social action and to solicit funds and members. Participants have remarked that the nucleus of the Free Speech Movement (FSM) came into existence there in the Dean's office, as student leaders discussed the situation and decided on united action.

There had been indications during the summer of 1964 that some students would be pressing for educational reforms, and there was talk among these students that if their arguments did not meet with a satisfactory response, they might, in order to gain a better hearing, resort to tactics similar to those used in the civil rights movement. In September 1964, the *SLATE* Supplement Report published "A Letter to Undergraduates," by Bradford Cleaveland, which contained a critique of undergraduate education at Berkeley, and ended with a series of demands:

1. Immediate commitment of the university to the total elimination of the course/grade/unit system of undergraduate learning in the social sciences and humanities.
2. Immediate disbanding of all university dorms and living group rules which prescribe hours and which provide for a system of student-imposed descipline, thereby dividing students against themselves.
3. Immediate negotiations on the establishment of a permanent student voice which is effective (that is, independent) in running university affairs.

10, 320–349. A review of the literature and an interpretation of student activism has been prepared for the U. S. Office of Education by Joseph Katz under the title *The Student Activists: Rights, Needs, and Powers of Undergraduates.* See also Sampson, Edward E. (Ed.). *Stirrings out of Apathy: Student Activism and the Decade of Protest. The Journal of Social Issues* (whole issue), 1967, *23.*

[2] See the chronology of events in Miller and Gilmore, xxiv–ix.

4. Immediate efforts to begin recruitment of an undergraduate teaching faculty to handle undergraduate learning in social sciences and humanities.

5. Immediate negotiations regarding two methods of undergraduate learning which provide for the basic freedom required in learning:

   a. A terminal examination system which will be voluntary, and an option with "b."

   b. Immediate creation of undergraduate programs of a wide variety in which the student will be given careful, but minimal, guidance, without courses, grades, and units.

6. Immediate establishment of a university committee to deal with these demands on the Berkeley campus.[3]

The publication of the above document did not create much of an impact. An editorial in the *Daily Californian* of September 17 called Cleaveland's letter a "needless noise." It rejected his demands as impractical in a university of 27,500 students. The editorial ended by saying that despite "university red-tape, instructors' disinterest, rules and academic deadlines, the individual student gets whatever he wants out of this University in direct proportion to what he puts in—no matter who is in charge, no matter what the rules." Nevertheless, these demands, which sounded rather utopian in 1964, have since become the center of discussion at Berkeley and elsewhere, and some have been met—in large part because of student pressure. What sort of students responded to academic strictures with resistance? In what ways were they different from their peers? Before we answer these questions, let us review briefly the genesis of the Free Speech Movement.

The students who were to visit the Dean's office on September 14 and form a nucleus of protestors against administrative restrictions on free speech were part of what was to become a vast, coalescing movement of student activists who were soon to demand academic freedom of various sorts on campuses all over the nation. Throughout its history, the FSM was a loose, at times internally

[3] Cleaveland, Bradford. "A Letter to Undergraduates." In Lipset, S. M., and Wolin, S. S. *The Berkeley Student Revolt.* New York: Anchor Books, 1965, p. 80.

dissenting, coalition of quite different groups of the student community. It was in this sense quite properly a "movement" rather than a "party." Much of the increasing élan and size of the movement resulted from the arousal of more student resentment by subsequent actions of the administration, until the issue became focused on the relatively simple principle of political freedom, rather than on the more complex one of educational reform, about which students and faculty differ considerably in involvement and sophistication.

A series of student protest actions including an all-night vigil, the setting up of tables in violation of University regulations, and a sit-in followed the Dean's pronouncement. This course of action culminated on October 1 in a crowd of students surrounding a police car in which a student under arrest had been placed, and preventing it from moving off. The roof of the car became a speaker's platform. This protest lasted until the following evening. It ended with an agreement between the students and the administration, and a victory for the students, which included the dropping of charges against those arrested.

The days that followed brought a series of arguments, charges, countercharges, and demonstrations. The FSM itself was split at times over what was the desirable course of action. Over the Thanksgiving holiday, the Chancellor sent out letters charging four members of the FSM with leading, organizing, and abetting the illegal demonstrations on October 1 and 2, and also charging a number of organizations that had participated in the FSM with violating campus regulations. It had generally been assumed that those events were officially forgotten. The Chancellor's letter resulted in increased mass protest, and an ultimatum was issued by the FSM. When the administration ignored the ultimatum, about a thousand students moved into Sproul Hall for a sit-in on December 2.

The sit-in was preceded by a noon rally that attracted thousands of students. Mario Savio, speaking at the rally, announced the broad purpose of the protest: "There comes a time when the operation of the machine becomes so odious, makes you so sick at heart, that you cannot take part; you cannot even tacitly take part. And you've got to put your bodies upon the wheels, and the gears, and all the apparatus, and you have to make it stop. And you have to make it clear to the people who own it, and to the people who run it, that until you are free, their machine will be prevented from running at all."

Eight hundred people prepared to spend the night inside Sproul Hall. In the words of a member of the FSM Steering Committee: "On the fourth floor, we set up a study area. On the third floor, classes were held. The number of classes soon became greater than the space available on that floor, and we spread to the stairwells and the basement. There were classes taught by TA's and others in Math, Anthropology, Genetics, several languages, and the civil rights movements in the Bay Area. A class on civil disobedience was taught in the fallout shelter. On the second floor we watched movies—on the serious side, about HUAC, on the light side, Charlie Chaplin. Joan [Baez] toured the building and led folk singing. On the first floor, a full-fledged Chanuka service was held, which eventually broke into dancing and other festivities."

At three the following morning, the Chancellor appeared, and went to each floor of Sproul Hall and urged the students to disband or face arrest. At about four the arrests began, and they lasted through the afternoon of the next day.

The sit-in was followed by a strike and a meeting of the university community called by the president of the student body in the Greek theater. At the end of the meeting, Mario Savio rose to make an announcement, and was seized by the throat and dragged from the platform by three policemen—an incident that freshly aroused the students, who shouted "Let him speak! Let him speak!" The following day, over 900 faculty members attending a session of the Academic Senate voted 824 to 115 in favor of a resolution against control of student speech and political advocacy. Regulations about time, place, and manner of political activity were to be restricted to those necessary for the normal functioning of the university, and disciplining of students in regard to political activities was to be in the hands of the faculty as the final authority. The FSM, viewing this proposal as an endorsement of the objectives they had been fighting for, immediately supported it. The Associated Students of the University of California (the official student government) did likewise.

On January 2, the Board of Regents named a new acting Chancellor. Things were quiet during the second semester. The new Chancellor appointed a select commitee of the Academic Senate to make a careful examination of the academic and non-academic situation of the students at Berkeley. This committee, under the chairmanship of Professor Charles Muscatine, worked for a full year, and in March 1966 published its report.[4] The Muscatine Report called for many changes, including the establishment of a Board of Educational Development, which was to be an agency of constant innovation and self-examination. Also, in the spring of 1965, Professor Joseph Tussman was given permission to start his experimental program involving radical changes in the academic program for the freshman and sophomore years. This program was put into operation in the fall of 1965 with a first group of 150 students.

A committee of the Board of Regents appointed Jerome C. Byrne, a lawyer, to prepare a special report on the recent events and to make proposals for reform. The report by Byrne and his staff, published in May 1965, concluded, among other things, that "the Free Speech Movement enjoyed widespread support among students on the Berkeley campus. The large numbers participating in the various demonstrations established this fact. A reliable survey of student opinion, which we have had reviewed by independent experts, concludes that, before the December sit-in, about two-thirds of the students said that they supported the FSM's objectives, and about a third supported its tactics. Subsequent surveys showed that support increased after the December sit-in." Upon its publication, the Byrne Report was strongly criticized by some of the regents.

While these events were going on at Berkeley, many other institutions across the country were experiencing student protests. According to a survey made by Richard E. Peterson of the Educational Testing Service, based on 849 accredited four-year institutions, 38 per cent of the colleges reported student protests over the issue of civil rights. Smaller percentages reported protests in

---

[4] Muscatine, Charles (Ed.). *Education at Berkeley: Report of the Select Committee on Education.* Berkeley: University of California, 1966.

the area of instructional quality, with 12 per cent reporting protests over poor quality of instruction, 8 per cent over the generally prevailing system of testing and grading, and 7 per cent over curriculum inflexibility.[5] Just as at Berkeley, students were mobilizing everywhere in larger numbers over political issues than over educational ones. Nevertheless, it would have been interesting to have the same survey repeated for 1965–66. We formed the impression, through observation of campuses and by reading the student press during 1965–66, that larger numbers of students have become involved in educational issues, and that the activists have increasingly become representative of the broad mass of students.[6]

Underneath the specific chain of events at Berkeley there were more superficial and deeper causes of the student revolution. On the more superficial side were lack of administrative flexibilty and sensitivity, and inadequate channels of communication between administration, faculty, and students. More deeply, there were (and are) such factors as increasing pressure on the student for high academic performance, preceded by similar pressures in high school and succeeded by the prospect, as required schooling lengthens into graduate institutions, of continuing years of being subjected to grading and testing. These more demanding standards are particularly hard for the student to accept because there has been no commensurate attempt to make the contents of the requirements more meaningful to him by relating them more fully to his own purposes, interests, and motivations. Further, there were the pressures and confusion over the military situation. (The ever-present possibility of the draft makes staying in school a necessity, and prevents the often desirable opportunity of a temporary break for work, travel, or self-renewal.) Finally, swelling numbers of students have enormously increased the size of the university populations, but no attendant attempts have been made to decrease the resulting dehumanizing effects.

Among the "positive" determinants of student activism are economic affluence, with its opportunities for the commodities

5 Peterson, Richard E. *The Scope of Organized Student Protest in 1964–1965.* Princeton, New Jersey: Educational Testing Service, 1966.
    6 See Katz, Joseph, and Sanford, Nevitt. "The New Student Power and Needed Educational Reforms." *Phi Delta Kappan,* 1966, *47,* 397–401.

and style of life that enhance the sense of self; the confidence gained by students at such prestige institutions as Berkeley by the academic successes they have achieved in their previous schooling; the experience of the civil rights movement, which not only has given students training in the tactics of dissent, but also a new sense of the power of individuals, or at least of groups of individuals, to influence the course of social and political events. Finally, throughout the 1960's there has been considerable mitigation of the "McCarthyism" that threw a pall over political life during the 1950's. After twenty years of affluence, values are being reexamined. Some members of the present college generation are taking a more fundamental look at social institutions.[7]

Reactions to the events at Berkeley have varied considerably. Many see them as a breach of law and order; many consider the FSM as pioneering a social renewal. Some observers have pointed out the similarity of the FSM to previous protest movements in educational history, while others have viewed it as one more instance of the conflict between generations, and of adolescent rebellion. Historical and psychological interpretations of the FSM have relevance. At the present, just as at times in the past, social circumstances are favorable to the universal tendency of adolescents to establish their own identity more firmly by simultaneously differentiating themselves from their parents and by redefining and modifying social institutions that they perceive as inimical to human growth. In this lies the particular contribution that adolescents can make to the self-renewal of society.

But the FSM may also be the first sign of a new form of consciousness in student society, just as labor has acquired a new form of consciousness during the last 100 years. Conceivably, the relationship between educators and educated is in the process of redefinition, with the students participating to a much greater degree than in the past. It may result in a change in who determines what about educational content, but also an earlier assumption of autonomy by the young—a redefinition of the role of the student, in which he is integrated into the work, social, and political processes of society in an active manner, rather than being

[7] For a more detailed discussion of the causes of the student revolution see Katz, J., and Sanford, N. "Causes of the Student Revolution," *Saturday Review*, December 18, 1965, pp. 64–66, 76, 79.

primarily a tacit consumer of culture developing academic or social skills for later use.

What were the characteristics of the students who took an active part in the FSM movement? We studied 62 Berkeley seniors (35 men and 27 women) who were arrested during the December 2 sit-in. (The names of these students were obtained by checking the list of those arrested against our master list of all entering Berkeley students in the fall of 1961.) We have Scholastic Aptitude Test data for 61 of these students, senior-year cumulative grade-point averages for 47, freshman Omnibus Personality Inventory (OPI) data for 42, senior OPI data for 23, and Senior Questionnaire data for 22. We had five of these students in our longitudinal interview sample, and we interviewed an additional six who were not part of the original interview sample. Forty-two of the arrested students had been given six OPI scales, and the Authoritarianism (F) and Ethnocentrism (E) Scales when they entered as freshmen in 1961; and 23 of them also responded to these same scales in the spring of 1965. The arrested men and women (Table 63) differed from their classmates as freshmen by scoring significantly higher on scales measuring Social Maturity (autonomy, flexibility, capacity to relate well to other people), Impulse Expression, Estheticism, and Developmental Status. They scored about the same as their classmates on a scale measuring Schizoid Functioning (social alienation and bizarreness of thinking). The men scored lower than their classmates on a scale measuring Masculinity-Femininity. (This scale is somewhat mislabeled and tends to measure interest: that is, low scorers express less interest in science and more in social and esthetic matters; they also admit to more awareness of adjustment problems and feelings of anxiety.) The arrested students scored significantly lower than their classmates did on scales measuring Authoritarianism and Ethnocentrism (see Table 64).

If one compares the personality scale scores of the arrested seniors with those of their classmates, the same differences are obtained as were obtained in the freshman year. (The difference between the two senior male groups on "masculinity," though about half a standard deviation, does not reach statistical significance.) The FSM students thus continued to rise on the personality measures between their freshman and senior years, and were con-

TABLE 63

SCORES ON EIGHT PERSONALITY SCALES OF MEN STUDENTS ARRESTED AND SAMPLES OF BERKELEY FRESHMAN AND SENIOR MEN

	Freshmen				Seniors		
	Arrested [a] (N = 10) Mean (SD)	Arrested (N = 20) Mean (SD)	Not arrested (N = 1026) Mean (SD)	p [b]	Arrested (N = 10) Mean (SD)	Not arrested (N = 286) Mean (SD)	p
Social Maturity [c]	60 (11)	61 (9)	50 (10)	< .001	67 (8)	57 (11)	< .01
Impulse Expression	55 (10)	57 (9)	50 (10)	< .01	62 (10)	52 (11)	< .01
Schizoid Functioning	52 (9)	52 (8)	50 (10)	n.s.	52 (12)	47 (11)	n.s.
Masculinity-Femininity	44 (7)	43 (8)	50 (10)	< .01	42 (9)	47 (13)	n.s.
Estheticism	60 (9)	61 (8)	50 (10)	< .001	65 (7)	52 (12)	< .001
Developmental Status	59 (13)	60 (11)	50 (10)	< .001	69 (9)	58 (11)	< .01
	(N = 11)	(N = 19)			(N = 11)		
Authoritarianism [d]	93 (25)	92 (26)	116 (26)	< .001	70 (29)	96 (26)	< .01
Ethnocentrism	45 (18)	42 (15)	56 (21)	< .01	30 (16)	44 (18)	< .02

[a] These are the students for whom we have both freshman and senior personality test responses. The two groups (freshman-senior and freshman only respondents) responded in nearly identical fashion.

[b] p is for the difference between students arrested (N = 20) and students not arrested (N = 1026).

[c] This and the following five scales are reported in standard scores. The standard scores were computed separately for each group on the basis of their freshman scores. A standard score of 50 is the mean raw score on each scale for the total male (N = 1026) and total female (N = 852) populations, respectively, tested in 1961. The following are percentile equivalents of the standard scores: 50 = 50, 55 = 70, 60 = 84, 66 = 95, 70 = 98.

[d] This and the following scale are reported in raw scores. The number of students arrested for whom we have responses on these two scales is slightly different from the number on the other scales.

395

TABLE 64

SCORES ON EIGHT PERSONALITY SCALES OF WOMEN STUDENTS ARRESTED AND SAMPLES OF BERKELEY FRESHMAN AND SENIOR WOMEN

	Freshmen				Seniors		
	Arrested [a] (N = 13) Mean (SD)	Arrested (N = 22) Mean (SD)	Not arrested (N = 852) Mean (SD)	p [b]	Arrested (N = 13) Mean (SD)	Not arrested (N = 265) Mean (SD)	p
Social Maturity [c]	60 (10)	60 (9)	50 (10)	< .001	66 (7)	58 (10)	< .01
Impulse Expression	57 (8)	55 (9)	50 (10)	< .05	59 (9)	52 (11)	< .02
Schizoid Functioning	47 (9)	47 (9)	50 (10)	n.s.	46 (12)	46 (11)	n.s.
Masculinity-Femininity	47 (8)	48 (10)	50 (10)	n.s.	49 (9)	48 (10)	n.s.
Estheticism	56 (10)	56 (8)	50 (10)	< .01	62 (8)	53 (10)	< .01
Developmental Status	60 (10)	59 (9)	50 (10)	< .001	69 (8)	59 (11)	< .01
	(N = 9)	(N = 20)			(N = 11)		
Authoritarianism [d]	87 (33)	81 (24)	113 (27)	< .001	70 (13)	89 (26)	< .02
Ethnocentrism	32 (12)	33 (9)	50 (18)	< .001	27 (4)	39 (16)	< .02

a See Note a, Table 63.
b See Note b, Table 63.
c See Note c, Table 63.
d See Note d, Table 63.

siderably ahead of their fellow seniors. Our data are in line with the data reported by Heist, and Watts and Whittaker.[8] Our own results enlarge on theirs by including personality inventory data for FSM students at the time of their entering Berkeley in 1961. Heist, and Watts and Whittaker, reporting on several samples of members of the FSM, including a sample of 130 arrested students, show that the FSM students scored considerably higher both on cognitive and affective personality scales when compared with samples of other Berkeley seniors. Thus, they scored higher on such measures as Thinking Introversion, Theoretical Orientation, Estheticism, Autonomy, and Impulse Expression. These authors also report that FSM students who participated in the Sproul Hall sit-in included Humanities and Natural Science majors in about the same proportion as the rest of the Berkeley student body. The social sciences had a larger representation in the FSM than in the rest of the student body; but only 1.3 per cent of the FSM respondents were majoring in Business and Engineering, in contrast to 17.8 per cent of the student population. The educational family background of the FSM respondents also is different: 26 per cent of the FSM students had fathers with advanced academic degrees (M.A. or Ph.D.), while this was true of only 11 per cent of a random sample of the Berkeley student population as a whole.

The FSM students were already different from their fellow students upon entrance. Their capacities for autonomy, awareness, and action were considerably higher than those of most of their classmates. One might raise the question, therefore, whether their personality characteristics, rather than the influence of the university, propelled them. But we know that personality characteristics are only a set of potentials. An environment other than Berkeley in 1962–63 might not have influenced them as much in the direction of increasing social awareness, capacity for self-exploration, and social action. One may even surmise that under other conditions, this psychological potential would have turned more in the direction of cynical rebelliousness or isolation.

With reference to the high scores of the FSM students on

---

[8] Heist, Paul. "Intellect and Commitment: The Faces of Discontent." Berkeley: Center for the Study of Higher Education, 1965 (mimeographed); Watts, W., and Whittaker, D. N. E. "Free Speech Advocates at Berkeley." *Journal of Applied Behavioral Science*, 1966, 2, 41–62.

Social Maturity and Impulse Expression, our interviews of people who have been measured by these scales have contributed to our belief that high scorers on these two scales tend to include a large proportion of people who are conflicted and have an eventual history of trying to resolve their conflicts. Interview and questionnaire data confirm this for the FSM students. They tended to come from family backgrounds marked by free expression of differences, and their histories in college often showed much turmoil. At the same time, these students also showed a high degree of reintegrative ability and self-awareness—a capacity for criticizing themselves, and seeing themselves in perspective. While they projected some of their inner conflict onto the outer world, they were also particularly keen observers of conflicts, discrepancies, and absurdities in the outer world. (One might argue that from the point of view of society and its perennial needs for reforms and self-renewal, people with these personality characteristics are particularly suitable for pointing out existing shortcomings and initiating reforms. In the process, they serve themselves as well as society.)

The FSM students reinforced impressions obtained with other students that a certain amount of dissent or even disagreement between parents and within the family is an incentive toward achieving greater autonomy. It is as if the expression of difference among their parents allows the child emotional freedom to explore his own individual inclinations and to express them. (Where, however, parental conflict is more hostile, or is responded to by the child with a greater degree of hostility, the child's attempt at self-assertion seems also to become more tortured and diffused.) We found that many parents of our interviewees turned out to have a history of involvement with relatively unorthodox ideas or actions.[9] This is of special interest in the light of the fact that the FSM students were particularly assertive in their rejection of adult authority and the middle-class way of life, and in their claim that no one over thirty could be trusted. They seemed, at the same time, to be attempting to realize their parents' ambitions

[9] Since this was written, Flacks has reported that data from two of his studies show that "activist students come predominantly from relatively liberal backgrounds." Flacks, Richard. "The Liberated Generation: An Exploration of the Roots of Student Protest." *Journal of Social Issues, 23, 3,* 52–75.

—ambitions their parents had been forced to suppress in part because of the depression and its aftermath. They criticized authority and held a purer version of the values that their parents also had held at their same age. We found that the arrested students received moral support from their parents. As the mother of one of the interviewees put it, when notified of her daughter's impending arrest: "As your mother, I'm worried and frightened for you, and I wish you wouldn't do it. As a person, I support your position. And as both, I am very proud of you."

In academic aptitude and performance, the arrested students scored above the rest of their classmates. On the verbal part of the Scholastic Aptitude Test, the arrested students' mean scores were significantly higher than those of the non-arrested students (Table 65). The spring 1965 cumulative grade-point averages of the arrested men and women are significantly higher than those of their fellow seniors (Table 66).

TABLE 65

FRESHMAN SCHOLASTIC APTITUDE TEST SCORES FOR ARRESTED STUDENTS
(RANDOM SENIOR SAMPLES [a] AND ALL ENTERING FRESHMEN IN 1960)

MEN

SAT	Arrested (N = 34) Mean	(SD)	Not Arrested (N = 400) Mean	(SD)	1960 [b] Freshmen (N = 1857) Mean	(SD)
Verbal	611	(81)	522	(84) ***	548	(93)
Mathematical	611	(86)	617	(76)	606	(88)

WOMEN

SAT	Arrested (N = 27) Mean	(SD)	Not Arrested (N = 400) Mean	(SD)	1960 Freshmen (N = 1494) Mean	(SD)
Verbal	610	(101)	559	(88) **	544	(86)
Mathematical	535	(95)	531	(87)	519	(88)

[a] Strictly speaking, these are fall 1961 entrants who were in school in the spring of 1965. Some of these had not attained senior standing.

[b] 1960 scores of all entering freshmen are provided for comparison purposes.

*** p < .001
** p < .01

TABLE 66

CUMULATIVE GRADE-POINT AVERAGES IN THE SPRING OF 1965 OF
ARRESTED SENIORS AND OF RANDOM SENIOR SAMPLES [a]

	Men				*Women*			
	Arrested (N = 25)		*Not Arrested* (N = 400)		*Arrested* (N = 22)		*Not Arrested* (N = 400)	
	Mean	*(SD)*	*Mean*	*(SD)*	*Mean*	*(SD)*	*Mean*	*(SD)*
GPA	2.93	(.40)	2.64	(.45) **	2.87	(.38)	2.65	(.39) *

[a] See Note a, Table 65.
** p < .01
* p < .05

Thus, even by conventional academic standards, these students were among the more highly achieving ones in the university.[10]

The picture that emerges from the Senior Questionnaire responses of the arrested students is one of a group of students who describe themselves as having been greatly influenced by ideas presented in courses, by teachers, and by close relations with teachers and other adults. They say they are primarily oriented toward the intellectual contents of their courses. More frequently than their peers, they describe themselves as having changed much in personal characteristics, freedom to express their feelings and

---

[10] Our data are in conflict with the reports by Watts and Whittaker, "Free Speech Advocates at Berkeley," in which there was no significant difference between the Fall 1964 GPA of 137 FSM undergraduates of all classes (2.62) when compared with a cross-section of 115 undergraduates (2.53). Our own data are corroborated by those reported by Heist, *Intellect and Commitment;* by those collected by Somers, a Berkeley sociologist; and by another survey cited by him (see Somers, R. H., "The Mainsprings of the Rebellion." In Lipset and Wolin, p. 344). Further corroboration of a link between high academic performance and activism comes from Robert Nichols, who reports that self-ratings and ratings by teachers and peers "all agree in characterizing Merit Finalists more frequently than less able students as independent, assertive, unconventional, cynical, rebellious, and argumentative." They are also described more frequently as "mature, dependable, well-adjusted, and honest." Merit Finalists "report more involvement in campus political activities, more organizational and leadership positions, and more discussion of political, social and religious issues with teachers and peers than do samples of average students." It is amazing how much this picture of the Merit Finalists agrees with our picture of the FSM students. (Nichols, Robert C. "The Origin and Development of Talent," in *National Merit Scholarship Corporation Research Reports,* 1966, 2, No. 10, 7.)

desires and their political views since entering college. They report greater struggle and conflict than their classmates in deciding on a major. They disagree more frequently with their fathers, and report their parents more frequently as strongly differing with each other.

There was little difference between the arrested and non-arrested students in their reported participation in social activities, but not unexpectedly, the arrested students had participated in civil rights activities and national or community political activities much more frequently than their classmates. The arrested students were much more permissive in sexual attitudes than their classmates, but in behavior, only the arrested men, not the women, reported a higher degree of sexual intimacy during college. A similar sex difference showed up with regard to drinking behavior: the arrested women are much like the non-arrested ones.

With regard to other questionnaire responses, a number of things should be noted: the arrested students named as their heroes various civil rights leaders and such literary figures as Hesse, Melville, and Orwell. The educational plans of the arrested students were focused on subjects and occupations involving other people and social objectives. Thirteen of the twenty-two students planned to do graduate work in education, social science, or social welfare. Thirteen also planned to be engaged ten years after graduation in teaching, social work, or social research. The arrested students also indicated a greater interest in the Peace Corps than their classmates did.

After their freshman year, most of the arrested students lived off-campus, rather than in university housing. They expressed dissatisfaction with the university administration more strongly than the rest. One hundred per cent of the men said that they were "very dissatisfied" with the relations of the administration to the students, while only 26 per cent of their classmates were "very dissatisfied"; 63 per cent of the arrested women were "very dissatisfied," while only 22 per cent of their female classmates were. (If one combines those who were "very dissatisfied" with those who were "moderately dissatisfied," the figures for their classmates are: men, 59 per cent, and women, 47 per cent.) In response to an open-ended question, half of the arrested students called for more personal communication between administration and students, and the other half called for more due process and student participation in or control of decision-making and policy.

An intense and aware struggle in reaching their present phase of development was reported by the arrested students. The women put developing their identity as a person before other values. The men reported themselves more frequently than their classmates as greatly influenced in their development by understanding themselves as persons, by dealing with crises in their relationships to other people, and by confronting problems in themselves. They described themselves more frequently than their fellow students did as having engaged in a struggle of conflicting thoughts and feelings when deciding on a major, and said that they had changed much in their freedom to express their feelings and desires. In response to an open-ended question, half of the arrested students stressed their gains in self-respect, self-knowledge, and sense of security. The other half stressed increased interest and ability in intellectual pursuits. Half of them singled out their participation in the FSM as an important influence for change. The other half said that either professors or close friends had affected them strongly.

The arrested students came face to face with dissent, and their passage through college was a stormy one, but their struggles and conflicts went hand-in-hand with increased awareness and active attempts at achieving integration. There were paradoxes in their lives, in that they felt in disagreement with established authority and yet were supported either by their parents, or by their parents' values. They organized themselves, temporarily, into a movement; but they retained reservations about organizations and bureaucracies, which have the power to thwart the expression of individuality. Thus, as we have indicated, the FSM was a movement at times well-organized and at times almost breaking apart. Its participants frequently saw themselves as Thoreau-type individualists who could join a movement only for a very limited time. In this regard, they differed greatly from the student activists of the 1930's, who accepted political organization much more readily. The current activists are almost conservatively American in their emphasis on individual autonomy. The contrast between the political and economic objectives of the activists of the 1930's and the more broadly humanistic and educational objectives of the activists of the 1960's is pronounced.

The "paradoxes" we have just noted do not point so much to inconsistency and conflict as they do to the attempts of the activists not to be impaled on either horn of such dilemmas as the need for joint social action and for individual freedom, and the need to be guided by adult models without becoming constricted by excessive acceptance of them.

The desire for meaningful human contact was especially marked among these young people. In spite of their attacks on authority, they had closer relationships to teachers and other adults than the rest of the students. Having closer relationships with peers and being able to do something for other people were particularly important objectives for them. Especially when they stress doing things for other people, activists mean to suggest a serious deficiency in present undergraduate education, which at its best seems to aim at preparing the person for better individual performance and to neglect, particularly in the academic sector, experience both in concerted action and in action that serves or is of use to other people. In spite of the appearance of gregariousness that colleges give, particularly residential ones, there is much social isolation. As one of our FSM interviewees remarked, the possibility of establishing closer relations with other students was a powerful secondary motivation in joining the movement. "A lot of honest relationships were made . . . it was great because you had 'instant relationships.' All the things that normally take days or weeks to find out about a person, you already discerned."

The activists strongly desired to see the world outside themselves more clearly. They tried to see the world objectively in its state of complexity, while at the same time attempting to do something about remedying the situation. They experienced conflict in others and in themselves, but this conflict seemed to sharpen their perception. Unlike the "neurotic," they did not turn to a frustrated self-involvement, but toward the community and the world. One might say that these students needed to make the world whole in order to make themselves whole: to bring psychological and social objectives into harmony. Adolescence is a particularly good time to aim at such psychological and social wholeness.

It is the time when a person can remake himself—expand beyond the possibilities and limitations established by his prior upbringing. In their search, adolescents invariably manage to touch upon factors that are inadequate in their environment—it is adult immaturity that tries to dismiss them as idealistic, impractical, or merely rebellious. Adolescent dissent gives society a tremendous chance. By virtue of their less encumbered vision and relative noncommitment to the established order, adolescents can make a major contribution toward society's self-renewal. (As a student writer pointed out recently, we have stressed the contribution of universities to society, but not said enough about their role in criticizing and reforming society.)

In their protest, the students actually put their fingers on many deficiencies in educational reality that had been neglected by faculty and administration. It would be missing much of the significance of this protest to think of it primarily in "housekeeping" terms—deficiencies in channels of communication or in "legal" arrangements. The fundamental thrust of the student protest was the result of a more or less deep dissatisfaction with the educational process, its content, methods, and personnel, and its inadequacies in meeting the students' developmental needs, including their intellectual ones. It is conceivable that the activists have succeeded in initiating a redefinition of the college adolescent's role, moving toward earlier autonomy, earlier participation in the social and political processes, including education, and earlier usefulness to other people.

We interviewed Tom, one of those who was arrested, on June 11, 1965. Among other things, we asked him to give us a retrospective account of events on the night of the sit-in, December 2. In Tom's case, we were dealing with a student whose moment of decision occurred during the very night of the sit-in; so that he may be describing in a condensed form what took place over longer periods of time for other students. Of course for our student, too, the decision was preceded by a long period of gestation. One of the most striking features of his description of the sit-in is that his decision to permit himself to be arrested not only came from a sense of public responsibility to contribute to reform and to underline the injustices of existing conditions, but also was seen by him as essential for establishing his own personal and private integrity. He was very aware of the possible external consequences of his act for himself, but he saw the situation as requiring a choice between his becoming an adult that he could respect, and diffusing and diluting his own life.

In quoting from the interview, we will focus on the student's process of arriving at his decision, but we will also include some of the things he said about what was going on around him. There is an existential feeling about the report given by this student, who is a science major. His account of his attitudes and behavior during the night of the sit-in, like the others we have collected, clashes sharply with many newspaper-engendered images of these students—images that feed the adult stereotype of the adolescent's dangerousness and tendency to delinquency. One wonders as one reads this student's description of the brutalities he experienced and witnessed during the night of the sit-in whether it was not quite an education for him to be confronted with the seamy side of the fabric of society—to be brought face-to-face with the evil in people and institutions. Such an "ordeal" with the "dragon" has always been considered a necessary rite of passage to adulthood. William James had something similar in mind when, in his *Moral Equivalent of War*, he called for a confrontation of the young with the "sour and hard foundations" of man's higher life. For purposes of such confrontation, society is not likely soon to run out of material illustrating injustice and stunted development; but one might perhaps expect the university to provide help and comfort in this confrontation rather than to be itself the scene of it.

Tom first heard about the sit-in on the afternoon of December 2. He had missed the rally, but in his opening remarks, he referred to the speech by Mario Savio from which we quoted earlier. He originally planned to spend only a short time at the sit-in, particularly because he had classes the following day—attending classes takes precedence over revolution.[11]

> I didn't hear the rally that day, the one where Mario made his speech—a very good speech, beautiful metaphors. I missed that, and I didn't even know that there

[11] The following excerpts from the tape-recorded interview have been edited slightly for the sake of readability.

was a sit-in til about five in the afternoon. I happened
to be walking to the student store, and so I found out
pretty fast, and I turned around and walked home. I
went back and made three or four sandwiches, and put
on two jackets that I could use as a pillow, and brought
Latin vocabulary cards so I could study. There was, of
course, no commitment to stay, but I definitely wanted
to go in. I met a few people in there I knew. We talked,
and sat around. That was a messy period, probably the
most confused period, because people were in there milling around. It was about five-thirty, maybe a little bit
later. They hadn't closed the doors yet, so the people
were walking inside and out. But after they closed the
doors, about seven, people were still milling around and
doing various things, and then they began to get more
organized. They started to have—it was some Jewish
holiday—the rabbi comes down and he's conducting a
service. It was very good. Then various people were
serving coffee. They sent down to the store and had
someone buy two cartons of cigarettes and put them in
a bag and threw them up.

I was just amazed at the organization of the whole
thing. It had been planned before, all the various aspects, including what to do about bathrooms, and what
happens if people get sick. They had all these things
planned: how to get food in and out, what types of food,
how much; cigarettes, coffee; what to do with the waste
paper; it was amazing. It turned out that at the most
crucial period during the whole sit-in, they didn't have
communication. When they had isolated us, we didn't
have windows to look out—we were surrounded by
police so we couldn't do anything. We had no connection with the outside for about twelve hours, so we
didn't know what was going on, and that became kind
of horrible for us after a while because of this one idea
that, I think, popped into everyone's head: this action
that you're doing personally has a meaning for you, but
it has a meaning outside for you, too—and whether
you're going to be a martyr or a traitor is divided by
a very slim line.

So we didn't know what was going on. And then I
watched the Charlie Chaplin movies, which were good,
and I studied Latin for a couple of hours, talked to various people all around, and then started to find a corner
somewhere so I could sit down and go to sleep. Then
about one-thirty in the morning, newspaper reporters
came and took everyone's picture, and turned on these

great big flood lights, and everyone was screaming obscenities all over the place, because they wanted to get some sleep. I felt that I would stick out the night, but I had an eight o'clock class the next day, and I was going to it; so I would do my part for the protest and stay the first night, and then if I could come back, I would the next day, but I was not going to miss my classes. Of course, I didn't consider seriously the possibility of being arrested. From a logical standpoint, it was the most ridiculous thing to do. It would essentially have made us all martyrs, which it did. It would have given the protest a great deal of popularity with everyone, including the professors, which again it did. So I would say that logically the best thing for the administration to have done would have been to let us sit there—and I'm sure that, let's say, four hundred people would have walked out by ten o'clock the next day, just because of classes. [The sit-in] would have lost all its emotion and probably would have been a tremendous failure. Well, I can't say that for sure. It just would not have been a climax. So, therefore, I supposed that the administration would do the most logical thing and not arrest people. Well, of course, I didn't realize then what the administration was composed of, and I didn't realize that they were very, really scared, frightened to death, and not very rational in making decisions, so again this leaves us with a particular insight into administrators. I'm a little more suspicious now than I was; a little more critical.

Around two in the morning, Tom heard for the first time that the police were on their way. He says there was a very tense period from about one-thirty to three, because he felt isolated and didn't know what was going on.

You have a general idea that the police are going to come. You don't know what they're going to do when they do come, and there's nothing you can do in the meantime. So there's a lot of tension going on, and again people are talking very nervously. They just didn't know what was about to happen. They had a lot of doubts and a lot of fears that came out too. But then someone again started singing. This is a tremendous emotional relief during a time like this, and everyone, whether he could sing or not, was screaming and yelling out the civil rights song, which is all very comforting, too, because it gives a feeling of unity.

Tom had been up since six on the morning of December 2. As it turned out, he was not arrested until the afternoon of December 3. He described how during the night the students were all packed in "like sardines," and when, at about five-thirty he got up to go to the bathroom, it took him twenty-five minutes to get there because he had to step between so many bodies. People were lying down, motionless and still, but they weren't asleep. "There was just too much doubt, fear, and tension; and you just couldn't sleep in that place. People were talking; they were just kind of lying and staring and thinking." So Tom sat down, and these thoughts went through his mind:

I figured if I was going to get arrested, let's have it over fast, so I won't have a chance to change my mind. That was the worst time. I was there from about nine-thirty, sitting in that position from nine-thirty to three o'clock, when they finally arrested me. So during that period I was just going over and over in my mind everything that happened up to that time—why I should get arrested or why I shouldn't—what were the arguments involved. One very strong argument was I had worked for the defense industry during one summer at college. I'd made a hell of a lot of money, and at that time, a lot of money represented my freedom to me. I wanted to be able to get a decent job afterwards; I didn't want to be dis-criminated against on the grounds that I'd been arrested before.

I wasn't sure how much my particular idea of the pro-test would be associated with the FSM's, so that was another thing that I was concerned with, because I wanted it to be a kind of tool of my arguments; I wanted to be able to express my individuality; and I just didn't know if this was going to have this effect. So again there was doubt in that area. But then after thinking over all these things, I realized that the real motivating force was education, and that I really was not too happy with the idea of going to school for four years just to get a degree, so that you can go on and on and on, and so that you can get good jobs in society and stuff like that. This was the big argument between myself and my par-ents. They both graduated from college before the de-pression; so they both had degrees, and it didn't matter what the degree was in, what subject, they could get good jobs. So this became all-important to them, and perhaps was the only concrete thing that they ever presented to me. So I realized then that I wasn't happy with this emphasis on getting a degree. I wanted the degree to mean something; I wanted it to represent a certain level of something that I had acquired after working for four years or fighting with myself for four years. So it finally occurred to me that here was a beautiful method —a beautiful way for me to rebel officially. I'd really had my freedom—been pretty independent all the way along —but I never established the type of rapport with my parents where they accepted me, not as their son, but as, let's say, another individual, another adult, which is very important. So I finally felt that this was going to be in one way a protest against my upbringing. It was also a justified protest—a criticism of the fact that they were striving for a degree instead of an education.

I don't like [to be locked up], so I began to get kind of excited. About two-thirty, I started getting this smile on my face that stayed with me throughout the night, I guess, because I knew I was going to enjoy what happened. I began noticing things around me—mostly these stupid police officers. When they came up to our floor to arrest us again, they changed their techniques. They had apparently got some sort of arresting engineers up there to determine what would be the most efficient way to do these things. I was also very concerned about whether to go limp or not. In the beginning I could not see really what relation this had to the protest as a whole—could not see why delay was so important, especially since it had been going on so long. But the penalty for resisting an officer is a $2,000 fine and a year in jail, so its something to seriously consider.

We had been given the phone number of a lawyer, if they asked. They didn't ask; they didn't inform us of our rights. So I didn't know what was going on, because I had never been arrested before, and I didn't know when to ask for legal counsel, which we were also instructed to do. By the time that I had finally made certain decisions and come to an understanding of what I was doing, and what I was about to do, I also began to see that going limp was important for other reasons, too. Within the whole area of the protest, the sit-in, we had not accepted those laws that we were supposedly violating. When they came up to me, there were four men all gathered around. One had a tape recorder, one was writing out a slip, and one was reading a speech that had been prepared. This one informed me that I was doing something against the law, and did I know it, and if I didn't leave I'd be arrested, something like that. He offered me an opportunity to get out, to get up and walk out, and I wouldn't be arrested or anything. I thought this was a contradiction—here I was under arrest and then I wasn't, and then he was giving me a chance to not be under arrest. So I asked him about it. I said I thought that I had already been under arrest and that I had been just waiting here to be taken out. He said, "Oh, no, no, no! You know it's not like that at all! You can get up and walk out. Do you want to?" I said no. So he was a little bit upset by that, and he was a little bit flustered, but finally went back to his speech. So he started reading on, and then they took my picture, and then got down to the last part of the speech which was— I'm trying to get the wording, which was so beautiful, so poetic: "Will you act like a gentleman and walk out with me?" It was like that—and I just about laughed. I didn't expect it to be this comical, and I was kind of stunned there for a while, because I didn't know exactly what to say.

What I had noticed was that when other people went limp they were still scared, and that they tensed up. Because of this, they had gotten some rough treatment. So when [the officers] grabbed me by the shoulders, two of them, and started grabbing me right here, on the shoulder blades, I felt these fingernails digging into my shoulders, I just raised my arms and they grabbed me underneath the arms, which was nice, and I really went limp. I almost fell asleep. I'd been waiting twelve hours in that one position, and you know this was the end, the climax, and it was getting pretty exciting, but I guess my nerves were shot—I'd been up thirty hours, something like that—it was unbelievable. But I was so limp they just dragged me across the floor, and they got going at a good pace and picked me up and threw me. So I was off the ground for a couple of seconds at least. By that time, I just didn't give a damn what happened—I didn't care whether I fell on my head or what. It just so happens that I didn't tense up, and because of that, I was caught when I fell.

About three-thirty in the afternoon, Tom finally got out and was put on a bus to be transported to prison. As he sat down, everyone in the bus "turned around and looked for half a second or so" and it made him "feel good." "They were saying that I may be doing something outside of myself which will be important outside of myself." His self-esteem and sense of usefulness thus bolstered, he began to feel anger and wondered how he could have been "so foolish" as to think that the police would treat him "like another human being" instead of "taking out their aggressions" on him. The last person to get on the bus was a fellow student. "They dragged him by his hair. I felt this was just going overboard; they were not being sane. Apparently he'd blacked out on the way down, so they had dragged him down by his hair instead of by his feet, and he was in a hell of a lot of pain when they got him out and put him in the seat."

The students were driven to the Santa Rita prison farm, and parked next to the booking office, but were not let out of the bus. They sat there for about three hours, discussing things, and yelling and screaming from time to time. They struck up conversations with some of the police officers and asked them how they viewed the protest. They also posed the question of what the officer would do if Governor Brown were his immediate commander and advised him to shoot them. The officer answered: "Well, of course not. I would be defying my own boss, but it would be because he was wrong. You don't deserve to be killed for doing this." Then a lieutenant got on the bus and said, "You know what I think? I think all you bastards are Commies, and this is a great big Commie conspiracy. My daughter wanted to go to Berkeley, but now I'm not going to let her." "Your daughter couldn't get into Berkeley," the students replied.

By this time, one of the big issues was when they were going to be let off the bus to go to the toilet. They were tired and hungry. Eventually one of the officers left the bus, then returned, saying that he couldn't find any authorities, and they would have to stay in the bus.

> So then we didn't know what to do. Some were suggesting we protest, and some were suggesting we climb out of the windows. So we divided up into debating teams. Somebody had a watch and was going to time the various arguments. We were going to have a ten-minute presentation on each side, and after that, we were going to vote on the action to take. Everyone joined in on this, and it made us feel better. Very passionate, strong argu-

ments were going up. The question involved was whether we were going to be silent to get our way, or protest to get our way. So after a very long, painfully democratic debate, we took a vote and it turned out to be pretty much fifty-fifty. But the protestors had it over the non-protestors. So what we decided to do was to protest for eight minutes, and then sit quietly for ten minutes and see what happened.

The students lifted up the windows of the bus and made as much noise as they could. The women students who had been arrested heard them in their barracks about 50 or 70 feet away, and they too began screaming and yelling. This protest brought results; they were let into the station and given a sandwich each. Booking took another three to four hours. Fifty-two of the students were crowded into a small, unventilated transfer cell for twenty minutes. They were then let into the barracks, but searching them took another hour. At one-thirty Tom finally got to lie down in an unheated bunkhouse.

Toward the end of the interview, the interviewer commented that Tom seemed to have a very good grasp of his whole involvement. Tom responded to this by saying:

Well, I'll tell you that I was frightened that if perhaps I didn't have a good grasp, I would end up going slightly insane too, because the problems were immense. I could see around me that people were very confused. They knew emotionally and intuitively they were doing something, but they didn't quite see what. They couldn't articulate it rationally, and that was quite a problem. Also, at certain times during the last semester I was busy studying, and I got left out on things that occurred. I found it very difficult to find a straight story about what had happened, even from the official FSM statements, which were often ambiguous and sometimes just wrong, incorrect. I couldn't trust them. I read them, and then I compared them with what other people had to say. I tried to get a statement from the administration, and I found out that such statements were so ambiguous you didn't know what was going on, or what happened. It was very important for me to have a grasp of what had actually happened before I could actually support anything or not. So at the time, if you didn't follow things specifically as they happened—and it took quite a lot of energy to get out and sort them out—but if you didn't, and the time came for action, and you wanted to participate but you didn't see things clearly and you couldn't justify it to yourself, there's a chance that you might hate yourself afterwards.

Finally, when Tom was asked what he had been doing in his last semester at college, after the arrest, he once more illustrated the discontent with educational procedures that had been a major base for the FSM protest. Tom reported studying a series of modern plays for one of his courses. He seems to have gone about it in a workmanlike, critical, and analytic fashion, but he received a "D" on his first midterm exam. He felt this was because he did not conform to the "rules" of test responses. After he had "psyched out" what was wanted, he performed better.

I used to read a lot of plays, but this was in high school, and I haven't for a long time, so I took a not very interesting English class and a course in modern British and American drama. I got to read up a lot on O'Neill and Shaw, and everyone else in between. It was very pleasurable, but my first midterm came back with a D minus on it. I didn't realize why. I finally found out it was the way I was approaching it—taking each individual play and analyzing it, showing where actions between characters would create this characterization that would lead to a full knowledge of the characters itself, to a place where you can anticipate the next action, given any particular situation, and then, how the actions of the characters relate to the theme of the play. But when you have to be tested on eighteen plays in an hour, and you're given two questions, then all you can do is say something that's general. They wanted a general comparison of themes of plays. So after I'd figured that out, I could look at the plays both individually, as units in themselves, and then as parts of other sets, and see general themes and compare them. I think I did fairly well, but it didn't require knowledge of any of the plays, which was too bad.

In spite of his involvement in the FSM and the activities connected with his trial, Tom said he "did quite a lot of thinking and learning academically even while participating full time in this other direction." "Maybe too much time is bad for an educational system like this. The questions I ask myself and find important to answer aren't necessarily the ones they are going to test me on." Tom seems to have implicitly raised the question of motivation. As we found elsewhere in our study, students who otherwise complained of insufficient time would find they could easily take on a time-consuming additional task if it was meaningful to them.

The strong intellectual interest and intellectual independence shown by Tom was typical of the students arrested during the sit-in. They were students whom most professors would rate as very desirable because of their motivations and their intellectual industry. We are confronted with a revolt of the intellectuals, not of the anti-intellectuals. Such students have taken the claims of the university to be an intellectual community seriously—in part because of the very excellence of the university they have been attending—and they simply want more of it, and want it better. There were students like this in the so-called "silent generation" of the "apathetic" Fifties; but their potential for involvement and activity did not coincide with as favorable a situation. Perhaps education might develop a psychological Keynesianism that would awaken students in "apathetic" times through the stimulation of autonomy and dissent. When students offer suggestions and dissent, we should consider them as an educational gift—a gift to their own education as well as to that of their teachers.

Activist students are a minority, but a rapidly growing one. There are many students who tend to accept their "education" passively, and who are insufficiently touched, stimulated, or awakened by their experience in college. The activists, by their example, have already helped to broaden these students' intellectual and valuational horizons. But closer attention to students different from themselves is likely to benefit the activists. From the perspective of their often generous and enthusiastic natures, many activists seem to see other students too easily in their own image. They would grow in tolerance and gain an enlarged perspective on human nature if they realized that theirs is only one way of achieving identity, and that other students may achieve their own particular "wholeness" in ways quite different from theirs. Intellectual awareness and excitement, enlarged social consciousness, and reform-mindedness are "universals"—qualities desirable in every educated person. In this lies the challenge and moral appeal of the activists.

PART FOUR

Recommendations

≉ 12 ≉

RECOMMENDATIONS FOR
POLICY AND
PHILOSOPHY

Joseph Katz

At this time, undergraduate education serves many different purposes. It is a further step in the socialization process; it provides channels for upward mobility; it provides some occupational preparation; and it gives professors a place to pursue their specialized investigations and to obtain some recruits for them. While serving these purposes, it also creates a learning environment in which, for many students, coercion predominates over curiosity and initiative.

We approached our study with the intent of examining as many of the student's experiences during his four college years as our methods and time would allow us. We did so because we suspected that the lives and development of the students were richer and more complex than the common articulations indicate. Our expectation was justified; and consequently our own views of the college situation underwent considerable modification and enlargement. We are particularly impressed with the great variety of people who are called "students." As our work progressed, we came to feel we were backsliding when we used the expression, "the college student." Noting the wide variety of styles, purposes, and personalities that college students exhibit, we began to wonder whether current institutional procedures and arrangements do not force them too much into the same mold.

Let us begin with a radical question and ask whether, if we were allowed to start from scratch, we would really design for most people between 17 and 22 the kind of collegiate institutions that we now have. We know that other societies, and our own society at other times, have provided quite different arrangements for people at this age. In some societies, people of college age have been married for several years and integrated into the work-world of their culture. In other societies, or particular social classes within them, they have spent these years wandering, or in military service, or in apprenticeship. These arrangements are often eminently satisfactory to the strivings that characterize the college-age years: the desire for movement, the thirst for experience, and the need for meaningful relationships with adults and peers. Contrast such solutions with those offered amid the vast impersonality of our campuses.

What social functions do colleges serve in our culture? One of the most obvious is that of general education, but there are other functions as well.[1] Colleges provide an avenue for social mobility; they contribute to socialization, from training in manners to the development of greater social and political tolerance; they provide a place for boys and girls to meet and prepare for marriage; and they give some preparation for the work-world be-

---

[1] Here, when one considers the college curriculum—in intent, a distillation of the accumulated wisdom and intellectual skills and competencies of our civilization—the question arises to what extent it is premature for people of college age, since the curriculum is not only the slow acquisition of the history of mankind, but requires, in order to be mastered by the individual, prolonged experience, testing, autonomy, and maturation.

yond school, and are indispensable stepping-stones to many occupations. Different types of colleges have tried to adapt themselves to the wide variety of class, caste, region, taste, and sophistication in American life. The more sophisticated and prestigious institutions have thus served as selecting devices by which people from the "lower" strata could be drawn into the business or intellectual classes. Colleges also provide parents with the opportunity to make a personal outlay for the sake of their children's education and enable society to keep the young "off the streets" at a particularly explosive and restless period in their lives. Finally, four years of schooling keep a large section of the population out of the labor market—a possible benefit in an economy in which it may be as important that some people not work as it is that others do. These functions are all socially useful, more or less. They do not include the possible role of the college in furthering individual development. This role, taken seriously, introduces a new element and a new challenge—one that has not been central, in spite of the familiar rhetoric according to which the development of character is one of the goals of a college education. This role has been the primary focus of our study.

We need to go beyond surface meanings. Definitions of the goals of education that list the development of character, or the production of gentlemen or "well-rounded" individuals are often, in spite of their individualistic cast, definitions of desired socialization, aimed at the production of reliable and predictable people for business and social purposes. Moreover, throughout history, schools and teachers have served not just to educate people, but also to control them. Literature abounds in accounts of the pedantic discipline—even sadism—of the schoolmaster, whether he be the ancient Greek slave in Rome, or the teacher in the Jewish Cheder, or the "Pauker" in the German Gymnasium. The rod and the teacher are readily associated with each other. The focus on social science and social welfare in this century has been one factor that has brought attention to human development more within the realm of possibility. This developed throughout the nineteenth century when the problems and rights of groups previously discriminated against—deviants, the insane, minorities, women, children—were thoroughly explored in literature and science.

But in many ways, attention to individual development is a luxury even today. Many people are more concerned with the task of getting increasingly large numbers of our young into college than with the task of increasing the quality of their lives. There are other environmental demands that compete or even conflict with the purposes of individual development. Among these are technological, bureaucratic, and political demands; parental expectations; the anticipatory influence of the graduate and professional schools, which, perhaps, more by habit than by design, exercise great control over the student's undergraduate course selection, the development of his interests, and his grade-getting activities; the often unspoken demands of his peers, stemming from the needs of human groups for solidarity, agreement, predictability, group cohesion, and the reduction of envy; and finally, the demands of the faculty, whose own education, experience, and loyalties make them strongly inclined to serve the interests of their specific department, or even of their specialty of method or content within it.[2] In response to the fact that the academic sector provides for a part of education only, there have sprung up other arrangements and institutions to complement and to oppose it. This is the extracurricular sector, with its fraternities, clubs, activities, and mores. (Our study has shown us its continued validity.) In recent years, this extracurricular sector has been particularly expanded in the areas of society-oriented activities, such as work with the underprivileged, political and civil rights activities, summer and vacation work camps, and service activities in this country and abroad. Extracurricular activities have traditionally been thought of as auxiliary, but in operation, they have been of primary significance for many students. For this reason, they furnish precedents for a more deliberately inclusive approach to education.

All relevant educational planning must begin with the recognition that students are greatly differentiated from each other not only in their ability and interests, but also in their purposes, learning styles, backgrounds, and personalities. Some students question their identity; others feel relatively comfortable in an

---

[2] The fact that professors are increasingly given the role of caretakers of the young between seventeen and twenty-two is perhaps an accident. Other societies have chosen other people to be in a guiding or controlling position during these years.

identity already achieved; still others anxiously cling to a shell of identity that protects them from threatening external stimuli. Some students view college as a deliberate stepping-stone to a career, while others are there simply because it is part of the many assignments that life will make. Some students have intellectual curiosity, others have conceptual ability of an almost "athletic" sort that they exercise without much intellectual involvement. Some like to collect college information the way other people collect money or stamps. For many, the cognitive-analytic dimension takes second place. They prefer to experience life esthetically, or kinetically. Others feel they are doing something "real" when they serve or manage to manipulate people. Some like to be left alone to brood and to indulge in fantasy. Others like to experience life in concert with other people, through working at a common task, or through friendship or conviviality.

Colleges have not sufficiently linked these varied styles and approaches to their educational tasks.[3] Some students respond to verbal and mathematical concepts directly, but for others, the full significance of such concepts becomes clear only when mediated through other activities. Imagine a group of students helping deprived children, learning the difficult skills of working constructively with other people, understanding their actions and motives, knowing when to support, challenge, or inhibit, when to take initiative and when not. Such experience would lend itself well to theoretical purposes, and it would verify for the students what they read about human development. The unsolved problems in their work experience would drive them to seek help from the experience of other people as embodied in past discussions and research.[4]

But even such an apparently simple arrangement as this might make for far-reaching changes. There is, for instance, the question of timing: when and how are theories to be introduced?

[3] See also the later discussion in this chapter of major areas of teaching.

[4] Our illustration is taken from the area of social service, but there are many other types of projects that can be devised in other areas. For instance, the understanding of literature or the capacity for expression and writing may be much enhanced by sending students into the community to observe and record the speech and expressions of people in different situations and different walks of life.

At what point in his exposure can each student best see the relevance of a theory to the data on hand? At what point does premature exposure to theory inhibit the development of personal articulations? Further, how much time is required to study a problem and integrate what one has learned? These are questions to be settled by experience. But the raising of them reveals the arbitrariness of our current ways of presenting subject matter and the regimenting of the student's time into four or five nearly equal "cognitive" strips.

Another difference between students consists in their varying preferences for lectures and discussions. Lectures seem particularly convenient for those students who do not care too much about the contents of what is offered or, whether they care or not, wish to have their material in a readily repeatable form at examination time. Though it is not a neat division, this grouping into those with an active orientation to learning and those with a passive orientation is indeed the underlying grouping we are looking for: a continuum from those students who approach subject matter with their own questions and desires to those who repeat what is said because they think they have to.

For a start then, one might offer students the option of having the same subject matter treated in two types of courses, lecture and discussion. One can expect that students by their choice of the one or the other option will sort themselves out naturally, and will thus facilitate our development of differing teaching techniques. It is not helpful to force a lecture-minded student into a discussion, because such a one can only gradually leave an externally imposed structure and move toward one that comes more from within. It would also be unwise to force an opinionated, discussion-minded student to submit himself to lectures.[5] He would simply continue his dogmatism or rebelliousness in silence. But students could gradually be made aware of the limitations of their initial mode of preference. This would call for the identification of teachers with special talents for reaching different kinds of students.

In the suggestion just made, a further underlying principle

[5] Some students seem to prefer discussion not so much to listen to others as to hear themselves.

is implied. The problem is how to select students for differing learning groups. One way, of course, would be to sort them out by way of tests and questionnaires. But there is often an alternative. By letting students sort themselves out in terms of their own preferences—if these are indices of underlying dispositions—one can obtain a grouping that is less externally imposed. It has the advantage of leaving the choice to the students and bypassing the implied passivity in grouping by tests or questionnaires.

People with different personalities learn quite differently. The authoritarian student is relatively closed to evidence in areas that arouse his prejudices, fears, and unacceptable desires. He will not easily open himself up to evidence in social science, or to the more subtle values in literature, unless his own fear of these alien and invading matters can be mitigated. The highly impulsive student will not sit down long enough to consider views that seem to threaten inhibitions of his propelling "needs," and he will often lack the patience to have regard for the inherent complexity of people or of things. His academic as well as his personal education depends on strengthening his capacity to control his impulses, and teaching him that to do so can be pleasant rather than restricting. The obsessive student will continue to transform facts and feelings into concepts, and he will think the one a substitute for the other. His concepts, because they are divorced from reality, will be barren and overgeneralized, and upon scrutiny, will reveal infantile preoccupations. While seemingly in love with words, he will have a secret contempt for thought, because on deeper levels he is aware of the defensive use he is making of it, or of the insufficient connection his concepts have with his feelings. There are other students who tend to feel comfortable only when they can relax, forget about the requirements of the classroom, and engage themselves on the level of narcissistic display of clothes, semi-drunken loss of consciousness, infantile power play, or sentimental dependency. Where there is such a ready tendency to regression, the ego capacities acquired in the classroom tend to remain underdeveloped because they are cut off from the person's vitality. (There are, of course, types of temporary "regressions" that appear to be in the service of ego expansion.)

How are we to have regard for personality without turning colleges into therapeutic institutions? This question is particularly vexing because therapeutic institutions are not brilliant models of effectiveness, and because psychotherapy is available to relatively small numbers. Teachers usually do not have the competence or the interest to serve as therapists, and they could not easily become competent without an improper mixing of two different roles. The answer lies in providing environmental conditions and experiences that are conducive to psychological development: that is, any experiences, academic or otherwise, that further a student's sense of competence, enhance his self-esteem, and affect his readiness for genuine self-awareness and self-criticism as well as his resistance to improper external pressures. Provisions for a proper timing of confrontation with heterodox ideas, flexible living arrangements, "leaves" from the college, and work experience, can have important psychological effects. The authoritarian student probably should not be confronted during his freshman year with a roommate who is likely to have some of the characteristics that he objects to in people. Such a confrontation may have to be reserved until later, after he has accepted smaller differences in ideas and people. The impulsive student will need to be provided with tasks congenial to his impulses, but requiring some disciplined self-control and tolerance of frustration; and he may best learn this by working together with peers who share some of his openness and unconventionality, but have developed personal discipline. The obsessive student needs both structure and gradually increasing opportunities for more spontaneous expression. It will help if we can join him with people who will not only respond to his words but also to his underlying feelings, and who are not trapped by the hostile component of his obsessiveness.

How can educators create such a beneficial situation? The starting point would be to make the student, not the course, the primary interest of the professor, the department, or the graduate or professional school; to make the student the "unit of education." This requires that we begin college with a different profile of the student than the number of courses and units he completed in high school. Instead, the profile would list strong proficiencies of the student, such as artistic talent, skills in languages, extended knowledge of an academic field, special skills as a community leader, and so on. This list would be followed by an indication of relevant areas in which the student is weak. For instance, a student who is capable in debating or other rhetorical skills might show underdevelopment of his esthetic capacities. A student gifted in the writing of poetry might be rather deficient in the capacity for detached and objective research and interpretation of evidence. A four-year plan for each student would then be geared to strengthen him further in selected areas in which he is already strong, and in which his interests persist, as well as to help him achieve a considerable strengthening in at least one area in which he is initially weak.

This profile should not be drawn up in terms of present departmental divisions of subject matter, but in terms of differently defined areas of human competence. After the initial profile has been drawn—and it should be revised at appropriate intervals—it is of great importance that the learning of students be "sequential," resulting in a cumulative growth of competence. The goals ought not to be defined as so and so many courses passed and so and so many units acquired, but rather as achievement in relatively well-defined areas of skills or competence. At the present time—though the requirements of having a major in principle call for it—there is too little opportunity for students to carry academic pursuits to some sort of closure. The fulfillment of a requirement gets the student often just to the beginning of a mastery of the subject matter, leaving him with one more bit of disconnected "knowledge."

If the focus is on selected areas of learning in which some mastery is possible, one may expect the sense of competence in doing something complicated well to generalize to other parts of the student's personality and increase his self-esteem and inner and outer identity. This may be particularly likely because the proposed plan calls for considerable expansion of the student's competence in an area in which he is initially weak but which is of special importance for his overall development—an example would be a somewhat exclusively machine-oriented engineer developing competence in the area of social relations or of esthetic sensitivity. Moreover, learning sequentially and achieving closure may develop psychological habits that go against the fragmentation of energies that is characteristic of many people in our society, and is strongly supported by our academic arrangements. Curricular planning dominated by the principles of sequentialness and closure would take the place of the present mechanical shuffling of requirements, requisites, and prerequisites. We also ought always to be mindful that four years is a very small amount of time, and that our present curriculum may try to do too much too soon. In psychotherapy, where our methods are more adjusted to human capacity, the sense of the slowness of time is widely shared by practitioners, but most attempts thus far to shorten the time required for more thoroughgoing therapeutic changes have not been successful. Although establishing and maintaining the student's profile might seem to require an unduly heavy outlay of personnel hours, particularly at the time of the student's entrance to college, there might be an eventual financial saving, because it would allow the student to be much more self-directed than he is under present conditions.

The question will be raised of what happens under the proposed system to "core" or "distribution" requirements, the implication being that the student needs to be exposed to some of our basic scientific and cultural achievements. One way to handle this would be to present these various intellectual areas in something like the traditional "courses." Some of the basic concepts of a particular field of inquiry could be presented in lecture form during each semester. These might be pure lecture courses, in which no grades or examinations would be given, and attendance would be voluntary. One can easily imagine that under such a system a group of teachers, particularly gifted for this kind of lecturing, would emerge. There might be several different people giving lecture series in the same area, in recognition of the fact that different students are attracted to different personalities and different approaches to the same subject matter.[6] Adequate course descriptions and the "grapevine" would take care of channeling students to the right professors. These "courses" should be open to students in any of the four college years so that each can determine for himself at what time he is most ready for exposure to a particular field. Discussion sections might be provided for those who wish to have them.

Such exposure ought to be carefully distinguished from

[6] There is, of course, always the possibility of a "Mickey Mouse" lecturer—these are plentiful under the present system—but an appropriate assessment of teaching and its effects would reduce this possibility.

the acquisition of the sustained competencies that have been suggested. These competencies, as indicated, would be in many different areas—the languages, the literature and culture of a people, interpersonal skills, such as teaching or working with children, journalistic observation and writing, and the like. This would require an expansion of the faculty to include persons competent in these fields. Ideally, the student himself would gradually take more and more initiative and responsibility for his own learning, so that one of the outcomes of attending college would be a much higher capacity for self-direction and for utilization of authoritative resources.

We must, however, be careful not to abandon one relatively coercive system for another, no matter how well-meaning and appropriate it might appear. Self-determination by the student ought to be a cardinal principle from the beginning. But what about those students, of which our research has found large numbers, who rely upon guidance, structuring, and being told what to do? They, too, should be allowed to choose for themselves, but be given the opportunity of being confronted with the consequences of their choice, so that they increasingly learn that even passivity has consequences—many of them not wished for and many of them alterable. (Thus, one might let entering freshmen determine whether they wanted the grade, pass-fail, or no-grade system.) It would not do at first to restrain students with a more passive conception of learning from indulging this bent, because it would deprive them of needed support, which they would reestablish by subterfuge. It is only by a gradual weaning process that they themselves can discover their own submerged interests and the pleasure that comes from choosing for themselves—a task that calls for particularly gifted teachers.

Our present curricular structure includes many requirements, particularly in the first two years of college. The standard student response to these is to get them out of the way as quickly as possible. Such requirements are often justified by reference to the "immaturity" of freshmen. But their "immaturity" may be assisted by a system that restricts their choices. I would urge expansion of the choices that freshmen and other students are allowed to make, but build into the system retrospective discussions with the students of the mistakes they feel they have made. We are in general too anxious to protect our students from mistakes, and thus we neglect both the benefits of initiative and the opportunities for learning that mistakes provide.

Finally, when we speak of the student as the primary "unit of education," we do not mean students separated from each other, as they now tend to be. Students not only would like to remove some of the barriers that now exist between them and others, but they also can learn many things much more effectively in joint projects with others. In college society, we have tended to assign peer-relatedness to the social realm and individualism to the intellectual realm. Perhaps some reversal is in order.

We have made several innovative proposals already and are going to make more. We stop, therefore, to suggest that when one thinks of putting any innovative idea into practice, one should not expect or perhaps even desire that one's institution adopt it wholesale. Not only would there be little chance that the faculty would accept such a package, but it would be premature to apply to many people so many untested arrangements. Perhaps one of the reasons for the relative stagnation in higher education has been the unwitting principle that reform ought to be college-wide. A more feasible alternative is to have new procedures tried out on the minimum number of students necessary. This allows greater latitude of experiment, bypasses "political" objections, and paves the way for an easier adoption of procedures that have proven themselves by example. The Board of Educational Development, proposed by the Muscatine Committee at Berkeley, is a step in this direction, in that it allows for experiments to be authorized for a period up to five years outside of the established jurisdictions of the faculty and faculty committees.

Our approach to undergraduate education deviates from the interests and experiences of a majority of current college faculty. In the populations studied by us, there was relatively little contact between students and faculty, but when it occurred, and particularly when the interaction was based on a coincidence of the professor's and the student's interests, its influence was profound. Thus, even for purely academic objectives it would be desirable to have more interaction, because of the need of adolescents for a part-model, for encouragement from an adult, and for something of the master-apprentice relationship. But we need to broaden our concept of faculty further if we wish to serve the interests of the student. We need faculty who can educate students in areas other than the present ones, and who can also address themselves to other developmental needs of the student. Obviously this does not mean that all faculty need to fill this role, but that this be a function filled by some faculty. We do in fact now have personnel other than the academic faculty, such as student deans, counselors, and resident advisors. But these people tend to be assigned the functions of administration, housekeeping, and policing. They are regarded as ancillary, and are not seen primarily as educators. Education is thought to be in the hands of the academic faculty, who view education primarily as presentation of subject matter.

It will strengthen our conception of the need for the expansion of the faculty if we outline some major areas of teaching and learning. First, there is the academic-conceptual area, under which is included much of the traditional subject matter, descriptions, theories, hypotheses, and so on.

The next area is the esthetic-artistic one, the area of feelings, emotions, intuitions, sensitivity, and sensibility. Some philosophers have described it in cognitive terms, and have spoken of the "language" of the emotions, the "language" of music, and so on, but the very paradoxical quality of the metaphor indicates that we are dealing here with a different interaction between the external world and inner experiences. This approach to reality requires its own sequence of training, and its own standards of performance, which, though sometimes subject to a wider range of argument than standards in the more exact sciences, can obtain some degree of consensus among qualified people. This mode of learning needs more recognition in colleges, and it needs more practitioners among the faculty. (The recent tendency towards resident artists and writers is a beginning.)

Then there is the area of people-oriented activity. This area is in some sense akin to the esthetic, since it also involves the affective and feeling modes of response. For some people, working with others, understanding them, and being of help to them, is a favorite mode of dealing with reality. The psychiatrist is a professional instance of this kind of orientation; his practice requires a certain amount of theory and cognitive apparatus, but in addition, his own feelings, perceptions, and hunches, in some sense his whole personality, are as much instruments as the merely cognitive skills. When we think of teaching this kind of "skill," we must bear in mind that its practitioners often are not as verbally facile as the ordinary academician.[7] In this they resemble the artist, whose teaching consists less in long lectures than in examples, in long looking or listening, and in the right words, sometimes quite few words, at the right time. These people like to teach in the face of some actual experience that the student is involved in. As faculty, they are probably most useful, not in performing verbally before a class, but in working together with students in life situations. Such faculty may also serve by being available to student groups who wish to submit problems in the affective domain of their own lives to a more searching and competent analysis.

A second group of people-oriented activities—salesmanship, politics, and administration—must be considered separately. Here we are dealing with a quite different manner of understanding people and being of service. It is a tricky area, because interests other than that of the person served are of major importance to the person rendering the service. Moreover, unlike the helping professions, there is no central obligation here to inquire into the motives of the people served, and it is often considered legitimate or even desirable to satisfy their irrational wants. There are many students strongly oriented towards the political or administrative life. They might be taught, in the manner of some of the ancient Sophists, to master the arts of manipulation and exploitation. But to teach them the art of satisfying divergent interests without injury to one or several of the parties will require some pioneering efforts. Some writers have deplored the lack of a tradition in this country (as contrasted with England) of motivating and training people for public service. The area of business service, too, seems to deserve more attention.

The fifth area is that of inanimate, man-made objects—instruments, machines, computers, and the like. Some people find that they can deal with reality best by creating artificial replicas or artificial extensions of it. As we know, they have been so suc-

[7] In the context of the college, this means faculty who can help students to understand healthy as well as unhealthy human and social functioning.

cessful that they have been able to crowd out much of the natural world that we inherited and have changed the ecology from one of natural surroundings to man-made ones. Here we need two sorts of faculty: those who are particularly adept with students who have a primary orientation towards man-made objects—who need to have it brought into connections with other human activities—and those who are able to impart some of the pleasures and skills of these pursuits to those with some other orientation.

The sixth area is that of motoric expression. In some respects, it is well taken care of already by our colleges. There is the large athletic apparatus: coaches are important people, and many students engage in sports as participants and as spectators. Nevertheless, the attitude toward motoric expression often is ambivalent, compounded by fears of its commercialism, its competition with academic pursuits, and perhaps also some influence from a European puritanic heritage that assigns the body, in ideology at least, a rather low place. But given the fact that there is a large number of students whose favorite mode of relating to reality is via motoric expression, the problem of connecting their motoric responses with other parts of their personality deserves much greater attention.

Finally, we come to the art of sociability. Though it tends to be regarded as incidental, it actually occupies a major place in the informal learning that takes place during college, and spans the range from learning manners to developing the capacity for friendships and intimacy. Given the fact that informal learning of it brings only moderately satisfactory results, more attention to the factors that foster good human relations seems desirable.

One could add to or modify this list of seven areas. But the essential thing is to move beyond a "single variable" conception of teaching. Present faculties tend to represent only one segment of humanity, primarily people with strong cognitive orientations and the tendency to exercise thought in a "non-applied" fashion.[8] The students represent a much larger variety of interests and orientations, and relatively few of them will go into

[8] The implied criticism is not of "cognition" which is a universal human function and merits strengthening in anyone, but of a particular mode of cognition, the academic-conceptual one, being fostered in neglect of the six other areas we have distinguished.

careers similar to those of their college teachers. Yet at the very time of their exposure to their specialized faculty, students are segregated from much of the adult world, so that a period in life when they are particularly open to change, they are secluded from potentially significant adults.

We need a considerable enlargement of the kind of people with whom we bring our students in contact. This may be done by enlisting faculty from non-academic occupations. Explorers, archeologists, journalists, businessmen, and government officials from many parts of the world might be asked to become associated for a period of time with the college.[9] In addition, there are available in almost any community a large group of adults, some of whom could serve as "auxiliary" faculty. These are people with a particularly exemplary knowledge of their own occupational field, who are able to communicate it, or people who have an outstanding knowledge of an area outside of their occupation, such as the psychiatrist who is also an expert on painting, or the lawyer who is an authority on Galileo. These people often have a great desire to teach and to be in contact with young people. They would benefit the students not only through their intellectual knowledge and skills, but also through what they stand for as people. What better model could there be for some college student heading into business than a businessman who is also learned and esthetically alive? We would give special care to matching the right student with the right man.

The auxiliary faculty would help solve what is both a qualitative and a quantitative problem. Qualitatively, it would present students with a larger variety of "models" than an academic faculty can provide. Quantitatively, it would enlarge the number of available teaching adults; there can never be enough people on a faculty if increased faculty-student contact is the goal. It is likely and perhaps desirable that most of the auxiliary faculty would serve only a limited number of years.

We have already stressed the importance of the proper phasing of learning. Our study has impressed us with the importance of the freshman year, particularly its early phases. The

---

[9] They might obtain teaching leaves from their employers—who would be well served by the fresh perspective their employees would gain.

entering student faces many sudden challenges and threats: separation from home, sudden exposure to large groups of strangers who may seem threatening or superior, new academic demands. Colleges usually give particular attention to the freshman. They often assign students to live with roommates of somewhat different backgrounds, so that their range of acquaintances and sympathies will be broadened, or they provide special introductory courses aimed at awakening and strengthening the student's interest in new subjects to new approaches. But the outcome is often quite different from what the planners intended. The student may find himself unable to respond to an "exciting" introductory course because of his failure to live up to his previous grade performance. The contact with "different" peers may be more painful and alienating than broadening. Thus, both the new academic testing and the exposure to strangers not necessarily perceived as friendly may intensify adolescent anxieties about one's identity, including one's capacity, and thus reactivate an earlier identity crisis. The resolution of the crisis is too often in a non-developmental direction: accommodation to the academic system by "psyching it out," and accommodation to the challenge of "difference" by withdrawal into groups of like-minded peers, or the establishment of a peer culture that keeps the values of the faculty at a distance.

It seems very desirable that colleges divert their best resources to the problems of the freshman. A combination of self-determination and guidance ought to be used to get the freshmen into the appropriate learning environments. Those freshmen who feel ready to assume independence, even if it seems a brash independence, ought to be given it, with the expectation that they will soon be confronted with the consequences of mistaken choices, and that mistakes will be made occasions for learning rather than censure. Those freshmen who expect to be told what to do, and to be graded and directed, ought to be given this opportunity, with the intent of confronting them with the consequences of passivity.

The freshman year is too often faced with academic values that are out of keeping with the student's status as an adolescent. The university is dedicated to a careful, sometimes a rather tidily limited, search for evidence, and to carefully defined conceptualization. The adolescent is much less a theoretical person than he is an ideological one. He likes to work with great ideas, and his concepts are closely related to his emotions and hopes. He uses ideas both as a guide out of his confusion and as a way to savor ideationally what he cannot yet experience emotionally, sensually, or in relations with other people. Football player and poet alike spend their freshman bull sessions discussing the grand topics of religion and sex. We propose that in the freshman year this ideological bent be given a full chance of expression. This may go against the grain of the academic orientation, for many professors are aghast at the inaccuracy, grandiosity, vagueness, and emotionality of the student's ideational production, and try to "clamp down" almost immediately and give the student a sense of what cool, detached, accurate scientific investigation is like, whether in history, literary criticism, or physics. The student can conform if he must, because his previous training has already taught him what the coin of the realm is, but it is not what he wants to do. He gets the sense that his own ideational products are unworthy, and feels humiliated and inept, wondering how good he is as a thinking person. Thus, to some extent, the colleges themselves produce the "anti-intellectuals" they complain about.

If we encourage the student's own experimentation, we will find that sooner or later he will want to refine his concepts and test some of his ideas, either by established methods of inquiry or by new and possibly unique ones. We should gratefully accept curosity where we find it, respond as fully as we can, and allow the student to proceed at his own pace wherever his investigations may lead him. We need to learn to listen and to follow the student's bent of thinking and his thinking devices. This requires a rather drastic revision of our standards. Instead of being guided by graduate-school standards of performance, we must develop new ones appropriate to the student's developmental situation in college, try to discern his purposes, and work with him towards their realization. If a student prefers philosophy to art, we should work with him so that he and we understand and, if desirable, can try to modify his avoidance of art. We must be alert to the ways in which he links ideas to current or anticipated actions or to his past—to parents, siblings, or events—because we cannot expect to clarify non-ideational entanglements by attention to subject matter alone. We need to determine where to rely on his own tendencies for growth, and where to step in with confrontation, or even restraint.

We must enlarge the freshman's opportunities for independent action. We constantly underestimate his intelligence and autonomy, misguided in part by the protective mask of submissiveness he wears before authority. The freshman should end his first year with feelings of success and competence. When there is little sense of success, both we and the student should seek to understand the causes of the failure, so that he will not feel overwhelmed or driven into a corner, but will be able to see the beginnings of a more promising path. (Colleges have a special obligation to their "dropouts," and therefore might consider setting up "Offices of Exit" to parallel their Offices of Admission.)

The possible question of whether our proposals would lead to a lowering of standards should have answered itself by now, for we have implicitly introduced the principle of the relevance of standards—and with relevant standards, it is possible to be "tough" and educative at the same time. The "profiles" recommended by us will ensure that the standards remain relevant to the individual. We suspect that if the student's incentive comes mainly from forces within himself, his desire to learn will increase with time, rather than diminish. Force and learning are largely contradictory; they produce temporary conformity at examination time and insufficient internalization. We assume that particularly people of college age, with their curiosity not yet overly stifled, and with overburdening demands of reality not yet upon them, will naturally work hard if impulse and work can be brought into some sort of harmony. Educators have relied too much on the superego and too little on the impulse and imagination as helps in education.

There is a certain degree of functionlessness in the present college. Much of what it now does for the sake of preparing students for their occupations, professions, or graduate schools could well be postponed. In fact, graduate or professional schools often repeat undergraduate material, and thus add to the student's dissatisfaction. The time thus freed could well be used for studying the possible expansion of the student's personality.

We propose a college with fewer walls separating it from

the community and a different structure within—a different conception of the faculty, a more complex conception of the students. We envision students participating in many more of the activities of the community, spending more time away from their parent institutions (facilities of exchange between different colleges might be developed), and studying abroad or working abroad in humanitarian activities during the college years. We see them taking responsibility earlier, becoming more self-determining, being more in control of and of use to other people. We see all this as the result of their achieving proficiency in certain explicit areas of competence, and integrating their capacity to learn with the rest of their personality.

Our discussion thus far has moved in the orbit of the traditional academic concerns of the college, though with considerable broadening of basic concepts. We now turn to the student's relations with other people, and to his personality development. Before considering peer relationships among students, we must remind ourselves how "artificial" living arrangements for students are, and how unlike anything that characterizes their lives either before or after college. The American model living unit is the one-family house, preferably with acreage around it, and with a separate room for each child. Within it there are several rings of "protection" between the child and other people. In college residences, students are thrown into huge building complexes, in which the rooms are often small, drab, and uniform. The student must often "room" with one or more other persons. A student who wants to express himself through furniture or decorations is often severely restricted: "functional" desks and beds are all he is allowed, and he may be forbidden to affix so much as a thumbtack to the wall. This type of communal living is thoroughly "un-American" and untypical, outside of the Army.

In most college housing facilities, the students are isolated from people other than those of their own age and sex; there are no adults, no children, not even pets. This situation is actually much like what Plato recommended when he proposed that the young be segregated from their parents and society for a period of years, and be raised in isolation outside the city, so as to become fit citizens of his new state. Such conditions would lend themselves nicely to "brainwashing," but since no one is interested in obtaining that kind of control over the student, the net effect is more one of omission.

Students live together in close proximity, without necessarily achieving deeper relationships. At the same time, many students long for more privacy, and find themselves unable to cope with the intrusions and noises of so many strangers. Sometimes a restrictive and narrow-minded director or supervisor makes their lives even less pleasant. In spite of all this, until recently students have been good boys and girls. "Griping," or occasionally raiding the kitchen seemed to satisfy their need to protest. But in the last two years, some of them have begun to raise more fundamental questions about the relations of housing to their intellectual and social lives. In thinking about college housing, we should remember that the trend toward building large complexes has considerably diminished. Hospitals and schools no longer resemble huge, forbidding armories, and yet colleges continue to build large, barracks-like structures. We need to give much more attention to the human aspects of student housing, and to ask how college living arrangements can be made to further both sociability and privacy.

We noted in an earlier chapter that in their passage through college, students acquire a degree of ease and skill in their daily interactions with other people, but we also found that many of them leave college with a sense of incompleteness as far as deeper involvements are concerned. Even joining a fraternity, which assures an immediate group of close associates, in no way assures personal closeness: some students feel quite alone in the midst of their "brothers." The emphasis of the college on individual performance contributes to this sense of isolation. So does the lack of opportunity for groups to work for a common purpose through mutually complementary activities. Moreover, the student's segregation from the world outside the campus increases his isolation, felt and actual. People outside the campus do not enter sufficiently into the work-world of the student, either as associates or as objects of concern. Finally, students do not receive sufficient support, including "feedback" at the right time in the right way, from older people. Young people need a sense of support from and acceptance by the older generation. The messages they get are often irrelevant to their deeper purposes, or even humiliating, if they stress how the student is not "measuring up."

It seems desirable to make possible the uniting of student groups in a common task. Such a task could involve anything: a project in the history of the opera, current styles in jazz, a study of the lives of a minority group, or teaching children in the elementary grades. The important thing is that it be a real and useful task, and one that can be accomplished only by a group acting in concert. It is easy to anticipate the effects: live discussions, new ideas, pleasure in the work, the forming of relationships. In our study, there was a somewhat isolated fraternity member whose greatest pleasure during his four years of college seems to have been occasioned by his building a boat together with some of his "brothers" in the basement of the fraternity house. This was a shared experience with a shared, meaningful purpose. Our proposal simply systematizes and enlarges this sort of happy experience. The new dimensions of interaction that the proposed groups would experience would also give rise to new thoughts, new feelings, and new conflicts within the members. These could, under the guidance of a competent adult, become occasions for fresh learning—not just about the work tasks, but also about the group process, and about oneself.

We assume such working groups would be composed of both males and females, and would thus provide a superior alternative and complement to the dating system. The dating system provides little opportunity for the men and women to learn about the characteristic aspects of the other's personality, or to form a better picture of his abilities. By providing occasions for more revealing association, we can help our young people to mate less under the dominance of the id and more under that of the ego; to make choices dependent less on their inhibited or frustrated impulses and the resultant fantasies, and more upon a clear knowledge of the other and the experience of cooperation in a common task.

The people to whom the student can be useful may be outside of the college walls, but they also can be within. We should make it much easier for students to be useful to one another. This might, for instance, be done by enlisting students to teach other students. One method is that of student-to-student teaching. (This has been tried occasionally in different places and, as far as I have been able to determine, usually with great success.) Such teaching not only is one of the best ways to learn subject matter, but it also enhances the teacher's self-esteem and sense of purpose. (Student-teachers would be under the supervision of a professor who himself would learn much about the teaching process through the experience. Using students as teachers may also be one device for individualizing instruction.)

Attention to housing arrangements ought to be a concern throughout the four years. Getting people together should be accomplished not through assignment, but through motivation, as in the work groups we have suggested. It becomes clear from a comparison of Berkeley and Stanford residence patterns that when official restraints are removed, residential choice is different from what some college authorities desire. Nevertheless, we feel that residential choice, at least beyond the freshman year, ought to be left to the student himself, as one exercise of his individuality. Work groups would serve to bring students together and thus balance the centrifugal pull of separate residences. At present, the classroom is a common meeting-place; but we have observed that it is not an environment particularly conducive to association and acquaintance.

The balance of coercion, structure, and freedom in the college milieu must be delicately handled. During a study we undertook of a large introductory course, one of the instructors conceived the idea that it would be a good thing for students to have meetings with their instructors in their dormitories, and to have men and women from the same corridors assigned to the same section, so that classroom discussion easily blended with dormitory conversation. This arrangement was put into effect, and we were told later that many students resented it, for they regarded it as an invasion of the academic world into their own private precinct. Although this reaction is in part a reflection of the present distance of the student culture from the academic culture, safeguarding the student's own territory will always be an important task of educational planning.

Concern for the student's personality development has pervaded this whole study, and for good reason. We do not think that the furtherance of personal growth would be a "nice" addition to present programs—we think it is an essential one. We also believe that no true intellectual development is possible when the intellect is treated not as a human component, but as an isolated depository for knowledge.

In our research, we have found it useful to work with the concepts of impulse and impulse control (in particular, superego and ego controls). One of our underlying assumptions has been that growth is facilitated by true, free expression of impulses in thought and in action, and by the development of more sophisticated and complex impulses. This implies a transformation of the infantile components of the impulses, but not a shutting-off, or an explosion, or some other non-integrated "relief" mechanism. Growth depends on a recognition and rejection of irrational impulse demands, particularly regressive and destructive ones.

In our study we found that a relatively small number of students had achieved, by the time of graduation, an integration of impulse and ego that pervaded their whole personality. We found more who had achieved a partial integration. An initial openness to one's own deeper feelings is a helpful predisposition to this sort of development. So is a willingness to expose oneself to new and different experiences. These new experiences may be found in associating with people who have different feelings, attitudes, and histories; or in doing innovative work on one's own initiative, for example, working with underprivileged children, or striking out on a painting style of one's own. Those students who were able to recognize their bondage to some external expectation or to a false self-image fared well in freeing themselves for deeper purposes and interests.

We also found much pathology in the development of students. A large percentage of students have personality handicaps that will make their future lives difficult, both for themselves and the people they will live and work with. Authoritarians project onto the external world some of their own unacceptable impulses, then seek to combat them by attacking other people. As citizens and alumni, such people constitute a social nuisance out of proportion to their numbers. It would be a service to all if these people could be made more accessible to education while in college. Another group of students at first seemed much like the authoritarians in their rigidity of attitude and tendency to look for external rules. On close inspection, they proved to be quite different in some respects. This group we termed "benevolent authoritarians." Such people do not view people who are unlike them in some salient feature of impulse expression as evil, or use them as targets of hostile aggression. Instead, they accept restrictions of their impulses quite submissively, and with little sign of rebelliousness: perhaps early in life they were encouraged to "play it safe" without conflicting stimulations to submission and defiance. They are *par excellence* the people who will let life happen to them. Their contributions to society are uprighteousness and docility. The educational task seems to be to wake them up, lead them beyond their reliance on external stimulation, and help them find stimulation within themselves.

While these two groups tend toward rigid impulse control or overcontrol, others are characterized by undercontrol. These people, for whom social expectations and forms and even personal constraints are no longer adequate, we called "drifters." They have broken free, but they have not yet found the means within themselves for integration, though they may be on the way. (This group is distinguished from a more disciplined group, which is able to conform to outer and inner demands, but does so at the expense of internal conflict.) We found that some of them make little progress toward abatement of their conflicts during the college years, and carry the consequences of their lack of resolution into their occupational and marital choices.

Since colleges cannot focus on all aspects of a student's development, they ought to identify areas in which attention is particularly strategic. Through our research, we have been especially impressed with the need for more attention to the student's occupational and marital choices. The occupational choice process is hampered in many ways. The student is forced to make decisions relating to his future occupation while he actually has very little concrete knowledge of it; hence, his anticipations may be more in the realm of fantasy or hearsay. His choice is hemmed in by the expectations of society, peers, and parents. Society has its prestige rankings, the peer group have their expectations based on a mixture of admiration, competition, and attempted control, and parents have their desires, often based on the unconscious wish to have their children compensate for what they think of as losses or failures in themselves. We found that parental influence sometimes takes a more devious form, in which the parents pay lip service to the idea that the student is free to choose whatever he wants. When there are so many demands, the student makes no firm decision, but somewhat halfheartedly moves along, doing the required things—declaring a major, choosing a graduate or professional school. All the while he has more or less strong mental reservations and does not really feel committed. In a sense, he makes no choice at all, but the many little steps he thinks relatively unimportant add up to a "choice" to which he finds himself committed.

Some parents and students see college primarily as vocational preparation, but the demands of the occupational market seem to make such preparation increasingly less necessary and desirable. Moreover, the student's need to do something useful and remunerative may be hampered rather than aided by the emphasis on liberal arts for their own sake. On the other hand, the student committed to a specific vocational program who keeps himself from realizing that a seemingly idle interest in a course outside his major really betokens a loss of interest in his "chosen" vocation may be headed for trouble, personal and vocational, in later life.

We suggest that students be more fully introduced to the world of work while still in college. The jobs should be real ones, and the work should be challenging. Moreover, appropriate procedures should be devised to enable students to become more aware of their true interests and to free themselves from preconceptions about what they "ought" to do or what they are "good" for.

As for the marital decision, greater exposure to the reality of human relationships would help to make it a more appropriate one. The intimacy of association in the student work groups we have suggested would allow for much more profound knowledge of the other. This in turn would give rise to questions, and sometimes problems, about which group discussions and other awareness-producing procedures could seek answers. As everyone knows, an enormous amount of preconceptions and anxieties hinders proper marital selection, yet educators have not taken enough responsibility for this developmental crisis. No adequate institutional or social procedures exist to aid college women in developing life-plans that will satisfy both their intellectual and emotional needs. We have observed that even in the freshman year, women students begin to be aware that theirs is a special situation with regard to marriage and career. Many women, anxious to continue their formal education, tend to flee from relationships that might threaten it. Others feel that their autonomy is at stake—that a choice must be made between marriage and career.[10] In view of what we earlier referred to as the ideological propensity of freshmen, we propose that experimental groups of freshman women be brought together for discussions of feminity, female roles, male-female relations, and related topics. We expect these discussions to be often more ideological than scientific. Their purpose would be to bring into the open the students' ideas, in all their complexity and emotional force, and to encourage the women to think about their problems and to gain confidence in their own ability to find solutions.[11] We suggest that in the second year, the students make various kinds of investigations in the library and in the field. They might collect data about the economic and social status of women in different periods and different regions, or they might conduct actual surveys among the surrounding population. From the third year on, we would expect these students to put their minds more and more to ideas that would lead to change. For instance, they might think of ways in which the occupational world could take account in work arrangements the differences in the life cycle of women, or of ways in which the cultivation of skills and interests can be carried into marriage. In short, we are once more combining intellectual and other developmental purposes. Our women students would learn about different fields

[10] Though we found many women more or less explicitly aware of this situation, it also was our impression that romantic expectations and social pressures toward marriage contributed to a lack of realism about this next stage of their lives.

[11] Similar programs ought to be devised for men; and at the appropriate times during the college year, men and women students ought to discuss these questions jointly.

such as economics, sociology, and psychology, and would have a chance to use their knowledge for the good of society. At the same time, participation in such a program would have profound personal effects on them. It would give them a kind of confidence in themselves that would make it less tempting for them to view themselves primarily as marital material or sex-objects.

There is deep resistance to a consideration of human development as important. At the beginning of psychotherapy, a patient often protests that his problem really is not big, and does not deserve much attention. The therapist may point out that this is a way of saying that the patient himself, not the problem, does not deserve attention. As a culture, we have not truly accepted the proposition that people deserve attention. We oscillate from creeds and acts asserting the dignity of the individual to permissive self-indulgence, or to depersonalized organization in business and schools. There are, of course, hazards in tying psychological understanding to educational problems. To begin with, the "language" of the emotions is by no means easy to decipher, and is subject to misinterpretation even by qualified observers. It would be regrettable if, in paying more attention to the affective domain, we allowed a hardening of concepts such as has taken place in the cognitive domain with its IQ's, SAT's, and GPA's, which force people into ill-fitting abstractions. Even the present chaos would be preferable, because the peer culture and individual resistance allow for escape into some affective freedom. We are only too familiar with the intrusive meddlings of the would-be helper, or the well-meaning but platitudinous efforts of those who are concerned with the "extracurricular."

For this reason, we have stressed the usefulness of applying psychological knowledge to institutional procedures, rather than engaging in wholesale psychotherapy. Colleges should, of course, make periodic examinations of how their procedures serve to facilitate or inhibit the development of their students. Such investigations, conducted at some length, ought to include the findings of qualified outsiders whose interests and thought patterns are not identified with the established ways of the college. We have misgivings about institutionalized research, for in the past it seems rarely to have risen beyond conventional assumptions. Perhaps new departures are possible. The institutional researcher need not and perhaps should not have power, so that he can neither threaten nor do favors; but he ought to be in a position to initiate experiment by persuasion.

We will conclude this chapter with an instance of such an experiment. We approached the staff of a large introductory humanities course for permission to study teacher-student interactions in the individually taught sections of the course. Permission was given, more because the teachers of the course thought we ought to have a chance than because of enthusiasm for our project. Part of our plan was to give a questionnaire to the students enrolled in the course, and in anticipation of this, we asked the staff to tell us about their objectives in their course. To our amazement, we found what we had thought would be a brief staff session turn into many hours of discussions. It seemed almost the first time that the staff had raised this fundamental question, and the instructors turned out not only to be interested but also to have quite different answers. Some stressed scholarly training as the primary objective, others historical interpretation, others moral reorientation. This reaction proved to be prophetic of a continuing involvement.

Our work in the classroom encompassed both observation and consultation. We observed one class per instructor per week, and immediately afterwards subjected the hour to detailed analysis. Part of our work in the beginning centered on alleviating the instructor's anxiety about being observed. Gradually more of the instructor's energies became free for looking at student's reactions and his own behavior. One instructor soon began to conduct his own independent investigations of how the students responded. He did so by means of informal class discussion, by giving a questionnaire, and by letting students take over some of his classes while he sat in the back and observed.

It turned out that we had met an unspoken need. Underneath the anxiety about teaching there was a desire to make teaching a more deliberate art, to obtain reliable information about what one was doing and how it could be improved. It was also discovered that such inquiry could be as intellectually challenging as the pursuit of subject matter. Soon we realized that syllabus planning and the grouping of students was in need of continuing investigation.

We offer this example to suggest that academic structures may not be as tight as they seem, and that this may be so because present procedures are not really very satisfactory to anyone. Although we have stressed the need for facilitating the development of students, we know that faculties, too, should be given full scope for development and provided with every opportunity for growth.

PART FIVE

Appendices

NOTE ON THE COLLECTION
AND ANALYSIS OF THE DATA

The data
collection of the Student Development Study began in the fall of
1961, when nearly the entire entering freshman class at Stanford
(N = 1303) and nearly two-thirds of the entering freshman class at
Berkeley (N = 2014) were administered six scales from the Omnibus Personality Inventory, and the Authoritarian and Ethnocentrism Scales (all described in Chapter 3). In addition, they were
given an experimental 54-item scale, Attitudes to Drinking (described in Chapter 9). These scales were readministered early in
1965 to over half the students who had taken the tests as freshmen and were still in school. The students in question were also
asked in 1965 to respond to a 19-page questionnaire. This questionnaire was based on the experience of intensive four-year interviewing and was intended to help determine to what extent it
was possible to generalize from the results obtained in the interviews.

The heart of the Student Development Study consisted in the longitudinal interviewing of selected student samples throughout their four college years. The subjects were selected at random, after being classified into five major categories and separated by sex. Half of the selected students were men and half were women. Seventy-five per cent of the students were selected in accordance with their responses on the Social Maturity (SM) and Impulse Expression (IE) Scales. One-third were high (one standard deviation or more above the mean) on both scales, one-third were at or near the mean, and one-third were low (one standard deviation or more below the mean). The remaining 25 per cent were equally divided between those who were high on the SM Scale and low on the IE Scale, and those who were low on the SM Scale and high on the IE Scale.

A total of 274 students were asked to participate in our interview program. At Stanford, only four out of 110 students refused initially to participate, and three of these were subsequently interviewed. Two students at Stanford refused to continue with the study after one and four interviews respectively. At Berkeley, seven out of 164 students refused initially to participate, and three students agreed to participate but did not show up for their first interviews (eight of these ten students dropped out of school subsequently). Twenty-four refused to continue after between one and four interviews (fifteen of these students subsequently dropped out of school). It was made clear to all participants in the test and interview sessions that their cooperation was voluntary. They were also assured that the information they gave us would be kept confidential.

The rationale of selecting students according to their responses to the Social Maturity and Impulse Expression Scales, which have some independence of each other (correlating about 0.45), was to obtain three groups of students who differed in such ego characteristics as flexibility, autonomy, and capacity for relationships, as well as in the degree of their imaginativeness and impulsivity. The underlying theoretical assumption was that development and education differ according to the degree to which the individual can utilize his impulses in his strivings for competence, instead of having more or less to defend himself against them. Differently put, we hoped to obtain in our high scorers people in whom the reality and the pleasure principles cooperated with each other rather than being isolated from or even antagonistic to each other. As a number of the reported analyses in this volume bear out, people who scored high on Social Maturity and Impulse Expression did have livelier careers through college, and more active, aware, and sensitive reactions to their college experiences and to the people in their environment. Sometimes the high scorers had too much impulse—and particularly too much conflict—to integrate, so that at the end of college their future was uncertain, and eventual integration was not clearly in sight. Many people in the middle group (those represented in the long case histories in Chapter 2, for example) have also moved steadily if less pronouncedly toward a restructuring of their lives, a better use of their potentialities, and a more effective utilization of their environment. The people who scored low on Social Maturity and Impulse Expression have a more passive and routine attitude toward themselves and their environment. They are a problem group, in spite of the fact that many of them are not likely to rock the boat of the educational and other institutions in which they find themselves.

The focus of our study was personality development between the ages of 17 and 22. Since all development takes place in a social context, we paid full attention to as many aspects of the students' environment as we could. Thus, in our interviews, we aimed particularly at obtaining student responses to (1) teachers and courses, (2) peers, (3) parents, (4) and the various campus living groups and other formal and informal organizations. We also attempted to trace the development of the students' moral, religious, and political values. We interviewed the students twice each year. These interviews extended from not much more than one hour in the freshman year to three hours or more for many in the senior year. We obtained information about the individual student's experiences in the intervals between interviews, and about the five areas of student life just enumerated. In addition, each interview centered on one area specifically: Interview 1 focused on the transition from home and high school to college; Interview 2, on parents and upbringing at home; Interview 3, on the use of the summer, when the student was not under direct control of the college; Interview 4, on the student's moral, religious, and political values; Interview 5, on his academic experience, that is, on his courses and teachers; Interview 6, on peer relations and sexual development; Interview 7, on self-concept and perception of change in one's self; Interview 8, on a final assessment of the college years and the special experience of being interviewed.

A 19-page Senior Questionnaire was administered to the seniors at Berkeley and Stanford early in 1965. The questions asked in this instrument were similar to those that we asked in our intensive interviews conducted during the four college years. Since we were able to administer the questionnaire to a much larger number of students than we had interviewed, the results give a more general, though also a more superficial, picture of the reported behavior and attitudes of the two college classes we studied. For a few of the items on the Senior Questionnaire, we had collected information at Stanford from the same students when they were freshmen. We also had administered an identical checklist of values to the Stanford freshmen of 1962. Other comparisons were made possible by the Omnibus Personality Inventory, originally given in 1961, and readministered in 1965 simultaneously with the Senior Questionnaire.

The following areas were covered in the Senior Questionnaire: academic life; choice of career; extracurricular activities; relationships with peers, and friendships; sexual development; anticipation of marriage and spouse; relationships with parents; and perception of self, change, and development.

The Senior Questionnaire was responded to by close to 60 per cent of the students who were in residence on both campuses early in 1965, and who had responded to the Omnibus Personality Inventory in the fall of 1961. The numbers of respondents were as follows: Stanford men, N = 272; Stanford women, N = 212; Berkeley men, N = 262; Berkeley women, N = 239. Two probes were made to determine to what extent the respondents were similar to those students for whom we do not have questionnaires. The first analysis, reported in Chapter 3, consisted in comparing the freshman scores on eight personality scales of (1) those who responded to the Personality Inventory in 1961 and 1965, and (2) random samples of students who responded only in 1961. The 32 t tests that were computed yielded only four significant differences at the .05 level: three of these were obtained for one of the four groups, the Berkeley women, and were of small magnitude.

The other analysis was based on the fact that at both Stanford and Berkeley, we constituted separate random samples of seniors and made special efforts to obtain a high rate of response. At Stanford, 80 per cent of the random sample responded, and at Berkeley, 75 per cent. The four random samples (Berkeley men, N = 71, Berkeley women, N = 79; Stanford men, N = 60, Stanford women, N = 40) were then compared with the other respondents on their Questionnaire reports of twenty-one activities engaged in during the college years. Forty-two chi-squares computed for Stanford men and women yielded statistically significant differences only two times out of forty-two—a difference that at the preassigned five per cent level of confidence can be the result of chance alone. For Berkeley, statistically significant differences were obtained five times out of forty-two. These differences (two for the men and three for the women) do not form any pattern, nor do they raise any serious questions about the representativeness of our Berkeley sample.

GUIDE TO FURTHER READING

The reader who wishes to familiarize himself with further research on the development of college students should turn first to Nevitt Sanford (Ed.), *The American College* (New York: Wiley, 1962). This book, now available in a paperback edition, brings together the studies of many leading researchers of student development, student culture, and the processes and outcomes of academic learning. It also contains numerous bibliographical references.

Several pioneer research projects undertaken during the 1940's are of continuing relevance. Theodore M. Newcomb's study of Bennington College is described in his *Personality and Social Change* (New York: Dryden, 1943). Newcomb and several associates restudied the same students after an interval of twenty-five years. The results are described in *Persistence and Change* (New York: Wiley, 1967). A series of studies at Sarah Lawrence College were particularly concerned with the emotional conditions of intellectual growth. Ruth Munroe's *Teaching the Individual* (New York: Columbia University Press, 1944) is representative of these studies. Esther Raushenbush, who was a prominent contributor to the Sarah Lawrence studies, uses the case-study method in her recent book *The Student and His Studies* (Middletown, Connecticut: Wesleyan University Press, 1964) to trace the intellectual development of students in several different institutions.

Robert W. White's *Lives in Progress* (New York: Holt, Rinehart and Winston, 2d ed., 1966) presents three extensive case histories that link the development of students in college to their earlier background and experiences, and follow the students into their later professional and personal lives. Kenneth Keniston, in *The Uncommitted* (New York: Harcourt, Brace and World, 1965), concentrates on those students who feel alienated from their society, tracing their history and discussing the social conditions that seem to encourage alienation.

For a vivid theoretical discussion of the developmental problems and tasks of late adolescence, the reader is referred to Erik H. Erikson's *Identity and the Life Cycle* (New York: International Universities Press, 1959).

Two recent books written from the same point of view as this volume present data and discussions of student development and the college environment. They are Mervin B. Freedman's *The College Experience* (San Francisco: Jossey-Bass, 1967), and Nevitt Sanford's *Where Colleges Fail* (San Francisco: Jossey-Bass, 1967). Readers who wish to keep themselves informed on current studies of higher education should turn to Lewis B. Mayhew's annual review of the literature in the *Educational Record*.

At the time of the second printing (September 1969), the following new studies have been published: Arthur W. Chickering, *Education and Identity* (San Francisco: Jossey-Bass, 1969); Kenneth A. Feldman and Theodore M. Newcomb's interpretive survey of forty years of research, *The Impact of College on Students* (San Francisco: Jossey-Bass, 1969); Douglas H. Heath, *Growing Up in College* (San Francisco: Jossey-Bass, 1968); Kenneth Keniston, *Young Radicals: Notes on Committed Youth* (New York: Harcourt, Brace and World, 1968); and Peter Madison, *Personality Development in College* (Reading, Mass.: Addison-Wesley, 1969).

✤ INDEX ✤

A

Academic program: noninvolvement with, 23–24; problems with, 17; variety of responses to, 25–26

Activist revolution, 1964, 386–414; interviews with arrested student, 404–414; nation-wide protest movements, 391–392 (*see also* Berkeley Sit-in of 1964)

Activities: engaged in during college, 15–16, 30–33, 261; importance of, 20, 23, 34–35, 65–66; sex differences in, 31, 32–33; summer, 21, 38–40

Administration, university: attitudes toward, 29–30, 299–300, 401–402; changes wanted by students, 29–30, 387–389, 401–402; student criticism of, 29–30, 386–389, 392

ADORNO, T. W., 163n, 376n, 378, 378n

Affection: importance to students, 56, 65; and sex, 55–56

ALFERT, E., 35, 35n, 322, 322n

Alienation, 293–297, 301–302

ALTBACH, P. G., 34, 386n

ALTUS, W. D., 320, 320n

Anti-intellectualism, 28–29

Antisocial behavior, 270–272

Authoritarianism: components of, 382–384; definitions of, 376–377; freshmen vs. seniors, 378–384; personality traits in, 379–381; as a stage of development, 377–378

Authoritarianism Scale, 163, 164, 378

Authority, attitudes toward, 299–300

Autonomy, development of, 154–155

Autonomy Scale, 163

B

Background shock, 84–86

BACON, S., 357, 357n

BECKER, H. S., 17n

Berkeley Sit-in of 1964, 386–414; basic causes of, 392–393; characteristics of participants, 394–404, 414; chronology of events, 386–391; Free Speech Movement, 386–391; inter-

457

Berkeley Sit-in of 1964 (*Cont.*):
views with arrested student, 404–414; Mario Savio, 389–390; Muscatine Report, 391; student demands, 387–388
BLANE, H., 352n
BLOCK, J., 353n
BOROW, H., 220, 220n
BROWN, R., 377, 377n
BUTTON, A. D., 352n
BYRNE, J. C., 391
Byrne Report, 391

C

California Psychological Inventory: in classification (a) of drinkers, 362–363, (b) of students, 196–197
Career choice, 5, 17, 18–24, 137–140, 149–150, 197–198, 207–238, 441–442; difficulties in, 12, 17, 19–21, 75–153, 229–238; of freshmen, 209–212; postgraduate status, 212–217; vs. postgraduate status (a) of men, 209–223, (b) of women, 224–229
Career vs. marriage, for women, 127–153, 442–444
Change: characterological, 5; of child self, 154–156; definitions of, 6–7; desired by students, 16–18; factors influencing, 13–15; and instability, 74; in relationships, 5, 9; self-perception of, 5, 9–12, 69–73
Child self, change of, 154–156
CLEVELAND, B., 387–388, 388n
College (s): factors in choice of, 125–126; factors militating against individual development, 420–421; as a liberalizing influence, 87; an overview of college years, 3–5; role of, 21, 87, 418–419; students (*see* Students)
Conflict: and development, 12–13, 61; in interpersonal relationships, 43–44; with parents, 62,

Conflict (*Cont.*):
63; students with high degree of, 12–13
Conformity, 9–10; pressures toward, 345–347
Constraint: dynamics of, 74–161; forces of, 75, 85, 87–88, 94–95, 98, 99, 250–252
Counseling Center, University of California at Berkeley, 324n
CPI (*see* California Psychological Inventory)
Curriculum: organization, 94; student response to, 187–206; suggestions for change in, 417–446

D

Dating, 130–131, 134–136; frequency, 51–52, 53–54; and intimacy, 51–52, 56; women's dating patterns, 52
Demonstrations (*see* Berkeley Sit-in of 1964)
Depression, 18, 68, 156–157, 324–326, 345–346
DEUTSCH, H., 279, 279n
Development during college years, 3–72; and conflict, 12–13, 61; dynamics of, 74–161; factors influencing, 75, 96; interviews with students with conflicts, 75–153; psychological problems of, 5, 345, 345n
Developmental Status Scale, 163, 164
Disciplines (*see* Career choice)
Discriminant analysis of students, 190–197
Dormitories, 35, 36–37, 257–258
Dormitory men: characteristics of, 282, 292, 302–311; family background of, 304–306; suggestions for better adjustment of, 313–314
DRAPER, H., 386n
Drinking: abstainers, 357, 359, 362, 363, 366–368; attitudes toward, 89–90; classification as escapist, facilitative, or inte-

Drinking (*Cont.*):
grative, 374; among fraternity men, 275–277; and personality, 348–375; problem drinkers, 370; Strassburger Scales in study of, 354–358, 364–366; student drinking patterns, 277, 355; among women, 357, 359, 362–364, 370–371
Dropouts: among psychiatric patients, 322; and residence, 35
DS Scale, 163, 164

E

E Scale, 163, 164
Eating clubs, 282–292; advantages and disadvantages of, 289–292; characteristics of members, 282, 283–292; family background of members, 284; suggestions for better adjustment of members, 312
Education, undergraduate: benefits of, 87; deficiencies in, 4, 249–252; recommended policy and philosophy of, 417–446; subjective impact on two medical students, 239–252; suggested use of student profile, 424–426
Ego: identity (*see* Identity); integration, 440–441; mechanisms, 92
EHRMANN, W., 55, 55n
EMERY, F., 352, 352n
Environment, academic, influence of, 13, 15
Equilibrium, 8, 74–75
ERIKSON, E. H., 7, 7n, 157, 157n, 455
Es Scale, 163, 164
Estheticism Scale, 163, 164
Ethnocentrism Scale, 163, 164
Extramarital relations, attitudes toward, 55

F

F Scale, 163, 164, 378
Faculty (*see* Teachers)

Family, 59–64, 130; family background of (a) dormitory men, 304–306, (b) eating club men, 284, (c) fraternity men, 262–263, 267–269, (d) off-campus men, 293, 294 (*see also* Parents)
FARNSWORTH, D., 345n
Father-attachment, resolution of, 143–144
FISHER, R. A., 190
FLACKS, R., 398n
Fraternities: advantages, 277–281; at Berkeley, 35; defects in, 270–272; at Stanford, 37, 258
Fraternity men: characteristics of, 258–281; family background, 262–263; "inheritor" group, 262–263, 265–267; suggestions for better adjustment of, 312–313
Free Speech Movement, 388–391; characteristics of members, 394–404, 414; implications, 393–394; inception and organization of, 388–389 (*see also* Berkeley Sit-in of 1964)
FREEDMAN, M. B., 179, 179n, 455
FRENKEL-BRUNSWICK, E., 376n, 378, 378n
Freshman year: social difficulties, 42–43; suggested treatment of students during, 432–435
Friendships: choice of friends, 107–111; closeness of, 46; precollege, 47; sex differences in, 45–47 (*see also* Interpersonal relationships)
FROMM, E., 346, 346n
FSM (*see* Free Speech Movement)

G

"Genius-isolates," 301–302, 308–309, 314
GILMORE, S., 386n
GIRAULT, E. S., 41, 41n
Grade-point average, 17, 17n; and personality characteristics, 193–196, 203; relation to post-

Grade-point average (*Cont.*):
graduate status, 217–219
Grades: and achievement, 25, 26; anxiety about, 25, 26; attitudes toward, 25, 117; emphasis on, 24; importance of, 17
Grading system: limitations, 17; student preferences for types of, 26; suitability to student types, 26
Graduate education (*see* Postgraduate status)
Group membership, 37; importance to students, 38
Guidance: effects of lack of, 17; need for, 30, 58
Guilt: and academic environment, 29; and sex, 49

H

HANFMANN, E., 352n
HARRIS, C., 184n
HEIST, P., 397, 397n, 400n
Heterosexual relations, 48–59
High school background, 69–71, 84–86
Home background, 59–64; effect on student, 88–94; punishment in the home, 60–61; relations in, 60, 64; separation from, 62–63 (*see also* Family; Parents)
Homosexuality, fears of, 45, 51
Housing, student, suggested changes in, 436–437, 439 (*see also* Dormitories; Eating clubs; Fraternities; Off-campus housing; Residences)

I

Identification with parents, 61
Identity, 47; identity crises, 7; importance of, 65; self-, establishment of, 157–158
Identity shock, 84–86
IE Scale, 163, 180–181, 182–184
Impulse control, development of, 440

Impulse Expression Scale, 163, 180–181, 182–184
Independence, desire for, 298
Individual development (*see* Development)
"Inheritor" group of fraternity men, 262–263, 265–267
Integration: desire for, 8; lack of, 8, 55–56; of personality, 440–441
Intellectual activity: increase in, 9, 10; influence of, 14
Intellectual development, 169–170
Interpersonal relationships; changes in, 9, 12–15; conflicts in, 43–44; difficulties in, 42–46; dissatisfaction in, 16, 42, 68, 69; effect of overseas campuses on, 41–42; and identity, 47; importance to students, 69; influence of, 13–15; sex differences in, 42–43, 45–46
Intimacy: and activities, 57; and conflict, 48, 49; and dating patterns, 51–52, 56, 57; and drinking, 57; of friendships, 45–46, 54; sexual, 48, 54–59
Intrapersonal relations: changes in, 9, 12, 14, 15; importance to student, 47–48; influence of, 13, 14, 15
Involvement, lack of: in academic pursuits, 23–24; in intellectual pursuits, 28–29; in professional world, 21

J

JELLINEK, E. M., 350–351, 351n
JONES, M. C., 353, 353n, 359, 369, 372n, 372–373

K

KATOPE, C. G., 386n
KATZ, J., 46–47, 47n, 78n, 387n, 392, 392n, 393, 393n
KENISTON, K., 455

L

Leadership: expected in marriage, 59; development in students, 111–114
Learning: methods, diversity of, 163, 165, 420–424, 427; orientation to, 28–29
"A Letter to Undergraduates," 387–388
LEVIN, M. M., 349, 349n
LEVINSON, D. J., 378, 378n
LIPSET, S. M., 34, 386n
LOEVINGER, J., 377, 377n
Loneliness in students, 18, 68, 156–157, 324–326, 345–346

M

MCCORD, J., 352n
MCCORD, W., 352n
Major fields of study (see Career choice)
Marriage: vs. career, for women students, 127–153, 442–444; expectations in, 58–59
Masculinity-Femininity Scale, 163, 164
Maturation, 6 (see also Development)
MAYHEW, L. B., 455
MEDSKER, L. L., 378, 378n
MF Scale, 163, 164
MILLER, M. V., 386n
Mobility: social, 21–22, 268–269, 301; upward, 21–22, 268–269, 301
MOGAR, R. E., 20–21, 21n
MOORE, N. I., 9n
MUNROE, R., 454
MUSCATINE, C., 391, 391n
Muscatine Report, 391

N

NEWCOMB, T. M., 454
NICHOLS, R. C., 400n

O

Objectives, educational, 204–206, 207, 234–236, 239–240, 418–419
Occupation, choice of (see Career choice)
Off-campus housing, 35, 37–38, 293
Off-campus men: characteristics, 282, 292–302; examples of "rootlessness" among, 293–294; family background, 293, 294; suggestions for better adjustment of, 314
Omnibus Personality Inventory: in classification of students, 190–197; scales of, 163–164; test results, freshman vs. senior years, 165–168, 171–178
On-campus housing (see Dormitories; Fraternities)
OPI (see Omnibus Personality Inventory)
Overseas campuses, 37; effects of, 14, 72–73, 315; importance of, 41–42

P

Parents: achieving independence from, 154–155; identification with, 61; influence of, 59–64, 131–134, 142, 152, 247–249
Passivity, 5, 18; in decision-making, 21, 77; in interpersonal relationships, 44; in use of vacation, 39
Peer groups, 257; influence of, 15; peer pressure, 28–29; relationships, 15, 28–29
Personality change, 9, 12, 13, 14, 66, 69, 162–184
Personality development, 4–13, 66, 68; personality scale changes during college, 162–184
Personality scales, 163–164
PETERSON, R. E., 23n, 391–392, 392n
PLANT, W. T., 377, 377n, 382, 382n
Postgraduate status: of men, 209–223, 260; of women, 224–229

Precollege experiences and development, 75

Premarital relations, attitudes toward, 48, 49, 50, 55

Privacy, need for, 36, 437

Promiscuity, 52

Psychiatric clinic, students using, 318–347 (*see also* Psychiatric patients)

Psychiatric patients: aptitudes and intelligence of, 321; complaints and problems, 322–323; diagnoses, 324–326; dropout rate among, 322; incidence, 320; personality traits of, 326–329; representative case histories, 326, 330–344

Psychotherapy, students receiving, 318–347 (*see also* Psychiatric patients)

Puberty, age of, relation to sexual behavior, 52–53

Punishment: as cause of depression, 345–347; in the home, 60–61

R

RASSCHAU, R., 352n

RAUSHENBUSH, E., 455

Reform, suggested, in educational policy and philosophy, 417–446

Residence, 35–38; choice of, 18, 35–36; dormitories, 35, 36–37, 257–258; eating clubs, 282–292; effects on students, 255–317; fraternities, 258–281; off-campus, 35, 36–37, 293; residence requirements, 35, 257–258; "special interest" houses, suggested, 314–315

Roomates, 105, 307–308

Rootlessness, 293–294

ROSEN, A. C., 352n

S

SAMPSON, E. E., 387n

SANFORD, N., 46–47, 47n, 74, 74n,

SANFORD, N. (*Cont.*):
179, 179n, 263, 374, 374n, 376n, 377, 377n, 378, 378n, 392, 392n, 393, 393n, 454, 455

SAT scores (*see* Scholastic Aptitude Test scores)

SAVIO, M., 389–390

Schizoid Functioning Scale, 163, 164

Scholastic Aptitude Test scores: Berkeley mean, 33; relation to postgraduate status, 217–219; Stanford mean, 33, 196

Security: desire for, 87; importance to students, 65n

Self-concept (*see* Identity)

Senior Questionnaire, analysis of replies to, 9–69, 188–190

Separation from home, 62–63

Sex differences: in activities 31, 32–33, 65; in dating patterns, 51–52, 53–54; in hero selection, 66; in SAT scores, 33; in sex attitudes, 48–51, 54–55

Sexual behavior: and affection, 55–56; attitudes toward sex, 48–59, 116–117; conflict in, 12, 49, 56; degree of intimacy in, 48, 54; freshman and senior attitudes to sex, comparison, 49–50; incidence of sexual intercourse, 54n, 54–56; and puberty, 52–53

SF Scale, 163, 164

SIEGEL, A. E., 382, 382n

SIEGEL, S., 382, 382n

SINGER, E., 352n

SKINNER, B. F., 347

Slate Supplement Report, 387–388

SM Scale, 163, 179

Social Alienation Scale, 163

Social development, 42–43 (*see also* Development during college years)

Social Maturity Scale, 163, 179; in classification of students, 198–200; cluster analyses, 171–184

Social mobility, 21–22, 268–269, 301

Social pressure, 134–136

Socialization and personality development, 168–171

SOKOLIK, B., 40n
Solitude, enjoyment of, 36, 47, 437
SOMERS, R. H., 400n
Sororities, 35–36
"Special interest" houses, suggested, 314–315
STRASSBURGER, F., 354, 354n
Strassburger Scales in study of drinking habits, and test results, 354–358, 364–366
STRASSBURGER, Z., 354, 354n
STRAUS, R., 357, 357n
Strong Vocational Interest Blank in analysis of career choice (a) of men, 220–223, (b) of women, 228–229
Student activists, characteristics of, 22, 46, 394–404, 414
Student Development Study: hypotheses of, 7; methodology, 449–453
Student protest (*see* Berkeley Sit-in of 1964)
Students: adjustment difficulties, means of ameliorating, 311–317; career group, characteristics of, 194–195, 198–199, 201, 205; classification by (a) aptitudes and interests, 190–197, (b) career choice, 197–198; conflicting forces in educative process and career choice, 229–238; differences in methods of learning, 420–424, 427; discriminant analyses of, 190–197; diversity of types, 103–107; "genius-isolates," 308–309, 314; grade group, characteristics of, 194–195, 198–199, 202, 205; "ideal," 193; intellectual interest group, characteristics of, 192–193, 195, 198–199, 201, 202, 205; needing psychiatric help, 318–347; relations with administration, 29–30; rootless, 293–294; vocational orientation, 87–88

Study, methods of, 163, 165, 420–424, 427
SUCZEK, R. F., 322, 322n
Summer activities, 21, 38–40
Support: lack of, in education, 65; need for adult, 46

T

t tests, 165
Teacher-student relations, 26–27, 114–116, 428–429, 445
Teaching and learning, major areas of, 429–431
TELFORD, C. W., 377, 377n
THOMPSON, C. M., 346, 346n
TRENT, J. W., 378, 378n
TROW, M., 33–34n
TRYON, R. C., 172, 172n
TUSSMAN, J., 391

V

Vacation, use of, 21, 38–40
Values, changes in, 64–68
VERDEN, P., 349, 349n
Vocational orientation of entering students, 87–88

W

WATTS, W., 397, 397n, 400n
WEBSTER, H., 179, 179n
WHITE, R. W., 455
WHITTAKER, D. N. E., 397, 397n, 400n
WOLIN, S. S., 386n
Women students, marriage vs. career conflict of, 22–23, 127–153, 442–444
Work experiences, during summer, 21, 38–40

Z

ZOLBROD, P. G., 386n